THE

POETICAL WORKS

OF

THOMAS CHATTERTON

WITH

Notices of his Life,

HISTORY OF THE ROWLEY CONTROVERSY,

A SELECTION OF HIS LETTERS,

AND NOTES CRITICAL AND EXPLANATORY.

VOL. I.

CAMBRIDGE:

PRINTED FOR W. P. GRANT.

MDCCCXLII.

CAMBRIDGE:
PRINTED BY METCALFE AND PALMER, TRINITY-STREET.

PREFACE.

PERHAPS there was never an age in which the literary world were more devoted to studies which involve metaphysical disquisition or analytical reasoning, than the present. The character of public men is the object of the most constant and the most curious investigation: it is not simply examined, but fairly dissected. Whether this predilection for analysis may not be carried too far, is certainly problematical; but that it has been attended with results both directly and remotely beneficial, admits of no doubt.

To gratify that class of readers who recognize in the study of man the proper and most ennobling study of their race, and who find a delight in examining into the darkest mysteries of the human heart, and exploring the most hidden springs of the human will, the present edition of Chatterton has been issued from the press. His fiery passions; his premature yet manly intellect; his plastic imagination; his affectionate nature; his dark destiny; his perpetual struggles; his brief but glorious career, and the solemn agony and terrific grandeur of his death, render him at once a sublime study for the poet, and a character of the most absorbing interest to the psychologist.

But besides the reasons for the republication of the Poems of Chatterton, which result from their intrinsic merit, and the wonderful genius and wild career of their author, we have another motive. The only edition which has any pretensions to completeness, is that which bears the names of Dr. Southey and Mr. Cottle. This edition is now extremely rare, and consequently of difficult attainment.

A new Life of Chatterton, of a more compre-
hensive nature than any that has hitherto been
published, has been prefixed to these volumes.
We have endeavoured to supply the defects of
preceding memoirs; and both public investigation
and private correspondence have been rendered
available in compiling the notices of his life. We
are therefore moderately certain that, however
future biographers may surpass us in a philo-
sophical estimate of the creator of the Rowley
Poems, or excel us in beauty and correctness
of style, they will find it nearly impossible to
adduce a new fact, or throw a clearer light on the
external life of Thomas Chatterton.

In order to furnish the general reader with some
account of the reception which these poems met
on their first publication, a history of the Rowley
Controversy has been drawn up, which it is be-
lieved will be found sufficiently explicit and satis-
factory.

The remarks of Sir Walter Scott, Southey,

Malone, and the greater part of the controver-
sialists, have been incorporated in the work; and
to those who come to the study of " Rowley" for
the first time, will offer a critical desideratum of
no trifling value.

A selection has been made from the prose
works of such pieces as are of peculiar interest, or,
from their connexion with the career of Chatterton,
appeared to require insertion.

In conclusion, we offer our sincerest thanks to
the friends who have so kindly rendered their as-
sistance. The readiness and ability with which
our questions have been answered, are gratefully
acknowledged; and the valuable information which
has been communicated, has, it is with pleasure
admitted, rendered our notices of the Life of Chat-
terton more complete and satisfactory than they
would otherwise have been.

CONTENTS TO VOLUME I.

THE LIFE

OF

THOMAS CHATTERTON.

"To wryte of a Mannes Lyfe mote bee enowe to sale of somme he was
ybore and deceased ; odher somme lacketh recytalle, as manie notable
matteres bee contained in yer storie."

Lyfe of W. Canynge, bie Rowley.

I.

His Birth—Parentage—Education.

THOMAS CHATTERTON,[*] whose life we are about to
record, was born at Bristol on the 20th of November,
1752. He was of humble origin. His father in the
early part of his life is said to have filled the office of
writing-usher to a classical school. He was after-
wards appointed one of the choir in the Cathedral of
Bristol, and subsequently became the master of the
Free-school, situated in Pyle-street, in the same city,

---

[*] The materials for this biography are derived from Dean Milles's
Preliminary Dissertation to Rowley's Poems; Dr. Gregory's Life of
Chatterton; Bryant's Observations; Sir Herbert Croft's Love and
Madness ; Warton's Enquiry into the Authenticity of the Poems attri-
buted to Rowley, and the eighth section of his History of English
Poetry ; Malone's Cursory Observations ; Barrett's History of Bristol ;
Life of Chatterton, by Chalmers ; Edition of his Works, by Southey
and Cottle ; Britton's History of Redcliffe Church ; Campbell's Speci-
mens of the British Poets ; Chatterton's Life, by Dix ; Cottle's Early
Recollections of Coleridge, and miscellaneous articles in various Maga-
zines and Reviews.—ED.

which latter situations he continued to hold conjointly
till the time of his death, which took place in August,
1752, three months before the birth of his son, who
was thus ushered, a posthumous child, into the world.
This parent, if we may credit the statements and au-
thorities of the poet's last biographer, was scarcely
competent to have supplied the careful attention and
control for which Dr. Gregory—on the boy's part—
deplores his premature loss.* That he was clever
and fond of study, there is evidence to prove. He
believed, moreover, in magic, and was deeply read in
Cornelius Agrippa.

Of the mother of Chatterton little is known pre-
vious to her husband's death. She appears to have
been a plain, worthy woman: of gentle, though some-
what melancholy disposition,—of mild and amiable
qualities, and possessing withal a most devoted at-
tachment to her children, of which Thomas, the
subject of this memoir, was the second,—the eldest,
a girl, being at the time of his birth, apparently some

---

* By the premature loss of his father he was deprived of that careful
attention which would probably have conducted his early years through
all the difficulties that circumstances or disposition might oppose to
the attainment of knowledge.—Dr. Gregory.

That he (Chatterton's father) was a man of some talent and shrewd-
ness, is evident from the various testimonials of those who knew him
well; but he was inclined to dissipated habits, and was of a "brutal
disposition." The house in which he lived had only two sitting-rooms,
and he often passed the whole night roaring out catches in one of them,
with some of the lowest rabble of the parish. His wife he always
treated with the greatest indifference, and once, on being asked why
he married her, he coolly replied, "*solely for a house-keeper*." That
he was not likely to experience much "careful attention" from his
father, may be inferred from the fact of the ill-usage Mrs. Chatterton
received from him; and few will doubt, that, as the *wife* was treated
with harshness and neglect, the *son* would have experienced similar
treatment.—Dix's *Life of Chatterton.*—(1837)

years old. In order to support her family, now rely-ing entirely on her own exertions, she opened a day-school, and advertised herself as a milliner or sempstress—a resource which the attention of her neighbours, who very greatly esteemed her, appears to have rendered valuable, both by their patronage and assistance.

The infancy of Chatterton is distinguished by little that is worthy of record. At the age of five years, he was sent to the school in Pyle-street, for-merly under the superintendence of his father, and then kept by a Mr. Love. Here, however, he exhi-bited no symptoms of that precocious genius which, ere long, was to "make grey-headed erudition bend before it." On the contrary, he was remarkably dull and stupid, receiving into his apparently obtuse skull no portion of the luminous instruction which the pedagogue of a free-school could be supposed to impart.*

Indeed, it seemed pretty plain that the young Chatterton was about to turn out an incorrigible dunce. The most ordinary attainments acquired by the generality of children while yet in the nurse's arms,—the commonest rudiments of knowledge,—the very letters of the alphabet, though insinuated by no harsh master, but by the care of a fond and anxious mother, seemed to baffle every attempt made to pene-trate the hopeless stupidity, which there was reason

---

* Either his faculties were not yet opened, or the waywardness of genius, which will pursue only such objects as are self-approved, inca-pacitated him from receiving instruction in the ordinary method.—Dr. Gregory.

to apprehend he would always exhibit. This circum-
stance appears to have caused his poor parent, to
whom he was sent back on the score of incapacity, a
great deal of uneasiness; and we are told by a neigh-
bour, that "until he was six years and a half old, she
thought him to be an absolute fool, and often when
correcting him, told him so."

But a change was soon to be displayed. There
chanced to be in her possession an old musical
manuscript, in French, and adorned with illuminated
capitals. It arrested the child's attention; to use his
mother's words, he "*fell in love*" with it.* He began
to read. An ancient black-letter Bible, which she
brought to her assistance, completed the attraction.
Thomas Chatterton was no more a dunce.

* How much of what is commonly called genius—or at least, how
much of the secondary direction of genius, which marks its varieties,
and gives it a specific distinctive character—depends on accidents of
the slightest kind, that modify the general tendencies of suggestion, by
the peculiar liveliness which they give to certain trains of thought. I
am aware, indeed, that in cases of this sort, we may often err—and
that we may probably err, to a certain extent, in the greater number of
them—in ascribing to the accident, those mental peculiarities which
existed before it was observed, and which would afterwards, as original
tendencies, have developed themselves in any circumstances in which
the individual might have been placed; but the influence of circum-
stances, though apt to be magnified, is not on that account the less real;
and though we may sometimes err, therefore, as to the particular ex-
amples, we cannot err as to the general influence itself.

We are told in the life of Chatterton, that, in his early boyhood, he
was reckoned of very dull intellect, till he "fell in love," as his mother
expressed it, with the illuminated capitals of an old musical manuscript,
in French, from which she afterwards taught him to read. It is impos-
sible to think of the subsequent history of this wonderful young man,
without tracing a probable connexion of those accidental circumstances,
which could not fail to give a peculiar importance to certain concep-
tions, with the character of that genius, which was afterwards to make
grey-headed erudition bend before it, and to astonish at least all those
on whom it did not impose.—Brown's *Philosophy of the Mind.*

He was taught to read from an old black-letter Testament, or
Bible. Perhaps the bent of most men's studies may, in some measure,

His mental cultivation now commenced in earnest.
He read with the utmost avidity. He stormed the
bookshelves of all his acquaintance. He devoured,
not volumes, but libraries. "At seven," says the
same neighbour, who was much in the house, "he
visibly improved: at eight years of age he was so
eager for books, that he read from the moment he
waked, which was early, until he went to bed, if they
would let him." And the dreams of ambition were
already commenced. A manufacturer promised to
make the children a present of some earthenware—
a cup or plaything that might gratify a child: he
asked the boy what device should be inscribed on his.
"Paint me," replied the future creator of Rowley—
"Paint me an angel, with wings and a trumpet, *to
trumpet my name over the world.*" This anecdote
rests upon credible authority—that of his sister.

"My brother," writes the same relation, in her
expressive letter to Sir Herbert Croft, "very early
discovered a thirst for pre-eminence. I remember,
before he was five years old he would always preside
over his playmates as their master, and they his hired
servants. He was dull in learning, not knowing
many letters at four years old, and always objected to
read in a small book. He learnt the alphabet from
an old folio music-book of my father's, my mother
was then tearing up for waste paper: the capitals at

be determined by accident, and frequently in very early life; nor is it
unreasonable to suppose that his peculiar attachment to antiquities
may, in a considerable degree, have resulted from this little circum-
stance.—DR. GREGORY.
  One of his biographers has expressed surprise that a person in his
mother's rank of life should have been acquainted with black-letter.

the beginning of the verses I assisted in teaching him. I recollect nothing remarkable till he went into the school, which was in his eighth year, excepting his promising my mother and me a deal of finery, when he grew up, as a reward of her care."

The affection with which he regarded his relatives, whom throughout his life he distinguished by every token of regard, forms indeed one of the most interesting traits of his character. Here it began to manifest itself in the promise of fine clothes—of gauds and frippery—which no doubt his pen was to procure; and the child's dream of greatness derived additional splendour from the imagined glories of his bedizened friends.

Another change became apparent in him.* He grew reserved and thoughtful. He was silent and gloomy for long intervals together, speaking to no one, and appearing angry when noticed or disturbed. He would break out into sudden fits of weeping, for which no reason could be assigned; would shut himself up in some chamber, and suffer no one to ap-

---

The writer might have known that books of the ancient type continued to be read in that rank of life long after they had ceased to be used by persons of a higher station.(1)—CAMPBELL.

* From this time forth throughout his life, he was the subject of what we may be allowed to call an intensity of mind. Who shall explain the spell which held such a spirit in impregnable torpor up to a particular moment, far beyond the age at which rudiments are mastered with ease by the generality of children, and then broke, and let it dart forth with impetuous energy? This energy was not, we may presume, suspended, or in a stagnant state, but only working reflexly and more deeply, in those moody intervals in which he would be long invincibly silent, not from sullenness of temper, and would sometimes weep, from no cause that was known, or that he afterwards assigned. The elements of his nature were in a state of fermentation, which threw out strange and capricious effects.—ECLECTIC REVIEW.

(1) The biographer alluded to was Chalmers.—ED.

proach him, nor allow himself to be enticed from his seclusion. Often he would go the length of absenting himself from home altogether, for the space, sometimes, of many hours: and his sister remembered his being most severely chastised for a long absence; at which he did not however shed one tear, but merely said, "It was hard indeed to be whipped for reading."

Not unfrequently a search was instituted. His mother's house was close to the fine structure of St. Mary Redcliffe, and they well knew that the boy's favourite haunts were the aisles and towers of that noble pile. And there they would find the truant, seated generally by the tomb of Canynge, or lodged in one of the towers, reading sometimes, or—what if thus early imagining Rowley? Stealing away in this manner, he would constantly awaken the solicitude of his friends, to whom his little eccentricities were already the source of much uneasiness.

In August, 1760, when he had not quite attained his eighth year, he was admitted into the school established at Bristol for charitable purposes, by one Edward Colston in 1708. This person, who was a merchant, and who by excess of industry possessed himself of almost unlimited wealth, has recorded his benevolent disposition in the numerous benefactions which he has bestowed on his native city. In this institution, which is situated in a part of that city called St. Augustine's Back, one hundred boys are clothed, boarded, and educated, and in many instances apprenticed at a suitable age to some credit-

able trade or profession. The rules are very strict:
the hours in summer are, from seven o'clock till
twelve in the morning, and from one to five in the
afternoon; in winter they assemble from eight till
twelve, and from one to four. Throughout the year
they are obliged to be in bed by eight o'clock, and are
never permitted to be absent from school, except on
Saturdays and Saints'-days, and then only from
between one and two in the afternoon, and seven and
eight in the evening. Into this school, and subject
to these regulations, was Chatterton admitted, at a
time when his faculties were ripe for cultivation, his
ambition eager for enterprize, his soul expanding with
desire for renown.

After all, however, it was only a charity-school;
and elated as he was with the prospect of acquiring
knowledge, he soon manifested his disgust. He is said
to have asserted " that he could not learn so much at
school as he could at home, for they had not books
enough there." It was but a kind of mercantile,
ledger and day-book education the young poet was
receiving : they taught him nothing but reading,
writing, and arithmetic,—made him each day pursue
the round of a gin-horse, while his brain was labour-
ing with the conception of Rowley, soon to issue
from that teeming womb. Who can wonder that
Chatterton was disgusted ?

But he was not so backward, even here: he kept
stirring, and made some progress, especially in the
arithmetic classes, in which the usher allowed him to
be amongst the foremost. This usher will be remem-

bered with the fame of Chatterton, for *he* too—in his
way—was a poet: and the reader of Chatterton's works
will recollect the Elegy on his death, composed in
later years, but bearing adequate testimony to the
warmth of their mutual attachment.   He appears to
have been an amiable and estimable man, and is indeed
so connected with the early life of Chatterton, and the
first production of Rowley, that Dr. Gregory is justi-
fied in lamenting the want of a more perfect memoir
of him.   One of his intimate acquaintances shall tell
us all that is known respecting him :—

  " In the summer of 1763, being then in the 12th year of
my age, I contracted an intimacy with one Thomas Phillips,
who was some time usher or assistant master of a hospital or
charity-school, founded for the education and maintenance of
youth at Bristol, by Edward Colston, Esquire.   Phillips,
notwithstanding the disadvantage of a very confined educa-
tion, possessed a taste for history and poetry; of the latter,
the magazines and other periodicals of that time furnish no
very contemptible specimen.

  " Towards the latter end of that year, by means of my in-
timacy with Phillips, I formed a connexion with Chatterton,
who was on the foundation of that school, and about four-
teen months younger than myself.   The poetical attempts of
Phillips had excited a kind of literary emulation amongst the
elder classes of the scholars ; the love of fame animated their
bosoms, and a variety of competitors appeared to dispute the
laurel with him : their endeavours however, in general, did
not meet with the success which their zeal and assiduity
deserved ; and Phillips still, to the mortification of his oppo-
nents, came off victorious and unhurt.

  " In all these trifling contentions, the fruits of which are
now, and have been long since, deservedly and entirely forgot-
ten, Chatterton appeared merely as an idle spectator, no ways
interested in the business of the drama: simply contenting
himself with the sports and pastimes more immediately
adapted to his age, he apparently possessed neither inclina-
tion, nor indeed ability, for literary pursuits ; nor do I believe
(notwithstanding the evidence adduced to the contrary by the
author of Love and Madness) that he attempted the composi-

tion of a single couplet during the first three years of my acquaintance with him." *

We shall presently find this opinion to be incorrect; in the meantime, as, in the writer's company, we have stepped over to the summer of 1763, we must look back and see how Chatterton has been employed. He is reported to have stood aloof from the society of his schoolmates—to have made few acquaintances, and only amongst those whose dispositions inclined them to reflection.

After his admission into the school—two years after say some authorities, but hardly so long—his mother allowed him a trifle for pocket-money, which found its way to the treasury of a bookseller, who supplied him, in return, with all the literature his circulating-shelves could afford. The bibliopole was liberal, too, for when the pence were not forthcoming, knowing the boy's family, he allowed him to select his volume,

* Letter from Mr. Thistlethwaite to Dean Milles, printed in the Dean's Edition of Rowley, and in Southey and Cottle's Edition of Chatterton, vol iii.—" Whatever grounds Mr. Thistlethwaite might have for this opinion, it however only serves to furnish an additional proof of the deceitfulness of those conjectures which are formed concerning the abilities of youth. The pert and forward boy, of active, but superficial talents, generally bears away the palm from the modesty and pensiveness of genius. Such a disposition, which is in reality the result of insensibility, too frequently meets with encouragement, which produces indolence, impudence, and dissipation; while the less shewy, but more excellent understandings are depressed by neglect, or disheartened by discouragement. Chatterton, doubtless, at that very period, was possessed of a vigour of understanding, of a quickness of penetration, a boldness of imagination, far superior to the talents of his companions. But that penetration itself led him, perhaps, to feel more strongly his own deficiencies; those delicate, yet vivid feelings which usually accompany real abilities, induced him to decline a contest, in which there was a danger of experiencing the mortification of being inferior. If he produced any compositions, his exquisite taste led him to suppress them. In the meantime he was laying in stores of information, and improving both his imagination and his judgment."—Dr. Gregory.

and even to make transcripts from new books.* His name deserves to be recorded ; he was a Mr. Goodal, and he kept his shop nearly opposite the Cider House Passage, in Broad Street.

The works thus procured were of a very miscellaneous character. Chatterton confined his studies to no particular head. In later life he pursued the same course, and amassed a confused heap of heterogeneous knowledge, which included subjects the most abstruse. Even at this early period he perused promiscuously, works on religion, history, biography, poetry, heraldry,—and betrayed a passionate attachment for antiquities. To be sure, the Burgum pedigree was engendering in his brain—a mere fœtus, to be delivered in due time. He was not very communicative, this poet in embryo; neither too obsequious, though incurring a favour ; he merely bowed his head, as he entered the shop, and made a similar obeisance on taking leave.

In fact, the pride, the reserve, the native and unconquerable haughtiness had already betrayed itself in his young character. One expression—that " God had sent his creatures into the world with arms long enough to reach anything, if they chose to be at the trouble," was frequently in his mouth. He was in arms for the omnipotence of the human intellect.

* Recorded on the authority of W. H. Ireland, the fabricator of the Shakespeare MSS. The reader can refer to his "Confessions" and allow the passage what credit he pleases. In this, as in one or two other incidents in the early life of Chatterton obtained from the same source, and inserted in this biography, the author observes nothing of a suspicious nature—even when the character of Ireland is taken into consideration. The name of the bookseller is derived from Dix.

Slight mistake, that; though he did his share, and something more: how many have performed one thousandth such a part?

Soon after this time he wrote a catalogue of all the books he had read; the number amounted to seventy,—not despicable for his contracted means. The subjects they embraced were chiefly history and divinity, all devoured, and digested perhaps—in a manner, after school-hours, and during the seasons allotted for recreation. Bingham, Young, and Stillingfleet were among them. No slender stock of theology he was accumulating; but then—Rowley's sermon was to follow.

It cannot be doubted that all this time the elements of his great work were arranging themselves in order, and silently shaping into Ella tragedies and Bawdin histories. During holidays and half-holidays, and leisure moments—whenever he could procure them—he would retire to a little room which he called his own, shutting himself in, and allowing no one to bear him company. Here he would remain for hours, in no way solicitous about external things. Of his meals he was even oblivious, letting the hour slip by, or disregarding the often repeated summons; and making his appearance at last begrimed with ochre, charcoal, and black-lead.

Now, that in this small head of a tonsure-becapped charity-boy—barely in his tenth year—there should be already fermenting Rowley poems, is a circumstance which our philosophers will find it hard to deal with; sufficiently probable, however, and a kind of "psychological romance" in its way. It is pretty well established, by the testimony of those who were likely to know something of the matter, that he had already commenced his preparations.

To many readers, there may savour something of offence in dwelling thus minutely upon every circumstance of his early life. Let such persons remember that the biography of Chatterton is that of a boy,—that he died before most boys have acquired the knowledge of walking across a room with propriety,—and further, that this is no Walter Scott-life, or Burns-life, or even Byron-life—but a Chatterton-life. And again, that Chatterton was a boy—and a charity-boy.

II.

Confirmed at ten years old by the Bishop—Is articled to an Attorney—Commences the Rowley fabrications.

At ten years old, Chatterton was confirmed; an age, apparently, when the meaning of the rite, the importance ascribed to it, or the nature of the responsibility, could hardly have been understood by him. But Chatterton, we repeat, was no common boy. Not only was he prepared for the occasion, but his sister adds, that he made very "sensible and serious remarks on the awfulness of the ceremony," and his own feelings in relation to it. This event is assigned by all his historians, whose authority indeed is the evidence of his sister, to a period full two years later.

The date commonly ascribed, however—that of his twelfth year—has been sufficiently invalidated by Mr. Tyson, to authorise the present biographer in assigning it to the earlier period. His sister, Mrs. Newton, made reference to the event many years after it had taken place, when her brother had been long dead, during an interval of ill-health, too, as she acknowledges; and no considerable time before her own disordered faculties rendered her a subject of painful attention. Her account is as follows:—

"At twelve years old, he was confirmed by the Bishop: he made very sensible, serious remarks on the awfulness of the ceremony, and his own feelings and convictions during it. Soon after this, in the week he was door-keeper, he made some verses on the last day, I think about eighteen lines; paraphrased the ninth chapter of Job; and, not long after, some chapters in Isaiah. He had been gloomy from the time he began to learn, but we remarked he was more cheerful after he began to write poetry. Some satirical pieces we saw soon after."[*]

Upon this Mr. Tyson remarks:—

"Mrs. Newton's communications in this letter are evidently what they profess to be, the result of recollection, and on a subject, as she acknowledges, painful to the writer, as well as undertaken at a period of ill-health. With respect to dates, therefore, it is exceedingly probable that mistakes should occur, and especially where they do not tend to affect the credibility of the circumstances to which they relate.

"That Mrs. Newton was incorrect in asserting that it was not till after he was twelve years old that Chatterton produced his first poetical attempts, is apparent from the statement of Sir Herbert Croft, that the satirical verses entitled "Sly Dick," as well as the Hymn for Christmas-Day, were written by Chatterton at about the age of eleven; information which he must have derived either from Mrs. Newton, or from her mother, Mrs. Chatterton. The inaccuracy of

---

[*] Letter to Sir Herbert Croft.

Mrs. Newton's memory with respect to the date of her brother's first poetical efforts, is further proved, beyond all controversy, by the fact that the verses entitled "Apostate Will" bear the date in Chatterton's own hand-writing, of April 14, 1764, when he was not quite eleven years and five months old.

"This point being established, it remains to determine to what limit Mrs. Newton's inaccuracy upon the subject may reasonably be supposed to extend.

"There can be no doubt of the correctness of Mrs. Newton's statement, that her brother began to write poetry soon after he was confirmed. Her error, as to his age when he produced his first poetical efforts, arose from the period she assigned to his confirmation; and the question about to be raised is, whether that event did not take place when he was ten years old, instead of twelve, as stated by Mrs. Newton.

"In support of the assumption of the inaccuracy of her memory, in reference to the date of her brother's confirmation, it should be recollected that her letter was written on the 22nd of September, 1778, fourteen years after the period assigned by her as that when the event took place; and when the circumstances under which she wrote are also considered, it appears but reasonable to conclude that, whether fourteen or sixteen years had elapsed since the period to which she refers, was a point on which her memory was not unlikely to prove fallacious.

"Neither is there any improbability to contend with, in assigning Chatterton's confirmation to so early a period of his life. More than five years had then elapsed since "the wond'rous boy" fell in love, to use his mother's expression, with the rudiments of literature: and such was the ardour he evinced in the pursuit of knowledge, that at the very time to which it is contended the circumstance of his confirmation should be assigned, he was in the habit, as his sister informs us, of expending what was given him for pocket-money in hiring books from a circulating library.

"In addition to these suggestions in favour of the supposition that Chatterton was confirmed at the age of ten instead of twelve years, the verses themselves, now produced as those which he wrote upon the occasion, combined with the circumstances connected with their publication, may be confidently adduced as tending in a very high degree to establish the position. Besides the identity of the subject, they consist of sixteen lines, approximating to Mrs. Newton's statement in that respect, as nearly as can be expected from the indeterminate manner in which she expresses herself; they contain abundant internal proof of the juvenility of the writer; they were inserted in the Bristol newspaper to which Chatterton, as well as his literary associates, were subsequently in the habit of communicating their productions; and they appeared in the seventh week after he had attained the tenth year of his age."*

Mr. Tyson then produces the lines, to which we shall presently refer.

Now, considering this position as established, we cannot but remark upon the wonderful prematurity which is evident in everything relating to the life of Chatterton; and the many ordinary existencies that were compressed into those seventeen years of his. Not by decades, and hardly by lustrums, could he reckon, who yet found time to consummate a creation. Calculating by what he has effected and left behind him, his genius, before his sixteenth year, seems to have attained the meridian of its vigour; and upon this circumstance in particular, his claim to admiration is founded.

Something too fast, however, at the age of ten, to comment upon sixteen.

With respect to Chatterton's first poetical productions Mr. Tyson is undoubtedly right. It was written in 1762, instead of 1764. His sister is positive to the subject, which she states to be "verses on the last day—about eighteen lines—written in the week he was door-keeper."* To Mr. Tyson's industrious

---

* From a communication respecting Chatterton's first poetical production, published as an Appendix to Dix's Life, and which I am permitted, by the kindness of Mr. Tyson, to make use of in this biography.

research we owe the preservation of these lines, which it was thought were entirely lost. " It is with a feeling of gratification," observes that gentleman, "that they are rescued from the obscurity in which they were enveloped, and placed before the public eye, as exhibiting the flutterings of the unfledged eaglet." They were published in *Felix Farley s Bristol Journal,* for January 8th, 1763, and are entitled—

ON THE LAST EPIPHANY, OR CHRIST COMING TO
JUDGMENT.

Behold ! just coming from above,
The JUDGE, with majesty and love !
The sky divides, and rolls away,
T' admit him through the realms of day !
The sun astonish'd, hides its face,
The moon and stars with wonder gaze
At JESU's bright superior rays !
Dread lightnings flash, and thunders roar,
And shake the earth and briny shore ;
The trumpet sounds at heaven's command,
And pierceth through the sea and land ;
The dead in each now hear the voice,
The sinners fear and saints rejoice ;
For now the awful hour is come,
When every tenant of the tomb
Must rise, and take his everlasting doom.

Nothing uncommon in these—even for ten years ; but then, in composition, as in everything else, when once fairly in progress, Chatterton made rapid strides towards perfection.

" *He had been gloomy from the time he began to*

---

* It was, and still is, I believe, customary for the boys educated at Colston's school to take the post of door-keeper in rotation, the office continuing for the space of a week at a time in the occupation of one boy. Of course the lad in office had much leisure time during this period.—DIX's *Life.*

learn, but he became more cheerful when he began to write poetry." Why, the weight—the incubus—was removed. He had burst his bonds—could flutter now, and prepare himself for higher flights. It was pleasant even to feel his liberty, and to know that what was within him he could speak out. The bandage was removed from the eyes of the mewed bird. He could behold the heaven, where his thoughts rested—whence his prophesyings had descended, and the living fire that had tipped his tongue. While he was yet musing, the flame had kindled. His beliefs, his aspirations, and his ardent yearnings—burning, struggling to be uttered—they might be uttered now.

"*Some satirical pieces we saw soon after.*" That is, after his twelfth, or, as it has been proved, his tenth year. Of his powers of satire, we shall, bye-and-by, have much to say. It has been generally thought that his verses entitled "Apostate Will" were his first essay in that line. The opinion was erroneous; and the proof in this case we likewise owe to Mr. Tyson. This " Apostate Will" was an unprincipled man, who for mercenary motives shifted his religion from one sect to another without compunction. Sir Herbert Croft transcribed it after his death from an old pocket-book in the possession of his relatives. This pocket-book had been given to him by his sister, as a New-year's present, after his confirmation, and he had subsequently returned it to her filled with attempts at poetry. " It appears," says the transcriber, "to be his first, perhaps his only copy of it, and is evidently his hand-writing. By the date, he was eleven years and almost five months old. It is not the most extraordinary performance in the world; but, from the circumstance of Chatterton's parentage and education, it is unlikely, if not impossible, that he should have met with any assistance or correction: whereas, when we read the Ode which Pope wrote at twelve, and another of Cowley at thirteen, we are apt to suspect a parent, friend, or tutor, of an amiable dishonesty, of which we feel perhaps that we should be guilty. Suspicions of this nature touch not Chatterton. He knew no tutor, friend, or parent, at least no parent who could correct or assist him."*

This is a lame and impotent conclusion. Pope's father was anything but friendly disposed towards his son's poetical powers. *He* would not, even if he could, have assisted him. And Chatterton *had* a tutor—which tutor was his intimate friend, and who himself made a pretence of writing poetry—Thomas Phillips. The verses, however, for which this question is begged, would confer as little credit on Phillips as they do on Chatterton. One or two of his critics, indeed, staunch for the existence of Rowley, have made them a pretence for undervaluing his genius, because, forsooth, he does not include the imbecile disciples of Wesley in the ranks of the Protestants, and—astonishing inference!—have discovered from this circumstance that he could not be the creator of Rowley.

But—somewhat wide of our mark. We do not

---

* "Love and Madness," by Sir Herbert Croft.

indeed mean to assert that Chatterton received assis-
tance from Phillips, or from any living being; on the
contrary, his unassisted powers were sufficient for
anything: but the observations of the Reverend
Baronet have always been as a beam in our eye, and
—we have now cast it out.

We must again have recourse to Mr. Tyson.

"In *Felix Farley's Bristol Journal* of Saturday, December
17, 1763, and some following numbers, a succession of satiri-
cal attacks, in verse and prose, are inserted, on a churchwar-
den who is accused of having ordered the levelling of the
church-yard entrusted to his care, and of hauling away the
clay to be used for the purposes of his trade as a brickmaker.
One of the pieces states that the church-yard alluded to "is
an appendage to the grandest structure in this city;" thus
clearly indicating it to be that of St. Mary Redcliffe, the
churchwarden of which, for the year 1763, was Joseph
Thomas; and by a familiar abbreviation of whose Christian
name, the person satirized is addressed in the lines about to be
produced. With respect to their authorship, the locality of
the circumstance to which they relate would directly point to
Chatterton, in whose mind the subject could not fail of ex-
citing an interest; in addition to which it presented a tempt-
ing opportunity of indulging the propensity to satire, which
formed so prominent a trait in his character.

"But Chatterton's title to the composition in question
requires no other proof than a comparison with the satire
entitled "Sly Dick," the commencement of which is here
transcribed to facilitate the reader's immediate reference.

> "Sharp was the frost, the wind was high,
> And sparkling stars bedeckt the sky:
> Sly Dick in arts of cunning skill'd,
> Whose rapine all his pockets fill'd,
> Had laid him down to take his rest,
> And soothe with sleep his anxious breast.
> 'Twas then a dark infernal sprite," &c.
>
> *   *   *   *   *

And then follows the "first satirical poem," which, as
we have not included it in the collection of his "Ac-
knowledged Poems," we proceed to transcribe. It

appeared in the Journal before mentioned for January 7, 1764.

THE CHURCHWARDEN AND THE APPARITION.

A FABLE.

The night was cold, the wind was high,
And stars bespangled all the sky;
Churchwarden J*E. had laid him down,
And slept secure on bed of down;
But still the pleasing hope of gain
That never left his active brain,
Expos'd the church-yard to his view,
That seat of treasure wholly new.
" Pull down that cross," he quickly cried,
The mason instantly complied;
When, lo! behold the golden prize
Appears—joy sparkles in his eyes.
The door now creaks,—the window shakes,
With sudden fear he starts and wakes;
Quaking and pale, in eager haste
His haggard eyes around he cast;
A ghastly phantom, lean and wan,
That instant rose and thus began:
" Weak wretch—to think to blind my eyes!
Hypocrisy's a thin disguise;
Your humble mien and fawning tongue
Have oft deceiv'd the old and young.
On this side now, and now on that,
The very emblem of the bat:
What ever part you take we know
'Tis only interest makes it so.
And tho' with sacred zeal you burn,
Religion's only for your turn.
I'm Conscience call'd!"—J*E. greatly fear'd;
The lightning flash'd—it disappear'd.*

---

* " The paper," continues Mr..Tyson, " from which this poem is extracted. contains a letter, addressed to the printer on the same subject, with the signature of " FULLFORD *the Grave-digger.*" To enter into any argument to prove that it was written by Chatterton would be trifling with the reader's judgment, for to no other person than the author of the " Bristowe Tragedy" would such a signature have occurred. The observation, however, should not be omitted, that this circumstance affords a decided proof of Chatterton's acquaintance with the subject of one of the finest of Rowley's poems, upwards of four

Nothing of "Kew Gardens" here,—and yet it was written in little better than five years afterwards.

These productions are sufficient to convict Mr. Thistlethwaite of inaccuracy in the opinion which he had formed of Chatterton's power, and the period at which he first began to join couplets together. The poems of "Sly Dick" and "Apostate Will" are in

years before the least intimation was given of the discovery of any ancient manuscripts. Here follows the letter :—

"MR. PRINTER,

"Being *old*, and having enjoyed my place many a long year, I have buried, or rather dug the graves for one half of our parish ; and could tell to an inch, *where* and *how* their bodies lie, and are ranged under ground ; and by this my skill am always consulted by my master, the sexton, where such and such a family are interred, and have never failed of giving great satisfaction in the discharge of my office. But, alas ! I am like to be robbed at once, of all my knowledge, procured at the expence of so many years' close study and application to business : for you must know, my READ MASTER, a great projector, has taken it into his head to level the church-yard ; and by digging and throwing about his *clay* there, and defacing the stones, makes such confusion among the *dead*, and will so puzzle me, if he goes on, that no man *living* will be able to find where to lay them properly, and then he may dig the graves himself ; for I foresee, I shall get the ill-will of the parish about it, for even the poor love to bury with their kindred : and all's but right that they should. I should be glad, therefore, to know the sense of the public, whether any body has a just right, or needful call to dig in the church-yard, besides ' FULLFORD *the Grave-digger*.'

"P.S. As I intend dropping the business of grave-digger, now rendered so very troublesome, I propose renting my old spot of ground (the church-yard) when the green turf is all removed, and for *decency's* sake, will prevent the *naked* appearance of it, by planting potatoes, raising some fine beds of onions, &c., as the mould is fat and good.— And I see no reason why I may not get a *profitable job* out of the church, as well as my GREAT MASTER,—as I find that's the game now-a-days, tho' decency, convenience or the like, be the pretence."

With all deference to Mr. Tyson's judgment, I do not think this *jeu d'esprit* to be the composition of Chatterton. Certainly the mere casual coincidence between the assumed name of the writer and that of Sir Baldwin Fulford, in the "Bristowe Tragedy," which I presume Mr. Tyson alludes to, is not sufficient to establish it. Besides, Chatterton has nowhere recorded that Sir Charles Bawdin and Sir Baldwin Fulford are the same,—there is a presumption that they are, but nothing more. I do not think that Chatterton in his twelfth year, was equal even to the very indifferent prose of the letter in question. He was never a good prose writer, and is no way tolerable in that line till 1770.—ED.

themselves a meagre evidence of his poetical faculties in his eleventh and twelfth years. But Thistlethwaite was an advocate for the genuineness of the Rowley Poems,—was a correspondent of Dean Milles on the subject,—and a bit of an author in his way.* He was no friend to Chatterton; and had an interest in depreciating his abilities.

Of the other juvenilities of Chatterton we shall not speak. Allowing him, which was undoubtedly the case, to have had his great work in contemplation, and to have been fitting his powers for the creation, we cannot help wishing that he had either not written at all such pieces as " Apostate Will"—or had written them better.

III.

Produces the Burgum pedigree — Leaves Colston's school, and is articled to one Lambert, an attorney.

In the house in which Mrs. Chatterton resided,—a poor back tenement, dismally situated in a kind of court, behind a row of somewhat better houses that fronted the street,—there was a small garret which had been used as a lumber-room. Of this apartment Chatterton possessed himself: he kept the key, and suffered no one, if he could help it, to have access to it. In it were deposited all his papers and

---

* He wrote some things which have been long since forgotten; " The Consultation"—" The Prediction of Liberty"—" The Tories in the Dumps"—and " Corruption," were among them. " He was a Colston's-school-boy, and apprenticed to Mr. Grant, bookseller and stationer. He afterwards went to London, and studied the law."—DIX.

parchments, and a variety of other articles, for which his relations found no other terms than "rubbish" and "litter," but which Chatterton managed to convert into uses that will confer immortality on his name. In short they were the materials, from which sprung to light the Manuscripts afterwards produced by him as the originals of Rowley, and which are now snugly preserved in the Library of the British Museum.

There were not many opportunities afforded him of labouring at his darling project. His hours of absence from Colston's school were wide apart—his half-holidays occurred but on Saturday afternoons. Punctually however as the day came round, he returned, arriving at home a few minutes after the boys were dismissed, and proceeded to shut himself in his chamber. What passed there remained a mystery; he revealed nothing to his friends.*

---

* From twelve to seven, each Saturday, he was always at home, returning punctually a few minutes after the clock had struck, to get to his little room, and shut himself up. In this room he always had by him a great piece of ochre in a brown pan, pounce-bags full of charcoal dust, which he had from a Miss Sanger, a neighbour; also a bottle of black-lead powder, which they once took to clean the stove with, and made him very angry. Every holiday almost he passed at home, and often, having been denied the key when he wanted it, (because they thought he hurt his health and made himself dirty,) he would come to Mrs. Edkins, and kiss her cheek, and coax her to get it for him, using the most persuasive expressions to effect his end;—so that this eagerness of his to be in this room so much alone, the apparatus, the parchments, (for he was not then indentured to Mr. Lambert,) both plain as well as written on, and the begrimed figure he always presented when he came down at tea-time, his face exhibiting many stains of black and yellow,—all these circumstances began to alarm them; and when she could get into his room, she would be very inquisitive, and peep about at every thing. Once he put his foot on a parchment on the floor, to prevent her from taking it up, saying, "You are too curious and clear-sighted—I wish you would bide out of the room—it is my room." To this she answered by telling him, it was only a general lumber room, and that she wanted some parchment to make thread-papers of;

The time thus spent, thus snatched from play and recreation, was indeed devoted to the production of his antique fabric. Immured in the solitude of his chamber, he was "creating poetry out of parchment, and calling beauteous spirits from antiquity to preside over their own apparently coeval relics." He seized a great conception, and wrote it down.

There were residing at this time in Bristol, two tradesmen, pewterers, and partners in that trade—Mr. Burgum, and Mr. George Catcott. Chatterton had attracted the notice of Mr. Burgum, as a remarkable boy, fond of reading, attached to antiquities, and of quick and lively intellect, and occasionally he had received from him small sums of money. There were few points of human character, which, young as he was, he had left unstudied. Burgum is described as having been a vain and credulous man, fond of notoriety and display,—a fit subject, undoubtedly, to practise a hoax upon; and Chatterton set about it.

He went to him one day, and told him that he had found his pedigree, from the time of William the Conqueror,—a pedigree that allied him to the proudest families in England,—a pedigree that deduced his descent from Simon de Leyncte Lyze, *alias* Senliz, who married Matilda, daughter of Waltheof, Earl of Nor-

but he was offended, and would not permit her to touch any of them, not even those that were not written on; but at last with a voice of entreaty, said, "Pray don't touch anything here," and seemed very anxious to get her away; and this increased her fears, lest he should be doing something improper, knowing his want of money, and ambition to appear like others. At last they got a strange idea that these colours were to colour himself, and that, perhaps, he would join some gipsies one day or other, as he seemed so discontented with his station in life, and unhappy.—*Communicated by G. Cumberland, Esq. in Dix's Life.*

thumberland, Northampton, and Huntingdon. He
assured the pewterer this, and the pewterer believed
it.

No doubt it *was* a pleasant thing to be told that the
blood which the scratch of a rusty nail might draw
was pure as the stream that flowed in lordly veins,—
to be conscious that after all he was nothing so despi-
cable,—no hop o' my thumb of yesterday,—not even
of the last batch of Baronets—but a lineal descendant
of a proud and almost princely Norman. It was some-
thing, this information, and well worth the crown with
which it was rewarded.

In the generosity of his elated heart, Mr. Burgum,
upon the production of this important document,—
presented its fortunate discoverer with the magnificent
sum of five shillings. From this recompense, and
some peculiarities displayed by the same gentleman,
Chatterton has handed him down to posterity in his
will :

> " Gods! what would Burgum give to get a name,
> And snatch his blundering dialect from shame !
> What would he give to hand his memory down
> To Time's remotest boundary ?—A crown.
> Would you ask more, his swelling face looks blue ;
> Futurity he rates at two pounds two.
> Well, Burgum, take thy laurel to thy brow ;
> With a rich saddle decorate a sow ;
> Strut in Iambics, totter in an ode,
> Promise, and never pay, and be the mode."

But where was this document found ?—and how
came it into the possession of a Bristol charity-boy ?
Rather important questions, in the estimation of those
at the Herald's office. Alas! Burgum, thy blue looks,
and thy blank looks—of what avail will they be ?

Thou must get thee back to thy pewterer's shop, and thy smelting pot.

The ancestors of Chatterton, for upwards of one hundred and fifty years, had filled the office of Sexton of the church of St. Mary Redcliffe. His uncle, indeed, John Chatterton, who died a few years- previous to his birth, had been the last of that name who had inherited it; but from the contiguity of his mother's house to that noble structure, the young Chatterton had generally a free access to all parts of the building. The affair is somewhat singular, and will be best told in the following extract from Dr. Gregory.

"Over the north porch of St. Mary Redcliffe church, which was founded, or at least rebuilt, by Mr. W. Canynge (an eminent merchant of Bristol in the fifteenth century, and in the reign of Edward the Fourth), there is a kind of muniment room, in which were deposited six or seven chests, one of which in particular was said to be *Mr. Canynge's cofre;* this chest, it is said, was secured by six keys, two of which were entrusted to the minister and procurator of the church, two to the mayor, and one to each of the churchwardens. In process of time, however, the six keys appear to have been lost; and about the year 1727, a notion prevailed that some title-deeds and other writings of value were contained in Mr. Canynge's cofre. In consequence of this opinion an order of vestry was made that the chest should be opened under the inspection of an attorney, and that those writings which appeared of consequence should be removed to the south porch of the church. The locks were therefore forced, and not only the principal chest, but the others, which were also supposed to contain writings, were all broken open. The deeds immediately relating to the church were removed, and the other manuscripts were left exposed as of no value. Considerable depredations had, from time to time, been committed upon them by different persons; but the most insatiate of these plunderers was the father of Chatterton. His uncle being sexton of St. Mary Redcliffe, gave him free access to the church. He carried off, from time to time, parcels of the parchments; and one time alone, with the assistance of the boys, is known to have filled a large basket with them. They were deposited in a cupboard in the school, and employed for different purposes, such as the covering of copy-books, &c.: in particular, Mr. Gibbs, the minister of the parish, having presented the boys with twenty bibles, Mr. Chatterton, in order to preserve these books from being damaged, covered them with some of the parchments. At his death, the widow being under the necessity of removing, carried the remainder of them to her new habitation. Of the discovery of their value by the younger Chatterton, the account of Mr. Smith, a very intimate acquaintance, which he gave to Dr. Glynn of Cambridge, is too interesting to be omitted. ' When young Chatterton was first articled to Mr. Lambert, he used frequently to come home to his mother, by way of a short visit. There, one day, his eye was caught by one of these parchments, which had been converted into a thread-paper. He found not only the writing to be very old, the characters very different from common characters, but that the subject therein treated was different from common subjects. Being naturally of an inquisitive and curious turn, he was very much struck with their appearance, and, as might be expected, began to question his mother what those thread-papers were, how she got them, and whence they came. Upon further inquiry, he was led to a full discovery of all the parchments which remained.' The bulk of them consisted of poetical and other compositions, by Mr. Canynge, and a particular friend of his, Thomas Rowley, whom Chatterton at first called a monk, and afterwards a secular priest of the fifteenth century. *Such at least appears to be the account which Chatterton thought proper to give, and which he wished to be believed.*"

That Chatterton was acquainted with these documents before he was articled to Mr. Lambert, is evident from the circumstance of his producing the Burgum pedigree, and his assertion that the materials from which it was compiled were found in the old chests in the muniment room of Redcliffe church.

Burgum never seems to have doubted the improbability of this story. We do not know that he even inquired about the originals, but appeared sufficiently contented with the *transcript* which Chatterton thought proper to give him. And lo!—in the charity-boy's hand-writing—in a small school-boy's copy-book, there came to Mr. Burgum a succinct account of all his ancestors, rescued from the gulph of all-devouring time. The document bore the following title: "An account of the family of the De Bergham, from the Norman Conquest to this time; collected from original records, tournament rolls, and the he-ralds of march and garter records, by T. Chatterton." The remuneration which Chatterton received, we have already stated to have been five shillings.

Elated with this success, and finding his poor dupe to be no way incredulous or suspicious of the hoax thus triumphantly practised upon him, Chatterton set to work again, and in a fortnight afterwards presented the pewterer with a second document, being nothing else than a supplement to the pedigree—in fact a "Continuation of the account of the family of the De Bergham, from the Norman Conquest to this time, by T. Chatterton." And indeed he had been even more liberal in this second communication than in the first, for *now* Mr. Burgum discovered that he might claim descent from an undoubted son of Par-nassus, who was, as Chatterton testified, "the greatest ornament of his age." The fact was truly undeniable; for here, preserved in the archives of Redcliffe church —amongst all the evidence that allied Mr. Burgum to nobility and royalty—appeared a poem written by his ancestor, one John De Bergham, and entituled "The Romaunte of the Cnyghte." This poem Chatterton had transcribed in all its genuine orthography, and the

better to elucidate its beauties—as Mr. Burgum was
unskilled in gothic lore—he accompanied it with a
modernized version, by *himself.* " To give you," says
he to the pewterer, " an idea of the poetry of the age,
take the following piece, wrote by him (John De
Bergham) about 1320." This was not all; he adds a
list of some of the works of which this said ancestor
was the author.

" This John was one of the greatest ornaments of the age
in which he lived. He wrote several books, *and translated
some part of the Iliad*, under the title ' Romance of Troy,'
which possibly may be the book alluded to in the following
French memoire.
" Un Lyvre ke parle de quartee principal gestes, et de
Charles: le romaunce Titus et Vespasian: le romaunce de
Agyres: le romaunce de Marchaunce: le romaunce de Ed-
mund et Agoland: le Ribaud par Monsieur Iscannus: le
romaunce de Tibbot de Arable: le romaunce de Troys, &c."

He brought likewise the De Bergham arms " la-
boriously painted" on parchment.

In this second portion of the pedigree the " ac-
count" is carried down to the reign of Charles the
Second; and there, as the pewterer was not unlikely
to know something of his ancestors—it being only re-
moved by a period of a hundred years—Chatterton
very wisely stopped.[*]

* Chatterton linked and gilded this splendid chain of ancestry
through all the ages remote enough to leave unbounded scope for
fiction: when he approached the regions of probability, he let the end
loose, that his friend might attach himself to it in the best way
he could.—SIR WALTER SCOTT.
[The " Romaunt of the Cnyghte" will be found in page 225 of this
edition; the modernised version is likewise inserted among the ac-
knowledged poems. As the Burgum pedigree is also reprinted among
the miscellaneous prose works of Chatterton at the end of the volume,
together with remarks upon it, by Mr. Cottle and others, I refer the
reader to it for further information.—ED.]

Long afterwards—after Chatterton's death, indeed—Mr. Burgum made a journey to London, and laid before the heralds of March and Garter, for their approval, this pedigree of the De Bergham family; the result was, that he returned to Bristol, carried on his pewtering, and thought no more of his ancestors!*

So much for the first creation of Thomas Chatterton.†

In the letter from Mr. Thistlethwaite to Dean Milles, to which we have before had occasion to refer, there is mention made of a circumstance, which, if true, will prove the composition of the Rowley poems to be already commenced.

"Going down Horse-street, near the school, one day during the summer of 1764, I accidentally met with Chatter-

---

* Messrs. Catcott and Burgum appear to have been respectable men, and to have carried on a good business. We can hardly laugh at the half-ennobled pewterer for swallowing the hoax, when we find the late editors of Chatterton's Works—Messrs. Southey and Cottle, 1803—not *daring* to say that they knew it to be such, but only questioning its authenticity.

† Chatterton had made essays in poetical composition, evincing remarkable prematurity of intellect, and, perhaps, had even begun to form the strange project which was to bring him into such notoriety, before he entered on the mechanical and always detested duties of his clerkship. It was, however, in that situation that the invisible forge was kept in constant heat to work out the scheme: and he gravely amused himself, at the expense of some young or elder acquaintance, by producing from time to time, some fragment or completed cast of composition, presented sometimes on an apparently old piece of parchment, drawn, as he pretended, out of the mass of that material which had come into his possession after being thrown as rubbish out of the famous chest. He duped and elated a foolish tradesman, who was in some sort his friend, but not much worth as such, by presenting to him, set forth in all heraldic formalities, a pedigree which deduced his descent, greatly to his surprise, from an ancestry high in antiquity and rank. He might have continued to enjoy, and might have transmitted the new-found honour, if he had not been at last so ill advised as to carry the document which awarded it to him to the test of the herald's office.—ECLECTIC REVIEW.

ton; entering into conversation with him, the subject of which I do not now recollect, he informed me that he was in possession of certain old MSS. which had been deposited in a chest in Redcliffe church, and that he had lent some, or one of them, to Phillips. Within a day or two after this I saw Phillips, and repeated to him the information I had received from Chatterton. Phillips produced a MS. on parchment or vellum, which I am confident was *"Elinoure and Juga,"* a kind of pastoral eclogue, afterwards published in the Town and Country Magazine for May 1769. The parchment or vellum appeared to have been closely pared round the margin, for what purpose or by what accident I know not, but the words were evidently entire and unmutilated.

" As the writing was yellow and pale, manifestly as I conceive occasioned by age, and consequently difficult to decipher, Phillips had with his pen traced and gone over several of the lines, (which, as far as my recollection serves, were written in the manner of prose, and without any regard to punctuation,) and by that means laboured to attain the object of his pursuit —an investigation of their meaning. I endeavoured to assist him, but from an almost total ignorance of the character, manners, language, and orthography of the age in which the lines were written, all our efforts were unprofitably exerted; and although we arrived at an explanation, and corrected many of the words, still the sense was notoriously deficient.

" For my own part, having little or no taste for such studies, I repined not at the disappointment; Phillips, on the contrary, was to all appearance mortified; indeed, much more so than at that time I thought the object deserved; expressing his sorrow at his want of success, and repeatedly declaring his intention of resuming the attempt at a future period."*

Little dependence, I believe, is to be placed on the veracity of Mr. Thistlethwaite's statement. It is true that his letter was written in 1781, seventeen years after the time to which he refers; and that at the

---

* If this narrative may be depended on, Chatterton had discovered these manuscripts before he was twelve years of age. It is, however, scarcely consistent with other accounts, since both Mrs. Chatterton and her daughter seem to be of opinion that he knew nothing of the parchments brought from Redcliffe church, which were supposed to contain Rowley's poems, till after he had left school. There appears good reason for suspecting some mistake in Mr. Thistlewaite's narrative, either as to the date, or some other circumstance.— DR. GREGORY.

period in question he was only *thirteen* years of age.
What could a charity-boy, like Thistlethwaite, of
hardly average talents, know about the antiquity of
parchment and vellum, and the genuineness of manu-
scripts of the fifteenth century? I must be pardoned
if I state that I believe the whole to be a fabrication.
Phillips and Chatterton were both dead, and no doubt
could be thrown on the story. And allowing—what
I will readily acknowledge—Chatterton to have been
the most remarkable youth upon record, I cannot,
with "Apostate Will" and the "Hymn to Christmas
Day" before me, as the evidence of his poetical
powers at eleven, believe, that in less than a year he
could have *produced*—though he might have contem-
plated—one of the finest of the Rowley Poems. Cer-
tainly, among the parchments which were preserved
as originals, there is no trace of "Elinoure and Juga."

It was on the 1st of July, 1767, that Chatterton
took his leave of Colston's school. He had been
there nearly seven years. On the same day he was
bound apprentice to a Mr. John Lambert, an at-
torney; the trustees of the school paying the usual
fee of ten pounds to his new master. The inden-
tures of his apprenticeship are preserved in the
Literary and Scientific Institution at Bristol. They
specify that he was to be found in food, clothing, and
lodging by his master; while his mother was to wash
and mend for him.

And here a new era opened in the life of Chatter-
ton. It does not indeed appear that he had any choice
offered him of a situation,—or whether his inclina-

tions were consulted,—whether, in short, he had any interest in the affair, further than a home found him for another seven years, which was the intended term of his apprenticeship. His mother was very poor; and he would not like to have remained a burden upon her, which in the choice of another occupation might have occurred; his every wish, on the contrary, seems to have been, to relieve and assist her.

But here he was removed from home altogether: no more Saturday afternoons, and whole holidays on saint's-days; no more of the little room, and hammering on the Rowley anvil—not, at least, in the neighbourhood of Redcliffe church, and the tomb of "dynge Maistre Canynge." A great mistake, Mr. Catcott seems to have made, when, in the Gentleman's Magazine for August 1788, he says that Chatterton first presented him with the poems of Rowley in 1768, while he wore on his head *the tonsure-cap of Colston's school.*

There was very little business transacted in Lambert's office, and, with the exception of about two or three hours, Chatterton had the whole day to himself. He was kept sufficiently strict however, being sent to the office every morning at eight o'clock, where he remained, omitting the sixty minutes allotted for dinner, till the clock stood at the same hour in the evening. He was then at liberty till ten o'clock, at which time the family went to bed. When in the house, which was distinct from the office, he was confined to the kitchen; he slept with the foot-boy, and was subjected to other indignities of a like nature.

His pride, which always characterised him, took offence at this mortifying treatment, and he became gloomy and sullen, exhibiting frequent fits of ill-temper.

Lambert, indeed, was a vulgar, insolent, imperious man, who, because the boy wrote poetry, was of a melancholy and contemplative disposition, and disposed to study and reading, thought him a fit object of insult and contemptuous usage. Yet, notwithstanding, he bears the highest testimony to the worth of Chatterton, to his regularity in his profession, his punctual attendance on all the duties required of him, and admits that he once only had occasion to correct him. And then Chatterton must needs satirize the head-master of the school he had just left, a Mr. Warner, in an anonymous letter, written in very abusive terms, but which the hand-writing, only partially disguised, and the texture of the paper—being the same as that used in the office—brought home to the real culprit. On this occasion he struck him a few blows.

Chatterton was a good apprentice. There are still extant in his hand-writing, a folio book of law forms and precedents, containing three hundred and thirty-four closely written pages; also thirty-six pages in another book of the same kind. In the noting book are thirty-six notarial acts, besides many notices and letters transcribed in the ordinary book. These were done independently of his regular duties. At night, punctually as the clock struck ten, he would be at Mr. Lambert's door. " We saw him," his sister writes, "most evenings before nine, and he would, in general, stay to the limits of his time, which was ten. He was seldom two evenings together without seeing us." The time, also, which was at his command, when he neglected to visit his friends, was generally spent in solitary rambles. Mr. Lambert says that he never knew him in bad company, or suspected him of any inclination thereto.

When we consider that he was now fifteen years of age, and that in less than three years more his career of existence was terminated, we begin to enquire where, and how, did he find time to produce the works which now bear his name? Let the reader examine the contents of this volume. A goodly quantity even here, to say nothing of the quality: and this without taking into account a series of Prose Works not of sufficient value to be reprinted; and many poems, some of considerable length, which are gone altogether, which perished with their author when he tore his manuscripts into fragments; or have been since lost by the carelessness of persons into whose possession they fell.*

That the greater part of his works were written during his stay with Mr. Lambert,—that the Creation, which will for ever confer immortality on his name, was consummated in these hours of leisure, of which, we have already intimated, many fell to his share,

---

* That this has been the case with many of his productions, there is no doubt. Walpole speaks of several which he *saw*, and which are now no where to be found. Among these were "The Flight," addressed to Lord Bute, in forty stanzas of six lines each; and "The Dowager, a Tragedy," unfinished.

there is abundant evidence to prove. We are indeed entering upon his life in earnest, when we arrive at this period. The proud and lonely boy, with those bright flashing eyes of his, and that wild unearthly look, did not wander about the banks of the river, when he could snatch an hour for exercise, swinging his arms to and fro, and talking rapidly to himself, without an object. Those fits of sullenness and stupidity of which he has been accused—of total abstraction from the all of the external world; those intervals of silence, when with difficulty he could be got to speak or make answer to an inquiry: when, by his sister's testimony, "for days together he would say very little, and apparently by constraint;" when he would sit and weep for hours, no cause or motive assigned,—were nothing less than the agonies of the poet—as of the inspired Pythonness, labouring beneath the transmission of the divine afflatus, and the spirit of unwonted prophecy.

There was much to bear with in the life they were leading him, portioning him with vulgar, illiterate menials, and confining him to strict office hours, sending to and fro men-servants and maid-servants to watch his actions, and, if possible, detect him off his post. There was much to endure in the insolent brutality of his master, who, as Chatterton complained, "was continually insulting him and making his life miserable;" tearing up and destroying his compositions, and annoying him with coarse and contemptuous allusions. But the ardour of the young poet was not so easily quenched,—of too obdurate and fierce a nature the spirit they meanly assailed. "The sleep of the eagle on the cliff-edge above the roar of cataracts, and in the heart of the thunder-cloud, is hushed and deep as that of the halcyon on the smooth and sunny main."

IV.

Astonishes the literati of Bristol with an account of the "Fryars' first passing over the old bridge."

Chatterton was devotedly attached to the study of heraldry. According to the evidence collected by his last biographer, he seized upon every opportunity to perfect himself therein.* I cannot help thinking, however, that the knowledge of that science which he acquired, and certainly the taste he displayed—judging by the shields and escutcheons he has left behind him — border very closely on the ridiculous. His ideas of architecture were perhaps more grotesque; the drawings of Bristol Castle, and other public edifices, which he palmed upon Mr. Barrett, and which the silly Dean Milles believed to be authentic, are

---

* He was also very partial to the study of heraldry, and used to inform persons what their arms were. He one day said to Mr. Palmer, "I'll tell you the meaning of your name. Persons used to go to the Holy Land, and returned from thence with palm branches, and so were called Palmers;" he said the arms of the Palmers were, three palm branches, and the crest a leopard, or tiger, with a palm branch in his mouth.—Chatterton was very anxious to understand the drawing of heraldry, and for this purpose he applied to Mr. Palmer for some instructions respecting it; the employment of the latter chiefly being that of engraving coats-of-arms and crests on plate. Mr. P. also taught him how to colour his designs. A number of these drawings of Chatterton were in Mr. Palmer's possession, which he afterwards gave up to some person who was making inquiries with a view to writing his life.—Dix's *Life of Chatterton.*

justly reprobated by Warton, as the representations
of buildings which never existed, in a capricious,
affected style of Gothic architecture, reducible to no
system. The *attempts*, however, in both sciences
display considerable ingenuity, and a wonderful talent
for *invention*.

In the meantime, while engaging himself in multi-
farious pursuits, the disgust which he had conceived
for his profession continued to increase. He was loud
in his complaints against the injustice of Lambert.
He despised the society into which he was cast; he
maintained a gloomy reserve, speaking to no one—re-
treating into his own invisible world—betraying only
by the curled lip and scornful smile, his consciousness
of anything that passed around him. What had *he* in
common with his vulgar associates?

Even with the better class of persons with whom
he occasionally mixed, he was not disposed to be over
communicative. His mind was growing antique from
the long contemplation of Rowley. His existence—
only partially, and when he gave the reins to his
satirical disposition—was of the eighteenth century,—
otherwhiles of the fifteenth; shrouded amongst dust
and cobwebs, musty parchments and obliterated in-
scriptions, and his imagination haunted with visions
of ghostly friars and trains of shaven monks pacing
in sable stole the cloisters of St. John's.

A friend named Baker, who had left Bristol and
gone to America, had requested Chatterton to main-
tain a correspondence with him: this friend had
been his bed-fellow while at Colston's school, and

the poet had conceived a great attachment for him. About his fifteenth year, soon after Baker had reached his destination, Chatterton sent him a letter composed of all the hard words he could think of, and requested him to answer in the same style. About nine months after he was articled to Mr. Lambert, he wrote again. The letter on this occasion, which is the earliest of Chatterton's epistles extant, is as follows:—

" Dear Friend,   " *March 6th*, 1768.

    " I must now close my poetical labours, my master being returned from London. You write in a very entertaining style ; though I am afraid mine will be the contrary. Your celebrated Miss Rumsey is going to be married to Mr. Fowler, as he himself informs me. Pretty children ! about to enter into the comfortable yoke of matrimony, to be at their own liberty ; just apropos to the old law—but out of the frying-pan into the fire ! For a lover, heavens mend him ! but for a husband, oh excellent ! what a female Machiavel this Miss Rumsey is ! A very good mistress of nature to discover a *demon* in the habit of a parson ; to find a spirit so well adapted to the humour of an English wife, that is, one who takes off his hat to every person he chances to meet, to shew his staring horns, and very politely stands at the door of his wife's chamber, whilst her gallant is entertaining her within. O mirabili ! what will human nature degenerate into! Fowler aforesaid declares he makes a scruple of conscience of being too free with Miss Rumsey before marriage. There's a gallant for you ! why a girl with anything of the woman, would despise him for it. But no more of him. I am glad you approve of the ladies in Charles-Town ; and am obliged to you for the compliment of including me in your happiness ; my friendship is as firm as the white rock when the black waves roar around it and the waters burst on its hoary top, when the driving wind ploughs the sable sea, and the rising waves aspire to the clouds, turning with the rattling hail. So much for heroics. To speak in plain English, I am, and ever will be, your unalterable friend. I did not give your love to Miss Rumsey, having not yet seen her in private, and in public she will not speak to me, because of her great love to Fowler ; and on another occasion. I have been violently in love these three-and-twenty times since your departure ; and not a few

times came off victorious. I am obliged to you for your curi-
osity, and shall esteem it very much, not on account of itself,
but as coming from you. The poems, &c. on Miss *Hoyland* I
wish better, for her sake and your's. The TOURNAMENT I
have only one canto of, which I send herewith; the remainder
is entirely lost. I am, with the greatest regret, going to sub-
scribe myself—Your faithful and constant friend, 'till death
do us part, "THOMAS CHATTERTON.
"Mr. Baker, Charles-Town, South Carolina."

The poem " To a Friend," in p. 415, was written
at the same time, and to the same correspondent.

This Miss Hoyland was Baker's *inamorata*. The
poems enclosed in the letter, and addressed to her,
were sufficiently "namby-pamby" to captivate the
intellect of any young lady. They are, in truth, with
one or two exceptions, but trashy compositions, hur-
ried over in a slovenly manner, when he could snatch
a moment from works of greater importance. Nor is
the taste of Chatterton to be at all impugned in the
matter. There are some ten or twelve of them,
exhibiting every mark of haste and carelessness; but
then it was only behind the bush that he was their
author, Baker having requested to exhibit them as
his own.

A question arises, from the perusal of this letter,
respecting the amatory inclinations of Chatterton.
His was scarcely a disposition to fall in love, though
he here confesses to three-and-twenty flames. Sparks
only they must have been,—not actual flames, with a
smoke to them. His sister asserts that, up to the
time of his apprenticeship, he was remarkably indif-
ferent to females. "One day," she says, "he was
remarking to me the tendency severe study had to

sour the temper, and declared he had always seen all
the sex with equal indifference, but those that nature
made dear. He thought of making an acquaintance
with a girl in the neighbourhood, supposing it might
soften the austerity of temper study had occasioned.
He wrote a poem to her, and they commenced cor-
responding acquaintance." This young lady was the
Miss Rumsey of the foregoing letter. The writer
continues, "He would frequently walk the college
green with the young girls that stately paraded there
to shew their finery, but I really believe he was no
debauchee, though some have reported it). The dear
unhappy boy had faults enough : I saw with concern
he was proud, and exceedingly imperious; but that of
venality he could not be justly accused with." Mrs.
Newton was no scholar; by the word "venality," she
means libertinism.

But was he, indeed, a libertine? Let us hear
the testimonies of his acquaintance. "He stands
charged," says Dr. Gregory, "with a profligate at-
tachment to women ; the accusation, however, is
stated in a vague and desultory manner, as if from
common report, without any direct, or decided evi-
dence in support of the opinion. His sister could
not perhaps have produced a better proof of his mo-
rality, than his inclination to associate with modest
women."

Mr. Thistlethwaite had certainly a good opportu-
nity for observing the course of Chatterton's conduct.
We have called in question some of his statements ;
they related however to a period when he was a mere

child; and were of too important a nature to be ad-
missible on such evidence. But at the time for which
we are now collecting references, he was old enough
—being nearly eighteen months older than Chatter-
ton—to be admitted as counsel for the prisoner. He
writes thus to Dean Milles :—

"It has been said that he was an unprincipled libertine,
depraved in his mind, and profligate in his morals ; whose
abilities were prostituted to serve the cause of vice, and whose
leisure hours were wasted in continued scenes of debauchery
and obscenity.

"I admit that amongst Chatterton's papers may be found
many passages, not only immoral, but bordering upon a liber-
tinism gross and unpardonable. It is not my intention to
attempt a vindication of those passages, which for the regard
I bear his memory, I wish he had never written ; but which I
nevertheless believe to have originated rather from a warmth
of imagination, aided by a vain affectation of singularity, than
from any natural depravity, or from a heart vitiated by evil
example.

"The opportunities a long acquaintance with him afforded
me, justify me in saying that whilst he lived in Bristol he was
not the debauched character represented. Temperate in his
living, moderate in his pleasures, and regular in his exercises,
he was undeserving of the aspersion. What change London
might have effected in him I know not ; but from the strain of
his letters to his mother and sister, and his conduct towards
them after he quitted Bristol, and also from the testimony of
those with whom he lodged, I have no doubt but the intem-
perancies and irregularities laid to his charge did either not
exist at all, or, at the worst, are considerably aggravated be-
yond what candour can approve."

When we reach his London life, we shall adduce
evidence even more satisfactory than this.

The fact is, that Chatterton's character has been
blackened by every slanderer who could trace scur-
rilous words upon paper. He was a kind of whipping-
post for every scribbling apprentice to try his hand on;
"a butt at which every callow witling made his proof-

shot." Not a few calumniators, whose judgment was
tested by the conventional rank which they held in lite-
rature, encouraged them to the flagellation, and even
dealt him a lash or two themselves sometimes. Of
these persons more hereafter.

In the meantime how stands it with this Bristol
proflicacy? All the evidence is for the accused, and
the charge amounts to nothing more than assertion
without proof,—nay, without the possibility of being
proved, or the indirectest limbo of a foundation on
which to establish it. Already it disappears, and,
shade like, while we attempt to observe it, fades into
the impalpablest æther. His writings, it is allowed,
occasionally exhibit a laxity of expression, which had
better been avoided. But even these instances are
only in his satires, and the satires too of the eighteenth
century, when Churchill was famous, and Wilkes'
'Essay on Woman,' though burnt by the common
hangman, was remembered. Chatterton was a youth
of strong and tumultuous passions, which he subdued
by his love of literature and his devotion to study:
small time indeed he had for the indulgence of amatory
propensities and lascivious inclinations, who died be-
fore he was eighteen, and besides a mass of other
productions, left his Genesis of Rowley behind him.

To proceed to another subject. We have not yet
clearly seen how Chatterton disposed of his time, and
managed to economize it with such success. Here
his sister lets us into a secret. He seldom slept, and
would even write by moonlight. "We heard him
frequently say that he found he studied best towards

the full of the moon; and would often *sit up all night and write by moonlight.*"

To be sure, he was all this time at work on the Rowley Poems: an engagement which not only occupied his mind, but influenced his every-day actions. He would seldom eat animal food; not like Byron, for fear of getting fat—but like Shelley, because he supposed it to impair the intellect. He never tasted strong or spirituous liquors, living upon a tart only, or a crust of bread and a draught of pure spring water. Sometimes his mother would tempt him, when he paid her a visit, with the offer of a hot meal, to which he would reply, that " he had a work in hand, and must not make himself more stupid than God had made him." Few such instances of temperance, especially among literary men, are on record. Byron dined, when in Italy, on a biscuit and a glass of soda-water; but he, we repeat, anticipated corpulency, and shuddered at the notion of a *fat* Childe Harold.

There was in Lambert's office-library, amongst a heap of law books possessing little interest to Chatterton, an old copy of Camden's Britannia. From a bookseller of Bristol he obtained, as a loan, an edition of Speght's Chaucer, which everybody knows to be in black letter; and for his own use, compiled from the scanty glossary which is appended to that work, a counter-glossary, having for its arrangement, in something like alphabetical order, so as to be easy of reference, the words in *modern* English, with the word corresponding to each in the antiquated diction of Chaucer. The books however, from which he derived

most assistance were the English dictionaries of Ker-
sey and Bailey, from which it has been incontestably
proved that nearly the whole of the obsolete words
employed in the Rowley poems were obtained. He
had access also to the old library at Bristol, in which
were to be consulted such works as Holinshed's
Chronicles, Geoffrey of Monmouth, and Fuller's
Church History. With these at his command, and
the exhaustless stores of an unconquerable mind and
an untiring energy to draw from, the creation of Row-
ley proceeded apace—indeed, by this time was almost
completed.

In the month of September, 1768, a new bridge
was completed at Bristol, superseding the old structure
that had spanned for centuries the river. On the day
upon which it was first opened to the public a kind of
ceremony seems to have taken place, and the thorough-
fare to have been proclaimed with all due honours.
Immediately afterwards there appeared in the weekly
newspaper already alluded to—Felix Farley's Bristol
Journal—an account of the ceremonies observed at
the opening of the old bridge, which had just been
demolished. It was accompanied by the following
note to the printer :—

MR. PRINTER,
        The following description of the Mayor's first
passing over the old bridge, taken from an old Manuscript,
may not [at this time] be unacceptable to the generality of
your readers.   Your's, &c.
                            DUNHELMUS BRISTOLIENSIS.

    " On Fridaie was the time fixed for passing the newe
Brydge : Aboute the time of the tollynge the tenth Clock,
Master Greggorie Dalbenye mounted on a Fergreyne Horse,

enformed Master Mayor all thyngs were prepared; whan two Beadils want fyrst streyng fresh stre, next came a manne dressed up as follows—Hose of goatskyn, crinepart outwards, Doublet and Waystcoat also, over which a white Robe without sleeves, much like an albe, but not so longe, reeching but to his Lends; a Girdle of Azure over his left shoulder, rechde also to his Lends on the ryght, and doubled back to his Left, bucklyng with a Gouldin Buckel, dangled to his Knee; thereby representyng a Saxon Elderman.—In his hande he bare a shield, the maystrie of Gille a Brogton, who painted the same, representyng Saincte Warburgh crossynge the Ford. Then a mickle strong Manne, in Armour, carried a huge anlace; after whom came Six Claryons and Six Minstrels, who sang the Song of Saincte Warburgh; then came Master Maior, mounted on a white Horse, dight with sable trappyngs, wrought about by the Nunnes of Saincte Kenna, with Gould and Silver; his Hayr brayded with Ribbons, and a Chaperon, with the auntient arms of Brystowe fastende on his forehead. Master Maior bare in his Hande a gouldin Rodde, and a congean squier bare in his Hande, his Helmet, waulking by the Syde of the Horse: than came the Eldermen and Cittie Broders mounted on Sable Horses, dyght with white trappyngs and Plumes, and scarlet copes and Chapeous, having thereon Sable Plumes; after them, the Preests and Freeres, Parysh, Mendicaunt and Seculor, some syngyng Saincte Warburgh's song, others soundyng clarions thereto, and otherssome Citrialles. In thilk manner reechyng the Brydge, the Manne with the Anlace stode on the fyrst Top of a Mound, yreed in the midst of the Bridge; then want up the Manne with the Sheelde, after him the Ministrels and Clarions. And then the Preestes and Freeres, all in white Albs, makyng a most goodlie Shewe; the Maior and Eldermen standyng round, theie sang, with the sound of Clarions, the Song of Saincte Baldwyn; which beyng done, the Manne on the Top threwe with greet myght his Anlace into the see, and the Clarions sounded an auntiant Charge and Forloyn: Then theie sang againe the songe of Saincte Warburgh, and proceeded up Chrysts hill, to the cross, where a Latin Sermon was preeched by Ralph de Blundeville. And with sound of Clarion theie agayne went to the Brydge, and there dined, spendyng the rest of the daie in Sportes and Plaies, the Freers of Saincte Augustine doeyng the Plaie of the Knyghtes of Bristowe, and makynge a great fire at night on Kynwulph Hyll.[*]

* In this small document, as carelessly printed by Southey and Dix, there are no less than 280 mistakes, many of which are considerable

Such a singular document produced at so critical a moment could scarcely fail to awaken curiosity, especially among the amateurs of that half-literary Bristol city. The Journal office was besieged. Where was the original manuscript? who was the transcriber? who the fortunate discoverer? where too was it discovered? amongst what cobwebs had it reposed for centuries? and what spiders had spun the cobwebs? Rapidly the interesting number was bought up; the description flew from mouth to mouth, intersecting broadways and bye-lanes, while the real author—the ex-charity boy—young Thomas Chatterton, sat silently laughing in his sleeve, upon his stool in Mr. Lambert's office.

To the disappointment of the *soi-disant* antiquarians, no satisfactory answer could be obtained to the numerous questions they propounded. There was the document, plain enough, and written in a small, neat, not un-lawyer-like looking hand; but to whom that *hand* belonged, or who Dunhelmus Bristoliensis was, was more than Mr. Farley or any of his devils could discover.

Encouraged by his success, however, Chatterton soon presented another paper for insertion, and was immediately recognised as the individual on whose account so much clamour had been raised. The alarm was sounded; the citizens hastened to the

importance. The original MS. in Chatterton's handwriting is preserved in the British Museum. It is there called "The description of the MAYOR's passing over the Bridge," and not the 'Fryars,' as hitherto printed. So likewise in Farley's Journal, with which the MS. has been carefully collated.—ED.

office; the musty original was of course demanded, only—as they said—for inspection.

Now Chatterton at this time was little more than a child, and as such they treated him. He was assailed with threats, to which he retaliated with haughtiness, and flatly refused to give any account.* Finding him invincible, they assumed another tone; spoke to him in a gentle manner, talked of patronage and assistance, and at last fairly won him over. He stated that he was employed to transcribe the contents of certain ancient manuscripts by a gentleman, who also had engaged him to furnish complimentary verses, inscribed to a lady with whom that gentleman was in love. This, of course, was an extempore invention, fabricated on the spot. It agrees, however, with what we have seen was really the case—an engagement which he was under to his friend Baker of Charlestown, to supply him with poems of that nature. Perhaps, as the first thought that entered his head, he caught at it on the spur of the necessity. Be it as it may, it was not deemed sufficiently satisfactory by his judges.

He next asserted that the original document was one of many ancient manuscripts in his possession, which had formerly belonged to his father, who had obtained them from a large chest in the muniment room of Redcliffe church. This information,

---

* The sages of Bristol, with a spirit of barbarism which the monks and friars of the fifteenth century could not easily have rivalled, having traced the letter to Chatterton, interrogated him with *threats* about the original. Boy as he was, he haughtily refused to explain upon compulsion.—CAMPBELL.

we must suppose, was considered authentic, as no
doubts appear to have been expressed. It is rather
singular, however, that an inspection of these manu-
scripts was not immediately demanded; and, consi-
dering the manner in which, according to Chatterton's
statement, his father possessed himself of them, carry-
ing them away without leave asked or given, that
some compulsion was not used to make the boy
restore them. What *was* the behaviour of the parties
on the occasion is buried in the uncertainty of time.

The real origin of the manuscript will be best
ascertained from the following statement sent to Dean
Milles, by a Mr. Rudhall, an early friend of Chatter-
ton.

"Mr. John Rudhall, a native and inhabitant of Bristol,
and formerly apprentice to Mr. Francis Gresley, an apothecary
in that city, was well acquainted with Chatterton whilst he
was apprentice to Mr. Lambert: during that time Chatterton
frequently called upon him at his master's house, and soon
after he had printed the account of the bridge in the Bristol
paper, told Mr. Rudhall that he was the author of it; but it
occurring to him afterwards that he might be called upon to
produce the original, he brought to him one day a piece of
parchment about the size of a half-sheet of foolscap paper:
Mr. Rudhall does not think that anything was written on it
when produced by Chatterton, but he saw him write several
words, if not lines, in a character which Mr. Rudhall did not
understand: which, he says, was totally unlike English, and,
as he apprehended, was meant by Chatterton to imitate or
represent the original from which this account was printed.
He cannot determine precisely how much Chatterton wrote in
this manner, but says, that the time he spent in that visit did
not exceed three-quarters of an hour; the size of the parch-
ment, however, (even supposing it to have been filled with
writing,) will in some measure ascertain the quantity which it
contained. He says also that when Chatterton had written on
the parchment, he held it over the candle, to give it the ap-
pearance of antiquity, *which changed the colour of the ink, and
made the parchment appear black and contracted ;* he never saw

him make any similar attempt, nor was the parchment pro-
duced afterwards by Chatterton to him, or (as far as he
knows) to any other person. Mr. Rudhall had promised
Chatterton not to reveal this secret, and he scrupulously kept
his word till the year 1779; but, on the prospect of procuring
a gratuity of ten pounds for Chatterton's mother, from a gen-
tleman who came to Bristol in order to collect information
concerning her son's history, he thought so material a benefit
to the family would fully justify him for divulging a secret by
which no person now living could be a sufferer."

V.

*Is introduced to Messrs. Catcott and Barrett, and is
of great service to the latter gentleman in his pro-
jected 'History of Bristol.'*

·Very soon after the description of the Mayor's
passing over the old bridge appeared in *Farley's
Journal*, as Mr. Catcott of Bristol, partner to Mr.
Burgum the pewterer, of pedigree memory, was
walking with a friend in Redcliffe church, he was in-
formed by him of several ancient pieces of poetry,
lately discovered there, and which were in the posses-
sion of an extraordinary young man with whom he
was acquainted. Mr. Catcott is described by those
who knew him to have been fond of study and at-
tached to literary pursuits. He had been the first to
enquire at Farley's office respecting the communica-
tion of the old-bridge document, and had evinced a
lively interest in the whole affair. Struck with his
friend's information, he desired an introduction to
the young man, whose turn of mind appeared so con-
genial to his own, and who proved, of course, to be
the youth he had anticipated—Thomas Chatterton.

With this gentleman, our friend is disposed to be somewhat communicative. He gives him a copy of the Bristowe Tragedy, Rowley's Epitaph upon Canynge's Ancestor, and other smaller pieces. In a few days afterwards he gives him the *yellow Roll.* About this period Mr. Barrett, a surgeon of Bristol, and a man of great respectability, has undertaken to publish a history of Bristol, and is anxiously collecting materials for that work. His friends, eager to procure him intelligence, fail not to apprise him of the treasure of ancient poems and other manuscripts relative to Bristol, which have been discovered in the oaken repository in Redcliffe church. Mr. Catcott hastens, specimens in hand, to his study. The poems are examined, pronounced authentic, and Chatterton is introduced to the believing historian, whom he immediately supplies, not only with poems, but with materials of the utmost value for his own work. It is Mr. Barrett's purpose to collect information on the subject of the churches and public edifices of Bristol. Chatterton undertakes to examine the papers of Rowley for that purpose, and in a few days brings him a true and particular account of the *ancient* churches of Bristol, which formerly occupied the sites of the existing structures. The historian entertains no doubt of the authenticity of the documents, rewards his young friend with a sum of money; and Chatterton, more elated than ever, goes off to coin his brain afresh, and invent, not only churches, but castles, and even palaces. We will give the reader a specimen. It is from what he entitles

" Turgot's Account of Bristol, translated by T. Rowley out of Saxon into English," and is to be found in p. 31 of Barrett's History of Bristol.

"SECT. II. OF TURGOTUS.—Strange as it male seem that there were Walles to Radclefte, yet fulle true ytte is, beynge the Walles of Brightrycus pallace, and in owre daies remain-ethe there a small piece neie Eselwynnes Towre. I conceive not it coulde be square, tho Tradytyon so saieth : the Inhabiters wythyn the Walle had ryghte of Tolle on the Ryvers Severne and a part of Avon. Thus much of Radclefte Walles. SECT. III. OF TURGOTUS.—Nowe to speake of Bryghtstowe, yttes Walles and Castelle beynge the fayrest buyldinge, of ytte I shalle speake fyrste. The pryncipall Streets meete in forme of a Cross, and is a goode patterne for the Cityes of Chrystyannes. Brightricus fyrst ybuylden the Walles in fashyon allmoste Square wythe four Gates : Elle Gate, Baldwynnes or Leonardes Gate, Froome or the Water Gate, and Nycholas or Wareburgha's."—&c. &c. &c.

And from time to time does he furnish Mr. Barrett with similar documents; of such magnitude, moreover, that as he does not hesitate to publish them, they occupy no inconsiderable portion of his large quarto volume, a work otherwise of considerable value and research.*

---

* In the republic of letters, as it used to be denominated, the laws have been conventionally so lax, so much licence has been taken and conceded for fictitious statements respecting the authorship, the long neglect or suppression, the accidental discovery, &c. of writings at length produced to the public, that it would seem harsh to lay any hard stress of condemnation on the freak of sham-antique poetry pretendedly detected in an old oaken repository. But a settled, complicated *system* of deception, carried into effect in a variety of ways, with a determination, in all appearance, to continue it as long as the practice could be maintained, with false asseverations never spared, and in a temper to regard suspicion and interrogation as a wrong and an insult, must be held, after every allowance pleaded in excuse or mitigation, to have betrayed at the least a great indifference to the moral principle. The same non-intervention of conscience is apparent in the last stage of his deplorable history, when he betook himself to writing in the political journals of the time. Like so many since, and so many now, he appears to have done it in the character and in the

But what are we to say to all this—this duping and deceiving, this inventing of pedigrees and histories? The fabrication of the poems, the mere poems of Rowley, must be forgiven him. No one was injured, no one was defrauded. "It must indeed," says Thomas Campbell, "be pronounced improper by the general law which condemns all falsifications of history; but it deprived no man of his fame; it had no sacrilegious interference with the memory of departed genius; it had not, like Lauder's imposture, any malignant motive, to rob a party or a country of a name which was its pride and ornament." Sir Walter Scott's testimony is scarcely so favourable. "I fear," he says, "the original source of the inconsistencies of Chatterton's conduct and character was in that inequality of spirit with which Providence, as in mockery of the most splendid gifts of genius and fancy, has often conjoined them. This strange disorder of the mind, often confounded by the vulgar with actual insanity, of which perhaps it is a remote shade, is fostered by the workings of an ardent imagination, as it is checked and subdued by mathematical or philosophical research. I cannot regard the imposture as of an indifferent or harmless nature." Southey, on the contrary, expresses it as his opinion, that "the deception might most assuredly have been

calculation of a mere literary adventurer; a partisan, if actually and generally on the one side, yet ready to write in the same heated invective on the other, at any more patronising opening of the way to patronage and profit. We find him writing for the newspapers on the very same day for Alderman Beckford against the ministry, and for the ministry against Beckford.—ECLECTIC REVIEW.

begun and continued without the slightest sense of criminality in Chatterton." And a writer in the Edinburgh Review remarks, " The pretended antiquity of his poems has been denounced as a crime against truth, with all the solemnity with which Ananias's lie is quoted from Scripture. The word 'forgery' does not apply to such an innocent deception." "Posterity," Mr. Britton feelingly observes, " may be excused, if, forgetting his errors in the contemplation of his neglected state and youthful sorrows, it speak only of his genius." Nor must we, though we have already cited him, forget the peroration of Campbell : " When we conceive the inspired boy transporting himself in imagination back to the days of his fictitious Rowley, embodying his ideal character, and giving to ' airy nothing a local habitation and a name,' we may forget the impostor in the enthusiast, and forgive the falsehood of his reverie for its beauty and ingenuity." *

* This biographer must be pardoned, if. in the form of a note, he enlist another quotation, in addition to the many cited above :—
" We have hardly sufficient data to enable us to judge what Chatterton's real character, moral or literary—and it is difficult to separate them in our enquiry—was, or would have been. I, for one, cannot help thinking that the vices of the former were adventitious, and that the imperfections of the latter would have been obviated or removed. His tale is but half told. Had not the curtain dropt so abruptly on the hero of the drama, succeeding scenes might have shewn him triumphing over all his follies, and atoning for all his faults. His ruling passion was the love of fame ; and the progress of fame is like the course of the Thames, which in its native fields will scarcely float the toy-ship which an infant's hand has launched, but when it has once visited the metropolis, mighty vessels may ride upon its bosom, and it rolls on irresistibly to the ocean. This Chatterton knew; and, in a blind confidence on his own unaided powers, he rushed to the capital in pursuit of competence and renown. The result, we all know, was neglect, penury, and self-destruction. —HENRY NEELE.

But a wide difference between the pseudo-poet
and the pretended historian. Heartily, for the fair
fame of Thomas Chatterton, is it to be wished that
he had never met with Barrett, or that Barrett, as he
afterwards did, had offended him at the first outset.
The Burgum pedigree, also, though innocent compa-
ratively—as it duped only a silly, ostentatious indivi-
dual—with this fabrication and falsification of history
for pecuniary motives, is too serious a deception to
be passed silently over. But let us be sparing of
blame, at least, till we have rightly unravelled the
mysteries of his character, and have seen how far the
passion of imposing upon the credulity of his fellows
made up the LIFE, the BEING (without which he
could not *be*) of this extraordinary boy. " For the
Past is all holy to us ; the Dead are all holy, even they
that were base and wicked while alive. Their base-
ness and wickedness was not *They*, was but the heavy
and unmanageable Environment that lay round them,
with which they fought unprevailing ; *they* (the ethe-
real god-given Force that dwelt in them, and was
their *Self*) have now shuffled off that heavy Environ-
ment, and are free and pure : their life-long Battle,
go how it might, is all ended, with many wounds or
with fewer ; they have been recalled from it, and the
once harsh jarring battle-field has become a silent
awe-inspiring Golgotha, and Field of God !"* Alas !
was Chatterton then, so "base and wicked?" He

* Thomas Carlyle. *Gottesacker*, or ' Field of God,' the expressive
German for a church yard, " the green back-ground of life," says Jean
Paul, sublimely.

was only a boy : who shall say, had his pride permitted him to live, how triumphantly hereafter he would have asserted his dignity of character, when experience had taught him the value of truth, and the security of virtue?

This introduction to Catcott and Barrett seems to have elevated Chatterton in his own importance. His sister's testimony is—

"He would often speak in great raptures of the undoubted success of his plan for future life. His ambition increased daily. His spirits were rather uneven, sometimes so gloomed that for days together he would say but very little, and apparently by constraint ; at other times exceedingly cheerful. When in spirits he would enjoy his rising fame ; confident of advancement, he would promise my mother and me should be partakers of his success. Mr. Barrett lent him many books on surgery, and I believe he bought many more, as I remember to have packed them up to send to him when in London, and no demand was ever made for them. About this time he wrote several satirical poems. He began to be universally known among the young men. He had many cap acquaintances, but I am confident but few intimates."

For some time he continued to be very communicative on the subject of Rowley. "He was always," says Mr. Smith, one of his intimate companions, "extremely fond of walking in the fields, particularly in Redcliffe meadows, and of talking about these manuscripts, and sometimes reading them there. 'Come, (he would say,) you and I will take a walk in the meadow; I have got the cleverest thing for you imaginable—it is worth half-a-crown merely to have a sight of it, and to hear me read it to you.' When we arrived at the place proposed, he would produce his parchment, shew it me and read it to me. There was one spot in particular, full in view of the church, in which he seemed to take a peculiar delight. He would frequently lay himself down, fix his eyes upon the church, and seem as if he were in a kind of trance. Then on a sudden, and abruptly, he would tell me, ' That steeple was burnt down by lightning: that was the place where they formerly acted plays.'* His Sundays were commonly spent in walking alone into the country about Bristol, as far as the duration of daylight would allow ; and from these excursions he never failed to bring home with him drawings of churches, or of some other objects which had impressed his romantic imagination."

* It is remarkable that in the course of the evidence afforded by Mr. Smith, there is mention made of Redcliffe church spire being destroyed by lightning. But how could either Mr. Smith or Chatterton have been apprised of this, as there was no history nor any *known record* concerning such an event? It is true that since the death of the latter, there has been a publication, by Mr. Nasmith, of William of Worcestre; this came out in the year 1778, and we find the fact there mentioned. ' Latitudo (lego altitudo) Turris de Radclyfe continet 300 pedes; de quibus 100 pedes sunt per fulmen dejecti.' p. 120. As the only history in which this is mentioned came out after the death of Chatterton, he could not have his intelligence from hence, but it *must* have come from one of the manuscripts of Rowley. Rowley must have been in some degree an eye-witness of the event; but Chatterton had no history of it, no record excepting what must have come from Rowley. He could not have mentioned it without some previous intimation from that quarter; for *no account was elsewhere to be had.*—BRYANT'S OBSERVATIONS.

Mr. Bryant was not aware that in the parlour of a person residing in Bristol, a Mr. Katar, whom Chatterton *used to visit*, hung a print of St. Mary Redcliffe church, engraved by Toms from a drawing by William Halfpenny, and published in the year 1746, seven years before Chatterton's birth, underneath which is the following inscription: " This church was founded by Simon de Burton, merchant, in ye 22nd year of ye reign of King Edward ye first. In the year 1446, the steeple of the said church was blown down in a great storm of thunder and lightning, wch did much damage to the same, but was by Mr. Wm. Canynge, a worthy merchant, wth the assistance of diverse other wealthy inhabitants, at a great expense, new covered, glazed, and repaired." &c. &c.—*Published May* 1746, *by* BENJAMIN HICKEY, *Bristol.*—A more detailed account of this engraving will be found in DIX's *Life of Chatterton,* p. 44.

The repeated sums of money which he obtained from Messrs. Catcott and Barrett enabled him to have frequent recourse to his old friends, the circulating libraries. From those gentlemen, too, he procured several volumes; from Mr. Barrett especially, many on surgery. He became a frequent purchaser moreover, as he acknowledges in his 'will'; but, discontented with the amount of the sums bestowed on him, he is said to have exclaimed against the parsimony of his patrons, who 'dribbled' their rewards in shillings and half-crowns.

Indeed, neither Catcott nor Barrett seem to have been regarded by him with deference. The reader of his Acknowledged Poems will remember numerous instances in which the former gentleman falls under his lash. But, when "the fit" was on him, that he "spared neither friend nor foe," was his own confession. Perhaps his sincere opinion of them both is to be found in the following lines of his "last Will and Testament:"—

"Catcott, for thee, I know thy heart is good,
But, ah! thy merit's seldom understood:
Too bigoted to whimsies, which thy youth
Receiv'd to venerate as Gospel truth,
Thy friendship never could be dear to me,
Since all I am is opposite to thee.
If ever obligated to thy purse,
Rowley discharges all—my first chief curse!
For had I never known the antique lore,
I ne'er had ventur'd from my peaceful shore,
To be the wreck of promises and hopes,
A Boy of Learning, and a Bard of Tropes;
But happy in my humble sphere had moved,
Untroubled, unsuspected, unbelov'd.

To Barrett next, he has my thanks sincere,
For all the little knowledge I had here.

> But what was knowledge? Could it here succeed,
> When scarcely twenty in the town can read?
> Could knowledge bring in interest to maintain
> The wild expenses of a poet's brain?
> I thank thee, Barrett—thy advice was right,
> But 'twas ordained by fate that I should write.
> Spite of the prudence of this prudent place,
> I wrote my mind, nor hid the author's face."

It is certain, at the time when Mr. Catcott first became acquainted with Chatterton, that the works now known as the Rowley poems were either in existence, or were so far matured in Chatterton's mind as to enable him to speak confidently of them. During the first conversation which Mr. Catcott held with him, he enumerated the titles of most of the poems which afterwards appeared. He confessed, moreover, that he had destroyed several; and a nearly completed tragedy, called "The Apostate," was seen by Mr. Catcott, but is now nowhere to be found. To this production Mr. Bryant makes allusion in his 'Observations.' "The subject of it," he tells us, "was the apostatizing of a person from the Christian to the Jewish faith." " A small part," says Dr. Gregory, " has been preserved by Mr. Barrett;" and a writer so late as 1835 asserts that a portion of it was printed by that gentleman in his History of Bristol. Four lines only, in a note to the " Parliament of Sprytes." It may, however, turn up some day, if not actually destroyed.

Whether he was offended by the repeated examinations, to which he was subjected, on the score of the original parchments, and the multiplied entreaties that he would produce them, or whether he was disgusted with the paltry sums with which his patrons requited his services, is uncertain; but he soon became suspicious and reserved, made fewer communications on the subject, and exhibited no more parchments, or fragments of Rowley's handwriting.

In the meantime his peculiarities were remarked by all who were thrown into contact with him. His pride was excessive. For days together he would scarcely utter a word. He would enter and quit his master's house without deigning to address a single inmate; would occupy his stool at the office in rigid silence, noticing the observations of his fellow-clerks only with a supercilious, sarcastic smile of contempt.

It was the general impression that he was going mad. His fits of absence were remarkable. " He would often look stedfastly in a person's face without speaking, or seeming to see the person, for a quarter of an hour or more." So says one of his companions; but perhaps for a quarter of an hour we should read five minutes. Some considered him dull, stupid, and sullen.* Yet Dr. Gregory asserts that " his pride,

---

* What was supposed to be dulness in Chatterton was genius. The symptoms of talent were misconstrued by his contemporaries. They were disgusted with his pride, which was a consciousness of preeminence of abilities. Mr. Capel, a brother apprentice in the same house with Chatterton, relates that there was " generally a dreariness in his look, and a wildness attended with a visible contempt for others." The silence, the solitude of this visionary boy, his eccentric habits, his singularities of behaviour, were not attributed to the true cause. His fits of melancholy were mistaken for sullenness. An old female relation, who undoubtedly thought him mad, has reported that "he talked very little, was very absent in company, and used very often to walk by the river side, talking to himself and flourishing his arms about." He despised discretion, a virtue allied to many meannesses; and in the place of worldly prudence, attention to proposals of economy, and a regular profession, substituted his anticipations of immortality. He

which perhaps should rather be termed the strong
consciousness of intellectual excellence, did not de-
stroy his affability. He was always accessible, and
rather forward to make acquaintance than apt to
decline the advances of others. There is reason
however to believe," he continues, "that the in-
equality of his spirits affected greatly his behaviour in
company."

There is extant a curious document in Chatter-
ton's handwriting, which there is ground for sup-
posing he actually sent to Mr. Catcott, with a view
of extorting money from him. Before we pass judg-
ment upon it, however, we should remember that
Chatterton had presented that gentleman with the
most valuable productions of his pen, and that they
were received and treasured by him as "a creation
from the old ages." We must further remember that
he afterwards disposed of them to Messrs. Payne and
Co., the London booksellers, for fifty pounds: so that
he might have liquidated the debt, and obtained "the
executors" receipt in full, without doing himself any
violent injury or injustice.

' Mr. G. Catcott
To the Exors. of T. Rowley.

' To pleasure rec⁴ in read⁶ his				
Historic works . . }	£5	5	0
—— his Poetic works .	£5	5	0
	£10	10	0

There is some levity in this, but it may easily be pardoned—" the labourer is worthy of his hire,"—and the sum after all is not so very exorbitant. But Mr. Catcott determined otherwise, and allowed the account to ' stand over.'

In the meantime he was not indolent, but, as we might say, was rather actively employed. Mr. Thistlethwaite has drawn a vivid picture of his engagements and pursuits at this period.

" One day he might be found busily employed in the study of heraldry and English antiquities ; the next discovered him deeply engaged, confounded, and perplexed amidst the subtleties of metaphysical disquisition, or lost and bewildered in the abstruse labyrinth of mathematical researches ; and these in an instant again neglected and thrown aside to make room for music and astronomy, of both which sciences his knowledge was entirely confined to theory. Even physic was not without a charm to allure his imagination, and he would talk of Galen, Hippocrates, and Paracelsus, with all the confidence and familiarity of a modern empiric."

He must needs learn Latin, moreover. He had borrowed from Mr. Barrett's library, Benson's Saxon Vocabulary, and Skinner's Etymologicon Anglicanæ, of which the interpretations are in Latin, and were consequently unintelligible to the Bristol charity-boy. But being dissuaded from the attempt by one of his friends, on account of the alleged difficulty of acquiring, by self-instruction only, anything like a competent knowledge of that language ; at the recommendation of the same friend he devoted himself for a few days to French, which he then, with his usual versatility, abandoned. The Benson and Skinner were returned to Mr. Barrett with an expression of disappointment ; and Kersey and Bailey, more

suitable for his purposes, were applied to with greater
diligence than ever.

Through Mr. George Catcott he obtained an in-
troduction to his brother, the Rev. Alexander Cat-
cott, an acquaintance the young bard was very vain
of. Indeed he would fain have persuaded his asso-
ciates that he was so necessary an assistant to the
clergyman's pursuits—which *were* something in his
own line—that he could not be dispensed with; and
he made it a boast, that he had access whenever he
pleased to the parson's study. Chatterton sometimes
shot with the long bow, and he is said to have done
so when he made this assertion. They got on very
well however, and were very good friends, though
their friendship did not prevent the shafts of Chat-
terton's ridicule from aiming at his reverend patron,
and making somewhat too free with his name. But
he made him amends, and even spoke of him at other
times with fondness. Mr. Catcott had written a work
to prove the truth of the scriptural account of the
Deluge. Numerous are the hits at that performance
which are scattered through Chatterton's satires. In
his "Kew Gardens" he is more than usually tolerant:

> If Catcott's flimsy system can't be prov'd,
> Let it alone, for Catcott's much belov'd.

And the apology in his ' Will,' is, as Dr. Gregory ob-
serves, " the best recompense he had in his power to
make."

"I leave the Reverend Mr. Catcott some little of my free-
thinking, that he may put on spectacles of reason, and see how
vilely he is duped in believing the Scriptures literally. I wish
he and his brother George would know how far I am their real

enemy, *but I have an unlucky way of raillery, and when the strong fit of satire is upon me I spare neither friend nor foe.* This is my excuse for what I have said of them elsewhere."

" We hardly know whether to laugh or grieve," remarks Sir Walter Scott, "when Chatterton reproaches Catcott, down whose throat he had crammed the improbable tale of Rowley, with gross *credulity* because he was a believer in revelation."

Before we take leave of these gentlemen, one circumstance must be mentioned. George Catcott, as before stated, was a pewterer by trade, and partner to Burgum, the man of pedigree notoriety, 'a presumptuous, vulgar, ignorant fellow, who boasted of his ancestry.' Will the reader pardon Chatterton his impudent but amusing hoax, when he is informed that this Burgum defrauded his partner of all the property he possessed, £3000 ? I wish we could release him with as little blame from the graver charge of inventing histories for Barrett.*

So much then up to his sixteenth year ; though as yet he has been only conning his part, which he will play finely presently, when he has a freer stage, and is not hampered by side-scenes and foot-lights. After all it is only a melodrame, and no complete

* The De Burgum pedigree was purchased by Mr. Joseph Cottle of Bristol, from Chatterton's family, for five guineas, and it is in his possession at this moment. I may, perhaps, be pardoned for tacking on an anecdote respecting this book. One evening it was shewn to Ireland, the person who palmed upon the public "the tragedy of Vortigern and Rowena,"which he asserted to be in Shakspeare's own handwriting. Ireland admired the fabrication of the De Burgum pedigree, and, at the request of Mr. Cottle, wrote on a vacant leaf, facsimiles of all the various ways in which good Queen Bess and Will Shakspeare have autographed their names. This book will for ever remain a great curiosity. —MR. RICHARD SMITH, *in the Gentleman's Magazine, Dec.* 1838.

tragedy : it would never be licensed as such by the Lord Chamberlain.

VI.

Corresponds with Dodsley and Walpole on the subject of the Rowley Poems.

We may suppose that by this period the creation of Rowley was nearly, if not all, completed. How long this shadowy renown might have contented Chatterton, had he met with the success he anticipated, it is difficult to determine. Whether, from under the supposititious mantle of Rowley, he might still have continued to hoodwink the world; or whether, casting aside the 'simulacrum, or ghost-defunct' of a poet, he would have stepped forth and cried, Lo! I am Cæsar! and gathering up his monkish habiliments, have hurled them back into the shadow of deep night, can only be matter for conjecture. For indeed he seemed little ambitious of his own renown, and preferred the applause showered upon Rowley to the astonishment that might have greeted Chatterton. And hence, in this acting of a dual part, arises the great difficulty of rightly estimating his character. For, in that unit of a body—that Chatterton, that one might see, and note, and laugh at—there dwelt, properly, two souls : a solution of which difficulty the Pythagoreans may assist us to. Into a still-born body, in that year 1427, must the soul of Rowley have been infused, and, being speedily ejected from its scarce possessed lodgings, must have wandered for more than three centuries through infinite nothingness, till it haply stumbled upon the embryo into which had already struggled the soul of a Bristol charity-boy. For, be positive, two souls there were —how they got there let others determine—uneasily occupying that corporeal tenement, which fighting in its nurse's arms, was carried to Redcliffe Church, and named Thomas Chatterton.

But, leaving it to the reader to solve the difficulty as he pleases, we find that we are now arrived at one of the most important eras of Chatterton's life. He had grown ambitious to appear in print, and here again not in the proper person of his one self, Chatterton, but of his other self, Rowley. To compass this end he made application to Dodsley, the noted publisher, in the following letter :—

"*Bristol, December* 21, 1768.

" Sir,—I take this method to acquaint you that I can procure copies of several ancient poems ; and an interlude, perhaps the oldest dramatic piece extant, wrote by one Rowley, a priest in Bristol, who lived in the reigns of Henry the VIth, and Edward the IVth. If these pieces will be of service to you, at your command, copies shall be sent to you by,

" Your most obedient servant,

" D. B.

" Please to direct for D. B., to be left with Mr. Thomas Chatterton, Redcliffe Hill, Bristol.

" *For Mr. J. Dodsley, bookseller, Pall Mall, London.*"

It is supposed that the bibliopole returned no answer. To correspondents of small notoriety, publishers are *so* uncourteous. In less than two months Chatterton addressed him again.

" *Bristol, Feb.* 15, 1769.

" Sir,

" Having intelligence that the tragedy of Ælla was in being, after a long and laborious search, I was so happy as to attain a sight of it. Struck with the beauties of

it, I endeavoured to obtain a copy of it to send to you ; but the present possessor absolutely denies to give me one unless I give him a guinea for a consideration. As I am unable to procure such a sum, I made search for another copy, but unsuccessfully. Unwilling such a beauteous piece should be lost, I have made bold to apply to you : several gentlemen of learning, who have seen it, join with me in praising it. I am far from having any mercenary views for myself in this affair, and, was I able, would print it at my own risque. It is a perfect tragedy ; the plot clear, the language spirited, and the songs (interspersed in it) are flowing, poetical, and elegantly simple ; the similies judiciously applied, and, though wrote in the reign of Henry the VIth, not inferior to many of the present age. If I can procure a copy, with or without the gratification, it shall be immediately sent to you. The motive that actuates me to do this is, to convince the world that the monks (of whom some have so despicable an opinion) were not such blockheads as generally thought, and that good poetry might be wrote in the dark days of superstition, as well as in these more enlightened ages. An immediate answer will oblige. I shall not receive your favour as for myself, but as your agent.—I am, sir, your most obedient servant,
"Thomas Chatterton.

"P. S.—My reason for concealing my name was, lest my master (who is now out of town) should see my letters, and think I neglected his business. Direct for me on Redcliffe Hill."

Then came an extract from the tragedy, by way of specimen ; and the letter concluded with this notice :—

"The whole contains about one thousand lines. If it should not suit you, I should be obliged to you if you would calculate the expenses of printing it, as I will endeavour to publish it by subscription on my own account.
"*For Mr. James Dodsley,*
"*Bookseller, Pall Mall, London.*" *

---

* These letters were for a long period preserved — by accident, apparently — among other loose papers in Dodsley's counting-house. They were subsequently advertised among the autograph rarities in Thorpe's catalogue, and were afterwards traced into the possession of Mr. Haslewood, a great Chattertonian collector. They were first published in 1813, by Mr. Britton, in his work on Redcliffe Church. A more detailed account, and a facsimile of one of the letters, will be

It is generally thought that Chatterton likewise received no answer to this second letter ;—I must say that I am of a different opinion. In his letter to his relation Stephens he speaks of Dodsley as his correspondent; and notwithstanding all the romance of that epistle, a vein of truth runs through his account of the affair with Walpole, and I see therefore no reason to question the accuracy of his other statement. But of course the scheme failed. Publishers do not remit the purchase-money for a copyright until they have the *quid pro quo* in hand. And a tragedy too, of the age of Henry VIth! *A perfect tragedy, the plot clear, the language spirited, and the songs flowing, poetical, and elegantly simple.* And this on the word of an unknown correspondent, whose 'master' might think he neglected his 'business.' There was not so much shrewdness in this manœuvre of Chatterton's to obtain a guinea, as might have been expected from him.

And now it was, that defeated in his application to Dodsley, he conceived the project of opening a correspondence with Horace Walpole—Lord Orford, —a man of eminence and high standing, both in literature and the world. And here he went to work in a different manner, as suited to the altered rank of the party on whom he intended to practise. He commenced with this letter, and manuscript :—

" SIR,—Being versed a little in antiquities, I have met with several curious manuscripts, among which the following

found in a periodical called " Sherwood's London Miscellany," for January, 1839.—ED.

may be of service to you, in any future edition of your truly entertaining Anecdotes of Painting. In correcting the mistakes (if any) in the notes, you will greatly oblige,

"Your most humble servant,

"THOMAS CHATTERTON.

"Bristol, March 25, Corn Street."

"The Ryse of Peyncteyne in Englande, wroten by T. Row-lie,[1] 1469, for Mastre Canynge.[2]

" Peynctynge ynn England, haveth of ould tyme bin yn use; for saieth the Roman wryters, the Brytonnes dyd depycte themselves, yn soundrie wyse, of the fourmes of the soune and moone wythe the hearbe woade: albeytte I doubte theie were no skylled carvellers. The Romans be accounted of all menne of cunnynge wytte yn peyncteynge and carvellynge; aunter theie mote inhylde theyre rare devyces ynto the mynds of the Brytonnes; albeytte att the commeynge of Hengeyst, nete appeares to wytteness yt, the Kystes are rude-lie ycorven, and for the moste parte houge hepes of stones. Hengeste dyd brynge ynto this reaulme herehaughtrie, whyche dydde peyncteynge. Hengeste bare an asce[3] ahreed bie an afgod. Horsa, an horse sauleaunte, whych eftsoones hys broder eke bore. Cerdyke, a sheld adryfene.[4] Cuthwar, a shelde afegrod:[5] whose ensamples were followed bie the latter of hys troope, thys emproved the gentle art of peyncteynge. Herehaughtrie was yn esteem amongste them: take yee these Saxon acheumentes. Heofmas[6] un æeced-fet was

---

[1] "T. Rowlie was a secular priest of Saint John's, in this city; his merit as a biographer, historiographer, is great; as a poet still greater: some of his pieces would do honour to Pope; and the person under whose patronage they may appear to the world, will lay the Englishman, the antiquary, and the poet, under an eternal obligation."*

[2] "The founder of that noble gothic pile, St. Mary Redclift Church, in this city; the Mæcenas of his time; one who could happily blend the poet, the painter, the priest, and the Christian, perfect in each: a friend to all distress, an honour to Bristol, and a glory to the church."

[3] *Asce,* &c., a ship supported by an idol.

[4] *Adryfene,* an embossed shield; being rudely carved with flowers, leaves, serpents, and whatever suited the imagination of the carver.

[5] *Afegrod,* a shield, painted in the same taste as the carving of the last.

[6] *Heofnas,* &c., azure, a plate; which is the signification of æeced-fed.

* [All these notes are by Chatterton, and are printed as they appear in the letter.—ED.]

ybore of Leof, au Abthane of Somertonne. Ocyre[1] added-ybore bic Elawolf of Mercier. Blae[2] border adronet an stowe adellice—the nuntiaunte armourie of Bristowe. A scelde[3] agrefen was the armourie of Ælle Lord of Bristowe Castle. Crosses in mayute nombere was ybore, albeyt chiefes and oder partytiones was unknowen, untill the nynth centurie. Nor was peyacteynge of sheeldes theire onlie emploie, walles maie be seene, whereyn ys auntiannte Saxonne peynteynge; and the carvellynge maie be seene yn imageies atte Keyneshame, Puckilchyrche, and the castel; albeyt largerre thane life, theie bee of feeytyre hondie warke. Affleredus was a peyncter of the eighth centurie, hys dresse bee yune menne, a longe alban, braced wyth twayne of azure gyrdles; labelles of redde clothe onne his arme and flatted beaver uponne the heade. Next Aylward in tenthe centurie ycorven longe paramentes; wyth-oute, of redde uponne pourple, wyth gould beltes and dukalle courounes beinge rems of floreated goulde. Afflem a peyncter lived ynne the reygne of Edmonde; whane, as storie saiethe was fyrst broughte ynto Englande, the connynge mysterie of steineynge glasse, of which he was a notable performer; of his worke maie bee seene atte Ashebyrne, as eke at the myn-ster chauncele of Seyncte Bede, whych doethe represente Seyncte Warburghe to whose honoure the mynstere whylome han bin dedycated. Of hys lyfe be fulle maint accountes. Goeynge to partes of the londe hee was taken bie the Danes, and carryed to Denmarque, there to bee forslagen bie shotte of arrowe. Inkarde, a soldyer of the Danes, was to slea hym; onne the nete before the feeste of deathe hee found Afflen to bee hys broder. Affryghte chaynede uppe hys soule. Ghaste-nesse dwelled yn his breaste. Oscarre, the greate Dane, gave hest hee shulde bee forslagen, with the commeynge sunne, no teares coulde availe, the morne cladde yn roabes of ghastness was come; whan the Danique kynge behested Oscarre, to arraye his knyghtes eftsoones, for warre: Afflem was put yn theyre flyeynge battailes, sawe his countrie ensconced wyth foemen, hadde hys wyfe ande chyldrene broghten capteeves to hys shyppe, and was deieynge wythe sorrowe, whanne the loude blataunte wynde hurled the battyle agaynst an heck. For fraughte wythe embolleynge waves, he sawe hys broder, wyfe, and chyldrenne synke to deathe: himselfe was throwen

[1] *Ocyre*, &c., or *Promeiso*, and in Saxon, was little green cakes offered to the afgods or idols.

[2] *Blae*, &c., sable, within a border under, a town walled and cre-nelled proper.

[3] *A scelde*, &c., a shield, carved with crosses.

onne a bank ynne Isle of Wyghte, to lyve hys lyfe forgarde to
alle emmorse : thus moche for Afflem. John,[10] second abbatte
of Seyncte Austyn mynsterre, was the fyrste Englyshe payn-
stere in oyles ; of hym have I sayde in odere places relateynge
to his poesies. He dyd wryte a boke of the Proportione of
Imageries, whereynne he saieth the Saxonnes dydde throwe
a mengleture over theyre coloures to chevie them from the
weder. Nowe methynkethe steinede glasse motte need no
syke a casinge, butte oile alleynge, botte albeytte ne peyncte-
ynge of the Saxonnes bee in oyle botte water, or as whylome
called eau. Chatelion, a Frenchmane, learned oyle peyncte-
ynge of abbot Johne. Carvellynge ynne hys daies gedered
new beauties, botte mostelie was wasted in small and dribelet
pieces, the ymageries beeynge alle cladde ynne longe para-
mentes, whan the glorie of a carveller shulde bee in ungar-
mented ymagerie, therebie showinge the semblamente to
kynde. Roberte of Glowster lissed notte his spryghte to
warre ne learnynge, butte was the sonne, under whose raies
the flourettes of the field shotte into lyfe ; Gilla a Brogtoune
was kyndelie noticed bie himme, who depycted notable ya
cau. Henrie a Thornton was a genson depyctor of counte-
nances ; he payncted the walles of master Canynge hys howse,
where bee the councelmenne atte dynnere ; a most dayntie
and fœtyve performaunce nowe yrased beeynge done M.CC.I.
Henrie a Londre was a curyous broderer of scarces ynne
sylver and golde and selkes diverse of hue. Childeberte West
was a depyctour of countenances. Botte above alle was the
peyncter, John de Bohunn, whose worke maie be seene yn
Westmynster halle. Of carvellers[11] and oder peyncters I shall

---

[10] " This John was inducted abbot in the year 1186, and sat in the
dies 29 years. He was the greatest poet of the age in which he lived ;
he understood the learned languages. Take a specimen of his poetry
on King Richard I.
      " Harte of lyone ! shake thie sword
         Bare thie mortherynge steinede honde ;
      Quace whole armies to the queede.
         Worke thie wylle yn burlie bronde.
      Barons here on bankers browded,
         Fyghte ya furres gayuste the cale ;
      Whilest thou ynne thonderynge armies
         Warriketh whole cytfyes bale.
      Harte of lyon ! sound the beme !
         Sounde ytte ynto inner londes,
      Feare flies sportine ynne the cleeme,
         Inne thie banner terror stondez."
[11] " I have the lives of several eminent carvers, painters, &c., of an-
tiquity, but as they all relate to Bristol, may not be of service in a

saie hereafter, fyrst Englyschynge from the Latyne cit to wytte. Peynctynge improveth the mynde, and smotheth the roughe face of our spryghtes.

"*For Horace Walpole, Esq.*
"*To be left with Mr. Bathoe, bookseller, near Exeter Change, Strand, London.*"

With what amazement must Walpole have greeted the receipt of this epistle! Heraldry introduced into England, by Hengist! and, Achievements borne by the Saxons! "Bathoe, my bookseller," writes Walpole, many years afterwards, "brought me a pacquet left with him. It contained an ode, or little poem of two or three stanzas, in alternate rhyme, on the death of Richard I.; and I was told, in very few lines, that it had been found at Bristol with many other old poems: and the possessor could furnish me with accounts of a series of great painters that had flourished at Bristol. Here I must pause to mention my own reflections. At first I concluded, that somebody having met with my Anecdotes of Painting, had a mind to laugh at me, I thought not very ingeniously, as I was not likely to swallow a succession of great painters at Bristol. The ode or sonnet, as I think it was called, was too pretty to be a part of the plan; and, as is easy with all the other supposed poems of Rowley, it was not difficult to make it very modern, by changing the old words for new; though yet more difficult than with most of them. I then imagined, and do still, that the success of Ossian's poems had suggested this plan."

general history. If they may be acceptable to you, they are at your service."

But Walpole was courteous, and, without hinting his suspicions, which perhaps were not so serious as he would have had the world believe when it began to laugh at him, sent Chatterton an immediate reply, couched in the following terms :—

"Arlington Street, March 28, 1769.

" Sir,—I cannot but think myself singularly obliged, by a gentleman with whom I have not the pleasure of being acquainted, when I read your very curious and kind letter, which I have this minute received. I give you a thousand thanks for it, and for the very obliging offer you make me of communicating your manuscript to me. What you have already sent me is valuable, and full of information ; but, instead of correcting you, sir, you are far more able to correct me. I have not the happiness of understanding the Saxon language, and without your learned notes, should not have been able to comprehend Rowley's text.

" As a second edition of my Anecdotes was published last year, I must not flatter myself that a third will be wanted soon, but I shall be happy to lay up any notices you will be so good as to extract for me, and send me at your leisure ; for as it is uncertain when I may use them, I would by no means borrow and detain your MSS.

" Give me leave to ask you, where Rowley's poems are to be found. I should not be sorry to print them, or at least a specimen of them, if they have never been printed.

" The abbot John's verses, that you have given me, are wonderful for their harmony and spirit ; though there are some words I do not understand. You do not point out exactly the time when he lived, which I wish to know ; as I suppose it was long before John al Ectry's discovery of oil painting ; if so, it confirms what I have guessed, and have hinted in my Anecdotes, that oil painting was known here much earlier than that discovery or revival.

" I will not trouble you with more questions now, sir ; but flatter myself, from the urbanity and politeness you have already shewn me, that you will give me leave to consult you. I hope too, you will forgive the simplicity of my direction, as you have favoured me with none other.

" I am, Sir, your much obliged

and obedient humble servant,

" HORACE WALPOLE.

"P.S.—Be so good as to direct to Mr. Walpole, Arlington-street."

Chatterton allowed no time for this enthusiasm to cool. He instantly forwarded a further communication; but unfortunately, of the letter that accompanied it, we have only a fragment remaining. It is probable that the mutilation took place after Walpole, at Chatterton's desire, had returned the letters. In the missing portion of this epistle, Chatterton had, with a generous but imprudent confidence,—relying upon the frankness and apparent liberality of Horace Walpole,—confessed his limited means, and deplored the humble sphere in which he was condemned to move. Then a change took place in Walpole's behaviour, which Chatterton always attributed to his unfortunate confession. We may imagine the indignant boy, in a fit of mingled pride and resentment, tearing and defacing the guilty document; and charging it with the ruin of those magnificent visions which Walpole's answer had raised and beautified. The remaining fragment is as follows:—

* * * * * *

" I offer you some further anecdotes and specimens of poetry, and am,

" Your very humble and obedient servant,

" THOMAS CHATTERTON.

" *March 30, 1769, Corn Street, Bristol.*"

Historie of Peyncters yn Englande.

BIE T. ROWLIE.

" Haveynge sayde yn oder places of peyncteynge and the ryse thereof, eke of somme peyncteres ; nowe bee ytte toe be sayde of oders wordie of note. Afwolde was a skylled wyghte yn laieynge onne of coloures ; hee lyved yn Merciæ, ynne the daies of Kynge Offa, ande depycted the countenaunce of Eadburga, his dawter, whyche depycture beeynge borne to Bryght-

rycke he toke her to wyfe, as maie be seene at large in Alfridus.[1]
Edilwald, Kynge of the Northumbers, understode peyncte-
ynge, botte I cannot fynde anie piece of hys nemped.[2] Inne a
mansion at Copenhamme I have seene a peyncteynge of moche
antiquite, where is sitteynge Egbryghte in a royaul mannere,
wythe kynges yn chaynes at hys fote, wythe meincte sembla-
ble[3] fygures, whyche were symboles of hys lyfe; and I haveth
noted the Saxons to be more notable yane lore and peyncte-
ynge thann the Normannes, nor ys the monies sythence the
dales of Willyame le Bastarde so fayrelie stroken as afore-
tyme. I eke haveth seene the armorie of East Sexe most
fetyvelie[4] depycted, yan the medst of an auntyaunte wall.
Botte nowe we bee upon peyncteynge, sommewhatte muie bee
saide of the poemes of these daies, whyche bee toe the mynde
what peyncteynge bee toe the eyne, the coloures of the fyrste
beeynge mo dureynge. Ecca Byshoppe of Hereforde yn D.LVII.
was a goode poete, whome I thus Englyshe :—

> Whan azure skie ys veylde yn robes of nyghte
>   Whanne glemmrynge dewe droppes stounde[5] the faytours[6]
>   eyne,
> Whanne flying cloudes, betinged wyth roddie lyghte,
>   Doth on the bryndlynge wolfe and wood bore shine,
> Whanne even star, fayre herehaughtes of nyghte,
>   Spreds the darke douskie sheene along the mees,[7]
> The wrethynge neders[8] sends a glumie[9] lyghte,
>   And houlets wynge from levyn[10] blasted trees.
> Arise mie spryghte and seke the distant delle,
> And there to echoing tonges thie raptured joies ytele.

Gif thys manne han no hande for a peynter, he had a head:
a pycture appearethe ynne each lyne, and I wys so fyne an
even sighte mote be drawn as ynne the above. In anoder of
hys vearses he saithe,

> Whanne sprynge came dauneynge onne a flourette bedde,
>   Dighte yane greene raimente of a chaungyage kynde ;
> The leaves of hawthorne boddeynge on hys hedde,
>   And wythe prymrosen coureynge to the wynde :

---

[1] "This is a writer whose works I have never been happy enough to
meet with."
  [2] *Nemped*, mentioned.
  [3] *Semblable*, metaphorical.
  [4] *Fetyvelie*, elegantly, handsomely.
  [5] *Stounde*, astonish.
  [6] *Faytours*, travellers.
  [7] *Mees*, mead.
  [8] *Neders*, adders, used here perhaps as a glow-worm.
  [9] *Glumie* dull, gloomy.
  [10] *Levyn*, blasted by lightning.

> Thanne dydd the Shepster[1] hys longe albaune[2] spredde
> Uponne the greenie bancke and daunced rounde
> Whilest the soest flowretes nodded onne his hedde,
> And hys fayre lambes besprenged[3] onne the grounde,
> Anethe hys fote the brooklette ranne alonge,
> Whyche strolleth rounde the vale to here his joyous songe.

Methynckethe these bee thoughtes notte oft to be metten wyth, and ne to bee excellede yn theyre kynde. Elmar, Byshoppe of Selseie, was fetyve yn workes of ghastlienesse,[4] for the whyche take yee thys speeche :

> Nowe maie alle helle open to glope thee downe,
>   Whylst azure merke[5] immenged[6] wythe the daie,
> Shewe lyghte on darkned peynes to be moe roune,[7]
>   O mayest thou die lyvinge deathes for aie :
> Maie floodes of Solfirre bear thie sprighte anoune,[8]
>   Synkeynge to depths of woe, maie levynne brondes[9]
> Tremble upon thie peyne devoted crowne,
>   And senge thie alle yn vayne emploreynge hondes ;
> Maie all the woes that Godis wrathe can sende
> Uponne thie heade alyghte, and there theyre furie spende.

Gorweth of Wales be sayde to be a wryter goode, botte I understande notte that tonge. Thus moche for poetes, whose poesies do beere resemblance to pyctures in mie unwordie opynion. Asserius was wryter of hystories ; he ys buryed at Seyncte Keynas College ynne Keynsham wythe Turgotte, anoder wryter of hystories, Inne the walle of this college ys a tombe of Seyncte Keyna[10] whych was ydoulven anie, and placed ynne the walle, albeit done yn the daies of Cerdyke, as appeared bie a crosse of leade upon the kyste ;[11] ytte bee moe notablie performed than meynte[12] of ymageries[13] of these daies. Inne the chyrche wyndowe ys a geason[14] peyncteynge of Seyncte Keyna syttynge yn a trefoliated chayre, ynne a long alban braced wythe golden gyrdles from the wayste upwarde to the breaste, over the whyche ys a small azure coape ;[15] benethe ys depycted Galfridus, MLV. whyche maie bee that Geoffroie who ybuylded the geason gate* to Seyncte Augustynes chapele once leadynge. Harrie Piercie of Northomberlande was a quaynte[16]

---

[1] *Shepster*, shepherd.
[2] *Albanne*, a large loose white robe.
[3] *Besprended*, scattered.
[4] *Ghastlieness*, terror.
[5] *Merke*, darkness.
[6] *Immenged*, mingled.
[7] *Roune*, terrific.
[8] *Anoune*, ever and anon.
[9] *Levynne Brondes*, thunderbolts.
[10] "This I believe is there now."
[11] *Kyste*, coffin.
[12] *Meynte*, many.
[13] *Ymageries*, statues, &c.
[14] *Geason*, curious.
[15] *Coape*, cloak or mantle.
[16] *Quaynte*, curious.

* This gate is now standing in this city, though the chapel is not to be seen.

peyncter; he lyvede yn M.C. and depycted severalle of the
wyndowes ynne Thonge Abbye, the greate windowe atte Bat-
taile Abbeie; he depycted the face verie welle wythalle, botte
was lackeynge yn the most-to-bee-loked-to accounte, propor-
tione. John a Roane payncted the shape of a hayre: he
carved the castle for the sheelde of Gilberte Clare of thek[17]
feytyve performaunce. Elwarde ycorne[18] the castle for the
seal of Kynge Harolde of most geason worke; nor has anie
seale sythence bynne so rare, excepte the seale of Kinge Hen-
rie the fyfthe, corven by Josephe Whetgyfte. Thomas a Baker
from corveynge crosse loafes, tooke to corveying of ymageryes,
whych he dyd most fetyvelie; he lyved ynne the cittie of
Bathe, beeynge the fyrste yn Englande, thatte used hayre
ynne the bowe of the fyddle,[19] beeynge before used wythe
peetched hempe or flax. Thys carveller dyd decase yn MLXXI.
Thus moche for carvellers and peyncters.

"John was inducted abbot in the year 1146, and sat in the
dies 29 years. As you approve of the small specimen of his
poetry, I have sent you a larger, which though admirable is
still (in my opinion) inferior to Rowley,[20] whose works when I
have leisure I will fairly copy and send you."

And with this document, as from the pen of Row-
ley, came a further specimen of Abbot John, in the
poem on "Warre," inserted at page 304.

The note on the antiquity of the violin is curious
enough, and affords another exemplification of Chat-
terton's ruling passion for falsifying history. There
can be no doubt, had Horace Walpole offered to
undertake such a work, that Rowley's pretended
manuscripts would have been forthcoming, and that
Chatterton would have suffered them to be printed

---

[17] *Thek*, very.
[18] *Ycorne*, a contraction of *ycorven*, carved.
[19] "Nothing is so much wanted as a History of the Antiquity of the
Violin, nor is any antiquary more able to do it than yourself. Such a
piece would redound to the honour of England, as Rowley proves the
use of the bow to be knowne to the Saxons, and even introduced by
them."
[20] "None of Rowley's pieces were ever made public, being, till the
year 1631, shut up in the iron chest in Redcliffe Church."

without throwing off the mask, or confessing the imposition; supposing, all this time, that Walpole had allowed himself to have been deceived by them.

But already, in the second letter only, here were *four* poets, of whom the world had never heard, rescued from oblivion by Thomas Chatterton. Rowley; Abbot John; Ecca, Bishop of Hereford; and Elmar, Bishop of ' Selseie.' He must have formed a liberal opinion of the measure of Horace Walpole's credulity, which perhaps was sufficiently ample, in the success of his former experiment, to warrant any test he might think fit to administer in a second.

However, Walpole declined being caught twice. Or, probably, Chatterton's confession, as its author persisted, was, after all, the real cause of the alteration —if indeed there was any, beyond a natural disinclination to be imposed upon—in Walpole's behaviour. Upon reading Chatterton's statement, which, according to the virtuoso, was in these terms—" he informed me that he was the son of a poor widow, who supported him with great difficulty; that he was clerk or apprentice to an attorney, but had a taste and turn for more elegant studies; and hinted a wish that I would assist him with my interest in emerging out of so dull a profession, by procuring him some place in which he could pursue his natural bent ;"—upon reading this statement, Walpole wrote to a relation, an old lady living at Bath, and desired her to make enquiries respecting Chatterton, and communicate the result to him. This was done, and the boy's story was verified, though "nothing was returned about his character," on which subject Walpole had particularly requested information : for, indeed, the authenticity of these extraordinary documents was being called in question. Walpole had communicated the poems to his friends, Gray and Mason—famous in their time, and the former, artificial as he is, still read and admired—who "at once pronounced them forgeries, and declared there was no symptom in them of their being the productions of near so distant an age ;" and "recommended the returning them without any further notice :" but overstepping their advice, Walpole wrote another letter to Chatterton, in which he told him that he had "communicated his transcripts to much better judges, and that they were by no means satisfied with the authenticity of his supposed MSS. ;" objecting the harmony and structure of the versification, which indeed is an insurmountable objection to the antiquity of any of the poems produced by Chatterton. For the substance of his observations, as the letter is lost, being probably destroyed by the angry boy, we cannot do better than quote Walpole's words, as he afterwards related the affair in his own defence :—

" Being satisfied with my intelligence about Chatterton, I wrote him a letter with as much kindness and tenderness as if I had been his guardian; for, though I had no doubt of his impositions, such a spirit of poetry breathed in his coinage, as interested me for him: nor was it a grave crime in a young bard to have forged false notes of hand that were to pass current only in the parish of Parnassus. I undeceived him about my being a person of any interest, and urged to him that in duty and gratitude to his mother, who had straitened herself to breed him up to a profession, he ought to labour in it, that in her old age he might absolve his filial debt ; and I told him that when he should have made a fortune, he might unbend himself with the studies consonant to his inclinations."

So far, good; but while we believe that no blame whatever attaches itself to Walpole—estimating his *action* only—in his conduct towards Chatterton, we must acknowledge that the above statement looks rather awkward when placed side by side with the following, which occurs in the same 'defence :'—

"I should have been blameable to his mother, and society, if I had seduced an apprentice from his master, to marry him to the nine muses ; and I should have encouraged a propensity to forgery, which is not the talent most wanting culture in the present age. *All of the house of forgery are relations ;* and though it is just to Chatterton's memory to say, that his poverty never made him claim kindred with the richest, or more enriching branches, yet his ingenuity in counterfeiting styles, and I believe, hands, *might easily have led him to those more facile imitations of prose, promissory notes.*"

This indeed is a 'damnatory clause ;' especially when we remember that Horace Walpole was the author of the " Castle of Otranto," in the preface to which work it is stated to have been discovered " in the library of an ancient Catholic family in the north of England, and printed at Naples in the black letter, in the year 1529 ;" assuming, in fact, to be a translation from the Italian; and then, in the second edition, casting off the mask, " the author flatters himself he shall appear excusable for having offered his work to the world under the *borrowed personage* of a translator." So might Chatterton have appealed —Was not *my* Rowley a " borrowed personage," and am not I therefore 'excusable?'* "Oh! ye," exclaims

* To be sure, the patrician author of the grave history with which the " Castle of Otranto" was preceded, and palmed on the public for an

the indignant Coleridge, coupling this fact with the foregoing heartless reference to the 'house of forgery,' "Oh! ye who honour the name of *man*, rejoice that this Walpole is called *a lord.*"* One fact, however, in Walpole's favour must be borne in mind; Chatterton did *not* so appeal, but still persisted in his first assertion. On the other hand, it should not be forgotten—what seems hitherto to have escaped notice—that Walpole, many years afterwards, had the cowardice to deny the receipt of these letters which Chatterton had sent him, with their history of Painters and Glass-stainers, and specimens of "time-shrouded minstrelsy," of which no other than himself was the "sweet harper." This the virtuoso did in a letter to Hannah More, dated September 1789, immediately after the publication of Barrett's History of Bristol, in which these letters were printed for the first time, and made public for all the world to read, and as a likely consequence to ridicule the poor dupe who had suffered himself to be, in his own words, "so bamboozled." Here runs his denial:—

ancient foreign production, had not the clearest right in the world to be severe on the poor plebeian for trying his hand in the same line. Some hints of conscience on this matter would not have been amiss. Perhaps he would plead that his was a *mere* literary fib; was not an imposition attempted on individuals personally; was not meant to be turned to any account of personal advantage; was not employed to cajole anybody's good nature into an obligation to serve his interests; and, besides, was not a falsification of the state of our poetry in an early age. He had to allege, also, when accused of having been virtually, and almost directly, the cause of the subsequent catastrophe, that Chatterton persisted in his course of artifice after what was represented as the fatal cruelty, and with anger against those who had not submitted to be deceived by his asseverations.—ECLECTIC REVIEW.

[* This must have been before he wrote "for the *Morning Post* its aristocracy."—ED.]

" I will not ask you about the new History of Bristol, because you are too good a citizen to say a word against your native place ; but do pray cast your eye on the prints of the cathedral* and castle, the *chef d'œuvres* of Chatterton's ignorance, and of Mr. Barrett's too, and on two letters, *pretended to have been sent to me, and which never were sent.* If my incredulity had wavered, they would have fixed it. I wish the milkwoman† would assert that Boadicea's dairymaid had invented Dutch tiles ; it would be like Chatterton's origin of heraldry and painted glass in these two letters.‡

This was indeed cowardly, and somewhat impudent. The man of science, who had desired further information—had particularly enquired about Abbot John and the discovery of oil-painting, shrank from the ridicule to which he had now become obviously exposed. And so pitifully done—not boldly denied,—*that* he dared not do, for he too well knew that his own answer was in existence, and might some day be produced against him,—but snivelling in a letter to an antiquated blue-stocking. This was mean enough.

Setting all this aside, however, and judging of Walpole's conduct by his actions during Chatterton's lifetime, we cannot think he was to blame. Sure we are that there was scarcely one person living who would have acted otherwise had the overture been made to himself. Besides the recent discovery of the Macpherson imposition, in which Walpole was implicated, as he was one of the first entrusted with specimens of Ossian's fragments, which he implicitly believed, was too fresh, and too galling, to have allowed him to weigh calmly the merits of another

* The print of the cathedral, in Barrett's History, is in no respect connected with Chatterton.—TYSON.
† Ann Yearsley, the poetical milkwoman, and a *protegé* of Hannah More's.
‡ Horace Walpole's Letters, vol. vi. 1840.

attempt at imposition. "I had not," he frankly confesses, "zeal enough to embark a second time in a similar crusade."

But we are forestalling our narrative by these remarks. Upon receiving Walpole's second letter and after pondering upon the advice it contained, Chatterton wrote, in reply, the following:—

"Sir,
"I am not able to dispute with a person of your literary character. I have transcribed Rowley's poems, &c. &c. from a transcript in the possession of a gentleman who is assured of their authenticity. St. Austin's minster was in Bristol. In speaking of painters in Bristol, I mean glass-stainers. The MSS. have long been in the hands of the present possessor, which is all I know of them. Though I am but sixteen years of age, I have lived long enough to see that poverty attends literature. I am obliged to you, sir, for your advice, and will go a little beyond it, by destroying all my useless lumber of literature, and never using my pen again but in the law.

"I am,
"Your most humble servant,
"THOMAS CHATTERTON."

As no immediate answer was returned to this, its writer became impatient, and in six days time sent again:—

"Sir,
"Being fully convinced of the papers of Rowley being genuine, I should be obliged to you to return me the copy I sent you, having no other. Mr. Barrett, an able antiquary, who is now writing the History of Bristol, has desired it of me; and I should be sorry to deprive him, or the world indeed, of a valuable curiosity, which I know to be an authentic piece of antiquity.

"Your very humble servant,
"THOMAS CHATTERTON.

"Bristol, Corn-street, April 14, 1769.

"P.S.—If you wish to publish them yourself, they are at your service."

There are two other letters to Walpole in the British Museum, one in Chatterton's handwriting, the second in that of Mr. Barrett, and both bearing the same date with this last, April 14. They were *never sent* however, and the fact only shews that their author had not determined what arguments to urge upon the occasion. That in Chatterton's writing, and which was probably the first copy, is as follows :—

"*For Horace Walpole, Esq., Arlington-street, London.*

"SIR,

"As I am *now* fully convinced that Rowley's papers are genuine, should be obliged to you if you'd send copies of them to the Town and Country Magazine, or return them to me for that purpose; as it would be the greatest injustice to deprive the world of so valuable a curiosity.

"I have seen the original from which the extracts first sent you were copied. The harmony is not so extraordinary, as Joseph Iscam is altogether as harmonious.

"The stanza Rowley writes in, instead of being introduced by Spenser, was in use 300 years before
   *　　*　　*　　*　　*　　*　　*
by Rowley; although I have seen some poetry of that age exceeding alliterations without rhyme.

"I shall not defend Rowley's pastoral; its merit can stand its own defence.

"Rowley was employed by Canynge to go to the principal monasteries in the kingdom to collect drawings, paintings, and all the MSS. relating to architecture: is it then so very extraordinary he should meet with the few remains of Saxon learning? 'Tis allowed by every historian of credit, that the Normans destroyed all the Saxon MSS., paintings, &c. that fell in their way; endeavouring to suppress the very language. The want of knowing what they were, is all the foundation you can have for styling them a barbarous nation.

"If you are not satisfied with these conspicuous
   *　　*　　*　　*　　*　　*　　*
the honour to be of my opinion.

"I am, sir,

"Your very humble and obedient servant,

"T. CHATTERTON.

"*Bristol, Corn-street, April* 14, 1769."

The other, of which Barrett has preserved a copy, runs thus :—

"SIR,   "Being fully convinced of the papers of Rowley being genuine, I should be obliged to you to return the copy I sent you, having no other. Mr. Barrett, who is now writing the History and Antiquities of the city of Bristol, has desired it of me; and I should be very sorry to deprive him, or the world indeed, of a valuable curiosity, which I know to be an authentic piece of antiquity. However barbarous the Saxons may be called by our modern virtuosos, it is certain we are indebted to Alfred, and other Saxon kings, for the wisest of our laws, and in part, for the British Constitution. The Normans, indeed, destroyed the MSS. paintings, &c. of the Saxons that fell in their way; but some might be, and certainly were, recovered out of the monasteries, &c. in which they were preserved. Mr. Vertue could know nothing of the matter—'twas quite out of his walk. I thought Rowley's Pastoral had a degree of merit that would be its own defence. Abbot John's verses were translated by Rowley out of the Greek, and there might be poetry of his age something more than mere alliterations, as he was so great a scholar. The stanza, if I mistake not, was used by Ischam, Gower, Ladgate, in the sense as by Rowley, and the modern gloomy seems but a refinement of the old word. Glomming, in Anglo-Saxon, is ye twilight.

"From, sir,
"Your humble servant,
"April 14th.   "T. CHATTERTON."

"As Joseph Iscam," remarks Sir Walter Scott, "is equally a person of dubious existence with Rowley, this is a curious instance of placing the elephant upon the tortoise."

The silence which Walpole continued to preserve towards Chatterton—notwithstanding the importunity with which the latter had urged the return of his manuscripts—does not tell much in his favour. When he received Chatterton's letter he was about to set out on a journey to Paris, where, according to his own statement, he remained six weeks. But why allow three months to elapse without taking any notice of his correspondent? In July we find Chatterton, with his patience exhausted, writing again in no very measured terms:

"SIR,

"I cannot reconcile your behavour to me with the notions I once entertained of you. I think myself injured, sir; and did not you know my circumstances, you would not dare to treat me thus. I have sent twice for a copy of the MS.—no answer from you. An explanation, or excuse for your silence, would oblige

"*July 24th.*"   "THOMAS CHATTERTON.

"Singularly impertinent!" cries Horace Walpole. "Dignified and spirited!" exclaims Robert Southey. We leave our readers, with a fair statement of the case before them, to decide whether Chatterton's conduct was the more *insolent*, or Walpole's behaviour the more *unjust*: in Southey's words, it is thus "particularly stated" that they may form a just conception of the whole of the correspondence between Mr. Walpole and the great but unfortunate Chatterton.

What Horace Walpole *did*, when he received this last epistle, will be best told by himself.

"He wrote me (says Walpole, referring to the fore-mentioned letter of advice) rather a peevish answer; said he could not contest with a person of my learning (a compliment by no means due to me, and which I certainly had not assumed, having mentioned my having consulted abler judges), maintained the genuineness of the poems, and demanded to have them returned, as they were the property of another gentleman.

"When I received this letter I was going to Paris in a day or two, and either forgot his request of the poems, or perhaps, not having time to have them copied, deferred complying till my return, which was to be in six weeks. I protest I do not remember which was the case; and yet, though in a cause of so little importance. I will not utter a syllable of which I am not positively certain; nor will charge my memory with a tittle beyond what it retains.

"Soon after my return from France I received another letter from Chatterton, the style of which was singularly impertinent. He demanded his poems roughly; and added, that I would not have *dared* to use him so ill, if he had not acquainted me with the narrowness of his circumstances.

"My heart did not accuse me of insolence to him. I wrote an answer expostulating with him on his injustice, and renewing good advice; but upon second thoughts, reflecting that so wrong-headed a young man, of whom I knew nothing, and whom I had never seen, might be absurd enough to print my letter, I flung it into the fire; and snapping up both his poems and letters, without taking a copy of either, for which I am now sorry, I returned all to him, and thought no more of him or them.*

---

* On these circumstances was founded the whole charge that was brought against Walpole, of blighting the prospects, and eventually contributing to the ruin of the youthful genius. Whatever may be thought of some expressions respecting Chatterton, which Walpole employed in the explanation of the affair which he afterwards published, the idea of taxing him with criminality in neglecting him, was manifestly unjust. But in all cases of misfortune, the first consolation to which human nature resorts, is, right or wrong, to find somebody to blame, and an evil seems to be half cured when it is traced to an object of indignation.—CAMPBELL.

Walpole's memory has suffered most on account of his conduct towards Chatterton, in which we have always thought he was perfectly defensible. That unhappy son of genius endeavoured to impose upon Walpole a few stanzas of very inferior merit as ancient, and sent him an equally gross and palpable imposture under the shape of a pretended List of Painters. Walpole's sole crime lies in not patronizing at once a young man who only appeared before him in the character of a very inartificial impostor, though he afterwards proved himself a gigantic one. The fate of Chatterton lies not at the door of Walpole, but of the public at large, who, two years (we believe) afterwards, were possessed of the splendid proofs of his natural powers, and any one of whom was as much called upon as Walpole to prevent the most unhappy catastrophe.—SIR WALTER SCOTT.

The periodicals of the day, and the tribe of those "who daily scribble for their daily bread," and for whom Walpole had, perhaps unwisely, frequently expressed his contempt, attacked him bitterly for his inhumanity to genius, and even accused him as the author of the subsequent misfortunes and untimely death of that misguided son of genius,—a fate which befell him, it is to be feared, more in consequence of his own dissolute and profligate habits, than from any want of patronage. However this be, Walpole clearly had nothing to say to it.—LORD DOVER.

Walpole regrets that he took no copy of Chatter-
ton's MSS. Had he done so, would such a proceed-

Mr. Walker compares the conduct of Dr. Blacklock towards Burns,
with that of Walpole to Chatterton. Had he read Walpole's defence,
he would not have fastened this accusation, which has been long since
exploded, upon the back of Walpole.—LOCKHART.

It has been the pride of modern literature to degrade the character
of Walpole. That as a man he was sarcastic, fretful, and fastidious;
prone to satirical comment on the failings of his friends; easily dis-
gusted by uncouthness of manners or impropriety of speech; accus-
tomed to regard the world of professional literature with the super-
cilious smile of conscious elevation, is evident from his letters, and the
memorabilia published in "Walpoliana." These imperfections and
eccentricities were the natural accompaniments of an irritable temper-
ament, and an aristocratic education; they were confirmed and
exasperated by the exquisite sensibility of his taste, which detected
with an intrinsic rapidity the slightest deviation from good manners.
To this individual, of habits so fastidious, so select in his intercourse,
and so tender of his literary fame, it was the misfortune of Chatterton
to apply: and had Walpole possessed the lights in which we at present
view the endowments of his supplicant, there seems no reason to doubt
that he would have sacrificed many of his jealousies and preposses-
sions to the encouragement of so extraordinary a phenomenon. As it
was, he must have felt indignant at the presumption and mercenary
spirit of a boy, who could first attempt to make him the dupe of his
forgeries, and afterwards endeavour to rest his claims for support, or
patronage, on the productions of his artifice. Walpole's discretion, or
his humanity, however, overcame his anger, and in a letter equally re-
markable for the gentleness of its reproof, and its good sense, he ex-
horts him to apply with industry and perseverance to the duties of his
profession, as the surest means of enabling him hereafter to discharge
the debt of gratitude to his relatives.—BRITTON.

An unsuccessful overture to Dodsley the noted publisher, reduced
him, at whatever cost to his pride, to look out for some personage in
whom there might be found a lingering remainder of the virtues of that
nearly departed age, when men of rank and wealth were the patrons of
indigent men of genius; and Mr. Horace Walpole was the man. To
him were conveyed some pieces of the Rowley fabrication, as samples
of the literary treasures so fortunately rescued from the oblivion in
which old Time believed he had buried them for aye. Walpole was
caught at first; returned the most courteous compliments and a "thou-
sand thanks," and would be gratified to be favoured with further com-
munications from a gentleman so much his superior in Saxon learning.
But after there had been time to consult Gray and Mason, who imme-
diately pronounced the compositions forgeries; and after (what might
have gone near to do the mischief) he had received from Chatterton
an account of his condition, as in humble circumstances, enslaved to
an employment which he could not endure, with a request that Walpole
would assist him to escape from it by exerting his interest to procure
for him some situation in which he might be free to prosecute the
course which nature intended him for;—the patron that was to be and

ing have been strictly honourable? However, the
world, after heaping upon him all the abuse it could

who had been drawn to make a first yielding movement with smiles
and gentle speech, turned sharp round, and would have no more to say
to him.

This refusal to take the duties and honours of patronage has been
maledicted in the name of all the gods and muses at once. Mr. Walpole's
vindication is a capital display of dexterous and pointed fencing. But,
also, we cannot help thinking it was in a great degree successful. It is pro-
bable the judgment passed on his conduct in the transaction has inad-
vertently been allowed to take its colours, less from the true merits of
the particular case, than from his known character, as a cold, selfish,
cynical, fastidious, but sycophantic aristocrat. In the first place, he
might fairly ask why *he* should be singled out as the individual to be,
independently of his will, so charged with the fortunes, as to be ac-
countable for the disasters of a young man unknown to him. But next
when he became convinced that this young man, while appealing to his
benevolence, and soliciting his assistance, was deliberately practising a
deception on him, and perhaps secretly exulting at the thought of in-
veigling so eminent and shrewd a person to serve him in the capacity
of dupe, who can wonder that he resented such an experiment on him,
or vehemently reproach him for declining, even in an unceremonious
manner, to become a patron on such terms? Let any one make the
case his own, and say whether he has so little pride, that he would not
be irritated at finding himself partly caught by a stratagem, which im-
plied a contempt of his discernment in the very act of petitioning his
favour. A man of benevolence extraordinary might, indeed, have con-
ceived a philanthropic solicitude for a young man of unquestionable
genius, in untoward circumstances, and entering on a course not tend-
ing to honourable distinction. He might have wished to devise some
way of rescuing such talents from perversion, and directing them to a
worthy application. But such gratuitous virtue could not be required
of Walpole, but by a law which not one, probably, of his censurers
would have obeyed in a similar case.—ECLECTIC REVIEW.

On the score of his transactions with Chatterton, Mr. Walpole has
incurred more censure than he really deserved. In an age when litera-
ture is so little patronized by those who wield all the powers of the
state, and have in trust for the public the distribution of its emolu-
ments; when men of the first abilities, actually engaged in the learned
professions are permitted to languish in obscurity and poverty, without
any of those rewards which are *appropriated* to the professions they ex-
ercise, and are compelled to depend for a precarious subsistence on the
scanty pittance which they derive from diurnal drudgery in the service
of booksellers, it can scarcely be deemed an instance of extraordinary
illiberality that a private man, though a man of fortune, should be in-
attentive to the petition of a perfect stranger, a young man whose birth
or education entitle him to no high pretensions, and who had only con-
ceived an unreasonable dislike to a profession both lucrative and re-
spectable. If Chatterton had actually avowed the poems, perhaps a
very generous and feeling heart, such as rarely exists at present, and
least of all in the highest circles of life, might have been more strongly

think of, and even charging him with having been the immediate cause of the pitiable catastrophe which succeeded, has at length, and of its own accord, pardoned him, and, I believe, only with justice. That he should be made accountable for Chatterton's suicide, was one of the maddest and most absurd persecutions ever urged against an individual. The proud boy held on his course, " unslacked of motion," for more than a twelvemonth afterwards, manifesting the same passion for imposing upon the credulity of others; nor did Walpole, during that time, nor till after his most mournful end had awakened public curiosity and solicitude, hear anything more of him.

Chatterton, indeed, had no right to expect patronage at the hands of Horace Walpole. What had he to do, sitting under the shadow of the great? He was, could he but have seen it, in a fair way of earn-

---

affected with their beauties, and might probably have extended some small degree of encouragement. But, considering things as they are, and not as they ought to be, it was a degree of unusual condescension to take any notice whatever of the application; and when Chatterton felt so poignantly his disappointment, he only demonstrated his ignorance of the state of patronage in this country, and acted like a young and ingenuous person, who judged of the feelings of courtiers by the generous emotions of his own breast, or the practice of times which exist only in records of romance. Mr. Walpole afterwards regretted, and I believe sincerely, that he had not seen this extraordinary youth, and that he did not pay a more favourable attention to his correspondence: but, to be neglected in life, and regretted and admired when these passions can be no longer of service, has been the usual fate of learning and genius. Mr. Walpole was certainly under no obligation of patronizing Chatterton. To have encouraged and befriended him, would have been an exertion of liberality and munificence uncommon in the present day; but to ascribe to Mr. Walpole's neglect (if it can even merit so harsh an appellation) the dreadful catastrophe which happened at the distance of nearly two years after, would be the highest degree of injustice and absurdity.—Dr. GREGORY.

Horace Walpole has been frequently inveighed against by the ardent admirers of Chatterton with more severity than justice.—SOUTHEY.

the worst, though for minds other than the strongest, the most dangerous knowledge we can acquire. Under the porch, where its schoolmen teach, at some stage or other, we must all sit, except perhaps the mere foolish, who would include anything in their blind belief, and who are only Christians because they are not Pagans. We believe Shelley—warring all his life against the *abuse* of religion—to have been the most religious of all men. There are many who cannot understand this, and to such will offence come. These see, not with the eye of faith, but with the fleshly vision only.

It is to be hoped at least of Chatterton, that he was sincere in his disbelief; for an affectation of scepticism is of all vices the most odious, though unfortunately not the most uncommon. In his writings he strove rather against the hypocrisy of professors, than against religion itself; he ridicules the Pharisee, but never the publican. His antique poems are uniformly of an exalted moral, and not unfrequently of a devotional character. In extenuation of his offence, be it remembered that he was ' literally and strictly' a boy : and let his accusers, who would be first to cast a stone at him, question of themselves what were their own religious principles, 'and whether they had any ' in their schoolboy era, at the age of sixteen.

Dealing with Chatterton's life, from this period till its most melancholy termination, we have many difficulties to encounter. "Few subjects of composition," says Sir Walter Scott, "equally affecting or elevating can ever occur, when we consider the strange ambiguity of his character, his attainments under circumstances incalculably disadvantageous, and his wish to disguise them under the name of another; his high spirit of independence, and the ready versatility with which he stooped to the meanest political or literary drudgery; the amiable and interesting affection which he displays towards his family, with a certain looseness of morality which approaches to profligacy,—a subject uniting so strong an alternation of light and shade." Regarding these 'conflicting elements' of his disposition in a generous and sympathising spirit, many of his admirers have endeavoured to excuse his failings, and at once to account for them by urging the plea of insanity,—a visitation which is likely to have been too true, and which is strongly countenanced by the fact that there were decided symptoms of such a malady in his family. His sister was placed under restraint, and her own child was subject to frequent fits of mental aberration. "A key," remarks his generous friend Southey, "to the eccentricities of his life, and the deplorable rashness of his death."*

* Scott laments that the life and character of Chatterton have never been drawn by the "hand of a master." Unfortunately there is no biography of Chatterton, worthy of the name, in existence. That by Dr. Gregory is wholly unworthy of the writer; it is meagre of facts, and affords us scarcely one opportunity of judging of the poet, or of deciding in what particular he differed from the herd of ordinary mortals. The Doctor expresses no opinion of his own, but leaves for the reader the summary of his scanty evidence.

Of the recently published Life by Dix, it may be as well to state, that there is little new in the work be-

Among the papers of Chatterton, preserved in the British Museum, there occurs the following curious document—being his boasted articles of Faith—writ-

---

side the appendices. That by Mr. Tyson, signed ℧., is important. Of the Life by Chalmers, "the hack of Grub-street for many a long year," we shall not speak ourselves; but, by way of evidence, append a review from the hand of a writer, who, as Lord Byron can well attest, had the power, when he so pleased, to castigate smartly. The memoir of Chatterton, by a person named Davis, which may occasionally be picked up for a few pence at the bookstalls, is in every respect beneath criticism.

"Mr. Chalmers' Life of Chatterton is written in the spirit of pharisaic morality, which blinds the understanding as much as it hardens the heart. He tells the history of the Rowley papers just as a pleader would have told it at the Old Bailey, if Chatterton had been upon trial for forging a bill of exchange! After saying that 'his general conduct during his apprenticeship was decent and regular; and that on one occasion only Mr. Lambert thought him deserving of correction, for writing an abusive letter, in a feigned hand, to his old schoolmaster;' he adds, in true Old Bailey logic, 'so soon did this young man learn the art of deceit, which he was now preparing to practise on a more extensive scale.' When this letter was written, Chatterton was hardly fifteen! Upon publishing his first modern antique in *Felix Farley's Bristol Journal*, the subject excited inquiry, and the paper being traced to him, he was consequently interrogated (says Mr. Chalmers), probably without much ceremony, where he obtained it. '*And here his unhappy disposition shewed itself in a manner highly affecting in one so young, for he had not yet reached his sixteenth year, and according to all that can be gathered, had not been corrupted either by precept or example.*'

"Mr. Chalmers is undoubtedly learned, for he writes about catalectics; and there is a well-known book within the compass of his classical studies, which must have taught him that—

Ingenuas didicisse fideliter artes
Emollit mores, nec sinit esse feros:

but unhappily he has not learnt those arts 'faithfully,' for if he had, his feelings upon this subject would not have been thus 'brutal.' However dangerous may be the distinction between venial and mortal sins in the practical casuistry of the Romish Church, that puritanical spirit, whose moral laws are framed in the temper of Draco, is more detestable, and not less pernicious. Mr. Chalmers refers the whole fiction of Rowley to original sin. Satan, no doubt, had about as much to do with it as with the burning of the missionaries' printing-office at Serampore—an affair of which they suppose him to have repented, because of the liberal subscriptions which were raised to repair its loss. The deception was not intended to defraud or injure one human being, and might most assuredly have been begun and continued without the

ten apparently about this period of his life, and (I
believe) never before published.

"*The Articles of the Belief of me, Thomas Chatterton.*"

"That God being incomprehensible, it is not required of us
to know the mysteries of the Trinity.

"That it matters not whether a man is a Pagan, Turk,
Jew, or Christian, if he acts according to the religion he pro-
fesses.

"That if a man leads a good moral life, he is a Christian.

"That the stage is the best school of morality :—and

"That the Church of Rome (some tricks of priestcraft ex-
cepted) is certainly the true Church.

"THOMAS CHATTERTON."

It is written on a fragment of foolscap paper, much
soiled and worn, apparently from having been long
carried in the pocket. I think it requires no com-
ment.

He had, some months since, commenced a corres-
pondence with the London periodicals. The first
notice to be found respecting his contributions is in

---

slightest sense of criminality in Chatterton. And for the other eccen-
tricities of his life, and its melancholy catastrophe, Mr. Chalmers
might have remembered that there were original diseases in the world,
as well as original sin ; and that when the coroner's inquest returned
a verdict of insanity after his death, that verdict might very possibly
be correct. It is at least rendered highly probable by the fact that
there was a decided insanity in his family. As for the fame of Thomas
Chatterton, which this biographer thinks it will not be possible to per-
petuate, Mr. C.'s opinion will never be weighed in the scale against it.
The history of the Bristol boy will always attract curiosity to his
poems, and that curiosity will be amply gratified: and whilst Mr.
Chalmers states that '*his deceptions, his prevarications, his political
tergiversations, &c. were such as should be looked for in men of ad-
vanced age, hardened by evil associations, and soured by disappointed
pride or avarice;*' let it be remembered that his 'deceptions' and
'prevarications' only relate to the poems and papers attributed to
Rowley, which are things very unlike the effect of disappointed pride
and avarice ! and to call his essays on political controversy *political
tergiversation*, is as preposterous an abuse of language, as it would be
to call Mr. Chalmers a judicious critic, or candid biographer."—
SOUTHEY, *in the Quarterly Review, No. XXII.*

Among the papers of Chatterton, preserved in the British Museum, there occurs the following curious document—being his boasted articles of Faith—writ-

---

side the appendices. That by Mr. Tyson, signed ℧., is important. Of the Life by Chalmers, "the hack of Grub-street for many a long year," we shall not speak ourselves; but, by way of evidence, append a review from the hand of a writer, who, as Lord Byron can well attest, had the power, when he so pleased, to castigate smartly. The memoir of Chatterton, by a person named Davis, which may occasionally be picked up for a few pence at the bookstalls, is in every respect beneath criticism.

"Mr. Chalmers' Life of Chatterton is written in the spirit of pharisaic morality, which blinds the understanding as much as it hardens the heart. He tells the history of the Rowley papers just as a pleader would have told it at the Old Bailey, if Chatterton had been upon trial for forging a bill of exchange! After saying that 'his general conduct during his apprenticeship was decent and regular; and that on one occasion only Mr. Lambert thought him deserving of correction, for writing an abusive letter, in a feigned hand, to his old schoolmaster;' he adds, in true Old Bailey logic, 'so soon did this young man learn the art of deceit, which he was now preparing to practise on a more extensive scale.' When this letter was written, Chatterton was hardly fifteen! Upon publishing his first modern antique in *Felix Farley's Bristol Journal*, the subject excited inquiry, and the paper being traced to him, he was consequently interrogated (says Mr. Chalmers), probably without much ceremony, where he obtained it. '*And here his unhappy disposition shewed itself in a manner highly affecting in one so young, for he had not yet reached his sixteenth year, and according to all that can be gathered, had not been corrupted either by precept or example.*'

"Mr. Chalmers is undoubtedly learned, for he writes about catalectics; and there is a well-known book within the compass of his classical studies, which must have taught him that—

Ingenuas didicisse fideliter artes
Emollit mores, nec sinit esse feros:

but unhappily he has not learnt those arts 'faithfully,' for if he had, his feelings upon this subject would not have been thus 'brutal.' However dangerous may be the distinction between venial and mortal sins in the practical casuistry of the Romish Church, that puritanical spirit, whose moral laws are framed in the temper of Draco, is more detestable, and not less pernicious. Mr. Chalmers refers the whole fiction of Rowley to original sin. Satan, no doubt, had about as much to do with it as with the burning of the missionaries' printing-office at Serampore—an affair of which they suppose him to have repented, because of the liberal subscriptions which were raised to repair its loss. The deception was not intended to defraud or injure one human being, and might most assuredly have been begun and continued without the

" *Curious Coats in and about Bristol.*
" Barry of 6. Or and Azure, counterchanged per Fess, by
Gilbert de Gaunt. Argent, a maunch Gules edged, Or, verdoy
of trefoils, by John Cosier. Or, a canton sable, by Delouvis.
A seal, Quarterly, first and fourth on bend, 3 annulets, second
and third a head couped gutté, by the name of Sancto Lovis,
to a deed dated 1204.
" Your most humble servant,
"THOMAS CHATTERTON."

About this period, too, we have another evidence
of his genius for fiction—in which he pretty largely
dealt at times—in his letter to a Mr. Stephens, a
breeches-maker, of Salisbury, who was in some sort
a relation of the family; at the "grave and sober ad-
vice" with which it concludes, " we are mute," says
Sir Walter Scott, " with astonishment."

" SIR,—If you think vanity is the dictator of the fol-
lowing lines, you will not do me justice. No, Sir, it is only
the desire of proving myself worthy your correspondence
has induced me to write. My partial friends flatter me with
giving me a little uncommon share of abilities. It is Mr. Ste-
phens alone, whose good sense disdains flattery, whom I ap-
peal to. It is a maxim with me that compliments of friends
is more dangerous than railing of enemies. You may enquire,
if you please, for the *Town and Country Magazine,* wherein all
signed ' D. B.' and ' Asaphides,' are mine. The pieces called
Saxon are originally and totally the product of my muse ;
though I should think it a greater merit to be able to trans-
late Saxon. As the said Magazine is by far the best of its
kind, I shall have some pieces in it every month ; and if I vary
from my said signature, will give you notice thereof. Having
some curious anecdotes of paintings and painters, I sent them
to Mr. Walpole, author of the Anecdotes of Painting, Historic
Doubts, and other pieces well known in the learned world.
His answer I make bold to send you. Hence I began a lite-
rary correspondence, which ended as most such do. I differed
with him in the age of a MS. He insists on his superior
talents, which is no proof of that superiority. We possibly
may publicly engage in one of the periodical publications ;
though I know not who will give the onset. Of my proceed-
ings in this affair I shall make bold to acquaint you. My next
correspondent of note is Dodsley, whose collection of modern

and antique poems are in every library. In this city my prin-
cipal acquaintance are Mr. Barrett, now writing, at a vast
expense, an ancient and modern History of Bristol—a task
more difficult than the cleansing the Augean stable. Many
have attempted, but none succeeded in it; yet will this work,
when finished, please not only my fellow-citizens, but all the
world. Mr. Catcott, author of that excellent treatise on the
Deluge, and other pieces, to enumerate which would argue a
supposition that you were not acquainted with the literary
world. To the studies of these gentlemen I am always admit-
ted, and they are not below asking my advice in any matters
of antiquity. I have made a very curious collection of coins
and antiques. As I cannot afford to have a goodlabine to
keep them in, I commonly give them to those who can. If
you pick up any Roman, Saxon, English coins, or other an-
tiques, even a sight of them would highly oblige me. When
you quarter your arms in the mullet, say: Or, a Fess, Vert
by the name of Chatterton. I trace your family from Fitz-
Stephen, son of Stephen, Earl of Aumerle, in 1095, son of
Od, Earl of Blays, and Lord of Holderness.

" I am, your very humble servant,
"THOMAS CHATTERTON."

In such and similar ways did our young poet
evince that he had a pleasant humour.

There is an anecdote preserved of him, which I
have never seen recorded, the circumstance of which
occurred about this period. Spending one evening
with a party of intimate companions, among other
subjects, the conversation turned upon suicide; and
some taking one side of the argument, and some
another—whether indeed it was of bravery or cow-
ardice, the act of self-destruction. Chatterton sud-
denly plucked from his breast a small pocket-pistol,
and, holding it to his forehead, with resolute accent
exclaimed, " Now—if one had but the courage to pull
the trigger!" It was then, for the first time, dis-
covered that he was in the constant habit of carrying
this loaded weapon about his person.

Mr. Edmunds' Journal it was *not* printed; but, after the posthumous publication of Chatterton's Miscellanies, and the Supplement to that work, there appeared, in the form of a " Supplement to the Supplement," a little pamphlet of eight pages, containing the first 376 lines of " Kew Gardens," which it is reasonable to conclude were furnished from the 'first packet' sent to Mr. Edmunds. Dr. Gregory asserts that the whole of the poem was "transmitted in different parcels" to the same party. It is not very likely, however, or the remainder would have appeared in the same publication, especially as the printed fragment breaks suddenly off, leaving the sense notoriously deficient. The existence of this pamphlet was unknown to Southey in 1803. About sixty of the concluding lines of the poem were published in his edition of Chatterton; and to these was annexed, as a note, " Every effort has been made to obtain the remainder of the poem, but without success." I am aware of only one copy of the fragment, which is in the library of the British Museum.*

* Dix published the " Kew Gardens" in his ' Life of Chatterton,' in 1837. He says, " I have been fortunate enough to procure a copy of the whole poem; and it is here for the first time printed entire." He did not, however, procure the whole poem; for the hiatus of 200 lines, above referred to, occurs in his publication. The real state of the case is, that out of the 1094 lines of " Kew Gardens," printed by Dix, only 120 appeared for the 'first time.' From line 496 to the end, it is little more than a transcript of " The Whore of Babylon;" indeed 550 lines are *literally* the same: add to these the 376 lines published many years before, with the fragment in Southey's edition, and we find that 974 lines of the poem had been before the public for upwards of thirty years. I may here remark that, not being myself aware of Mr. Edmunds' pamphlet till after the sheets of " Kew Gardens" had gone to press, I inadvertently ascribed to Dix two or three short notes, which occur in the course of the poem. Dix, in reality, has nothing to do with them; they are by Chatterton.—ED.

Ready-made satire Chatterton always had at hand, without the labour of producing fresh material. He had but to transcribe three hundred couplets from " Kew Gardens," with here and there a slight alteration or transposition, and the " Whore of Babylon" was completed, the old metal being fused in a fresh die. Several instances of this mode of manufacture occur in his " Acknowledged Poems," (the Rowley Creation was too sacred to be thus tampered with); but, except in the above-mentioned instance, and in that of " The Exhibition," where fifty consecutive lines are taken likewise from " Kew Gardens," the number of couplets thus borrowed from one composition and transferred to a second, seldom exceeds nine or ten. Undoubtedly this poetical laboratory, and chemical transfusion and transformation, were easy of construction, and no wise difficult in the process. *Stans pede in uno;* one might write a bookseller's shop full so.

VIII.

Literary career in London.

Little now remains to be said of Chatterton, and that little consists of no stirring adventures, and of no incidents that can satisfy curiosity or afford amusement to any but those who love a simple story, and sufficiently admire the poet to trace the history of the man. There are no documents to which we can refer for facts; there are no biographical notices which we can consult for a record of Chatterton's town life. All that is to be told must be gathered from his own letters, and woven, as best it can, into the form of a narrative.

In our last chapter we intimated the Poet's resolution to try his fortune in London. To enable him to defray the expences of the journey, his friends and acquaintance contributed a guinea a-piece.* It may seem a strange inconsistency that he, nineteen-twentieths of whose composition was pride, should thus be a dependant on the bounty of others : but no man who has any acquaintance with the workings of the human heart will wonder at this. This nature of ours is full of contradictions ; and pride and meanness, and generosity and injustice, are not seldom found in close alliance. Perhaps, too, in his dreams of future greatness, and his anticipated discoveries of El Dorados, he expected to repay, and doubly repay, the debt which, after all, Circumstance, that unspiritual god, had obliged him to contract.

Full of hope, and thirsting to attain the golden goal —not only of fame, but of wealth and station—Chatterton entered on his London career. The clouds which had covered the sky in the morning of life seemed fast floating away ; his moral atmosphere grew clearer. The sun came out in all its strength. A soft ideal light lent enchantment to the world of thought in which he moved ; he went on his path hoping and singing, and trusting soon to reach the bright and shining gate which his imagination had erected at the end of that path : yet if we consider

* Mr. Barrett.

his actual circumstances, there was but little ground
for hope. Who and what were his allies? " Patrons,
booksellers, printers, publishers of *Freeholders' Ma-
gazines*, and proprietors of *Towns* and *Counties ;*"
to these men the young poet sold himself—say rather,
sold, Esau-like, his birthright—the vision and the
faculty divine—for a mess of pottage. How could
any good come out of such a Galilee as this? What
could be looked for but that the creator should sink
into the scribbler, the poet into the buffoon—a
spirit, free, uncompromising, integral, into a character
compromised, factional, and slavish?

We must not, however, be too severe on the
young poet. If he threw away his genius, was there
not a reason? Perhaps none grieved more than him-
self over the new character which he was obliged to
assume. But if man doth not live by bread alone, it
is equally true that he cannot live without it; and
the soul which should feed only on angels' food must
bow itself down to the flesh-pots of Egypt, in order
that its frail co-mate, the body, may have " bread and
meat in the morning, and bread and meat in the
evening."

Chatterton's first letter to his mother, which bears
date April 26, shews that he was full of heart and
hope. He reached London at five o'clock in the
evening; called immediately on his friends Mr. Ed-
munds, Mr. Fell, Mr. Hamilton, and Mr. Dodsley,
and met with great encouragement from them. In a
short time we find him settled, apparently much to his
own satisfaction, at Mr. Walmsley's. Mr. Walmsley

Mr. Edmunds' Journal it was *not* printed ; but, after the posthumous publication of Chatterton's Miscellanies, and the Supplement to that work, there appeared, in the form of a " Supplement to the Supplement," a little pamphlet of eight pages, containing the first 376 lines of " Kew Gardens," which it is reasonable to conclude were furnished from the 'first packet' sent to Mr. Edmunds. Dr. Gregory asserts that the whole of the poem was "transmitted in different parcels" to the same party. It is not very likely, however, or the remainder would have appeared in the same publication, especially as the printed fragment breaks suddenly off, leaving the sense notoriously deficient. The existence of this pamphlet was unknown to Southey in 1803. About sixty of the concluding lines of the poem were published in his edition of Chatterton ; and to these was annexed, as a note, " Every effort has been made to obtain the remainder of the poem, but without success." I am aware of only one copy of the fragment, which is in the library of the British Museum.*

* Dix published the " Kew Gardens" in his ' Life of Chatterton,' in 1837. He says, " I have been fortunate enough to procure a copy of the whole poem ; and it is here for the first time printed entire." He did not, however, procure the whole poem ; for the hiatus of 200 lines, above referred to, occurs in his publication. The real state of the case is, that out of the 1094 lines of " Kew Gardens," printed by Dix, only 120 appeared for the ' first time.' From line 496 to the end, it is little more than a transcript of " The Whore of Babylon ;" indeed 550 lines are *literally* the same : add to these the 376 lines published many years before, with the fragment in Southey's edition, and we find that 974 lines of the poem had been before the public for upwards of thirty years. I may here remark that, not being myself aware of Mr. Edmunds' pamphlet till after the sheets of " Kew Gardens " had gone to press, I inadvertently ascribed to Dix two or three short notes, which occur in the course of the poem. Dix, in reality, has nothing to do with them ; they are by Chatterton.—ED.

gentleman in Cheapside, who was a partner in a music-shop. When he discovered that Chatterton could write, he desired him to compose a few songs for him. These were shewn to a Doctor of Music, and he was invited to treat with the Doctor on the footing of a composer, for Ranelagh and the Gardens. He now grew affluent—comparatively at least, for all things in this world go by comparison. He employed his money in dressing fashionably—but only as a means to an end—an introduction into good society. He informs us that he had engaged to live with the brother of a Scotch Lord, who was speculating in the book-selling branches. As a compensation he was to have board and lodging gratis. Chatterton considered this a great step in his royal-road to fame and wealth. In the first flush of joy and hope he promised his sister a handsome provision; every month was to end to her advantage—she was " to walk in silk attire, and siller hae in store." His mother was not forgotten; for her too there were presents,—London gauds and Parisian vanities, and intimations of more substantial assistance. And why should we omit to mention the tobacco for his grandmother—British herb too—and the trifles for Thorne? Simplest articles of household use, but not without a meaning to the thoughtful heart; for surely they shadow forth, darkly and im-perfectly though it be, the character of this Boy-King of Song. Tameless, and swift, and proud—contem-ning the world, and scorning the herd of mankind—he had yet a heart full of home-affections, and an intellect that could descend to things of mean and trifling nature when they had reference to a mother, a sister, or a friend. Let us do justice to Chatterton ; and if we are to make the most of his vices, let us not forget to make the most of his virtues.

Chatterton next projected a voluminous History of London, which was to appear in numbers. He anticipated great success, and no small profit : and, in his letter to his sister, exults in the idea that this design would not involve him in those expences which his other literary labours obliged him to incur, as he should not be compelled to go to the coffee-house : and thus, he adds, "*I shall be able to serve you the more by it.*" It is needless to add that this scheme was abandoned; the beautiful sentiment which it was the means of suggesting can never die.

Chatterton was unusually elated. He had forwarded an essay to Beckford, the Lord Mayor. It was received favourably. This encouraged the author to wait on the patriot, to procure his approbation to address a second letter to him on the subject of the remonstrance and its reception. His lordship received him politely, and warmly invited him to call again. *The rest was a secret.* He evidently magnifies the advantages which he thought awaited him ; he sees through a false medium, and the distant prospects look fairer and more dilated in the discoloured atmosphere of thought, just as the walls and towers of a city rise larger and brighter in the purple mist of a summer's morning. The last clause which I have quoted evinces that, like Byron, Chatterton loved a little mystification.

We come now to his political career—one more difficult to excuse, perhaps, than any other; at any rate the most unpleasant to touch upon. It is not fair, however, to deal with Chatterton as we should with one who had come to the full stature of a man, and who had no temptation to induce him to trifle with his principles.

Let us reflect that the writer was but a boy,—a boy of an ardent and passionate temperament, thirsting for distinction, anxious to acquire a name, thwarted by fortune, without friends, save those who were so in word only, and without hopes, save such as arose from the light of his own genius. He looked forward to the time when he should be able to build up a strong and durable monument of fame; when his imagination should be strengthened, his intellect matured, and his ambition become clear and well defined: but meanwhile, it was necessary to do something. The daily bread must be had, and the warm coat purchased, and a thousand other poor necessities satisfied; and to attain such consummation, the essay must be produced, and the guinea earned. Something of vanity, too, undoubtedly prevailed in Chatterton's "moral man," and in this instance it forcibly demonstrates itself. He was delighted to have an opportunity of shewing the world what he could do; it was a sort of petty triumph, a kind of literary ovation, to find himself necessary as a political partizan,—to find that the despised apprentice of Bristol was able to deal the cards at the state *soirées*, and to dream that there was some probability of his holding all the trumps, or at least having the honours in his own hand. No wonder that the gin-and-water of notoriety and vulgar applause intoxicated the young aspirant, and led him to *shuffle*, when he should have played his game boldly and candidly. There was more of levity than licentiousness in this conduct; more of the desire—silly and low enough for him who could *create* as well as *scribble*—to shew with what facility the child of seventeen could prove a point one day and refute it the next; more of the acuteness of the special pleader than the apostacy of the statesman; and, to finish the climax, more of scorn for his employers, and for mankind generally, we fear, than anxiety for either the good or the bad cause. By what figure of rhetoric such a transaction as this could be styled *political tergiversation*, we confess ourselves at a loss to discover, unless, as Southey intimates, it be by the same figure which associates the ideas of " Chalmers and infallibility."

Chatterton thought but little of the merits of the popular leaders at that time, although his inclination would necessarily have led him to espouse what has been called the cause of the people, had he ever ventured in real earnest to contend in the arena of politics. This is evident from many passages in his letters, but from none so strongly as this.

" Essays," he writes to his sister, " fetch no more than what the copy is sold for; as the patriots themselves are searching for a place, they have no gratuities to spare. On the other hand," he continues, " unpopular essays will not even be accepted, and you must pay to have them printed; but then you seldom lose by it. Courtiers are so sensible of their deficiency in merit, that they generally reward all who know how to daub them with an appearance of it."

Strong evidence this, if any were wanted, that penury, not policy, was Chatterton's principle of action, and that his contempt was equally directed against both parties. To reflect on the poverty, pain of heart, distress, and solitude of the marvellous boy; to see the creative genius descend from his throne of melodious thought, to mingle with the creeping things that went into the great Noah's-ark of Mammon, gives one far more sorrow than his *political tergiversation*, as one of his biographers has chosen to style this juvenile display of intellectual sleight-of-hand.

We shall make but few remarks on these celebrated letters. Chatterton's model appears to have been Junius, and he has cleverly imitated the inimitable. The structure of the sentence is not dissimilar, and there is no deficiency of trope and antithesis; but the delicate irony and the caustic sarcasm of that fearless writer, and the polished diction, and the exquisite unfolding of the expression, are sought in vain. Instead of these, we have what Shelley would call a mixture of wormwood and verdigrease; well turned periods, full of sound and fury, but signifying nothing, and a sort of Bombastes Furioso taking to task, infinitely amusing when we reflect on the age and circumstances of the writer. Still the political letters are remarkable productions, and really wonderful for a boy. They are remarkable for their energy, for

their spirit, and for the readiness which they evince
their author to have possessed, in assuming and sus-
taining the style of thought and language of an old and
practised composer. Chatterton put on the lion's skin,
and if we may be allowed so colloquial an expression,
made an ass of himself: had he thought fit, he might
have raised his human voice—for like Homer's heroes
he was an articulate-speaking man—and have put the
lion himself to flight.

It may be as well to indicate the two letters which
called down on poor Chatterton the indignation of
this virtuous biographer. They were written after
the death of Beckford: one of them was addressed
to Lord North, signed MODERATOR, complimenting
Administration, for rejecting the City remonstrance;
the other, which bore the same date, and was signed
PROBUS, was addressed to the Lord Mayor, probably
in consequence of the permission which Chatterton
obtained from him, and contained a virulent invective
against the government, for the identical measure
which had been reprobated by the former. Both
bear date May 26th, 1770. The one commenced,
"My Lord, it gives me painful pleasure;" and the
other, "When the endeavours of a spirited people to
free themselves from insupportable slavery."

There is a hectic gaiety about Chatterton's letters
to his mother and sister, a boastful proclamation and
unnatural iteration of his importance, and of the mag-
nificent prospects which awaited him, as though it
were only by the continued reassertion that he himself
could believe in the wealth and fame which he anti-

cipated. Thus in one place he speaks of "*an author who would have introduced him as a companion to the young Duke of Northumberland, in his intended general tour;*" in another of his future recognition by "*a ruling power in the Court party;*" and in a third, in a burst of enthusiastic vanity, he tells us, "My company is courted everywhere—I must be among the great: state matters suit me better than commercial." Poor Chatterton! well sung the poet of Christabel, Life is thorny and youth is vain; and the thorniness of the one fostered, if it did not engender, the vanity of the other, in the instance which we are considering.

The history of Chatterton's literary career in London must not be *recorded* without some annotations on the remainder of his prose compositions. These are readily enumerated—Adventures of a Star, Maria Friendless, The Unfortunate Fathers, Tony Selwood, The False Step, The Hunter of Oddities,* Cutholf, a Saxon poem, and a few other slight pieces. They appeared in the Gospel Magazine, Town and Country, Court and City, London, and the Political Register. Some of them are of considerable merit, though utterly unworthy of the minstrel who sang "how dauntless Ælla frayed the Dacyan foes." They are light essays, modelled on those of Steele, Addison, and other writers of the eighteenth century, but scarcely deserving of a second perusal. Their characteristics are, accuracy of observation, a tolerable acquaintance with the more prominent features of a town life,

---

* The genuineness of many of these pieces is exceedingly questionable.

humorous expression, and a facile adaptation of the peculiarities which are required for this species of composition. Indeed, they are chiefly valuable for the light which they throw on the intellectual organization of Chatterton; evincing the readiness with which he could attain any knowledge whose acquisition he coveted; the perfect management which he possessed of his pen, his mastery of any style of thought or expression, and the diversatility and prodigal luxuriance of his permaturely ripened genius. Chatterton's favourite maxim was, that man is equal to anything, and that there was nothing which could not be achieved by diligence. Unlike others, he was not satisfied with the bare enunciation of the proposition; every action of his life and every exercise of his mind was employed in its demonstration. His knowledge of antiquities was wonderful, but it was a study which he pursued *con amore.* The letter of Tony Selwood derives its principal charm from this circumstance. It is quite unnecessary to comment on each of these productions: the tales apparently do not aim at originality—indeed one of them, the story of Maria Friendless, is an old acquaintance in a new dress; it is a "masqued resurrection" of Misella in the Rambler.

Chatterton seems to have been fond of the poetical memoranda which Macpherson was pleased to christen the Poems of Ossian; probably more from their pretensions to ancientry, than any real admiration of those turgid heroics. At Bristol he favoured the world with a host of imitations. He had observed, as Wordsworth remarks, how few critics were able to distinguish between a real ancient medal, and a counterfeit of modern manufacture; and he set himself to the work of filling a magazine with *Saxon poems*, counterparts of those of Ossian, as like his as one of his misty stars is to another. The last of his efforts in this line was Cutholf; it seems to be no way dissimilar from those which he published at Bristol; and, if not stolen from the smithie of the "impudent Highlander," it bears every appearance of being forged on his anvil.

Among the poetical productions which he published in London, are the African Eclogues, characterised by himself in a letter to a friend "as the only two pieces of mine I have the vanity to call poetry." The versification is strong, melodious, and original. The loves of Narva and Mored are powerfully recited. There is a picturesque liveliness in this pastoral which is exceedingly alluring. It has many felicitous expressions, and perhaps may be natural in Africa, but it certainly is not so in England. The same criticism may be applied to The Death of Nicou.

We shall only mention one more metrical production of Chatterton's—The Revenge, a Burletta. He is said to have received five guineas for it, from the proprietor of Mary-le-bone Gardens, where it was performed after his death. It is light, airy, amusing, and comic,—but like most of his acknowledged poems, confers but little honour on the author: it is useful as a further illustration of the varied powers of the Bristol Boy; but we sigh to think that the royal child of song should abdicate the throne of his wide their spirit, and for the readiness which they evince their author to have possessed, in assuming and sustaining the style of thought and language of an old and practised composer. Chatterton put on the lion's skin, and if we may be allowed so colloquial an expression, made an ass of himself: had he thought fit, he might have raised his human voice—for like Homer's heroes he was an articulate-speaking man—and have put the lion himself to flight.

It may be as well to indicate the two letters which called down on poor Chatterton the indignation of this virtuous biographer. They were written after the death of Beckford: one of them was addressed to Lord North, signed MODERATOR, complimenting Administration, for rejecting the City remonstrance; the other, which bore the same date, and was signed PROBUS, was addressed to the Lord Mayor, probably in consequence of the permission which Chatterton obtained from him, and contained a virulent invective against the government, for the identical measure which had been reprobated by the former. Both bear date May 26th, 1770. The one commenced, "My Lord, it gives me painful pleasure;" and the other, "When the endeavours of a spirited people to free themselves from insupportable slavery."

There is a hectic gaiety about Chatterton's letters to his mother and sister, a boastful proclamation and unnatural iteration of his importance, and of the magnificent prospects which awaited him, as though it were only by the continued reassertion that he himself could believe in the wealth and fame which he anticipated. Thus in one place he speaks of "*an author who would have introduced him as a companion to the young Duke of Northumberland, in his intended general tour;*" in another of his future recognition by "*a ruling power in the Court party;*" and in a third, in a burst of enthusiastic vanity, he tells us, " My company is courted everywhere—I must be among the great: state matters suit me better than commercial." Poor Chatterton! well sung the poet of Christabel, Life is thorny and youth is vain; and the thorniness of the one fostered, if it did not engender, the vanity of the other, in the instance which we are considering.

The history of Chatterton's literary career in London must not be *recorded* without some annotations on the remainder of his prose compositions. These are readily enumerated—Adventures of a Star, Maria Friendless, The Unfortunate Fathers, Tony Selwood, The False Step, The Hunter of Oddities,* Cutholf, a Saxon poem, and a few other slight pieces. They appeared in the Gospel Magazine, Town and Country, Court and City, London, and the Political Register. Some of them are of considerable merit, though utterly unworthy of the minstrel who sang "how dauntless Ælla frayed the Dacyan foes." They are light essays, modelled on those of Steele, Addison, and other writers of the eighteenth century, but scarcely deserving of a second perusal. Their characteristics are, accuracy of observation, a tolerable acquaintance with the more prominent features of a town life,

* The genuineness of many of these pieces is exceedingly questionable.

in the school of Epicurus to learn the vanity of the
no-faith which he had adopted. A few years more of
doubt and darkness, and his vigorous intellect would
have enabled him to explore his way through the sub-
terranean gloom of scepticism, and to reach the upper
world where the true light shineth. Alas! those few
years never came.

Early in July, Chatterton changed his residence.
From Shoreditch he removed to No. 4, Brook-street,
Holborn.* Mrs. Angel was now his landlady. Her
occupation was that of a *sac*, or dress-maker; and
whatever be its own appropriate degree of estimation,
it derives an adventitious honour from its association
with the latest memories of the gifted Boy of Bristol.
The cause of his removal is unknown—some impute it
to necessity, and some to the pride that would conceal
from the inquisition of friends the fall of the golden
image which he had set up. Most probably the latter
motive was the real one.

It may not be uninteresting to state in this place the
remuneration which the poet received for the slavery
in which he was held by the booksellers who favoured
him with their magnificent patronage. We give the
following extract from Chatterton's pocket-book. It

* Since this paragraph was written, we have learnt that the occupa-
tion of Mrs. Angel was that of a dressmaker. At that period ladies
wore a dress called a sack, and the makers were called sack-makers.
Mrs. Angel resided at No. 4, Brook-street, Holborn. In 1789, Mr. Old-
ham purchased this house, together with the adjoining houses on either
side of it, and converted them into a stove and grate manufactory.
The premises exist at the present time as left by Mr. Oldham, and are
now occupied by an upholsterer and cabinet-maker; they extend
from Holborn to No. 6, Brook-street. It is hardly necessary to inform
our readers, that it is no longer possible to recognise the house in which
Chatterton closed his life of sorrow, in despair and madness.—ED.

sufficiently demonstrates the futility of his literary projects.

	£.	s.	d.
Received to May 23, of Mr. Hamilton for Middlesex	1	11	6
„ of B.	1	2	3
„ of Fell, for the Consuliad	0	10	6
„ of Mr. Hamilton, for Candidus and Foreign Journal	0	2	0
„ of Mr. Fell	0	10	6
„ Middlesex Journal	0	8	6
„ Mr. Hamilton, for 16 Songs	0	10	6
	4	15	9

In another part of this little book, shortly before he found himself confronted by starvation and death, he has inserted a memorandum intimating that the sum of eleven pounds was due to him from the London publishers. It was a cruel fate to be compelled to turn literary drudge with five-and-twenty shillings a month for wages; and more cruel still to be doomed to suffer all the pains of hunger, because those wages were not paid.

But the dream was not quite completed yet. There was still one hope left—a straw on the waters for the drowning man to grasp. In his misery and poverty he applied to his friend Mr. Barrett, to procure him a situation as surgeon's mate to the coast of Africa. This was a downfall indeed for the aspirant after wealth and distinction: the enthusiasm and the glory and the exultation of his bright and shining youth were gone; the ladder on which he had hoped to have climbed to the heaven of greatness was withdrawn: and the sleeper awoke to find that his only pillow was a stone, and that he must exchange his communings with angels for intercourse with cold and heartless men.

The application was made in vain. Mr. Barrett
refused him the recommendatory letter which was
required ; and as Chatterton was manifestly incom-
petent to discharge the duties of the appointment
which he had hoped to procure through his interest,
Mr. Barrett's refusal was perfectly justifiable,—in fact,
great blame would have attached to him if he had
acted otherwise. It was at this period that the African
Eclogues were written. Chatterton could still solace
himself with the divine employment of the muse, and
the inspiration which a transient gleam of hope lent
him, enabled him to sing, but in no very truthful or
natural strains,

> " Of Tiber's banks where scarlet jasmines bloom,
> And purple aloes shed a rich perfume :
> Where, when the sun is melting in his heat,
> The reeking tigers find a cool retreat ;
> Bask in the sedges, lose the sultry beam,
> And wanton with their shadows in the stream."

Chatterton's last hope had failed. He was friendless,
lone, and unassisted. He had fallen on evil days, and
could now only look forward to the time, fast approach-
ing, in which he should be a wanderer and an outcast.
What wonder then if in his dark and deep distress,
" self-contempt drowned youth's starlight smiles in
tears," and the victim proudly and angrily refused to
be fed—to be *kept alive*—by the bread of charity.
Once only the pride of the heart was subdued by the
frailty of the flesh, and he partook of the proffered
bounty. It is Warton who records that an oyster
feast prevailed on him to forego his dignity for a while,
and to accept the hospitality of Mr. Cross, an apothe-
cary, of Brook street. This was Chatterton's last

desire which genius did not hallow, and possessed of a
heart which kept pure the holy forms of young imagi-
nation.* His temperance should be imitated by all, and
his abstinence might be emulated, but hardly surpassed
by the anchorite. The morsel of bread, the penny tart
and draught of spring water, the wine-cup untasted,
and the strong drink avoided, will surely exonerate
Chatterton from the imputation of being a voluptuary,
even if he escape not the taint of dissolute tongues,
and jealousy and hate. His affection, his brotherly and
filial love, the undeviating kindness and attentive soli-
citude, which he exhibited towards the members of his
own family, and substantial assistance which he ren-
dered his mother and his sister, when in actual want
himself, demonstrate the natural excellency and amia-
bility of his heart, and afford a convincing proof that
poetry and piety are in closer conjunction than many
suppose.

Chatterton had now lived nine weeks at Shoreditch.
The month of July had commenced, the summer was
far advanced—but the golden visions of the young en-
thusiast were still the baseless fabric of a dream. His
patron, Beckford, was dead, and with him his political
hopes seem to have expired: his finances were con-
tracted; the liberality of the booksellers had proved a
delusion; hope no longer encouraged him to look to
the future, and faith in the saviour had no existence in
the heart of the inspired lyrist. The boy of seventeen
had learnt to doubt, and he had not lived long enough

* Wordsworth.

in the school of Epicurus to learn the vanity of the no-faith which he had adopted. A few years more of doubt and darkness, and his vigorous intellect would have enabled him to explore his way through the subterranean gloom of scepticism, and to reach the upper world where the true light shineth. Alas! those few years never came.

Early in July, Chatterton changed his residence. From Shoreditch he removed to No. 4, Brook-street, Holborn.* Mrs. Angel was now his landlady. Her occupation was that of a *sac*, or dress-maker; and whatever be its own appropriate degree of estimation, it derives an adventitious honour from its association with the latest memories of the gifted Boy of Bristol. The cause of his removal is unknown—some impute it to necessity, and some to the pride that would conceal from the inquisition of friends the fall of the golden image which he had set up. Most probably the latter motive was the real one.

It may not be uninteresting to state in this place the remuneration which the poet received for the slavery in which he was held by the booksellers who favoured him with their magnificent patronage. We give the following extract from Chatterton's pocket-book. It

---

* Since this paragraph was written, we have learnt that the occupation of Mrs. Angel was that of a dressmaker. At that period ladies wore a dress called a sack, and the makers were called sack-makers. Mrs. Angel resided at No. 4, Brook-street, Holborn. In 1789, Mr. Oldham purchased this house, together with the adjoining houses on either side of it, and converted them into a stove and grate manufactory. The premises exist at the present time as left by Mr. Oldham, and are now occupied by an upholsterer and cabinet-maker; they extend from Holborn to No. 6, Brook-street. It is hardly necessary to inform our readers, that it is no longer possible to recognise the house in which Chatterton closed his life of sorrow, in despair and madness.—ED.

knew him well,* and according to the general evidence he was as remarkable for the prematurity of his person as he was for that of his intellect and imagination. His mien and manner were exceedingly prepossessing; his eyes were grey, but piercingly brilliant; and when he was animated in conversation or excited by any passing event, the fire flashed and rolled in the lower part of the orbs in a wonderful and almost fearful way. Mr. Catcott characterized Chatterton's eye "as a kind of hawk's eye, and thought one could see his soul through it." As with Byron, one eye was more remarkable than the other, and its lightning-like flashes had something about them supernaturally grand.

It is difficult to form a just appreciation of the character of Chatterton. We are all in some measure the creatures of circumstance; and the more we are subjected to external influences, the more our will is weakened, and the less able are we to do battle with the hostile array of our passions, and to resist the temptations which are presented on all sides by a deceitful and untried world. The moral nature of Chatterton was essentially manly,—there is nothing in it which even approximates to the puerile or the feminine; his faults are all the growth of a strong and vigorous heart, and of a searching and masculine intellect. His indomitable pride, his premature but natural adoption of the habits and expressions of men, his love of reasoning, his earnest and unornamented

* Mrs. Edkins.

The application was made in vain. Mr. Barrett
refused him the recommendatory letter which was
required; and as Chatterton was manifestly incom-
petent to discharge the duties of the appointment
which he had hoped to procure through his interest,
Mr. Barrett's refusal was perfectly justifiable,—in fact,
great blame would have attached to him if he had
acted otherwise. It was at this period that the African
Eclogues were written. Chatterton could still solace
himself with the divine employment of the muse, and
the inspiration which a transient gleam of hope lent
him, enabled him to sing, but in no very truthful or
natural strains,

" Of Tiber's banks where scarlet jasmines bloom,
And purple aloes shed a rich perfume :
Where, when the sun is melting in his heat,
The reeking tigers find a cool retreat ;
Bask in the sedges, lose the sultry beam,
And wanton with their shadows in the stream."

Chatterton's last hope had failed. He was friendless,
lone, and unassisted. He had fallen on evil days, and
could now only look forward to the time, fast approach-
ing, in which he should be a wanderer and an outcast.
What wonder then if in his dark and deep distress,
"self-contempt drowned youth's starlight smiles in
tears," and the victim proudly and angrily refused to
be fed—to be *kept alive*—by the bread of charity.
Once only the pride of the heart was subdued by the
frailty of the flesh, and he partook of the proffered
bounty. It is Warton who records that an oyster
feast prevailed on him to forego his dignity for a while,
and to accept the hospitality of Mr. Cross, an apothe-
cary, of Brook street. This was Chatterton's last

his friends at Bristol, and remembering their wants and administering to their necessities. For his love of truth he was eminent even from his boyish years; for surely the creation of Rowley and Ischam, and the fiction of the discovered parchments, cannot be considered in any other light than a literary invention, in fact a part and parcel of the glorious imaginings which this royal child of song has left us. For his temperance, and the mastery which he had over his passions, he is surpassed by none: he was remarkable for his endurance, although not for his patience; if he was irritable and scornful, it is hardly to be wondered at, "for he moved about in worlds not realized," and felt acutely how this outward universe, with its false shows and cruel mockeries, gave the lie to that inward paradise of love and justice and harmony, which was shadowed forth in the heart of the poet, as the fields and trees and flowers in the clear and quiet waters.

Chatterton was unfortunate in the education which he received. Boys of his order of mind and disposition of heart require a teaching very different from that which is found to answer sufficiently well with the majority of children. Those who neither think nor feel, may be taught without any endeavour on the part of the instructor to discover and aid in the development of their mental faculties or the affections of their hearts; but for those who are conscious of a higher destiny, who come trailing clouds of glory fresh from God's hand, who cherish dim recollections of their Father's palace,* and are haunted with obsti-

---

* See Wordsworth's Ode on Childhood.

nate questionings as to the significance of this many-coloured thing called life; who observe that wonderful processes are going on in that inward man of theirs, and feel that they are greater than they know,—for such children there must be instituted an investigation into the capacities of their hearts and minds, their faculties must be developed harmoniously with the laws which nature has written on their minds, and their sensibilities must be trained, and their good qualities cultivated, and their evil passions checked in their growth, by a wise and loving superintendence. Such superintendence Chatterton never had. The ideal of such teaching is perhaps not to be found—but at least an approximation may be made to it; and in proportion as any man has approached towards this absolute standard is he a teacher, but in no other sense and in no other proportion has he the slightest pretensions to the sacred title.

For want of the true system of instruction, Chatterton, like most other poets, was obliged to have recourse to self-teaching. Without a guide, with no illumination but that of his own intellect, which blinded him with excess of light, he wandered widely from the narrow path which leads to perfection. He was true, to a certain extent, to the principles of his own nature, and generally sincere in the evolution of the good, and in his submission to their guidance; but he could not clearly distinguish the divine voice from the satanic whisper, and he too often obeyed the sugges-tions of the evil heart, when he was self-deceived into the belief that he was following the oracular intimations of the good conscience. Had Chatterton lived longer, he would doubtless have come to a full knowledge of the truth. Let any man be true to himself and his God-given nature; let " him love the truth and pursue it," through darkness and distress and solitude and despair; and the great Father, whose name is love, will never abandon a sincere and single-hearted, although erring, child. If the poet had continued his self-education, he would have learnt reverence for others, mistrust of himself, contempt for nothing that is, charity for all, humility and the fear of God; till at length, instead of being naked and miserable and poor, he would have been found clothed and in his right mind, and sitting at the feet of Jesus.

Such were the virtues, and such the faults and failings, of Thomas Chatterton. We have characterized the man—we must now sit in judgment on the poet.

It will not be possible to enter very largely upon a critical estimation of his creative powers ; and indeed we have said so much of Chatterton as a satirist, and made so many remarks on his acknowledged poems, that our wisest course will be to confine ourselves to a philosophical summing-up of his abilities as the creator of the Rowley Poems.

Between his fourteenth and his sixteenth year, Chatterton conceived and executed this wonderful imagination. As might have been expected, the traces of extreme youth, of inexperience, of ignorance of the human heart, or at least of the more secret workings of it, are discoverable in many of his poems. Frequently there is much harshness, his diction is occasionally obscure, and a verse deficient in idea receives its legitimate number of feet, by the introduction of redundant epithets signifying nothing. In general, however, the language is vigorous and well chosen, and the versification melodious. Indeed, Chatterton has the rare merit of having studied the principles of harmony, in an age when music in poetry was universally allowed to consist of a repetition of similarly modulated sounds, and when the concentration of different tones into one sustained and solid harmony was either neglected or unknown.

The exquisite pathos of the muse of Chatterton must be evident even to the most careless reader. In the pathetic we recognize the exercise of the highest and most perfect of his intellectual endowments. There is an Euripidæan tenderness in his poetry at times, which is capable of giving intense delight to the admirer of the Athenian dramatist; it emanates from a heart full of the softest and purest emotions, and vibrates beneath the touch of sorrow as the lyre under the fingering of some skilful master. When he speaks of a flower or a star or a bird, it is with an affectionate regard, and with a full recognition of its right to be included in the synthesis of humanity. Although he penetrates not into the inner mysteries of our nature, yet he never pourtrays it in false colours. His men are brave, generous, and heroic, and true to the impulses of the heart in a barbarous age; and his women gentle, loving, and faithful, and not less wise than women should be. There is usually

knew him well,* and according to the general evidence he was as remarkable for the prematurity of his person as he was for that of his intellect and imagination. His mien and manner were exceedingly prepossessing; his eyes were grey, but piercingly brilliant; and when he was animated in conversation or excited by any passing event, the fire flashed and rolled in the lower part of the orbs in a wonderful and almost fearful way. Mr. Catcott characterized Chatterton's eye "as a kind of hawk's eye, and thought one could see his soul through it." As with Byron, one eye was more remarkable than the other, and its lightning-like flashes had something about them supernaturally grand.

It is difficult to form a just appreciation of the character of Chatterton. We are all in some measure the creatures of circumstance; and the more we are subjected to external influences, the more our will is weakened, and the less able are we to do battle with the hostile array of our passions, and to resist the temptations which are presented on all sides by a deceitful and untried world. The moral nature of Chatterton was essentially manly,—there is nothing in it which even approximates to the puerile or the feminine; his faults are all the growth of a strong and vigorous heart, and of a searching and masculine intellect. His indomitable pride, his premature but natural adoption of the habits and expressions of men, his love of reasoning, his earnest and unornamented

* Mrs. Edkins.

eloquence, all demonstrate the essential manliness of his character. Chatterton, when he complains, never pules; his lamentations have often a deep pathos, but are quite free from that affected sentimental misery which disgrace the pages of our modern writers. There was a strength and energy and Roman *virtus* in his spirit, which sustained him in his most fearful struggles and in the most depressing circumstances. He looked no more than fact constrained him to the dark side of things; he ever hoped for the best, and anticipated the fairest prospects, even when a burden rested on him which would have crushed to the earth a less Titanic heart. This too was effected by the sheer force of his proud and unconquerable will, for Chatterton was naturally the subject of morbid feelings and gloomy apprehensions; and if the heroism of his nature had not been wonderfully predominant, would have doubtless fallen a victim to the destroying operations of the weaker and inferior mental organism. Instead of madness, idiocy would probably have been the fate of the creator of Rowley.

The hardships and the disappointments which Chatterton experienced, although they had necessarily a tendency to indurate the heart and to stifle the softer and finer feelings of our nature, never extinguished or even impaired that high sense of filial affection and brotherly love, which throughout was so conspicuous in his conduct. The charities of home had a permanent dwelling-place in the spirit of the young poet; and we have seen him, even in the distress and agony of his London career, speaking comfort and hope to

his friends at Bristol, and remembering their wants
and administering to their necessities. For his love
of truth he was eminent even from his boyish years ;
for surely the creation of Rowley and Ischam, and the
fiction of the discovered parchments, cannot be con-
sidered in any other light than a literary invention, in
fact a part and parcel of the glorious imaginings which
this royal child of song has left us. For his temperance,
and the mastery which he had over his passions, he is
surpassed by none: he was remarkable for his en-
durance, although not for his patience; if he was
irritable and scornful, it is hardly to be wondered at,
" for he moved about in worlds not realized," and felt
acutely how this outward universe, with its false shows
and cruel mockeries, gave the lie to that inward para-
dise of love and justice and harmony, which was
shadowed forth in the heart of the poet, as the fields
and trees and flowers in the clear and quiet waters.

Chatterton was unfortunate in the education which
he received. Boys of his order of mind and dispo-
sition of heart require a teaching very different from
that which is found to answer sufficiently well with the
majority of children. Those who neither think nor
feel, may be taught without any endeavour on the
part of the instructor to discover and aid in the
development of their mental faculties or the affec-
tions of their hearts ; but for those who are conscious
of a higher destiny, who come trailing clouds of glory
fresh from God's hand, who cherish dim recollections
of their Father's palace,* and are haunted with obsti-

* See Wordsworth's Ode on Childhood.

HISTORY

OF THE

ROWLEY CONTROVERSY.

It will be requisite, before we commence our account of the Rowley Controversy, briefly to re-capitulate the different notices relative to the dis-covery of the manuscripts which have appeared in various parts of our memoir.

The Church of St. Mary of Redcliffe* was erected in the year 1470, by William Cannynge, an opulent merchant of Bristol. An iron chest was placed in a muniment room over the northern portico, designed to receive instruments, inventories, and the parish accounts. It was ordered by the Founders that this chest should be annually inspected by the Mayor and the members of the Corporation; and that a feast should be held, after the inspection was concluded. This order was soon disregarded.

---

* The lovers of old English architecture will experience no ordinary gratification, on learning that the clusters of miserable tenements, with the dilapidated premises by which the north-east portion of St. Mary Redcliff has for centuries been excluded from public view, are now in the course of demolition.—*Bristol Mirror*, March 12, 1842.

When the new bridge at Bristol was finished, in the year 1768, there appeared in one of the Bristol Journals an account of the ceremonial which was observed when the old bridge was opened to the public, purporting to be transcribed from an ancient MS. Curiosity was excited; an enquiry was instituted; and the result was the discovery that the letter had been forwarded by a youth of the name of Chatterton, whose father had been for many years a sexton in the Church of St. Mary of Redcliffe, and master of a writing-school in that parish. The father, however, was dead, and no threats or persuasions could, at first, induce the son to acknowledge by what means the original memoir had come into his possession. After much altercation, he asserted that he had received this manuscript, with many others, from his father, who found them in the iron chest which we have already mentioned.

It is said that Chatterton the sexton was permitted by the churchwardens to take from the chest several pieces of parchment, for the purpose of covering the writing books of his scholars. The value of these despised manuscripts was immense, and the parish pædagogue, who had some pretensions to refinement of taste, discovered amongst them a vast number of poems, of which the greater part were composed by Thomas Rowlie, priest of St. John's Church, in Bristol, and the confessor of Alderman Cannynge. These were laid by with care, and after the death of the accomplished sexton, became the property of his son.

The son, it is stated, perceived the importance of

quently there is much harshness, his diction is occasionally obscure, and a verse deficient in idea receives its legitimate number of feet, by the introduction of redundant epithets signifying nothing. In general, however, the language is vigorous and well chosen, and the versification melodious. Indeed, Chatterton has the rare merit of having studied the principles of harmony, in an age when music in poetry was universally allowed to consist of a repetition of similarly modulated sounds, and when the concentration of different tones into one sustained and solid harmony was either neglected or unknown.

The exquisite pathos of the muse of Chatterton must be evident even to the most careless reader. In the pathetic we recognize the exercise of the highest and most perfect of his intellectual endowments. There is an Euripidæan tenderness in his poetry at times, which is capable of giving intense delight to the admirer of the Athenian dramatist; it emanates from a heart full of the softest and purest emotions, and vibrates beneath the touch of sorrow as the lyre under the fingering of some skilful master. When he speaks of a flower or a star or a bird, it is with an affectionate regard, and with a full recognition of its right to be included in the synthesis of humanity. Although he penetrates not into the inner mysteries of our nature, yet he never pourtrays it in false colours. His men are brave, generous, and heroic, and true to the impulses of the heart in a barbarous age; and his women gentle, loving, and faithful, and not less wise than women should be. There is usually

lieve the heaviness of the present essay we shall give
a few specimens of the glossarial observations of the
erudite Doctor extracted from his "Introduction to
an Examination of the Rowleian Controversy." He
asserts that the *evening* means the equalizing or ren-
dering day and night as to light *even,* or equal; that
the eaves of a house take their name from the exact-
ness of the line; that *hers,* a water-cress, means a
curse; that *lane* implies a path so narrow as to render
it necessary for passengers to go *alane;* that a barbde
hall and a barbde horse were so called, for the same
reason that the defensive parapet was called barbican—
what this reason was he omits to inform us; that
hancel differs only in one letter from *cancel,* which it
will be easy to shew is radically the same; for as
mihri was written mihi, and nihil nichil, it follows
therefore that hancelled, cancelled, chancelled, con-
vey literally and identically the same meaning; and
lastly that *Pentland* Frith is a corruption of *peincte-
land,* as that is synonimous with pict-land, *i. e.*
pinch'd, pink't, pick't, pict, *Anglice* painted land.

Leaving Dr. Sherwin and his "curious felicity" of
words, we next meet with the name of Chalmers, an
Anti-Rowleyan, whose depreciating and puritanical
Life of Chatterton has so righteously drawn down
the severe castigation of the present Laureate. Scott
and Southey himself are also to be included in the
same ranks, and their illustrious names will probably
carry conviction to the minds of those readers who
are unable or unwilling to decide the question them-
selves. Stevens and Malone and Pinkerton, Jamieson

and Herbert Croft, the author of "Love and Madness, have all drawn the sword for Chatterton, and wielded it with skill, energy, and effect.

Of all the vindicators of the reality of Rowley, none is more learned than Jacob Bryant; and so ably is his argument conducted, and so perfect a mastery of the subject does he exhibit, that it would not excite the least wonder in us, if the reader, after a perusal of his laborious work, were to side with the intrepid denier of the existence of Troy, and the bold asserter of the ancient origin of the Rowley poems, provided that he came to the investigation for the first time, and had not read the arguments with which Bryant has been confuted.

Our controversialist reasons in this manner. He asserts that the diction of Rowley is provincial, and after adducing many examples to support his affirmation, he remarks—" The transcriber has given some notes, in order to explain words of this nature. But he is often very unfortunate in his solutions. He mistakes the sense grossly: and the words have often far more force and significance than he is aware of. This could not have been the case if he had been the author. His blunders would not have turned out to his advantage; nor could there have been more sense in the lines than in the head which conceived them. In short, chance could never have so contrived that the poetry should be better than the purpose."

After a few more remarks on the dialects of the English language, and some observations on Chatterton's ignorance of French, Latin, and Greek, whence he deduces the impossibility of his making such an "exotic collection" of words, Bryant proceeds:

"I lay it down for a fixed principle, that if a person transmits to me a learned and excellent composition, and does not understand the context, he cannot be the author.

"I lay it down for a certainty, if a person in any such composition has, in transcribing, varied any of the terms through ignorance, and the true reading appears from the context, that he cannot have been the author. If, as the ancient Vicar is said to have done in respect to a portion of the Gospel, he for *sumpsimus* reads uniformly *mumpsimus*, he never composed the treatise in which he is so grossly mistaken. If a person in his notes upon a poem mistakes *Liber* Bacchus, for *liber* a book; and when he meets with *liber* a book, he interprets it *liber* free, he certainly did not compose the poem where those terms occur: he had not parts nor learning to effect it. In short, every writer must know his own meaning; and if any person, by his glossary or any other explanation, shews that he could not arrive at such meaning, he affords convincing proof that the original was by another hand. This ignorance will be found in Chatterton; and many mistakes in consequence of it will be seen,—of which mistakes and ignorance I will lay before the reader many examples. When these have been ascertained, let the reader judge whether this inexperienced and unlettered boy could have been the author of the poems in question."

Mr. Bryant, in accordance with this intimation, has

favoured the world with a treatise of six hundred pages, containing instances of Chatterton's inaccuracy, with his own corrections and improvements, and occasional recurrences to his first positions, and clever and forensic vindications of those positions. There is a great deal of historical, topographical, and critical information; a vast amount of antiquarian lore and erudite research; a strange display of patience and partiality; and a fixed determination never to believe in the genius of Chatterton, and always to maintain the claims of the imaginary Rowley. We will subjoin one instance of what Mr. Bryant terms the misconceptions of Chatterton, with Mr. Malone's explanation.

"In the song to Ælla, which was given to Mr. Barrett in Chatterton's hand writing, two lines are found to be expressed in the following manner:

> Orr seest the hatchedd stede
> *Ifrayninge* o'er the mede.

But when the original parchment, which was brought the next day, had been cleaned and examined more accurately, the true reading was found to be, not *ifrayninge*, but *yprauncynge;* which makes, in respect to sense, a material difference."

This is Mr. Bryant's account of the matter. Mr. Malone draws a very different deduction from the variation on which he lays so much stress.

"In one copy of the 'Songe to Ælla,' which Chatterton gave to Mr. Barrett, these lines were found—

> 'Or seest the hatched steed
> *Ifrayning* o'er the meed.

Being called upon for the original, he the next day produced a parchment containing the same poem, in which he had written *yprauncing*, instead of *ifrayning ;* but by some artifice he had obscured the MS. so much, to give it an ancient appearance, that Mr. Barrett could not make out the word without the use of galls. What follows from all this, but that Chatterton found, on examination, that there was no such word as *ifrayning*, and that he substituted another in its place? In the same poem he at one time wrote 'locks,' 'burlie,' 'brasting,' and 'kennest'; at another, 'hairs,' 'valiant,' 'bursting,' and 'hearest.' Variations of this kind he could have produced without end. What he called originals, indeed, were probably in general more perfect than what he called copies; because the former were always produced after the other, and were, in truth, nothing more than second editions of the same pieces."

Malone was a most vigorous and acute reasoner, and is deservedly ranked among the first controversialists on the Chatterton side of the question. He thus deals with the "fixed principles" of the asserter of the authenticity of Rowley's poems :

"I cannot dismiss Mr. Bryant without taking notice of a position which he has laid down, and which is indeed the basis of almost all the arguments that he has urged to prove the authenticity of the Bristol MS. It is this—that as every author must know his own meaning, and as Chatterton has sometimes given wrong interpretations of words that are found in the

these poems, and transcribed them. Some of them he sold to Mr. Catcott and Mr. Barrett, the former a merchant, the latter a surgeon, of Bristol. Most of these were transcripts; what few parchments there were have since been deposited in the British Museum. Chatterton was often questioned as to the source from which he derived the originals; but no satisfactory or definite answer could be elicited. In process of time the Rowley poems were given to the world. The army of literary men was dazzled, perplexed, and divided. One phalanx considered them to be a fabrication of Chatterton; another was positive that none but Rowley was the author of the poems which bore his name. The contention grew sharp—the combatants were drawn up in hostile array—and the Rowley war commenced in earnest.

It is not our intention to give the whole of the arguments which were brought forward by either party, for this essay would then be enlarged beyond all reasonable dimensions. It will be sufficient for our purpose to give a list of the principal champions of the identity of Rowley, and his claims to the authorship of the poems to which he has stood godfather, and of the impugners of that identity and of those pretensions.

First and foremost, Horace Walpole,* the author of Otranto, and lord of Strawberry-hill, rushed into the fight. He struggled manfully, in his " Vindication," to prove that the Bristol Boy, whom he had

---

* Not first in point of time, but first from his position, and from his influence over the destinies of Chatterton.

often more apposite than he imagined, and have a
latent and significant meaning that never occurred to
him, this will only show that a man's book is some-
times wiser than himself; a truth of which we have
every day so many striking instances, that it was
scarcely necessary for this learned antiquarian to have
exhibited a new proof of it.

Let it be considered, too, that the glossary and the
text were not always written at the same time; that
Chatterton might not always remember the precise
sense in which he had used antiquated words: and,
from a confused recollection, or from the want of the
very same books that he had consulted while he was
writing his poems, might add sometimes a false, and
sometimes an imperfect interpretation. This is not
a mere hypothesis—for in one instance he knew that
the comment was written at some interval of time
after the text. The glossary of the poem entitled
' The English Metamorphosis,' was written down by
Chatterton extemporally, without the assistance of
any book, at the desire, and in the presence, of
Mr. Barrett."

Mr. Malone thus satisfactorily accounts for the
inconsistency of Chatterton's interpretations, and for
the misapprehension under which it must be admit-
ted that Mr. Bryant has very convincingly demon-
strated that the young poet laboured. Whether his
misconceptions really originated in the precise sources
which Mr. Malone indicates, is foreign to the argu-
ment, and no way affects the correctness of his logic.
He was not obliged to show how they *did* arise, but

only how they *might* have arisen. It was enough for him to account for the existence of error, without tracing the mode and processes of its existence.

If it be conceded that the positions which the stout old sceptic laid down at the commencement of his work are fairly shown to be untenable, the reader will not find any difficulty in refuting the arguments which are adduced in the remainder of his volume, grounded on Chatterton's incapacity and ignorance, and on the fact that there are *some* verses, or scraps of verses, to be found in ancient poetry equally melodious with the tragedy of Ælla, or the Battle of Hastings. When we add that, to establish the antiquity of the versification of Rowley, and to prove that the appearance of novelty which it exhibits is no argument against that antiquity, the critic cites two passages from the poems of Spenser, one of which is harsh and feeble, the other musical and nervous, the reader will not entertain a very high character of the candour, or the poetical judgment of this celebrated controversialist.

The last of the combatants engaged in the Chattertonian war, whom we shall mention, is Thomas Warton, the Professor of Poetry in the University of Oxford. In the twenty-sixth section of his "History of English Poetry," he has furnished us with a complete analysis of the Rowley Poems, and perhaps a more judicious method of conducting the argument could not have been adopted. He supports his view of the question by demonstrating that the writing of the parchment which contained the Ode to Ælla, the Epistle to Lydgate, with his Answer, was, in the opinion of an ingenious critic and an intelligent anti-quary, a gross and palpable forgery ; that the form of the letters in the parchment differed very essentially from every one of our earlier alphabets ; that the characters wanted consistency and uniformity; that the appearance of antiquity had been attempted by the application of ochre, which was easily rubbed off with a linen cloth ; that the original manuscript, containing the Accounte of W. Cannynge's Feast, is totally unlike the three or four authentic manuscripts of the time of Edward the Fourth, with which it was compared ; and that the style and drawing of the armorial bearings depicted in it discover the hand of a modern herald. This is an analysis of his external argument.

The internal evidences of the fabrication of the Poems are, an unnatural affectation of ancient spelling and of obsolete words not belonging to the period assigned them ; combinations of old words which never existed in the unpolished state of the English language; an artificial misapplication of antiquated diction ; and the poet's forgetfulness of his assumed character, displayed in the perspicuity and freedom from uncouth expressions which not unfrequently characterize his productions.

Among the internal evidences he numbers many anachronisms. In the Battle of Hastings, Turgot has anticipated every conjecture of the moderns as regards the origin of Stonehenge. It is called by him a Druidical temple ; whereas the established and uniform opinion of the Welsh and Armorican bards, and of the historians and chroniclers through successive ages, indicates that it was erected in memory of Hengist's massacre.

In the Epistle to Lydgate, the impropriety of religious dramas is condemned, and some great story of human manners is recommended as most suitable for theatrical representation : but when we reflect that this opinion would have exposed the writer to the censures of the Church, and that it was not till the lapse of another century that the true philosophy of the drama was understood in the lowest degree in this country, we are constrained to acknowledge that this could not be the doctrine inculcated by a priest in the reign of the Fourth Edward.

Warton next adduces the inequality so conspicuous in the productions of our old writers, but without its counterpart in the Rowley Poems, as an additional proof of their modern origin. In the former splendid descriptions, poetical imagery and ornamental comparisons occur but rarely; while the latter are, throughout, poetical and animated. Our old English bards abound in unnatural conceptions, strange imaginations, and ridiculous absurdities ; but Rowley's poems present us with no incongruous combinations, no mixture of manners, institutions, customs, and characters. The anachronisms in the Battle of Hastings are such as no old poet could possible have fallen into, and betray an unskilful imitation of ancient manners. The verses of Lydgate and his immediate successors are often rugged and unmusical ; but Rowley's poetry sustains one uniform tone of harmony ; and if we

he deduces the impossibility of his making such an
"exotic collection" of words, Bryant proceeds:

"I lay it down for a fixed principle, that if a
person transmits to me a learned and excellent com-
position, and does not understand the context, he
cannot be the author.

"I lay it down for a certainty, if a person in any
such composition has, in transcribing, varied any of
the terms through ignorance, and the true reading
appears from the context, that he cannot have been
the author. If, as the ancient Vicar is said to have
done in respect to a portion of the Gospel, he for
sumpsimus reads uniformly *mumpsimus*, he never
composed the treatise in which he is so grossly mis-
taken. If a person in his notes upon a poem mistakes
Liber Bacchus, for *liber* a book ; and when he meets
with *liber* a book, he interprets it *liber* free, he cer-
tainly did not compose the poem where those terms
occur : he had not parts nor learning to effect it.
In short, every writer must know his own meaning ;
and if any person, by his glossary or any other
explanation, shews that he could not arrive at such
meaning, he affords convincing proof that the original
was by another hand. This ignorance will be found
in Chatterton ; and many mistakes in consequence of
it will be seen,—of which mistakes and ignorance I
will lay before the reader many examples. When
these have been ascertained, let the reader judge
whether this inexperienced and unlettered boy could
have been the author of the poems in question."

Mr. Bryant, in accordance with this intimation, has

favoured the world with a treatise of six hundred pages, containing instances of Chatterton's inaccuracy, with his own corrections and improvements, and occasional recurrences to his first positions, and clever and forensic vindications of those positions. There is a great deal of historical, topographical, and critical information; a vast amount of antiquarian lore and erudite research; a strange display of patience and partiality; and a fixed determination never to believe in the genius of Chatterton, and always to maintain the claims of the imaginary Rowley. We will subjoin one instance of what Mr. Bryant terms the misconceptions of Chatterton, with Mr. Malone's explanation.

" In the song to Ælla, which was given to Mr. Barrett in Chatterton's hand writing, two lines are found to be expressed in the following manner :

> Orr seest the hatchedd stede
> *Ifrayninge* o'er the mede.

But when the original parchment, which was brought the next day, had been cleaned and examined more accurately, the true reading was found to be, not *ifrayninge*, but *yprauncynge;* which makes, in respect to sense, a material difference."

This is Mr. Bryant's account of the matter. Mr. Malone draws a very different deduction from the variation on which he lays so much stress.

" In one copy of the ' Songe to Ælla,' which Chatterton gave to Mr. Barrett, these lines were found—

> ' Or seest the hatched steed
> *Ifrayning* o'er the meed.

being called upon for the original, he the next day produced a parchment containing the same poem, in which he had written ꝑƿƿ—ing, instead of ſtropping; but by some artifice he had obscured the MS. so much, to give it an ancient appearance, that Mr. Barrett could not make out the word without the use of galls. What follows from all this, but that Chatterton heard, on examination, that there was no such word as ſtropping, and that he substituted ſtropping in its place? In the same poem he at one time wrote 'heris,' 'purfle,' 'trasting,' and 'kennest'; at another, 'hairs,' 'valiant,' 'trusting,' and 'knowest.' Variations of this kind he could have produced without end. What he called originals, indeed, were probably in general more perfect than what he called copies; because the former were always produced after the other, and were, in truth, nothing more than second editions of the same piece."

Malone was a most vigorous and acute reasoner, and is deservedly ranked among the first controversialists on the Chatterton side of the question. He thus deals with the "fixed principles" of the asserter of the authenticity of Rowley's poems:

"I cannot dismiss Mr. Bryant without taking notice of a position which he has laid down, and which is indeed the basis of almost all the arguments that he has urged to prove the authenticity of the Bristol MS. It is this—that as every author must know his own meaning, and as Chatterton has sometimes given wrong interpretations of words that are found in the poems attributed to Rowley, he could not be the author of those poems."

If Chatterton had originally written these poems in the form in which they now appear, this argument might, in a doubtful question, have some weight: but although I have as high an opinion of his abilities as perhaps any person whatsoever, and do indeed believe him to have been the greatest genius that England has produced since the days of Shakspeare, I am not ready to acknowledge that he was endued with any miraculous powers.

Devoted as he was from his infancy to the study of antiquities, he could not have been so conversant with ancient language, or have had all the words necessary to be used so present to his mind, as to write antiquated poetry of any considerable length off-hand. He, without doubt, wrote his verses in plain English, and afterwards embroidered them with such old words as would suit the sense and metre. With these he furnished himself, sometimes probably from memory, and sometimes from glossaries; and annexed such interpretations as he found or made. When he could not readily find a word that would suit his metre, he invented one. If then his old words afford some sense, and yet are sometimes interpreted wrong, nothing more follows than that his glossaries were imperfect, or his knowledge inaccurate: still, however, he might have had a confused, though not a complete idea of their import. If, as the commentator asserts, the words that he has explained, not only suit the places in which they stand, but are

often more apposite than he imagined, and have a
latent and significant meaning that never occurred to
him, this will only show that a man's book is some-
times wiser than himself; a truth of which we have
every day so many striking instances, that it was
scarcely necessary for this learned antiquarian to have
exhibited a new proof of it.

Let it be considered, too, that the glossary and the
text were not always written at the same time; that
Chatterton might not always remember the precise
sense in which he had used antiquated words: and,
from a confused recollection, or from the want of the
very same books that he had consulted while he was
writing his poems, might add sometimes a false, and
sometimes an imperfect interpretation. This is not
a mere hypothesis—for in one instance he knew that
the comment was written at some interval of time
after the text. The glossary of the poem entitled
' The English Metamorphosis,' was written down by
Chatterton extemporally, without the assistance of
any book, at the desire, and in the presence, of
Mr. Barrett."

Mr. Malone thus satisfactorily accounts for the
inconsistency of Chatterton's interpretations, and for
the misapprehension under which it must be admit-
ted that Mr. Bryant has very convincingly demon-
strated that the young poet laboured. Whether his
misconceptions really originated in the precise sources
which Mr. Malone indicates, is foreign to the argu-
ment, and no way affects the correctness of his logic.
He was not obliged to show how they *did* arise, but

only how they *might* have arisen. It was enough for him to account for the existence of error, without tracing the mode and processes of its existence.

If it be conceded that the positions which the stout old sceptic laid down at the commencement of his work are fairly shown to be untenable, the reader will not find any difficulty in refuting the arguments which are adduced in the remainder of his volume, grounded on Chatterton's incapacity and ignorance, and on the fact that there are *some* verses, or scraps of verses, to be found in ancient poetry equally melodious with the tragedy of Ælla, or the Battle of Hastings. When we add that, to establish the antiquity of the versification of Rowley, and to prove that the appearance of novelty which it exhibits is no argument against that antiquity, the critic cites two passages from the poems of Spenser, one of which is harsh and feeble, the other musical and nervous, the reader will not entertain a very high character of the candour, or the poetical judgment of this celebrated controversialist.

The last of the combatants engaged in the Chattertonian war, whom we shall mention, is Thomas Warton, the Professor of Poetry in the University of Oxford. In the twenty-sixth section of his " History of English Poetry," he has furnished us with a complete analysis of the Rowley Poems, and perhaps a more judicious method of conducting the argument could not have been adopted. He supports his view of the question by demonstrating that the writing of the parchment which contained the Ode to Ælla, the Epistle to Lydgate, with his Answer, was, in the

opinion of an ingenious critic and an intelligent anti-
quary, a gross and palpable forgery ; that the form of
the letters in the parchment differed very essentially
from every one of our earlier alphabets; that the
characters wanted consistency and uniformity; that
the appearance of antiquity had been attempted by
the application of ochre, which was easily rubbed off
with a linen cloth ; that the original manuscript, con-
taining the Accounte of W. Cannynge's Feast, is
totally unlike the three or four authentic manuscripts
of the time of Edward the Fourth, with which it was
compared ; and that the style and drawing of the
armorial bearings depicted in it discover the hand of
a modern herald.   This is an analysis of his external
argument.

The internal evidences of the fabrication of the
Poems are, an unnatural affectation of ancient spelling
and of obsolete words not belonging to the period
assigned them ; combinations of old words which
never existed in the unpolished state of the English
language; an artificial misapplication of antiquated
diction ; and the poet's forgetfulness of his assumed
character, displayed in the perspicuity and freedom
from uncouth expressions which not unfrequently
characterize his productions.

Among the internal evidences he numbers many
anachronisms. In the Battle of Hastings, Turgot
has anticipated every conjecture of the moderns as
regards the origin of Stonehenge. It is called by him
a Druidical temple; whereas the established and
uniform opinion of the Welsh and Armorican bards,

and of the historians and chroniclers through suc-
cessive ages, indicates that it was erected in memory
of Hengist's massacre.

In the Epistle to Lydgate, the impropriety of
religious dramas is condemned, and some great story
of human manners is recommended as most suitable
for theatrical representation : but when we reflect
that this opinion would have exposed the writer to
the censures of the Church, and that it was not till
the lapse of another century that the true philosophy
of the drama was understood in the lowest degree in
this country, we are constrained to acknowledge that
this could not be the doctrine inculcated by a priest
in the reign of the Fourth Edward.

Warton next adduces the inequality so conspicuous
in the productions of our old writers, but without its
counterpart in the Rowley Poems, as an additional
proof of their modern origin. In the former splendid
descriptions, poetical imagery and ornamental com-
parisons occur but rarely; while the latter are,
throughout, poetical and animated. Our old English
bards abound in unnatural conceptions, strange ima-
ginations, and ridiculous absurdities ; but Rowley's
poems present us with no incongruous combinations,
no mixture of manners, institutions, customs, and cha-
racters. The anachronisms in the Battle of Hastings
are such as no old poet could possible have fallen into,
and betray an unskilful imitation of ancient manners.
The verses of Lydgate and his immediate successors
are often rugged and unmusical ; but Rowley's poetry
sustains one uniforn tone of harmony ; and if we

brush away the asperities of the antiquated spelling,
conveys its cultivated imagery in a polished and
agreeable strain of versification.

In conclusion, Warton gives it as his opinion that
the real author of these poems was Chatterton : he
supports this opinion by the merit of his acknow-
ledged compositions; by the testimony of those who
were acquainted with his conversation; by the vast
acquisitions of knowledge which he had attained; and
by the possession of that comprehensiveness of mind,
and activity of understanding, which predominated
over his situation in life, and his opportunities of
instruction; by his propensity to literary forgery;
by his predilection for the study of antiquities; and by
his enterprising and ambitious character; and the
necessity which constrained him to subsist by expedi-
ents.

Such is the acute and simple reasoning of the Ox-
ford Professor. To the writer of this essay it seems
unanswerable. It is based not on probabilities, or
arguments drawn from incidental verisimilitudes, but
on the eternal and indestructible principles of poetical
thought and composition; on analogy, on experiment,
on comparison.

We have endeavoured to furnish the reader with a
brief but comprehensive account of this celebrated
controversy. It would have been easy to analyse
the whole works of the different controversialists on
each side of the question : but as in that case we
must have added at least another volume to the
edition of Chatterton's poems now given to the world,

we concluded that it would be the more advisable
course to draw up a short account of the principal
asserters of the ancient origin of the Rowley Poems,
with the answers which have been returned by those
who believe in the genius and acquirements of the
marvellous Boy of Bristol.

ROWLEY POEMS.

Bristowe Tragedie;

Or, The Dethe of Syr Charles Bawdin.[1]

I.

The feathered songster chaunticleer
  Han wounde hys bugle horne,
And tolde the earlie villager
  The commynge of the morne:

II.

Kynge Edwarde sawe the ruddie streakes
  Of lyghte eclypse the greie;
And herde the raven's crokynge throte
  Proclayme the fated daie.

---

[1] The person here celebrated under the name of Sir Charles Bawdin, was probably Sir Baldwin Fulford, Knt., a zealous Lancastrian, who was executed at Bristol in the latter end of 1461, the first year of Edward the Fourth.

III.

"Thou'rt ryghte," quod hee, "for, by the Godde
    That syttes enthron'd on hyghe!
Charles Bawdin, and hys fellowes twaine,
    To daie shall surelie die."

IV.

Thenne wythe a jugge of nappy ale
    Hys Knyghtes dydd onne hymm waite;
"Goe tell the traytour, thatt to daie
    Hee leaves thys mortall state."

V.

Syr Canterlone thenne bendedd lowe,
    Wythe harte brymm-fulle of woe;
Hee journey'd to the castle-gate,
    And to Syr Charles dydd goe.

VI.

But whenne hee came, hys children twaine,
    And eke hys lovynge wyfe,
Wythe brinie tears dydd wett the floore,
    For goode Syr Charleses lyfe.

VII.

"O goode Syr Charles!" sayd Canterlone,
    "Badde tydings I doe brynge."
"Speke boldlie, manne," sayd brave Syr Charles,
    "Whatte says thie traytor kynge?"

VIII.

"I greeve to telle, before yonne sonne
    Does fromme the welkin flye,
Hee hathe uponne hys honnour sworne,
    Thatt thou shalt surelie die."

IX.

" Wee all must die," quod brave Syr Charles,
    " Of thatte I'm not affearde;
    Whatte bootes to lyve a little space?
    " Thanke Jesu, I'm prepar'd:

X.

" Butt telle thye kynge, for myne hee's not,
    I'de sooner die to daie
    Thanne lyve hys slave, as manie are,
    Tho' I shoulde lyve for aie."

XI.

Thenne Canterlone hee dydd goe out,
    To tell the maior straite
    To gett all thynges ynn reddyness
    For goode Syr Charles's fate.

XII.

Thenne Maisterr Canynge saughte the kynge,
    And felle down onne hys knee;
" I'm come," quod hee, " unto your grace
    To move your clemencye."

XIII.

Thenne quod the kynge, " youre tale speke out,
    You have been much oure friende;
    Whatever youre request may bee,
    Wee wylle to ytte attende."

XIV.

" My nobile leige! alle my request
    Ys for a nobile knyghte,
    Who, tho' mayhap hee has donne wronge,
    Hee thoughte ytte stylle was ryghte:

XV.

" Hee has a spouse and children twaine,
    Alle rewyn'd ' are for aie;
Yff thatt you are resolv'd to lett
    Charles Bawdin die to daie."

XVI.

" Speke nott of such a traytour vile."
    The kynge ynne furie sayde;
Before the evening starre doth sheene,
    Bawdin shall loose hys hedde:

XVII.

" Justice does loudlie for hym calle,
    And hee shalle have hys meede :
Speke, Maister Canynge ! Whatte thynge else
    Att present doe you neede ? "

XVIII.

" My nobile leige," goode Canynge sayde,
    " Leave justice to our Godde,
And laye the yronne rule asyde ;
    Be thyne the olyve rodde.

XIX.

" Was Godde to serche our hertes and reines,
    The best were synners grete ;
Christ's vycarr only knowes ne synne,
    Ynne alle thys mortall state.

---

* The word ' rewyn,' as used by Chaucer, and the old poets, signifies
' pity,' ' compassion.'

XX.

" Lette mercie rule thyne infante reigne,
   'Twylle faste thye crowne fulle sure ;
From race to race thy familie
   Alle sov'reigns shall endure :

XXI.

" But yff wythe bloode and slaughter thou
   Beginne thy infante reigne,
Thy crowne uponne thy childrennes brows
   Wylle never long remayne."

XXII.

" Canynge, awaie ! thys traytour vile
   Has scorn'd my power and mee :
Howe canst thou thenne for such a manne
   Intreate my clemencye ?"

XXIII.

" Mie nobile leige ! the trulie brave
   Wylle val'rous actions prize,
Respect a brave and nobile mynde,
   Altho' ynne enemies."

XXIV.

" Canynge, awaie ! By Godde ynne Heav'n
   Thatt dydd mee being gyve,
I wylle nott taste a bitt of breade
   Whilst thys Syr Charles dothe lyve.

XXV.

" Bie Marie, and alle Seinctes ynne Heav'n,
   Thys sunne shall be hys laste ;"
Thenne Canynge dropt a brinie teare,
   And from the presence paste.

XXVI.

Wyth herte brymm-fulle of gnawynge grief,
  Hee to Syr Charles dydd goe,
And satt hymm downe uponne a stoole,
  And teares beganne to flowe.[*]

XXVII.

" Wee alle must die," quod brave Syr Charles;
  " Whatte bootes ytte howe or whenne;
Dethe ys the sure, the certaine fate
  Of all wee mortall menne.

XXVIII.

" Saye, why, my friend, thie honest soul
  Runns overr att thyne eye;
Is ytte for my most welcome doome
  Thatt thou doste child-lyke crye ?"

XXIX.

Quod godlie Canynge, " I doe weepe,
  Thatt thou soe soone must dye,
And leave thy sonnes and helpless wyfe ;
  'Tys thys thatt wettes myne eye."

XXX.

" Thenne drie the teares thatt out thyne eye
  From godlie fountaines sprynge ;
Dethe I despise, and alle the power
  Of Edwarde, traytor kynge.

---

[*] " And now and then a sigh he stole;
  And tears began to flow."
          Dryden, *Ode on St. Cecilia's Day.*

XXXI.

" Whan through the tyrant's welcom means
    I shall resigne my lyfe,
The Godde I serve wylle soone provyde
    For bothe mye sonnes and wyfe.

XXXII.

" Before I sawe the lyghtsome sunne,
    Thys was appointed mee ;
Shall mortal manne repyne or grudge
    Whatt Godde ordeynes to bee ?

XXXIII.

" Howe oft ynne battaile have I stoode,
    Whan thousands dy'd arounde ;
Whan smokynge streemes of crimson bloode
    Imbrew'd the fatten'd grounde :

XXXIV.

" Howe dydd I knowe thatt ev'ry darte,
    That cutte the airie waie,
Myghte nott fynde passage toe my harte,
    And close myne eyes for aie ?

XXXV.

" And shall I nowe, forr feere of dethe,
    Looke wanne and bee dysmayde ?
Ne l fromme my herte flie childyshe feere,
    Bee alle the manne display'd.

XXXVI.

" Ah! goddelyke Henrie! Godde forefende,
    And guarde thee and thye sonne,
Yff 'tis hys wylle; but yff 'tis nott,
    Why thenne hys wylle bee donne.

XXXVII.

" My honest friende, my faulte has beene
    To serve Godde and mye prynce;
And thatt I no tyme-server am,
    My dethe wylle soone convynce.

XXXVIII.

" Ynne Londonne citye was I borne,
    Of parents of grete note;
My fadre dydd a nobile armes
    Emblazon onne hys cote:

XXXIX.

" I make ne doubte butt hee ys gone
    Where soone I hope to goe;
Where wee for ever shall bee blest,
    From oute the reech of woe:

XL.

" Hee taughte mee justice and the laws
    Wyth pitie to unite;
And eke hee taughte mee howe to knowe
    The wronge cause fromme the ryghte:[1]

XLI.

" Hee taughte mee wythe a prudent hande
    To feede the hungrie poore,
Ne lette mye servants dryve awaie
    The hungrie fromme my doore:

[1] Chatterton's conduct and opinions were early tinctured with irreligion. How must his mind have laboured under the burden of describing pathetically the pleasures of virtue and the rewards of religion; which are so frequently mentioned in these poems, though they had not made their proper impression on his heart!—DEAN MILLES.

[There was more of truth in this remark, and less of irony, than the worthy Dean imagined.—ED.]

XLII.

" And none can saye butt alle mye lyfe
I have hys wordyes kept ;
And summ'd the actyonns of the daie
Eche nyghte before I slept.[1]

XLIII.

" I have a spouse, goe aske of her,
Yff I defyl'd her bedde?
I have a kynge, and none can laie
Blacke treason onne my hedde.

XLIV.

" Ynne Lent, and onne the holie eve,
Fromme fleshe I dydd refrayne ;
Whie should I thenne appeare dismay'd
To leave thys worlde of payne?

XLV.

" Ne! hapless Henrie! I rejoyce,
I shalle ne see thye dethe ;
Moste willynglie ynne thye just cause
Doe I resign my brethe.

---

[1] If we look to the ballad of Sir Charles Bawdin, and translate it into modern English, we shall find its strength and interest to have no dependence on obsolete words. In the striking passage of the martyr Bawdin standing erect in his car to rebuke Edward, who beheld him from the window, when
" The tyrant's soul rushed to his face,"
and when he exclaimed,
" Behold the man! he speaks the truth,
He's greater than a king;"
in these, and in all the striking parts of the ballad, no effect is owing to mock antiquity, but to the simple and high conception of a great and just character, who
" Summ'd the actions of the day,
Each night before he slept."
What a moral portraiture from the hand of a boy!—CAMPBELL.

XLVI.

" Oh, fickle people ! rewyn'd londe !
　　Thou wylt kenne peace ne moe ;
　Whyle Richard's sonnes exalt themselves,
　　Thye brookes wythe bloude wylle flowe.

XLVII.

" Saie, were ye tyr'd of godlie peace,
　　And godlie Henrie's reigne,
　Thatt you dydd choppe youre easie daies
　　For those of bloude and peyne ?

XLVIII.

" Whatte tho' I onne a sledde* bee drawne,
　　And mangled by a hynde,
　I doe defye the traytor's pow'r,
　　Hee can ne harm my mynde ;

XLIX.

" Whatte tho', uphoisted onne a pole,
　　Mye lymbes shall rotte ynne ayre,
　And ne ryche monument of brasse
　　Charles Bawdin's name shall bear ;

L.

" Yett ynne the holie booke above,
　　Whyche tyme can't eate awaie,
　There wythe the servants of the Lorde
　　Mye name shall lyve for aie.

---

* ' Sledde,' sledge ; described by Bailey as the hurdle on which trai-
tors were dragged to execution. Used by Chaucer in the sense of a
travelling vehicle—" So that al tribulacion ydone away thou by my
giding and by my pathe *and by my sledes* shalte mowen retourne whole
and sounde into thy countrie."—*Translation of Boethius,* book iv.

LI.

"Thenne welcome dethe! for lyfe eterne
  I leave thys mortall lyfe:
Farewell, vayne worlde, and alle that's deare,
  Mye sonnes and lovynge wyfe!

LII.

"Nowe dethe as welcome to mee comes,
  As e'er the moneth of Maie;
Nor woulde I even wyshe to lyve,
  Wyth my dere wyfe to staie."

LIII.

Quod Canynge, "'Tys a goodlie thynge
  To bee prepar'd to die;
And from thys world of peyne and grefe
  To Godde ynne Heav'n to flie."

LIV.

And nowe the bell beganne to tolle,
  And claryonnes to sounde;
Syr Charles hee herde the horses' feete
  A prauncing onne the grounde:

LV.

And just before the officers
  His lovynge wyfe came ynne,
Weepynge unfeigned teeres of woe,
  Wythe loude and dysmalle dynne.

LVI.

"Sweet Florence! nowe I praie forbere,
  Ynne quiet lett mee die;
Praie Godde, thatt ev'ry Christian soule
  Maye looke onne dethe as I.

LVII.

"Sweet Florence! why these brinie teeres?
    Theye washe my soule awaie,
And almost make mee wyshe for lyfe,
    Wythe thee, sweete dame, to staie.

LVIII.

"'Tys butt a journie I shalle goe
    Untoe the lande of blysse ;
Nowe, as a proofe of husbande's love,
    Receive thys holie kysse."

LIX.

Thenne Florence, fault'ring ynne her saie,
    Tremblynge these wordyes spoke,
"Ah, cruele Edwarde! bloudie kynge!
    My herte ys welle nyghe broke :

LX.

"Ah, sweete Syr Charles! why wylt thou goe,
    Wythoute thye lovynge wyfe?
The cruelle axe thatt cuttes thye necke,
    Ytte eke shall ende mye lyfe."

LXI.

And nowe the officers came ynne
    To brynge Syr Charles awaie,
Whoe turnedd toe hys lovynge wyfe,
    And thus to her dydd saie :

LXII.

"I goe to lyfe, and nott to dethe ;
    Truste thou ynne Godde above,
And teache thye sonnes to feare the Lorde,
    And ynne theyre hertes hym love :

LXIII.

" Teache them to runne the nobile race
    Thatt I theyre fader runne :
Florence! shou'd dethe thee take—adieu !
    Yee officers, leade onne."

LXIV.

Thenne Florence rav'd as anie madde,
    And dydd her tresses tere ;
" Oh! staie, mye husbande ! lorde! and lyfe !"—
    Syr Charles thenne dropt a teare.

LXV.

'Tyll tyredd oute wythe ravynge loud,
    Shee fellen onne the flore ;
Syr Charles exerted alle hys myghte,
    And march'd fromme oute the dore.

LXVI.

Uponne a sledde hee mounted thenne,
    Wythe lookes fulle brave and swete ;
Lookes, thatt enshone ' ne more concern
    Thanne anie ynne the strete.

LXVII.

Before hym went the council-menne,
    Ynne scarlett robes and golde,
And tassils spanglynge ynne the sunne,
    Muche glorious to beholde :

---

⁷ 'Enshone.' This word is of doubtful authority. Its signification, as rendered by Dean Milles, and evidently by the sense of the passage, is 'shewed,' ' exhibited.'

LXVIII.

The Freers of Seincte Augustyne next
    Appeared to the syghte,
Alle cladd ynne homelie russett weedes,
    Of godlie monkysh plyghte :

LXIX.

Ynne diffraunt partes a godlie psaume
    Moste sweetlie theye dydd chaunt ;
Behynde theyre backes syx mynstrelles came,
    Who tun'd the strunge bataunt.[8]

LXX.

Thenne fyve-and-twentye archers came ;
    Echone the bowe dydd bende,
From rescue of kynge Henrie's friends
    Syr Charles forr to defend.

LXXI.

Bolde as a lyon came Syr Charles,
    Drawne onne a clothe-layde sledde,
Bye two blacke stedes ynne trappynges white,
    Wyth plumes uponne theyre hedde :

LXXII.

Behynde hym fyve-and-twentye moe
    Of archers stronge and stoute,
Wyth bended bowe echone ynne hande,
    Marched ynne goodlie route :

---

[8] 'Bataunt.' The name seems to imply that it was a stringed instru-
ment, like a dulcimer, played on by striking the wires with a piece of
iron or wood.—DEAN MILLES.

LXXIII.

Seincte Jameses Freers marched next,
   Echone hys parte dydd chaunt ;
Behynde theyre backes syx mynstrelles came,
   Who tun'd the strunge bataunt :

LXXIV.

Thenne came the maior and eldermenne,
   Ynne clothe of scarlett deck't ;
And theyre attendyng menne echone,
   Lyke Easterne princes trickt :*

LXXV.

And after them, a multitude
   Of citizenns dydd thronge ;
The wyndowes were alle fulle of heddes,
   As hee dydd passe alonge.

LXXVI.

And whenne hee came to the hyghe crosse,
   Syr Charles dydd turne and saie,
" O Thou, thatt savest manne fromme synne,
   Washe mye soule clean thys daie !"

LXXVII.

At the grete mynsterr wyndowe sat
   The kynge ynne myckle state,
To see Charles Badwin goe alonge
   To hys most welcom fate.

---

* Dean Milles, thoroughly persuaded of the authenticity of the Rowley
poems, remarks, " The procession here described was probably real, at
least it was so orderly in point of form, *that no modern pen could have
disposed it with so much propriety.*"

LXXVIII.

Soone as the sledde drewe nyghe enowe,
  Thatt Edwarde hee myghte heare,
The brave Syr Charles hee dydd stande uppe,
  And thus hys wordes declare:

LXXIX.

" Thou seest mee, Edwarde! traytour vile!
  Expos'd to infamie;
Butt bee assur'd, disloyall manne!
  I'm greaterr nowe thanne thee.

LXXX.

" Bye foule proceedyngs, murdre, bloude,
  Thou wearest nowe a crowne;
And hast appoynted mee to dye,
  By power nott thyne owne.

LXXXI.

" Thou thynkest I shall dye to-daie;
  I have beene dede 'till nowe,
And soone shall lyve to weare a crowne
  For aie uponne my browe;

LXXXII.

" Whylst thou, perhapps, for som few yeares,
  Shalt rule thys fickle lande,
To lett them knowe howe wyde the rule
  'Twixt kynge and tyrant hande:

LXXXIII.

" Thye pow'r unjust, thou traytour slave!
  Shall falle onne thye owne hedde"—
Fromme out of hearyng of the kynge
  Departed thenne the sledde.

LXXXIV.

Kynge Edwarde's soule rush'd to hys face,
 Hee turn'd hys hedde awaie,
And to hys broder Gloucester
 Hee thus dydd speke and saie:

LXXXV.

" To hym that soe-much-dreaded dethe
 Ne ghastlie terrors brynge,
Beholde the manne ! hee spake the truthe,
 Hee's greater thanne a kynge !"

LXXXVI.

" Soe lett hym die !" Duke Richard sayde ;
 " And maye echone oure foes
Bende downe theyre neckes to bloudie axe,
 And feede the carryon crowes."

LXXXVII.

And nowe the horses gentlie drewe
 Syr Charles uppe the hyghe hylle ;
The axe dydd glysterr ynne the sunne,
 Hys pretious bloude to spylle.

LXXXVIII.

Syr Charles dydd uppe the scaffold goe,
 As uppe a gilded carre
Of victorye, bye val'rous chiefs
 Gayn'd ynne the bloudie warre :

LXXXIX.

And to the people hee dydd saie,
 " Beholde you see mee dye,
For servynge loyally mye kynge,
 Mye kynge most rightfullie.

xc.

" As long as Edwarde rules thys lande,
　　Ne quiet you wylle knowe;
Youre sonnes and husbandes shalle bee slayne,
　　And brookes wythe bloude shalle flowe.

xci.

" You leave youre goode and lawfulle kynge,
　　Whenne ynne adversitye;
Lyke mee, untoe the true cause stycke,
　　And for the true cause dye."

xcii.

Thenne hee, wyth preestes, uponne hys knees,
　　A pray'r to Godde dydd make,
Beseechynge hym unto hymselfe
　　Hys partynge soule to take.

xciii.

Thenne, kneelynge downe, hee layd hys hedde
　　Most seemlie onne the blocke;
Whyche fromme hys bodie fayre at once
　　The able heddes-manne stroke;

xciv.

And oute the bloude beganne to flowe,
　　And rounde the scaffolde twyne;
And teares, enowe to washe't awaie,
　　Dydd flowe fromme each mann's eyne.

xcv.

The bloudie axe hys bodie fayre
　　Ynnto foure parties cutte;
And ev'rye parte, and eke hys hedde,
　　Uponne a pole was putte.

XCVI.

One parte dydd rotte onne Kynwulph-hylle,[9]
One onne the mynster-tower,
And one from off the castle-gate
The crowen dydd devoure;

XCVII.

The other onne Seyncte Powle's[10] goode gate,
A dreery spectacle;
Hys hedde was plac'd onne the hyghe crosse,
Ynne hyghe-streete most nobile.

XCVIII.

Thus was the ende of Bawdin's fate:
Godde prosper longe oure kynge,
And grante hee maye, wyth Bawdin's soule,
Ynne heav'n Godd's mercie synge![11]

---

[9] 'Kynwulph.'—So called from Kenwulf, king of Mercia, and probably the same spot which still bears the name of King's Down, a very eminent part of the city. DEAN MILLES.

[10] St. Paul's gate.

[11] The Bristowe Tragedy, or the Dethe of Syr Charles Bawdin, has little but its pathetic simplicity to recommend it. There is nothing ingenious in the plot, or striking in the execution; and it only ranks upon a par with a number of tragic ballads, both ancient and modern, in the same style.—DR. GREGORY.

In a letter from Chatterton's sister, first published in Southey's edition of his works in 1803, we learn that he privately acknowledged to his mother that he was the author of this poem. It will not prove uninteresting to the reader to peruse the various opinions of our most eminent literary men, on the subject of the forgery, if we must so term it,—but forgery is an ugly word.

The inconsistencies of Chatterton's conduct and character may be, in some measure, ascribed to his situation and extreme youth; yet we fear their original source was in that inequality of spirit with which providence, as in mockery of the most splendid gifts of genius and fancy, has often conjoined them. This strange disorder of the mind, often confounded by the vulgar with actual insanity, of which perhaps it is a remote shade, is fostered by the workings of an ardent imagination, as it is checked and subdued by mathematical or philosophical research.

Without considering the forgery of Rowley's poems in so heinous a light as if they had been a bill or bond, and pecuniary advantage the object of the fraud, we cannot regard the imposture as of an indifferent or harmless nature. Neither was the end proposed, being apparently the mere internal satisfaction of imposing upon the world, or, at best, the sullen obstinacy of maintaining an assertion which had been hastily made, apparently adequate to the immense labour necessary to sustain the credit of Rowley. But the ardent mind of Chatterton, who had pitched the standard of his honour on this particular ground, urged him to maintain it at the sacrifice of the poetical reputation he might have acquired by renouncing a phantom of his imagination, and at the yet more important dereliction of personal truth and moral rectitude.—WALTER SCOTT.

The heart which can peruse the fate of Chatterton without being moved is little to be envied for its tranquillity : but the intellects of those men must be as deficient as their hearts are uncharitable, who, confounding all shades of moral distinction, have ranked his literary fiction of Rowley in the same class of crimes with pecuniary forgery, and have calculated that if he had not died by his own hand, he would have probably ended his days upon a gallows. This disgusting sentence has been pronounced upon a youth who was exemplary for severe study, temperance, and natural affection. His Rowleian forgery must indeed be pronounced improper by the general law which condemns all falsifications of history; but it deprived no man of his fame; it had no sacrilegious interference with the memory of departed genius; it had not, like Lauder's imposture, any malignant motive, to rob a party or a country, of a name which was its pride and ornament.—CAMPBELL.

The deception was not intended to defraud or injure one human being, and might most assuredly have been begun and continued without the slightest sense of criminality in Chatterton.—SOUTHEY.

The moral character of Chatterton has been basely insulted by bigots, and by ignorant men. The pretended antiquity of his poems has been denounced as a crime against truth, with all the solemnity with which Ananias's lie is quoted from Scripture. The word 'forgery' does not apply to such an innocent deception.—EDINBURGH REVIEW.

AELLA,

a

Tragycal Enterlude,

or

Discoorseynge Tragedie,

wrotenn bie
THOMAS ROWLEIE;

plaiedd before

Mastre Canynge,

Atte hys Howse nempte the Rodde Lodge;
Alsoe before the Duke of Norfolck,

Johan Howard.

Chatterton's own opinion of his Tragedy appears from the following letter, written by him to Dodsley, the bookseller:—

"Bristol, Feb. 15, 1769.

"Sir,

"Having intelligence that the Tragedy of Ælla was in being, after a long and laborious search, I was so happy as to obtain a sight of it. Struck with the beauties of it, I endeavoured to obtain a copy of it to send you; but the present preserver absolutely denied to give me one, unless I give him a guinea for a consideration. As I am unable to procure such a sum I made search for another copy, but unsuccessfully. Unwilling such a beauteous piece should be lost, I have made bold to apply to you; several gentlemen of learning, who have seen it, join with me in praising it. I am far from having any mercenary views for myself in this affair, and, was I able, would print it at my own risque. It is a perfect tragedy; the plot clear, the language spirited, and the songs (interspersed in it) are flowing, poetical, and elegantly simple. The similes are judiciously applied, and though wrote in the reign of Henry VI., not inferior to many of the present age. If I can procure a copy, with or without the gratification, it shall be immediately sent to you. The motive that actuates me to do this is, to convince the world that the monks (of whom some have so despicable an opinion) were not such blockheads as is generally thought, and that good poetry might be wrote in the dark days of superstition, as well as in these more enlightened ages. An immediate answer will oblige me. I shall not receive your favour as for myself, but as your agent.

"I am, Sir,

"Your most obedient Servant,

"THOMAS CHATTERTON."

Mr. Dix says, "The recommendatory letter of Chatterton failed to impress the matter-of-fact bookseller with the importance of giving this Tragedy to the world, and the poor poet's offer was rejected, although he only asked the modest sum of *one guinea* for the copy."

EPISTLE TO MASTRE CANYNGE
ON ÆLLA.*

I.

'Trs songe bie mynstrelles, thatte yn auntyent[1] tym,
Whan Reasonn hylt[2] herselfe in cloudes of nyghte,
The preeste delyvered alle the lege[3] yn rhym;
Lyche peyncted[4] tyltynge-speares to please the syghte,
The whyche yn yttes felle[5] use doe make moke[6] dere,[7]
Syke dyd theire auncyante lee[8] deftlie[9] delyghte the eare.

---

[1] Ancient.	[2] Hid, concealed.	[3] Law.
[4] Painted.	[5] Bad, pernicious.	[6] Much.
[7] Hurt, damage.	[8] Song.	[9] Sweetly, agreeably.

II.

Perchaunce yn Vyrtues gare[10] rhym mote bee thenne,
Butte efte[11] nowe flyeth to the odher syde;
In hallie[12] preeste apperes the ribaudes[13] penne,
Inne lithie[14] moncke apperes the barronnes pryde:
But rhym wythe somme, as nedere[15] widhout teethe,
Make pleasaunce to the sense, botte maie do lytte scathe[16]

III.

Syr Johne, a knyghte, who hath a barne of lore,[17]
Kenns[18] Latyn att fyrst syghte from Frenche or Greke;
Pyghtethe[19] hys knowlachynge[20] ten yeres or more,
To rynge upon the Latynne worde to speke.
Whoever spekethe Englysch ys despysed,
The Englysch hym to please moste flyrste be latynized.[21]

IV.

Vevyan, a moncke, a good requiem[22] synges;
Can preache so wele, eche hynde[23] hys meneynge knowes;
Albeytte these gode guyfts[24] awaie he flynges,
Beeynge as badde yn vearse as goode yn prose.
Hee synges of seynctes who dyed for yer Godde,
Everych wynter nyghte afresche he sheddes theyr blodde.

---

[10] Cause.   [11] Oft.   [12] Holy.   [13] Rake, lewd person.
[14] 'Lithie,' humble, according to Chatterton. But its sense among old writers was *soft, gentle*.
   "So oft falleth the *lethy* water on the hard rock."—CHAUCER.
[15] 'Nedere,' adder.
   "Anonne the *nedirs* gonne her for to sting."—CHAUCER.
[16] Hurt, damage.
[17] Learning.   [18] Knows.   [19] Plucks or tortures.   [20] Knowledge.
[21] We find a very similar line in one of Chatterton's acknowledged poems—
   "Who damns good English if not latinized."—HAPPINESS, 1769.
[22] A service used over the dead.   [23] Peasant.   [24] Gifts.

v.

To maydens, huswyfes, and unlored²⁵ dames,
Hee redes hys tales of merryment and woe.
Loughe²⁶ loudlie dynneth²⁷ from the dolte²⁸ adrames;²⁹
He swelles on laudes³⁰ of fooles, tho' kennes³¹ hem soe,
Sommetyme at tragedie theie laughe and synge,
At merrie yaped³²fage³³somme hard-drayned water brynge.

vi.

Yette Vevyan ys ne foole, beyinde³⁴ hys lynes.
Geofroie makes vearse, as handycraftes theyr ware;
Wordes wythoute sense full groffyngelye³⁵ he twynes,
Cotteynge³⁶ hys storie off as wythe a sheere;
Waytes³⁷ monthes on nothynge, and hys storie donne,
Ne moe you from ytte kenn, than gyf³⁸ you neere begonne.

vii.

Enowe of odhers; of mieselfe to write,
Requyrynge whatt I doe notte nowe possess,
To you I leave the taske; I kenne your myghte
Wyll make mie faultes, mie meynte³⁹ of faultes, be less.
ÆLLA wythe thys I sende, and hope that you
Wylle from ytte cast awaie, whatte lynes maie be untrue.

---

²⁵ Unlearned.   ²⁶ Laugh.   ²⁷ Sounds.   ²⁸ Foolish.
²⁹ ' Adrames,' churls.—This word is unauthorized. The adjective
' adraming,' churlish, is to be found in old writers, and likewise in
Bailey.
³⁰ Praises.   ³¹ Knows.   ³² Laughable.   ³³ Tale, jest.
³⁴ Beyond.   ³⁵ Foolishly, vulgarly, abjectly.   ³⁶ Cutting.
³⁷ This word is probably a mistake for 'waystes.'—SOUTHEY.
³⁸ If.   ³⁹ Many, or rather, amount.

VIII.

Playes made from hallie[40] tales I holde unmeete;
Lette somme greate storie of a manne be songe;
Whanne, as a manne, we Godde and Jesus treate,
In mie pore mynde, we doe the Godhedde wronge.
Botte lette ne wordes, whyche droorie[41] mote ne heare,
Bee placed yn the same. Adieu untylle anere.[42]

THOMAS ROWLEIE.[43]

[40] Holy.   [41] 'Modesty,' according to Chatterton; but its sense
among old writers is uncertain, and capable of a very wide interpre-
tation. In Gower it evidently means 'friendship,' and in Southey's
quotation from 'The Bruce,' it would seem to signify 'illicit love.'

[42] Another.

[43] It was not in books only that this boy shewed his amazing intui-
tion and comprehension. He looked on life with the same penetrating
and pervading eye. His observation on things was equally quick and
extensive. His humour, his knowledge of the world, his attention to
character, and his general perception of the modes of life, appear in
his numerous satirical pieces, both in prose and verse. We wonder
at the address, the command, the facility, the versatility of mind, with
which in a short space of time he composed a variety of pieces, and
on subjects which usually require long observation and experience.—
WARTON.

LETTER

TO THE DYGNE MASTRE CANYNGE.*

I.

STRAUNGE dome ytte ys, that, yn these daies of oures,
Nete[1] butte a bare recytalle can hav place;
Nowe shapelie poesie hath loste yttes powers,
And pynant[2] hystorie ys onlie grace;
Heie[3] pycke up wolsome[4] weedes, ynstedde of flowers,
And famylies, ynstedde of wytte, theie trace;
Nowe poesie eanne meete wythe ne regrate,[5]
Whylste prose, and herehaughtrie,[6] ryse yn estate.

---

* There can be no doubt concerning the existence of Master Can-
ynge, since it is attested by such a number of contemporary historians,
and his remains lie interred in the church of which he was the
founder. He was the younger son of a citizen of Bristol, and in his
youth afforded early prognostics of wisdom and ability. He was
a handsome person, and married for love without a fortune. Of his
native city he was mayor five times; and in the year 1461, when Sir
Baldwin Fulford was executed for treason, Canynge pleaded for him
in vain. Among the proofs of his munificence there still exist an
alms house or hospital, with a chapel, and the beautiful church of
St. Mary Redcliffe, in Bristol.—DR. GREGORY.

   [1] Nought.   [2] Languid, insipid.   [3] They.
   [4] Noxious, loathsome.   [5] Esteem.   [6] Heraldry.

II.

Lette kynges, and rulers, whan heie gayne a throne,
Shew whatt theyre grandsieres, and great grandsieres
    bore,
Emarschalled[7] armes, yatte, ne before theyre owne,
Now raung'd wythe whatt yeir fadres han before;
Lette trades, and toune folck, lett syke[8] thynges alone,
Ne fyghte for sable yn a fielde of aure;[9]
Seldomm, or never, are armes vyrtues mede,
Shee nillynge[10] to take myckle[11] aie dothe hede.

III.

A man ascaunse[12] uponn a piece maye looke,
And shake hys hedde to styre hys rede[13] aboute;
Quod he, gyf I askaunted[14] oere thys booke,
Schulde fynde thereyn that trouthe ys left wythoute;
Eke,[15] gyf[16] unto a view percase[17] I tooke
The long beade-rolle of al the wrytynge route,
Asserius, Ingolphus, Torgotte, Bedde,
Thorow hem[18] al nete lyche ytte I coulde rede.—

IV.

Pardon, yee Graiebarbes,[19] gyff I saie, onwise
Yee are to stycke so close and bysmarelie[20]
To hystorie; you doe ytte tooe moche pryze,
Whyche amenused[21] thoughtes of poesie;

---

[7] Blazoned.   [8] Such.   [9] Gold, a term in heraldry.
[10] Unwilling.   [11] Much.   [12] Obliquely.
[13] Wisdom, council.
    " Who having three times shook his head,
      To stir his wit up, thus he said."—BUTLER's *Hudibras.*
[14] Glaunced.   [15] Also.   [16] If.   [17] Perchance.
[18] Them.   [19] Greybeards.   [20] Curiously.   [21] Lessened.

Somme drybblette[22] share you shoulde to yatte[23] alyse,[24]
Nott makynge everyche thynge bee hystorie;
Instedde of mountynge onn a wynged horse,
You onn a rouncy[25] dryve ynn dolefull course.

v.

Canynge and I from common course dyssente;
Wee ryde the stede, botte yev[26] to hym the reene;
Ne wylle betweene crased[27] molterynge[28] bookes bepente,
Botte soare on hyghe, and yn the sonne-bemes sheene;
And where wee kenn somme ishad[29] floures besprente,[30]
We take ytte, and from oulde rouste doe ytte clene;
Wee wylle ne cheynedd to one pasture bee,
Botte sometymes soare 'bove trouthe of hystorie.

vi.

Saie, Canynge, whatt was vearse yn daies of yore?
Fyne thoughtes, and couplettes fetyvelie[31] bewryen,[32]
Notte syke as doe annoie thys age so sore,
A keppened[33] poyntelle[34] restynge at eche lyne.
Vearse maie be goode, botte poesie wantes more,
An onlist[35] lecturn,[36] and a songe adygne;[37]
Accordynge to the rule I have thys wroughte,
Gyff ytt please Canynge, I care notte a groate.

---

[22] Small.   [23] That.   [24] Allow.
[25] 'Rouncy,' cart-horse. Used by Chaucer for a pony.
    "He rode upon a rouncy."—*Prologue to Canterbury Tales.*
    See likewise ' Runcilus' in Spelman's Glossary.
[26] Give.   [27] Broken.   [28] Musty, mouldy, scattered.
[29] Spread.   [30] Scattered.   [31] Elegantly.
[32] Declared, expressed, displayed.   [33] Studied.
[34] A pen, used metaphorically as a muse or genius.
[35] Boundless.   [36] Subject, lecture.   [37] Nervous.

VII.

The thynge ytts moste bee yttes owne defense;
Som metre maie notte please a womannes ear.
Canynge lookes notte for poesie, botte sense;
And dygne, and wordie³⁸ thoughtes, ys all hys care.
Canynge, adieu! I do you greete from hence;
Full soone I hope to taste of your good cheere:
Goode Byshoppe Carpynter dyd byd mee saie,
Hee wysche³⁹ you healthe and selinesse⁴⁰ for aie.

T. ROWLEIE.

---

³⁸ Worthy.　　　　³⁹ Wishes.　　　　⁴⁰ Happiness.

The simplicity, the unity, the moral intent of this Tragedy, are too striking not to affect the reader upon the first perusal. Is there a picture more striking to the moralist than the death of Celmonde, the virtue of Birtha expressed in her pious and charitable wish for Celmonde's future fame, or the conduct of Hurra, who, in the pursuit of a barbarous resolution, feels generously for a distressed female; checks his own resentment; prevents the bloody design of his comrades, and restores to the arms of his enemy, his wife, the chaste but unhappy Birtha. The whole transaction is included within the space of three days. The tragedy opens with Ælla's wedding-day. In the evening he is summoned to join the army: on the next day, "having done his mattynes and his vowes," he engages, defeats the Danes, and is wounded. Celmonde attempts his act of treachery against Birtha that night; and on the succeeding morning she is conveyed to her distracted lord, expiring, not under the wounds that he had received from his enemies, but from those he had given to himself, in which the distress of the tragedy consists. —Dean Milles.

ENTRODUCTIONNE.

I.

Somme cherisaunei[1] 'tys to gentle mynde,
Whan theie have chevyced[2] theyre londe from bayne,[3]
Whan theie ar dedd, theie leave yer name behynde,
And theyre goode deedes doe on the earthe remayne;
Downe yn the grave wee ynhyme[4] everych steyne,[5]
Whylest al her[6] gentlenesse ys made to sheene,
Lyche fetyve[7] baubels[8] geasonne[9] to be seene.

II.

Ælla, the wardenne of thys[10] castell[11] stede,
Whylest Saxons dyd the Englysche sceptre swaie,
Who made whole troopes of Dacyan men to blede,
Then seel'd[12] hys eyne, and seeled hys eyne for aie,
Wee rowze hym uppe before the judgment daie,
To saie what he, as clergyond,[13] can kenne,
And howe hee sojourned in the vale of men.

----

[1] 'Cherisaunei,' comfort. [The proper word is 'cherisaunce.' But in Kersey's Dictionary, a book which is known to have been frequently in the hands of Chatterton, through some error of the printer, it is spelt as we have it in the text. This is by no means the only instance in which Chatterton, in searching for obsolete words, has ignorantly copied the mistakes of his authorities.—Ed.]

[2] Preserved, redeemed.	[3] Ruin.	[4] Inter.	[5] Fault, blot.
[6] Their.	[7] Neat, comely.	[8] Jewels.
[9] Rare.	[10] Bristol.	[11] Castle.
[12] Closed.	[13] Taught.

ÆLLA.

PERSONNES REPRESENTEDD.

ÆLLA,   bie Thomas Rowleie, Preeste, the Aucthoure.
CELMONDE,   Johan Iscamm, Preeste.
Hurra,   Syrr Thybbotte Gorges, Knyghte.
Birtha,   Mastre Edwarde Canynge.

Odherr Partes bie Knyghtes, Minstrelles, &c.

CELMONDE, (att *Bristowe*).

Before yonne roddie sonne has droove his wayne
Throwe half his joornie, dyghte[1] yn gites[2] of goulde,
Mee, happeless me, hee wylle a wretche behoulde,
Mieselfe, and al that's myne, bounde ynne myschaunces
    chayne.
Ah! Birtha, whie did Nature frame thee fayre?
Whie art thou all thatt poyntelle[3] canne bewreene?[4]
Whie art thou nott as coarse as odhers are?—
Botte thenn thie soughle woulde throwe thy vysage
    sheene,
Yatt shemres[5] on thie comelie semlykeene,[6]

---

[1] Clothed.   [2] Robes, mantles.   [3] A pen.
[4] Express.
    "Is she not more than painting can express."
                Rowe's *Fair Penitent.*
[5] Shines.   [6] Countenance.

Lyche nottebrowne cloudes, whann bie the sonne
    made redde,
Orr scarlette, wyth waylde[1] lynnen clothe ywreene,[2]
Syke[3] would thie spryte upponn thie vysage spredde.
Thys daie brave Ælla dothe thyne honde and harte
Clayme as hys owne to be, whyche nee fromm hys moste
    parte.
And cann I lyve to see herr wythe anere![4]
Ytt cannotte, muste notte, naie, ytt shalle not bee.
Thys nyghte I'll putte stronge poysonn ynn the beere,
And hymm, herr, and myselfe, attenes[5] wyll slea.
Assyst mee, Helle! lett Devylles rounde mee tende,
To slea mieselfe, mie love, and eke mie doughtie[6] friende.

ÆLLA, BIRTHA.

ÆLLA.

Notte, whanne the hallie[7] prieste dyd make me
    knyghte,
Blessynge the weaponne, tellynge future dede,
Howe bie mie honde the prevyd[8] Dane shoulde blede,
Howe I schulde often bee, and often wynne, ynn fyghte;
Notte, whann I fyrste behelde thie beauteous hue,
Whyche strooke mie mynde, and rouzed my softer
    soule;
Nott, whann from the barbed[9] horse yn fyghte dyd
    viewe

---

[1] Chosen.	[2] Covered.	[3] Such.
[4] Another.	[5] At once.	[6] Mighty, valiant.
[7] Holy.	[8] Hardy, valourous.	[9] Armed.

The flying Dacians oere the wyde playne roule,
Whan all the troopes of Denmarque made grete dole,[1]
Dydd I fele joie wyth syke reddoure[2] as nowe,
Whann hallie preest, the lechemanne[3] of the soule,
Dydd knytte us both ynn a caytysnede[4] vowe:
Now hallie[5] Ælla's selynesse[6] ys grate;
Shap[7] haveth nowe ymade hys woes for to emmate.[8]

BIRTHA.

Mie lorde, and husbande, syke[9] a joie is myne;
Botte mayden modestie moste ne soe saie,
Albeytte thou mayest rede ytt ynn myne eyne,
Or ynn myne harte, where thou shalte be for aie;

---

[1] Lamentation.   [2] Violence.   [3] Physician.
[4] ['Caytysnede,' properly a participle, and not an adjective, as it is here used by Chatterton.
In Chaucer's translation of Boethius, we find it in the sense of 'separated by imprisonment;' or, if derived, as Skinner thinks, from the Latin *catenatus*, 'chained,' 'tied up.' " Thus witlesse, thoughtfull, sightlesse lokynge, I endure my penaunce in this derke prisonne *caitised* fro frendshlippe and aequaintaunce." In line 1103 of this tragedy, we find it again in the sense of 'being taken captive.' Its signification in Balley (Chatterton's probable authority) is 'chained,' 'bound with chains.' His own interpretation of the word in the passage before us is 'enforcing.' 'Caytysnede vowe,' a vow that may not be broken.—ED.]
[5] Happy.   [6] Happiness.
[7] ['Shap,' fate. Bailey and Kersey; not found in Chaucer, or other old writers. In the translation of the Æneid, by Gawin Douglas, 'fate' is rendered by 'werdissehap,' where it does not signify 'fate,' but the shaping or disposition of the fates. Kersey, who is often a blunderer, in his misapprehension of Skinner, affixed to it the meaning of 'fate,' 'destiny,' and this error was copied by Chatterton.—ED.]
[8] Lessen, decrease.   [9] Such.

Inne sothe, I have botte meeded[1] oute thie faie;[2]
For twelve tymes twelve the mone hath bin yblente,[3]
As manie tymes hathe vyed[4] the Godde of daie,
And on the grasse her lemes[5] of sylverr sente,
Sythe thou dydst cheese[6] mee for thie swote[7] to bee,
Enactynge[8] ynn the same moste faiefullie to mee.

Ofte have I seene thee atte the none-daie feaste,
Whanne deysde[9] bie thieselfe, for wante of pheeres,[10]
Awhylst thie merryemen[11] dydde laughe and jeaste,
Onn mee thou semest all eyne, to mee all eares.
Thou wardest[12] mee as gyff[13] ynn hondred feeres,
Alest[14] a daygnous[15] looke to thee be sente,
And offrendes[16] made mee, moe thann yie compheeres,[17]
Offe scarpes[18] of scarlette, and fyne paramente;[19]
All thie yntente to please was lyssed[20] to mee,
I saie ytt, I moste streve[21] thatt you ameded[22] bee.

ÆLLA.

Mie lyttel kyndnesses whyche I dydd doe,
Thie gentleness doth corven[23] them soe grete,
·Lyche bawsyn[24] olyphauntes[25] mie gnattes doe shewe;
Thou doest mie thoughtes of paying love amate.[26]

---

[1] Recompensed.   [2] Faith, constancy.   [3] Blinded.
[4] Viewed.   [5] Lights, rays.   [6] Chuse.
[7] Sweetheart, bride.   [8] Acting.   [9] Seated under a canopy.
[10] Fellows, equals.   [11] Followers.   [12] Watchest.
[13] If.   [14] Least.   [15] Disdainful.
[16] Presents, offerings.   [17] Equals, companions.
[18] Scarfs.   [19] Robes of scarlet.   [20] Bounded, confined.
[21] Strive.   [22] Rewarded.   [23] Represent.
[24] Large.   [25] Elephants.   [26] Destroy.

Botte hann mie actyonns straughte[1] the rolle of fate,
Pyghte[2] thee fromm hell, or brought heaven down
    to thee,
Layde the whol worlde a falldstole[3] atte thie feete,
One smyle would be suffycyll[4] mede[5] for mee.
I amm loves borro'r, and canne never paie,
Bott be hys borrower stylle, and thyne, mie swete, for aie.

BIRTHA.

Love, doe notte rate your achevments[6] soe smalle;
As I to you, syke love untoe mee beare;
For nothynge paste will Birtha ever call,
Ne on a foode from heaven thynke to cheere.
As farr as thys frayle brutylle[7] flesch wylle spere,[8]
Syke, and ne fardher I expecte of you;
Be notte toe slack yn love, ne overdéare;
A smalle fyre, yan a loud flame, proves more true.

ÆLLA.

Thie gentle wordis toe thie volunde[9] kenne[10]
To bee moe clergionde[11] thann ys ynn meyncte of menne.

ÆLLA, BIRTHA, CELMONDE, MYNSTRELLES.[1]

CELMONDE.

Alle blessynges showre on gentle Ælla's hedde!
Oft maie the moone, yn sylverr sheenynge lyghte,
Inne varied chaunges varyed blessynges shedde,
Besprengeynge[2] far abrode mischaunces nyghte;
And thou, fayre Birtha! thou, fayre dame, so bryghte;
Long mayest thou wyth Ælla fynde muche peace,
Wythe selynesse[3] as wyth a roabe, be dyghte,[4]
Wyth everych chaungynge mone new joies encrease!
I, as a token of mie love to speake,
Have brought you jubbes[5] of ale, at nyghte youre
    brayne[6] to breake.

---

[1] Of old English poetry, one of the striking characteristics is a continued tenor of disparity, not so much in the style as in the sentiment: but the bad predominates. In this sort of reading, we are but rarely relieved from disgust, or roused from indifference: we are suddenly charmed with a beautiful thought in the midst of a heap of rubbish. Like Addison's 'Traveller in the Desert,' who finds an unexpected fountain, if in the barren extent of a thousand lines we discover a solitary simile,

    "We bless our stars, and think it luxury."

In the unpolished ages, the Muse was too awkwardly or too weakly courted to grant many favours to her lovers. In Gower, Chaucer, and Lydgate, elegant descriptions, ornamental images, and melodious couplets, bear no proportion to pages of languor or mediocrity, to prolix, prosaic details, in rhyme, uninteresting and tedious. But the poems before us are uniformly supported; they are throughout poetical and animated; they have, to speak in general terms, no imbecilities either of thought or diction.—WARTON.

[2] Scattering, dispersing.   [3] Happiness.   [4] Clothed.
[5] Jugs.   [6] Care.

ÆLLA.

Whan sopperes paste we'lle drenche youre ale soe
    stronge,
Tyde[1] lyfe, tyde death.

CELMONDE.

      Ye mynstrelles, chaunt your songe!

Mynstrelles Songe, bie a Manne and Womanne.[2]

MANNE.

    Tourne thee to thie Shepsterr[3] swayne;
    Bryghte sonne has ne droncke the dewe
    From the floures of yellowe hue;
    Tourne thee, Alyce, backe agayne.

WOMANNE.

    No, bestoikerre[4] I wylle go,
    Softlie tryppynge o'ere the mees,[5]
    Lyche the sylver-footed doe,
    Seekeynge shelterr yn grene trees.

MANNE.

    See the moss-growne daisey'd banke,
    Pereynge[6] ynne the streme belowe;
    Here we'lle sytte, yn dewie danke;[7]
    Tourne thee, Alyce, do notte goe.

---

[1] Betide or happen.

[2] The first chorus, or 'Mynstrelles Songe,' is a perfect pastotal. It abounds in natural and tender sentiments and opposite imagery, and the fertility of the author's genius is displayed in this little ballad; since, short as it is, it contains a complete plot or fable.—DR. GREGORY.

[3] Shepherd.

[4] 'Bestoikerre,' deceiver. Bailey has the verb 'to bestoike,' to betray.

[5] Meadows.   [6] Appearing.   [7] Damp, moisture.

WOMANNE.

I've hearde erste[1] mie grandame saie,
Yonge damoyselles[2] schulde ne bee,
Inne the swotie[3] moonthe of Maie,
Wythe yonge menne bie the grene wode tree.

MANNE.

Sytte thee, Alyce, sytte, and harke,
Howe the ouzle[4] chauntes hys noate,
The chelandree,[5] greie morn larke,
Chauntynge from theyre lyttel throate.

WOMANNE.

I heare them from eche grene wode tree,
Chauntynge owte so blatauntlie,[6]
Tellynge lecturnyes[7] to mee,
Myscheefe ys whanne you are nygh.

MANNE.

See alonge the mees[8] so grene
Pied daisies, kynge-coppes swote;
Alle wee see, bie non bee seene,
Nete botte shepe settes here a fote.

WOMANNE.

Shepster swayne, you tare mie gratche,[9]
Oute uponne ye! lette me goe.
Leave mee swythe,[10] or I'lle alatche.[11]
Robynne, thys youre dame shall knowe.

---

[1] Formerly. [2] Damsels. [3] Pleasant. [4] The blackbird.
[5] Goldfinch. [6] Loudly. [7] Lectures. [8] Meadows.
[9] Apparel. [10] Quickly. [11] Accuse, cry out.

MANNE.

See! the crokynge[1] brionie
Rounde the popler twyste hys spraie;
Rounde the oake the greene ivie
Florryschethe[2] and lyveth aie.

Lette us seate us bie thys tree,
Laughe, and synge to lovynge ayres;
Comme, and doe notte coyen[3] bee;
Nature made all thynges bie payres.
Drooried[4] cattes wylle after kynde;
Gentle doves wylle kyss and coe.

WOMANNE.

Botte manne, hee moste bee ywrynde,[5]
Tylle syr preeste make one of two.
Tempte mee ne to the foule thynge;
I wylle no mannes lemanne[6] be;
Tyll syr preeste hys songe doethe synge;
Thou shalt neere fynde aught of mee:

MANNE.

Bie oure ladie her yborne,[7]
To-morrowe, soone as ytte ys daie,
I'll make thee wyfe, ne bee forsworne,
So tyde me lyfe or dethe for aie.

---

[1] Crooked, twisting.   [2] Flourishes.   [3] Coy.
[4] Modest.   [5] Separated.   [6] Mistress.
[7] Son.

WOMANNE.

Whatt dothe lette, botte thatte nowe
Wee attenes,[1] thos honde yn honde,
Unto divinistre[2] goe,
And bee lyncked yn wedlocke bonde?

MANNE.

I agree, and thus I plyghte
Honde, and harte, and all that's myne;
Goode syr Rogerr, do us ryghte,
Make us one, at Cothbertes shryne.

BOTHE.

Wee wylle ynn a bordelle[3] lyve,
Hailie,[4] thoughe of no estate;
Everyche clocke moe love shall gyve;
Wee ynn godenesse wylle bee greate.

ÆLLA.

I lyche thys songe, I lyche ytt myckle well;
And there ys monie for yer syngeyne nowe;
Butte have you noone thatt marriage-blessynges telle?

CELMONDE.

In marriage, blessynges are botte fewe, I trowe.[5]

MYNSTRELLES.

Laverde,[6] we have; and, gyff you please, wille synge,
As well as owre choughe-voyces[7] wylle permytte.

---

[1] At once.	[2] A divine.	[3] A cottage.
[4] Happy.	[5] Think.	[6] Lord.
[7] Hoarse, as raven voices.		

ÆLLA.

Comme then, and see you swotelie[1] tune the strynge,
And stret,[2] and engyne[3] all the human wytte,
Toe please mie dame.

MYNSTRELLES.

We'lle strayne owre wytte and synge.

Mynstrelles Songe.

FYRSTE MYNSTRELLE.

The boddynge[4] flourettes bloshes[5] atte the lyghte;
The mees[6] be sprenged[7] wyth the yellowe hue;
Ynn daiseyd mantels ys the mountayne dyghte;[8]
The nesh[9] yonge coweslepe bendethe wyth the dewe;
The trees enlefed,[10] yntoe heavenne straughte,[11]
Whenn gentle wyndes doe blowe, to whestlyng[12] dynne[13]
    ys broughte.

The evenynge commes, and brynges the dewe alonge;
The roddie[14] welkynne[15] sheeneth to the eyne;
Arounde the alestake[16] mynstrells synge the songe;
Yonge ivie rounde the doore poste do entwyne;
I laie mee onn the grasse; yette, to mie wylle,
Albeytte alle ys fayre, there lackethe somethynge stylle.

---

1 Sweatly.	3 Stretch.	5 Rack.	4 Budding.
5 Blush.	6 Meadows.	7 Sprinkled.	8 Clothed.
9 Tender.	10 Full of leaves.	11 Stretched.	12 Whistling.
13 Sound.	14 Red.	15 Sky.	16 Maypole.

SECONDE MYNSTRELLE.

So Adam thoughtenne,[1] whann, ynn Paradyse,
All heavenn and erthe dyd hommage to hys mynde;
Ynn womman alleyne[2] manaes pleasaunce lyes;
As instrumentes of joie were made the kynde.
Go, take a wyfe untoe thie armes, and see
Wynter, and brownie[3] hylles, wyll have a charme for
    thee.

THYRDE MYNSTRELLE.

Whanne Autumpne blake[4] and sonne-brente[5] doe
    appere,
Wyth hys goulde honde guylteynge[6] the falleynge lefe,
Bryngeynge oppe Wynterr to folfylle[7] the yere,
Beerynge uponne hys backe the riped shefe;
Whan al the hyls wythe woddie sede ys whyte;
Whanne levynne-fyres[8] and lemes[9] do mete from far the
    syghte;

Whann the fayre apple, rudde[10] as even skie,
Do bende the tree unto the fructyle[11] grounde;
When joicie[12] peres,[13] and berries of blacke die,
Doe daunce yn ayre, and call the eyne arounde;
Thann, bee the even foule, or even fayre,
Meethynckes mie hartys joie ys steynced[14] wyth somme
    care.

---

[1] Thought.   [2] Alone.   [3] Brown.   [4] Naked.
[5] Sun-burnt.   [6] Gilding.   [7] Fill up.   [8] Flashes of lightning.
[9] Meteors.   [10] Red.   [11] Fertile.   [12] Juicy.
[13] Pears.   [14] Stained, alloyed.

SECONDE MYNSTRELLE.

Angelles bee wrogte[1] to bee of neidher kynde;
Angelles alleyne fromme chafe[2] desyre bee free:
Dheere[3] ys a somwhatte evere yn the mynde,
Yatte, wythout wommanne, cannot stylled bee;
Ne seyncte yn celles, botte, havynge blodde and tere,[4]
Do fynde the spryte to joie on syghte of wommanne
        fayre:

Wommen bee made, notte for hemselves botte manne,
Bone of hys bone, and chyld of hys desire;
Fromme an ynutylle[5] membere fyrste beganne,
Ywroghte[6] with moche[7] of water, lyttele fyre;
Therefore theie seke the fyre of love, to hete
The milkyness of kynde, and make hemselves complete.

Albeytte, wythout wommen, menne were pheeres[8]
To salvage kynde, and wulde botte lyve to slea,
Botte wommenne efte[9] the spryghte of peace so
        cheres,[10]
Tochelod[11] yn Angel joie heie[12] Angeles bee;
Go, take thee swythyn[13] to thie bedde a wyfe,
Bee bante[14] or blessed hie[15] yn proovynge marryage
        lyfe.

---

[1] Formed. [2] Hot. [3] There. [4] Health.
[5] Useless. [6] Composed. [7] Much. [8] Fellows, equals.
[9] Often. [10] Cherishes, soothes. [11] Joined.
[12] They. [13] Quickly. [14] Cursed. [15] Highly.

Anodher Mynstrelles Songe bie Syr Thybbot Gorges.

As Elynour bie the green lesselle[1] was syttynge,[2]
  As from the sones hete she harried,[3]
She sayde, as herr whytte hondes whyte hosen was
    knyttynge,
  Whatte pleasure ytt ys to be married!

[1] Arbour.

[2] From the sublime irregularity of the Pindaric and the stately solemnity of the Rithme royal, our author sometimes descends to sport in lighter strains. The desultory genius of Rowley disdained the dull identity, not only of a beaten, but of a common track. In the 'Tragedy of Ella,' we have an ode, of which this is one of the stanzas:—

  "Mie husbande, lorde Thomas, a forrester boulde,
    As every clove pynne, or the baskette,
  Does no cherysauncys from Elynoure houlde,
    I have ytte as soon as I aske ytte."

In Durfey's 'Pills to purge Melancholy,' or some other book of Pills for the same salutary purpose, I remember an old Somersetshire ballad, yet certainly not older than the latter end of the last century, which exhibits, I believe for the first time, the same structure of stanza.

  "Go find out the vicar of Taunton Dean,
    And he'll tell you the banns they were asked,
  A thumping fat capon he had for his pains,
    And I skewer'd her up in a basket."

The old Chaucerian word 'cherisauncey,' in Chatterton's stanza, never danced so gaily before. But it is not so much to the movement, as to the double rhymes, that I here object.

There are I confess some double rhymes in Chaucer's 'Romant of the Rose,' but they are accidental, and they were suggested by correspondent French words and couplets in the French original. In our present instance, the double rhyme is constitutive of a peculiar conformation of stanza, of which it is one of the essential properties. An ode was to be written with a regular and imposed return of this duplication. To say nothing in the mean time, that Chatterton took, perhaps imperceptibly, the two words here employed for double rhymes, from the ballad I have cited. The double rhyme is now adapted to the comic and familiar style: and the unexpected consonancy often gives an air of burlesque. Not one example occurs in Chaucer's burlesque poem of Sir Thopas. Nor was it scarcely ever used under any circumstances by the elder poets, except in translation.—WARTON.   [3] Hastened.

Mie husbande, Lorde Thomas, a forrester boulde,
  As ever clove pynne,[1] or the baskette,[2]
Does no cherysauncys[3] from Elynour houlde,
  I have ytte as soone as I aske ytte.

Whann I lyved wyth my fadre yn merrie Cloud-dell,
  Tho' twas at my liefe[4] to mynde spynnynge,
I stylle wanted somethynge, botte whatte ne coulde telle,
  Mie lorde fadres barbde[5] haulle[6] han ne wynnynge.[7]

Eche mornynge I ryse, doe I sette mie maydennes,
  Somme to spynn, somme to curdell,[8] somme bleachynge,
Gyff any new entered doe aske for mie aidens,[9]
  Thann swythynne[10] you fynde mee a teachynge.

---

[1] It is a part of Sir Thomas's character that he was—

> "—— A forester bold,
> As ever clove pin, or the basket."

Alluding probably to his skill in archery and backsword, two principal
amusements of gentlemen in those days, and both connected with the
character of a forester. The 'pin' was the centre of a butt or shield
erected as a mark for the archers; and the cleaving it with the arrow
showed the perfection of the archer's skill. In allusion to this, in a trial
of archery (Love's Labour Lost, Act v. sc. 1), Costard says of Marcia:
"Then will she get the upshot by 'cleaving the pin.'" The shields
with which they protected themselves, or the guard that surrounded
the wrist of their sword arm, were made of *basket or wicker-work*, and
it shewed the strength and dexterity of the combatant to cleave it with
his sword.—DEAN MILLES.

[2] Terms in archery.   [3] Comforts.   [4] Choice.
[5] The word 'barbde' is peculiarly appropriated to horses, and there-
fore misapplied here.—SOUTHEY. Its meaning in the text is, "Hung
with armour.

[6] Hall.   [7] Allurements.   [8] Card.
[9] Assistance.   [10] Immediately.

Lorde Walterre, mie fadre,[1] he loved me welle,
  And nothynge unto mee was nedeynge,
Botte schulde I agen goe to merrie Cloud-dell,
  In sothen[2] twoulde bee wythoute redeynge.[3]

Shee sayde, and lorde Thomas came over the lea,
  As hee the fatte derkynnes[4] was chacynge,
Shee putte uppe her knyttynge, and to hym wente shee;
  So wee leave hem bothe kyndelie embracynge.

ÆLLA.

I lyche eke thys; goe ynn untoe the feaste;
  Wee wylle permytte you antecedente[5] bee;
There swotelie synge eche carolle,[6] and yaped[7] jeaste;
  And there ys monnie, that you merrie bee;
Comme, gentle love, wee wylle toe spouse-feaste goe,
And there ynn ale and wyne bee dreyncted[8] everych woe.

ÆLLA, BIRTHA, CELMONDE, MESSENGERE.

MESSENGERE.

Ælla, the Danes ar thondrynge onn our coaste;
Lyche scolles[9] of locusts, caste oppe bie the sea,
Magnus and Hurra, wythe a doughtie[10] hoaste,
Are ragyng, to be quansed[11] bie none botte thee;

---

[1] Father. [2] Truth. [3] Wisdom, deliberation.
[4] Young deer. [5] To go before. [6] Song. [7] Laughable.
[8] Drowned. [9] Shoals. [10] Valiant. [11] Stilled, quenched.

Haste, swyfte as Levynne[1] to these royners[2] flee :
Thie dogges alleyne can tame thys ragynge bulle.
Haste swythyn, fore[3] anieghe[4] the towne theie bee,
And Wedecesterres rolle of dome bee fulle.
Haste, haste, O Ælla, to the byker[5] flie,
For yn a momentes space tenne thousand menne maie
          die.

ÆLLA.

Beshrew thee for thie newes ! I moste be gon,
Was ever lockless dome so hard as myne !
Thos from dysportysmente[6] to warr to ron,
To chaunge the selke[7] veste for the gaberdyne ![8]

BIRTHA.

O ! lyche a nedere,[9] lette me rounde thee twyne,
And hylte[10] thie boddie from the schaftes of warre.
Thou shalte nott, must not, from thie Birtha ryne,[11]
Botte kenn the dynne of slughornes[12] from afarre.

ÆLLA.

O love, was thys thie joie, to shewe the treate,
Than groffyshe[13] to forbydde thie hongered guestes to
          eate ?

---

[1] Lightning.   [2] Ravagers.   [3] Before.   · [4] Near.
[5] Battle.   [6] Enjoyment.   [7] Silk.   [8] Military cloak.
[9] Adder.   [10] Hide.   [11] Run.
[12] Warlike instruments of music.   [13] Rudely, sternly.

O mie upswalynge[1] harte, whatt wordes can saie
The peynes, thatte passethe ynn mie soule ybrente?[2]
Thos to bee torne uponne mie spousalle daie,
O! 'tys a peyne beyond entendemente.[3]
Yee mychtie Goddes, and is yor favoures sente
As thous faste dented[4] to a loade of peyne?
Moste wee aie holde yn chace the shade content,
And for a bodykyn[5] a swarthe[6] obteyne?
O! whie, yee seynctes, oppress yee thos mie sowle?
How shalle I speke mie woe, mie freme,[7] mie dreerie[8]
    dole?[9]

CELMONDE.

Sometyme the wyseste lacketh pore mans rede.[10]
Reasonne and counynge wytte efte[11] flees awaie.
Thanne, loverde[12] lett me saie, wyth hommaged drede,
(Bieneth your fote ylayn[13]) mie counselle saie;
Gyff thos wee lett the matter lethlen[14] laie,
The foemenn, everych honde-poyncte,[15] getteth fote.
Mie loverde, lett the speere-menne, dyghte[16] for fraie,[17]
And all the sabbataners[18] goe aboute.
I speke, mie loverde, alleyne[19] to upryse
Youre wytte from marvelle, and the warriour to alyse.[20]

---

[1] Swelling.   [2] Burnt up.   [3] Comprehension.   [4] Joined.
[5] Body, substance.   [6] Ghost, or shadow.   [7] Strange.
[8] Dire, grievous.   [9] Sorrow.   [10] Counsel, advise.   [11] Often.
[12] Lord.   [13] Prostrate, lying.   [14] Still, dead
[15] Moment.   [16] Prepared.   [17] Battle.
[18] Booted soldiers.—"Answering," says Dean Milles, "to Homer's ἐυκ-
νημίδες Ἀχαιοι."   Lidgate uses the word 'sabaton' for a soldier's
boot, and 'sabot' is the modern French name for a slipper.
[19] Only.   [20] Set free. See additional Note at the end of Ælla.

ÆLLA.

Ah! nowe thou pottest takells[1] yn mie harte;
Mie soulghe[2] dothe nowe begynne to see herselle;
I wylle upryse mie myghte, and doe mie parte,
To slea the foemenne yn mie furie felle.[3]
Botte howe canne tynge[4] mie rampynge fourie[5] telle,
Whyche ryseth from mie love to Birtha fayre?
Ne coulde the queede,[6] and alle the myghte of Helle,
Founde out impleasaunce[7] of syke blacke ageare.[8]
Yette I wylle bee mieselfe, and rouze mie spryte
To acte wythe rennome,[9] and goe meet the bloddie
    fyghte.

BIRTHA.

No, thou schalte never leave thie Birtha's syde;
Ne schall the wynde uponne us blowe alleyne;
I, lyche a nedre,[10] wylle untoe thee byde;
Tyde[11] lyfe, tyde deathe, ytte shall behoulde us
    twayne.
I have mie parte of dreerie[12] dole[13] and peyne;
Itte brasteth[14] from mee atte the holtred[15] eyne;
Ynne tydes of teares mie swarthynge[16] spryte wyll
    drayne,
Gyff drerie dole ys thyne, tys twa tymes myne.
Goe notte, O Ælla; wythe thie Birtha staie;
For wyth thie semmlykeed[17] mie spryte wyll goe awaie.

---

1 Arrows, darts.	2 Soul.	3 Pernicious.	4 Tongue.
5 Fury.	6 Devil.	7 Unpleasantness.	
8 Appearance, dress.	9 Renown.	10 Adder.	11 Betide.
12 Grievous.	13 Sorrow.	14 Bursteth.	15 Hidden.
16 Dying.	17 Countenance.		

ÆLLA.

O! tys for thee, for thee alleyne I fele ;
. Yett I muste bee mieselfe; with valoures gear
I'lle dyghte mie hearte, and notte[1] mie lymbes yn stele,
And shake the bloddie swerde and steyned spere.[*]

BIRTHA.

Can Ælla from hys breaste hys Birtha teare?
Is shee so rou[2] and ugsomme[3] to hys syghte?
Entrykeynge[4] wyght![5] ys leathall[6] warre so deare?
Thou pryzest mee belowe the joies of fyghte.
Thou scalte notte leave mee, albeytte the erthe
Hong pendaunte[7] bie thie swerde, and craved for thy
    morthe.[8]

---

[1] Cloathe, prepare, fasten.

[*] These poems exhibit, both in the connection of words and sentences, a facility of combination, a quickness of transition, a rapidity of apostrophe, a frequent variation of form and phrase, and a firmness of contexture, which must have been the result of a long establishment of the arts and habits of writing. The versification is equally vigorous and harmonious, and is formed on a general elegance and stability of expression. It is remarkable, that whole stanzas sparkle with that brilliancy, which did not appear in our poetry till towards the middle of the present century. The lines have all the tricks and trappings, all the sophistications of poetical style, belonging to those models which were popular when Chatterton began to write verses.

Our old English poets are minute and particular. They do not deal in abstraction and general exhibition, the effects of affectation and a restless pursuit of novelty. They dwell on realities. Even in the course of narration or description, where poets of the fourteenth or fifteenth centuries would have used the literal expression, and represented the subject by the mention of natural circumstances, the writer of these pieces adopts ideal terms and artificial modes of telling a fact, and too frequently falls into metaphor, metaphysical imagery, and incidental personification.—WARTON.

[2] Horrid, ugly.   [3] Terrible.   [4] Deceitful.   [5] Man.
[6] Deadly.   [7] Depending.   [8] Death.

ÆLLA.

Dyddest thou kenne howe mie woes, as starres ybrente, [1]
Headed bie these thie wordes doe onn mee falle,
Thou woulde stryve to gyve mie harte contente,
Wakyng mie slepynge mynde to honnoures calle.
Of selynesse[2] I pryze thee moe yan all
Heaven can mee sende, or counynge wytt acquyre,
Yette I wylle leave thee, onne the foe to falle,
Retournynge to thie eyne with double fyre.

BIRTHA.

Moste Birtha boon[3] requeste and bee denyd?
Receyve attenes[4] a darte yn selynesse and pryde?
Doe staie, att leaste tylle morrowes sonne apperes.

ÆLLA.

Thou kenneste welle the Dacyannes myttee[5] powere;
Wythe them a mynnute wurchethe[6] bane[7] for yeares;
Theie undoe reaulmes wythyn a syngle hower.
Rouze all thie honnoure, Birtha; look attoure[8]
Thie bledeynge countrie, whych for hastie dede
Calls, for the rodeynge[9] of some doughtie[10] power,
To royn yttes royners,[11] make yttes foemenne blede.

BIRTHA.

Rouze all thie love; false and entrykyng[12] wyghte!
Ne leave thie Birtha thos uponne pretence of fyghte.

---

[1] Burning. [2] Happiness. [3] A favour.
[4] At once. BAILEY, KERSEY, and SPEGHT, who evidently copied it
from one another. "I very much suspect that the word *attenes* stands
upon no better authority than a misprint in Chaucer, C. T. ver. 4072."
—TYRWHITT.
[5] Mighty. [6] Worketh. [7] Calamity, damage. [8] Around.
[9] Command. [10] Valiant. [11] Ravagers. [12] Deceitful.

Thou nedest notte goe, untyll thou haste command
Under the sygnette¹ of oure lord the kynge.

ÆLLA.

And wouldest thou make me then a recreande?²
Hollie Seyncte Marie, keepe mee from the thynge!
Heere, Birtha, thou hast potte a double stynge,
One for thie love, anodher for thie mynde.

BIRTHA.

Agylted³ Ælla, thie abredynge⁴ blynge.⁵
'Twas love of thee thatte foule intente ywrynde.⁶
Yette heare mie supplycate, to mee attende,
Hear from mie groted⁷ harte the lover and the friende.

Lett Celmonde yn thie armour-brace⁸ be dyghte;⁹
And yn thie stead unto the battle goe;
Thie name alleyne wylle putte the Danes to flyghte,
The ayre thatt beares ytt woulde presse downe the foe.

ÆLLA.

Birtha, yn vayne thou wouldste mee recreand doe¹⁰;
I moste, I wylle, fyghte for mie countries wele,¹¹
And leave thee for ytt. Celmonde, sweftlie goe,
Telle mie Brystowans to [be] dyghte yn stele;

---

¹ Seal.   ² Coward.   ³ Offended.   ⁴ Upbraiding.
⁵ 'Blynge,' to cease, desist. The verb 'to blyn,' is in Bailey.
⁶ 'Ywrynde,' revealed, whispered. [The proper word is 'yrowned.'
Thus Chaucer, in the *Wife of Bath's Prologue*—
   "What rown'st 'ow with our maid?'
for ' What rownest (or whisperest) thou?' &c.—ED.]
⁷ Swollen.   ⁸ Suit of armour.   ⁹ Cloathed.
¹⁰ Persuade me to be a coward.   ¹¹ Welfare.

Tell hem I scorne to kenne hem from afar,
Botte leave the vyrgyn brydall bedde for bedde of warre.

ÆLLA, BIRTHA.

BIRTHA.

And thou wylt goe: O mie agroted[1] harte!

ÆLLA.

Mie countrie waites mie marche; I muste awaie;
Albeytte I schulde goe to mete the darte
Of certen dethe, yette here I woulde notte staie.
Botte thos to leave thee, Birtha, dothe asswaie[2]
Moe torturynge peynes yanne canne be sedde bie
    tyngue.[3]
Yette rouze thie honoure uppe, and wayte the daie,
Whan rounde aboute mee songe of warre heie[4] synge.
O Birtha, strev[5] mie agreeme[6] to accaie,[7]
And joyous see mie armes, dyghte oute ynn warre arraie.

BIRTHA.

Difficile[8] ys the pennaunce, yette I'lle strev
To keepe mie woe behyltren[9] yn mie breaste.
Albeytte nete maye to mee pleasaunce yev,[10]
Lyche thee, I'lle strev to sette mie mynde atte reste.

---

[1] ['Agroted,' swollen. Used by Chaucer in the sense of 'surfeited,' as
in *The Legend of Phyllis*. Perhaps ægroted, or sick.—ED.]
[2] Assay.   [3] Tongue.   [4] They.   [5] Strive.
[6] ['Agreeme,' torture. Chaucer has the participle 'agramed,' in the
sense of 'grieved.' Chatterton might have found it by reference to
Bailey.—ED.]
[7] Assuage.   [8] Difficult.   [9] Hid.   [10] Give.

Yett oh! forgeve, yff I have thee dystreste;
Love, doughtie love, wylle beare no odher swaie.
Juste as I was wythe Ælla to be bleste,
Shappe[1] foullie thos hathe snatched hym awaie.
It was a tene[2] too doughtie to bee borne,
Wydhout an ounde[3] of teares and breaste wyth syghes
 ytorne.[4]

ÆLLA.

Thie mynde ys now thieselfe; why wylte thou bee
All blanche,[5] al kyngelie, all soe wyse yn mynde,
Alleyne to lett pore wretched Ælla see,
Whatte wondrous bighes[6] he now muste leave behynde?
O Birtha fayre, warde[7] everyche commynge wynde,
On everych[8] wynde I wylle a token sende :
Onn mie longe shielde ycorne[9] thie name thoul't fynde
Butte here commes Celmonde, wordhie[10] knyghte and
 friende.

ÆLLA, BIRTHA, CELMONDE speaking.

Thie Brystowe knyghtes for thie forth-comynge lynge[11]
Echone athwarte hys backe hys longe warre-shield
 dothe slynge.

ÆLLA.

Birtha, adieu; but yette I cannotte goe.

BIRTHA.

Lyfe of mie spryte, mie gentle Ælla, staie.
Engyne[12] mee notte wyth syke a dreerie woe.

---

[1] Fate	[2] Pain or torment.	[3] Flood.	[4] Rent.
[5] Fair.	[6] Jewels.	[7] Watch.	[8] Every.
[9] Engraved.	[10] Worthy.	[11] Stay.	[12] Torture.

ÆLLA.

I muste, I wylle ; tys honnoure cals awaie.

BIRTHA.

O mie agroted¹ harte, braste,² braste ynn twaie.³
Ælla, for honnoure, flyes awaie from mee.

ÆLLA.

Birtha, adieu ; I maie notte here obaie.⁴
I'm flyynge from mieselfe yn flying thee.

BIRTHA.

O Ælla, housband, friend, and loverde,⁵ staie.
He's gon, he's gone, alass ! percase⁶ he's gone for aie.

CELMONDE.*

Hope, hallie⁷ suster,⁸ sweepeynge thro' the skie,
In crowne of goulde, and robe of lillie whyte,

| ¹ Swelling. | ² Burst. | ³ Twain. |
| ⁴ Wait, abide. | ⁵ Lord. | ⁶ Perhaps, by chance. |

* This soliloquy of Celmonde is indisputably one of the most distinguished passages in the play for its lofty ideas, powerful imagery, and poetic expression; nor is it, in point of reasoning, unlike or unequal to Shakspeare. How far does Spenser's description of Hope fall short of our poet's image !

" With Fear went Hope in rank ; a handsome maid,
And of a cheerful look, and lovely to behold ;
In silken samite she was light array'd,
And her fayre locks were woven up in gold,
She always smiled."   DEAN MILLES.

The piece of most conspicuous merit is 'Ella,' a Tragical Interlude, which is a most complete and well written tragedy. The plot is both interesting and full of variety, though the dialogue is in some places tedious. The character of Celmonde reminds us of Glenalvon in Douglas, but it is better drawn. His soliloquy is beautiful and characteristic.
—DR. GREGORY.

⁷ Holy.   ⁸ Sister.

Whyche farre abrode ynne gentle ayre doe flie,
Meetynge from dystaunce the enjoyous [1] syghte,
Albeytte [2] efte thou takest thie hie flyghte
Hecket [3] ynne a myste, and wyth thyne eyne yblente, [4]
Nowe commest thou to mee wythe starrie lyghte ;
Ontoe thie veste the rodde sonne ys adente ; [5]
The Sommer tyde, the month of Maie appere,
Depycte [6] wythe skylledd honde upponn thie wyde
aumere. [7]

I from a nete [8] of hopelen [9] am adawed, [10]
Awhaped [11] atte the fetyveness [12] of daie ;
Ælla, bie nete [13] moe thann hys myndbruche [14] awed,
Is gone, and I moste followe, toe the fraie.
Celmonde canne ne'er from anie byker [15] staie.
Dothe warre begynne ? there's Celmonde yn the place
Botte whanne the warre ys donne, I'll haste awaie.
The reste from nethe [16] tymes masque must shew yttes
face.
I see onnombered joies arounde mee ryse ;
Blake [17] stondethe future doome, and joie dothe mee
alyse. [18]

O honnoure, honnoure, what ys bie thee hanne? [19]
Hailie [20] the robber and the bordelyer, [21]

---

[1] Enraptured, joyful.   [2] Although.   [3] Wrapped closely, covered.
[4] Blinded.   [5] Fastened.   [6] Painted.
[7] Robe or girdle. See the additional Notes at the end of Ælla.
[8] Night.   [9] Hopelessness.
[10] Awakened.   [11] Astonished.   [12] Agreeableness.
[13] Nought.   [14] Emulation.   [15] Contest, battle.
[16] Beneath.   [17] Naked.   [18] Quit.
[19] Had.   [20] Happy.   [21] Peasant, cottager.

Who kens ne thee, or ys to thee bestanne,[1]
And nothynge does thie myckle[2] gastness[3] fere.
Faygne woulde I from mie bosomme all thee tare.
Thou there dysperpellest[4] thie levynne-bronde;[5]
Whylest mie soulgh's[6] forwyned,[7] thou art the gare;[8]
Sleene[9] ys mie comforte bie thie ferie[10] honde;
As somme talle hylle, whann wynds doe shake the
    ground,
Itte kerveth[11] all abroade, bie brasteynge[12] hyltren[13]
    wounde.

Honnoure, whatt bee ytte? tys a shadowes shade,
A thynge of wychencref,[14] an idle dreme;
On of the fonnis[15] whych the clerche[16] have made
Menne wydhoute sprytes, and wommen for to fleme,[17]
Knyghtes, who efte kenne the loude dynne of the
    beme,[18]
Schulde be forgarde[19] to syke enfeeblynge waies,
Make everych acte, alyche[20] theyr soules, be breme,[21]
And for theyre chyvalrie alleyne have prayse.
    O thou, whatteer thie name,
        Or Zabalus[22] or Queed,[23]
    Comme, steel mie sable spryte,
        For fremde[24] and dolefulle dede.

---

[1] Opposed, lost.   [2] Great.   [3] Terribleness.   [4] Scatterest.
[5] Lightning.   [6] Soul.   [7] Withered.   [8] Cause.
[9] Slain.   [10] Fiery.   [11] Cutteth, layeth waste.
[12] Bursting.   [13] Hidden.
[14] Witchcraft.—KERSEY and BAILEY.
                                                        [15] Devices.
[16] Church.   [17] Terrify.   [18] Trumpet.   [19] Lost.
[20] Like.   [21] Furious   [22] The devil.   [23] The devil.
[24] Strange.

MAGNUS, HURRA, *and* HIE PREESTE, *wyth the*
ARMIE, *neare* WATCHETTE.

MAGNUS.

Swythe¹ lette the offrendes² to the Goddes begynne,
To knowe of hem the issue of the fyghte.
Potte the blodde-steyned sword and pavyes³ ynne;
Spreade swythyn all arounde the hallie⁴ lyghte.

HIE PREESTE *syngeth.*⁎

Yee, who hie yn mokie⁵ ayre
Delethe seasonnes foule or fayre.
Yee, who, whanne yee weere agguylte,⁶
The mone yn bloddie gyttelles⁷ hylte,
Mooved the starres, and dyd unbynde
Everyche barriere⁸ to the wynde;

---

¹ Quickly.   ² Offerings.   ³ Daggers.   ⁴ Holy.

⁎ The ancient language of these Poems is affected and unnatural.
Antiquated expressions are engrafted on present modes of speech. The
diction and versification are at perpetual variance. Our author is
smooth and mellifluous as Pope and Mason, and yet more obscure and
inexplicable than Gower or Chaucer. The conclusion must be that he
borrowed his language from glossaries and etymological English lexi-
cons, and not from life or practice. But he borrowed without selection
or discernment. He seems to have been persuaded that no other in-
gredient was necessary for his fiction than old words. He viewed an-
cient language as all of one age and one district. In dictionaries of
old English he saw words detached and separated from their context:
these he seized and combined with others, without considering their
relative or other accidental significations.—WARTON.

⁵ Mùrky, gloomy.

⁶ 'Agguylte,' offended. Thus in *The Romaunt of the Rose*—
  " He hathe her wrathe for evermore,
    He agilte her nere in odher case."—CHAUCER.

⁷ Mantles.   ⁸ Boundary.

Whanne the oundynge[1] waves dystreste,
Storven[2] to be overest,[3]
Sockeynge[4] yn the spyre-gyrte towne,
Swolterynge[5] wole natyones downe,
Sendynge dethe, on plagues astrodde,[6]
Moovynge lyke the erthys[7] Godde ;
To mee send your heste[8] dyvyne,
Lyghte eletten[9] all myne eyne,
Thatt I maie now undevyse[10]
All the actyonnes of th' empprize.[11]

　　　　　　　　[*falleth downe and efte[12] rysethe.*
Thus sayethe the Goddes; goe, yssue to the playne;
Forr there shall meynte of mytte[13] menne bee slayne.

MAGNUS.

Whie, soe there evere was, whanne Magnus foughte.
Efte have I treynted[14] noyance[15] throughe the hoaste,
Athorowe[16] swerdes, alyche the Queed[17] dystraughte,[18]
Have Magnus pressynge wroghte hys foemen loaste,[19]
As whanne a tempeste vexethe soare the coaste,
The dyngeynge[20] ounde[21] the sandeie stronde doe tare.
So dyd I inne the warre the javlynne toste,[22]
Full meynte[23] a champyonnes breaste received mie
　　spear.

---

1 Foaming, undulating.	2 Strove.	3 Uppermost.
4 Sucking.	5 Overwhelming.	6 Astride.
7 Earth's.	8 Command.	
9 Enlighten.	10 Explain.	11 Understanding.
12 Afterwards.	13 Mighty.	14 Scattered.
15 Destruction.	16 Through.	17 The devil.
18 Distracted.	19 Loss.	20 Noisy, sounding.
21 Wave.	22 Toss.	23 Many.

Mie sheelde, lyche sommere morie [1] gronfer [2] droke, [3]
Mie lethalle [4] speere, alyche a levyn-mylted [5] oke.

HURRA.

Thie wordes are greate, full hyghe of sound, and eeke [6]
Lyche thonderre, to the whych dothe comme no rayne.
Itte lacketh notte a doughtie [7] honde to speke ;
The cocke saiethe drefte, [8] yett armed ys he alleyne.
Certis thie wordes maie, thou motest have sayne
Of mee, and meynte of moe, who eke canne fyghte,
Who haveth trodden downe the adventayle, [9]
And tore the heaulmes [10] from heades of myckle
    myghte.
Sythence [11] syke myghte ys placed yn thie honde,
Lette blowes thie actyons speeke, and bie thie corrage
    stonde.

MAGNUS.

Thou are a warrioure, Hurra, thatte I kenne,
And myckle famed for thie handie dede.
Thou fyghtest anente [12] maydens and ne menne,
Nor aie thou makest armed hartes to blede.
Efte [13] I, caparyson'd on bloddie stede,
Havethe thee seene binethe mee ynn the fyghte,
Wythe corses I investynge [14] everich mede,
And thou aston, [15] and wondrynge at mie myghte.
Thanne wouldest thou comme yn for mie renome, [16]
Albeytte thou wouldst reyne [17] awaie from bloddie dome. [18]

---

1 Marshy.	2 Fen-fire, or meteor.	3 Dry.	4 Deadly.
5 Melted with lightning.		6 Amplification, or boast.	
7 Valiant.	8 Least.	9 Beaver.	10 Helmets.
11 Since.	12 Against.	13 Often.	14 Clothing.
15 Astonished.	16 Renown.	17 Run.	18 Fate.

Thou beest a worme so groffile¹ and so smal,
I wythe thie bloude woulde scorne to foul mie sworde,
Botte wythe thie weaponnes woulde upon thee falle,
Alyche thie owne feare, slea thee wythe a worde.
I Hurra amme miesel, and aie wylle bee,
As greate yn valourous actes, and yn commande as thee.

MAGNUS, HURRA, ARMYE, AND MESSENGERE.
MESSENGERE.

Blynne⁰ your contekions,² chiefs ; for, as I stode*
Uponne mie watche, I spiede an armie commynge,
Notte lyche ann handfulle of a fremded⁴ foe,
Botte blacke wythe armoure, movynge ugsomlie,⁵
Lyche a blacke fulle cloude, thatte dothe goe alonge
To droppe yn hayle, and hele⁶ the thonder storme.

MAGNUS.

Ar there meynte of them?

MESSENGERR.

Thycke as the ante-flyes ynne a sommer's none,
Seemynge as tho' theie stynge as persante⁷ too.

HURRA.

Whatte matters thatte? lettes sette oure warr-arraie.
Goe, sounde the beme,⁸ lette champyons prepare;
Ne doubtynge, we wylle stynge as faste as heie.
Whatte? doest forgard⁹ thie blodde? ys ytte for feare?

---

1 Abject.   2 Cease.   3 Contentions.
* [This is the first specimen of blank verse in the poem. There cer-
tainly is no reason for its introduction.—ED.]
4 Frighted.   5 Terribly.   6 Help.   7 Piercing.
8 Trumpet.   9 Lose.

Wouldest thou gayne the towne, and castle-stere,[1]
And yette ne byker[2] wythe the soldyer guarde ?
Go, hyde thee ynn mie tente annethe[3] the lere ;[4]
I of thie boddie wylle keepe watche and warde.

MAGNUS.

Oure goddes of Denmarke know mie harte ys goode.

HURRA.

For nete[5] uppon the erthe, botte to be choughens[6] foode

MAGNUS, HURRA, ARMIE, SECONDE MESSENGERRE.
SECONDE MESSENGERRE.

As from mie towre I kende[7] the commynge foe,
I spied the crossed shielde, and bloddie swerde,
The furyous Ælla's banner; wythynne kenne
The armie ys.   Dysorder throughe oure hoaste
Is fleynge, borne onne wynges of Ælla's name;
Styr, styr, mie lordes !

MAGNUS.

What? Ælla? and soe neare ?
Thenne Denmarques roiend ;[8] oh mie rysynge feare!

HURRA.

What doeste thou mene ? thys Ælla's botte a manne.
Nowe bie mie sworde, thou arte a verie berne.[9]

---

1 The hold of the castle. 2 Battle. 3 Underneath.
4 Leather, stuff. 5 Nought. 6 Ravens.
7 Perceived. 8 Ruined. 9 Child.

Of late I dyd thie creand [1] valoure scanne,
Whanne thou dydst boaste soe moche [2] of actyon derne. [3]
Botte I toe warr mie doeynges moste atturne,
To cheere the Sabbataneres [4] to deere [5] dede.

MAGNUS.

I to the knyghtes onne everyche syde wylle burne, [6]
Telleynge 'hem alle to make her foemen blede;
Sythe shame or deathe onne eidher syde wylle bee,
Mie harte I wylle upryse, [7] and inne the battelle slea.

ÆLLA, CELMONDE, AND ARMIE *near* WATCHETTE.

ÆLLA.

Now havynge done oure mattynes [8] and oure vowes,
Lette us for the intended fyghte be boune, [9]
And everyche champyone potte the joyous crowne
Of certane masterschyppe [10] upon hys glestreynge [11]
    browes.

As for mie harte, I owne ytt ys, as ere
Itte has beene ynn the sommer-sheene of fate,
Unknowen to the ugsomme [12] gratche [13] of fere;
Mie blodde embollen, [14] wythe masterie elate,
Boyles ynne mie veynes, and rolles ynn rapyd state,
Impatyente forr to mete the persante [15] stele,

---

1 Cowardly.   2 Much.   3 Terrible.
4 Booted soldiers.   5 Terrible.
6 [" Burne," says Dean Milles, " is probably a mistake for ' turne,' "
in which sense it must be read in the text.—ED.]
7 Rouse up.   8 Morning devotion.   9 Ready.
10 Victory.   11 Glittering.   12 Hideous.
13 Garb, dress.   14 Swelling.   15 Piercing.

And telle the worlde, thatte Ælla dyed as greate
As anie knyghte who foughte for Englondes weale.
Friends, kynne, and soldyerres, ynne blacke armore
    drere,[1]
Mie actyons ymytate, mie presente redynge[2] here.

There ys ne house, athrow thys shap-scurged[3] isle,
Thatte has ne loste a kynne yn these fell fyghtes,
Fatte blodde has sorfeeted[4] the hongerde soyle,
And townes enlowed[5] lemed[6] oppe the nyghtes.
Inne gyte[7] of fyre oure hallie[8] churche dheie dyghtes;[9]
Oure sonnes lies torven[10] ynne theyre smethynge[11] gore;
Oppe bie the rootes oure tree of lyfe dheie pyghtes,[12]
Vexynge oure coaste, as byllowes doe the shore.
Yee menne, gyf ye are menne, displaie yor name,
Ybrende[13] yer tropes, alyche the roarynge tempest flame.

Ye Chrystyans, doe as wordhie of the name;
These roynerres[14] of oure hallie houses slea;
Braste,[15] lyke a cloude, from whence doth come the
    flame,
Lyche torrentes, gushynge downe the mountaines, bee.
And whanne alonge the grene yer champyons flee,
Swefte as the rodde for-weltrynge[16] levyn-bronde,[17]
Yatte hauntes the flyinge mortherer oere the lea,
Soe flie oponne these royners of the londe.

---

1 Terrible.   2 Advice.   3 Fate-scourged.   4 Surfeited, cloyed.
5 Flamed, fired.   6 Lighted.   7 Dress.
8 Holy.   9 Cloath.   10 Dead.   11 Smoking.
12 Pluck.   13 Consume. 14 Ravagers.   15 Burst.
16 Blasting.   17 Flash of lightning.

Lette those yatte¹ are unto yer battayles² fledde,
Take slepe eterne³ uponne a feerie 'lowynge⁵ bedde.

Let cowarde Londonne see herre towne on fyre,
And strev⁶ wythe goulde to staie the royners honde,
Ælla and Brystowe have the thoughtes thattes hygher,
Wee fyghte notte forr ourselves, botte all the londe.
As Severnes hyger⁷ lyghethe⁸ banckes of sonde,
Pressynge ytte downe binethe the reynynge⁹ streme,
Wythe dreerie¹⁰ dynn enswolters¹¹ the hyghe stronde,
Beerynge the rockes alonge ynn fhurye¹² breme,¹³
Soe wylle wee beere the Dacyanne armie downe,
And throughe a storme of blodde wyll reache the cham-
    pyon crowne.

Gyff ynn thys battelle locke¹⁴ ne wayte oure gare,¹⁵
To Brystowe dheie wylle tourne yeyre fhuyrie dyre;
Brystowe, and alle her joies, wylle synke toe ayre,
Brendeynge¹⁶ perforce wythe unenhantende¹⁷ fyre:

---

1 That.   2 Ships, boats.   3 Eternal.
4 Fiery.   5 Flaming.   6 Strive.
7 The most favourite allusion of Rowley, because it is three times
mentioned, (Battle of Hastings, ver. 326, 691, and above in Ælla,) is the
'hygra,' or as it is vulgarly called 'The bore of the Severn,' which con-
sists of a high wall of water, gradually accumulated from the strong
influence of the Atlantic ocean into the Bristol channel, and contracted
by the narrowing banks on each side, till at last it breaks with fury
against them, and on the channel of the river. Drayton has given
a picturesque description of this 'hygra' at the beginning of his seventh
Canto.—DEAN MILLES. See additional notes at the end of Ælla.
8 Lodgeth.   9 Running.   10 Terrible.
11 Swallows, sucks in. 12 Fury.   13 Fierce.
14 Luck.   15 Cause.   16 Burning.
17 Unaccustomed.

Thenne lette oure safetie doublie moove oure ire,
Lyche wolfyns,[1] rovynge for the evnynge pre,[2]
Seeing the lambe and shepsterr[3] nere the brire,
Doth th'one forr safetie, th'one for hongre slea;
Thanne, whanne the ravenne[4] crokes uponne the playne,
Oh! lette ytte bee the knelle to myghtie Dacyanns slayne.

---

1 Wolves.   2 Prey.   3 Shepherd.

4 It is asked, how Chatterton could have gained a knowledge of the raven-standard of the Danes, or that the raven was revered by that people? We have these instances in the tragedy of Ella, a Danish story :—

> "The Danes, wythe terroure rulynge at their hedde,
> Threw downe their banner talle, and lyche a raven fledde."

Again, the Danish soldiers say,

> "Onne, Ella, onn, we long for bloddie fraie,
> We longe to heare the raven," &c.

And the Danish leader Ella says,

> "Thanne, whanne the ravenn crokes uponne the playne,
> Oh lette ytt be the knelle to myghtie Dacians slayne."

And the chorus says,

> "Harke the ravenne flaps hys wing."

Mr. Bryant supposes that this piece of recondite northern mythology was inaccessibly shut up in Spelman, Asser, the Saxon Chronicle, Pontanus, and Olaus Wormius." But Chatterton seems to have had his intelligence from Thomson's *Masque of Alfred*, a common play-book, where the raven-standard of the Danes is thus poetically described :—

> ———— Is not yon pictured raven
> Their famous magic standard? Emblem fit
> To speak the savage genius of the people.——
> ———— 'Tis the same,
> Wrought by the sisters of the Danish king,
> Of furious Ivar, in a midnight hour;
> While the sick moon, at their enchanted song,
> Wrapt in pale tempest, labour'd through the clouds :
> The demons of destruction then, they say,
> Were all abroad, and mixing with their woof
> Their baleful power : the sisters ever sung,
> "Shake, standard, shake this ruin on our foes!"

And the hermit says,

> "The raven droops his wing—and, hark! the trumpet," &c.

Let me add, that Chatterton's idea of writing a play on a Danish story might have been suggested by this very masque. He is allowed to have

Lyche a rodde gronfer,[1] shalle mie anlace[2] sheene,
Lyche a strynge[3] lyoncelle[4] I'lle bee ynne fyghte,
Lyche fallynge leaves the Dacyannes shall bee sleene,[5]
Lyche aloud dynnynge[6] streeme scalle[7] be mie myghte.
Ye menne, who woulde deserve the name of knyghte,
Lette bloddie teares bie all your paves[8] be wepte ;
To commynge tymes no poyntelle[9] shalle ywrite,
Whanne Englonde han her foemenn, Brystow slepte.
Yourselfes, youre chyldren, and youre fellowes crie,
Go, fyghte ynn rennomes[10] gare,[11] be brave, and wynne
    or die.

I saie ne moe ; youre spryte the reste wylle saie ;
Youre spryte wylle wrynne,[12] thatte Brystow ys yer
    place ;
To honoures house I nede notte marcke the waie ;
Inne youre owne hartes you maie the foote-pathe trace.
'Twexte[13] shappe[14] and us there ys botte lyttelle space ;
The tyme ys nowe to proove yourselves bee menne ;

---

been a reader of Thomson. It is also to be observed, that both dramas
are built on the same point of the Danish history in England, the land-
ing of the Danes in Somersetshire. One of Chatterton's persons is
'Hurra.' Mr. Bryant says, that the proper name 'Hubba' might by
an unexperienced transcriber be easily taken for 'Hurra.' It is very
true, that Hubba is the right reading, as Chatterton well knew from
these lines in his favourite Thomson's *Masque:*
    "The valiant Hubba bites the bloody field,
        With twice six hundred Danes around him strow'd."
Chatterton, I presume, might have his reasons for converting 'Hubba'
into 'Hurra.'—WARTON.

1 Fen meteor.	2 Sword.	3 Strong.	4 Lion's whelp.
5 Slain.	6 Sounding.	7 Shall.	8 Daggers.
9 Pen.	10 Reputation.	11 Cause.	12 Discover.
13 Between.	14 Fate.		

Drawe forthe the bornyshed[1] bylle wythe fetyve[2] grace,
Rouze, lyche a wolfynne rouzing from hys denne.
Thus I enrone[3] mie anlace;[4] go thou shethe ;
I'lle potte ytt ne ynn place, tyll ytte ys sycke wythe
    deathe.

SOLDYERS.

Onn, Ælla, onn ; we longe for bloddie fraie ;
Wee longe to here the raven synge yn vayne ;
Onn, Ælla, onn ; we certys gayne the daie,
Whanne thou doste leade us to the leathal[5] playne.

CELMONDE.

Thie speche, O Loverde,[6] fyreth the whole trayne ;
Theie pancte for war, as honted wolves for breathe ;
Go, and sytte crowned on corses of the slayne ;
Go, and ywielde[7] the massie swerde of deathe.

SOLDYERRES.

From thee, O Ælla, alle oure courage reygnes ;
Echone yn phantasie do lede the Danes ynne chaynes.

ÆLLA.

Mie countrymenne, mie friendes, your noble sprytes
Speke yn youre eyne, and doe yer master telle.
Swefte as the rayne-storme toe the erthe alyghtes,
Soe wylle we fall upon these royners felle.

---

1 Burnished.   2 Agreeable, comely.   3 Unsheath.   4 Sword.
5 Deadly.   6 Lord.   7 Wield.

Oure mowynge swerdes shalle plonge hem downe to
    helle ;
Theyre throngynge corses shall onlyghte[1] the starres;
The barrowes[2] brastynge[3] wythe the sleene schall
    swelle,
Brynnynge[4] to commynge tymes our famous warres;
Iune everie eyne I kenne the lowe[5] of myghte,
Sheenynge abrode, alyche a hylle-fyre ynne the nyghte.

Whanne poyntelles[6] of oure famous fyghte shall saie,
Echone wylle marvelle atte the dernie[7] dede,
Echone wylle wyssen[8] hee hanne seene the daie,
And bravelie holped to make the foemenn blede;
Botte for yer holpe oure battelle wylle notte nede ;
Oure force ys force enowe to staie theyre honde;
Wee wylle retourne unto thys grened mede,
Oer corses of the foemen of the londe.
Nowe to the warre lette all the slughornes[9] sounde,
The Dacyanne troopes appere on yinder[10] rysynge grounde.
Chiefes, heade youre bandes, and leade.

DANES *flyinge, neare* WATCHETTE.

FYRSTE DANE.

Fly, fly, ye Danes! Magnus, the chiefe, ys sleene ;
The Saxonnes come wythe Ælla atte theyre heade ;
Lette's strev[11] to gette awaie to yinder greene ;
Flie, flie; thys ys the kyngdomme of the deadde.

---

1 Darken.	2 Tombs.	3 Bursting.	4 Declaring.
5 Flame.	6 Pens.	7 Valiant.	8 Wish.
9 Warlike instruments of music.	10 Yonder.	11 Strive.	

SECONDE DANE.

O goddes ! have thousandes bie mie anlace[1] bledde,
And muste I nowe for safetie flie awaie ?
See ! farre besprenged[2] alle oure troopes are spreade,
Yette I wylle synglie dare the bloddie fraie.
Botte ne ;[3] I'lle flie, and morther[4] yn retrete ;
Deathe, blodde, and fyre, scalle[5] marke the goeynge of
    my feete.

THYRDE DANE.

Enthoghteynge[6] forr to scape the brondeynge[7] foe,
As nere unto the byllowd beche I came,
Farr offe I spied a syghte of myckle woe,
Oure spyrynge[8] battayles[9] wrapte ynn sayles of flame.
The burled[10] Dacyannes, who were ynne the same,
Fro syde to syde fledde the pursuyte of deathe ;
The swelleynge fyre yer corrage doe enflame,
Theie lepe ynto the sea, and bobblynge[11] yield yer
    breathe ;
Whylest those thatt bee uponne the bloddie playne,
Bee deathe-doomed captyves taene, or yn the battle
    slayne.

HURRA.

Nowe bie the goddes, Magnus, dyscourteous[12] knyghte,
Bie cravente[13] havyoure[14] havethe don oure woe,

---

1 Sword.   2 Scattered.   3 No.   4 Murder.
5 Shall.   6 Thinking.   7 Furious, enflamed.
8 Lofty.   9 Ships.   10 Armed.
11 The noise made by a man in drowning.   12 Ungenerous.
13 Coward.   14 Behaviour.

Despendynge[1] all the talle menne yn the fyghte,
And placeyng valourous menne where draffs[2] mote goe.
Sythence[3] oure fourtunie[4] havethe tourned soe,
Gader[5] the souldyers lefte to future shappe,[6]
To somme newe place for safetie we wylle goe,
Inne future daie wee wylle have better happe.
    Sounde the loude slughorne for a quicke forloyne;[7]
Lette all the Dacyannes swythe[8] unto oure banner joyne.

    Throw hamlettes[9] wee wylle sprenge[10] sadde dethe and
        dole,[11]
Bathe yn hotte gore, and wasch[12] ourselves thereynne:
Goddes! here the Saxonnes lyche a byllowe rolle.
I heere the anlacis[13] detested dynne.
    Awaie, awaie, ye Danes, to yonder penne;[14]
Wee now wylle make forloyne yn tyme to fyghte agenne.

CELMONDE, *near* WATCHETTE. *

O forr a spryte al feere![15] to telle the daie,
The daie whyche scal[16] astounde[17] the herers rede,[18]
    Makeynge oure foemennes envyynge hartes to blede,
Ybereynge[19] thro the worlde oure rennomde[20] name for aie.

1 Expending.
2 'Draffa' is an Anglo-Saxon word, signifying 'things thrown away
as unfit for use.' See Mr. Tyrwhitt's Glossary on Chaucer.—DEAN
MILLES.
    3 Since then.   4 Fortune, or conflict.   5 Collect.   6 Fate.
    7 Retreat.   8 Quickly.   9 Villages.   10 Scatter.
    11 Lamentation. 12 Wash.   13 Sword.   14 Eminence.
    15 "O! for a Muse of fire."—*Prologue to Henry V.*
    16 Shall.   17 Astonish.   18 Wisdom.
    19 Bearing.   20 Renowned.
    * The following soliloquy of Celmonde is very different from the
former, which related solely to his love, and his future intended treach-
ery against Ælla and Birtha. The present speech, which is a recapitu-
lation of the battle, consists of encomiums, very properly introduced,

Bryghte sonne[1] han ynn hys roddie robes byn dyghte,[2]
From the rodde Easte he flytted[3] wythe hys trayne,
The howers drewe awaie the geete[4] of nyghte,
Her sable tapistrie was rente yn twayne.
The dauncynge streakes bedecked heavennes playne,
And on the dewe dyd smyle wythe shemrynge[5] eie,
Lyche gottes[6] of blodde whyche doe blacke armoure
     steyne,
Sheenynge upon the borne[7] whyche stondeth bie;[*]
The souldyers stoode uponne the hillis syde,
Lyche yonge enlefed[8] trees whyche yn a forreste byde.

Ælla rose lyche the tree besette wyth brieres;
Hys talle speere sheenynge as the starres at nyghte,
Hys eyne ensemeynge[9] as a lowe[10] of fyre;
Whanne he encheered everie manne to fyghte,
Hys gentle wordes dyd moove eche valourous knyghte;

---

on Ælla's conduct, and no less impartially contrasted with his own principles and behaviour. Without the least suspicion of plagiarism, it corresponds with the speech of Richard III., in Shakspeare; the former imputes the deformities of his mind to the qualities of his parents, the latter connects them with the deformities of his body.— DEAN MILLES.

1   " Heaven's gates, spontaneous, open to the powers,
       Heaven's golden gates, kept by the winged hours;
       Commission'd in alternate watch they stand,
       The sun's bright portals, and the skies command;
       Involve in clouds th' eternal gates of day,
       And the dark barrier roll with ease away."
                 POPE's *Iliad*, book v. 927.
         —— " Till morn
       Wak'd by the circling hours, with rosy hand,
       Unbarr'd the gates of light."—*Paradise Lost*, bk. 6.

[*] See the additional notes at the end of Ælla.

2 Clothed.	3 Flew.	4 Mantle.	5 Glittering.
6 Drops.	7 Hill.		8 In leaf.
9 Appearing.	10 Flame.		

Itte moovethe 'hem, as honterres lyoncelle;
In trebled armoure ys theyre courage dyghte;
Eche warrynge harte forr prayse and rennome swelles;
Lyche slowelie dynnynge of the croucheynge' streme,
Syche dyd the mormrynge² sounde of the whol armie
    seme.

Hee ledes 'hem onne to fyghte; oh! thenne to saie
How Ælla loked, and lokyng dyd encheere,
Moovynge alyche a mountayne yn affraie,
Whanne a lowde. whyrlevynde doe yttes boesomme
    tare
To telle howe everie loke wuld banyshe feere,
Woulde aske an angelles poyntell³ or hys tyngue.⁴
Lyche a talle rocke yatte ryseth heaven-were,⁵
Lyche a yonge wolfynne brondeous⁶ and strynge,⁷
Soe dydde he goe, and myghtie warriours hedde;
Wythe gore-depycted wynges masterie arounde hym
    fledde.

The battelle jyned; swerdes uponne swerdes dyd
    rynge;
Ælla was chafed as lyonns madded bee;
Lyche fallynge starres, he dydde the javlynn flynge;
Hys mightie anlace mightie menne dyd slea;
Where he dydde comme, the flemed⁸ foe dydde flee,
Or felle benethe hys honde, as fallynge rayne,
Wythe sythe a fhuyrie he dydde onn 'hemm dree,⁹
Hylles of yer bowkes¹⁰ dyd ryse opponne the playne;

---

1 Crooked, winding.   2 Murmuring.   3 Pen.   4 Tongue.
5 Towards heaven.   6 Furious.   7 Strong,   8 Frighted.
9 Drive.   10 Bodies.

Ælla, thou arte—botte staie, mie tynge; saie nee;
Howe greate I hymme maye make, stylle greater hee
    wylle bee.

Nor dydde hys souldyerres see hys actes yn vayne.
Heere a stoute Dane uponne hys compheere[1] felle;
Heere lorde and hyndlette[2] sonke uponne the playne;
Heere sonne and fadre trembled ynto helle.
Chief Magnus soughthyswaie, and, shame to telle!
Hee soughte hys waie for flyghte; botte Ælla's speere
Uponne the flyynge Dacyannes schoulder felle,
Quyte throwe hys boddie, and hys harte ytte tare,
He groned, and sonke uponne the gorie greene,
And wythe hys corse encreased the pyles of Dacyannes
    sleene.

Spente wythe the fyghte, the Danyshe champyons
    stonde,
Lyche bulles, whose strengthe and wondrous myghte
    ys fledde;
Ælla, a javelynne grypped[3] yn eyther honde,
Flyes to the thronge, and doomes two Dacyannes
    deadde.
After hys acte, the armie all yspedde;[4]
Fromm everich on unmyssynge javlynnes flewe;
Theie straughte[5] yer doughtie[6] swerdes; the foemenn
    bledde;
Fulle three of foure of myghtie Danes dheie slewe;

---

1 Companion.   2 Peasant.   3 Grasped.   4 Dispatched.
5 Stretched.   6 Valiant.

The Danes, wythe terroure rulynge att their head,
Threwe downe theyr bannere talle, and lyche a ravenne
fledde.

The soldyerres followed wythe a myghtie crie,
Cryes, yatte welle myghte the stouteste hartes affraie.
Swefte, as yer shyppes, the vanquyshed Dacyannes
flie ;
Swefte, as the rayne uponne an Aprylle daie,
Pressynge behynde, the Englysche soldyerres slaie.
Botte halfe the tythes of Danyshe menne remayne ;
Ælla commaundes 'heie shoulde the sleetre [1] staie,
Botte bynde 'hem prysonners on the bloddie playne.
The fyghtynge beynge done, I came awaie,
In odher fieldes to fyghte a moe unequalle fraie.
Mie servant squyre !

CELMONDE, SERVITOURE.

CELMONDE.

Prepare a fleing horse,
Whose feete are wynges, whose pace ys lycke the
wynde,
Whoe wylle outestreppe the morneynge lyghte yn
course,
Leaveynge the gyttelles [2] of the merke [3] behynde.
Somme hyltren [4] matters doe mie presence fynde.
Gyv oute to alle yatte I was sleene ynne fyghte.
Gyff ynne thys gare [5] thou doest mie order mynde,
Whanne I returne, thou shalte be made a knyghte ;

---

1 Slaughter.   2 Mantle, clothing.   3 Darkness.
4 Hidden.   5 Cause.

Flie, flie, be gon ; an howerre ys a daie ;
Quycke dyghte[1] mie beste of stedes, and brynge hymm
    heere—awaie !

CELMONDE. [*solus.*]

Ælla ys woundedd sore, and ynue the toune
He waytethe, tylle hys woundes be broghte to ethe.[2]
And shalle I from hys browes plocke off the croune,
Makynge the vyctore yn hys vyctorie blethe?
O no! fulle sooner schulde mie hartes blodde smethe,[3]
Fulle soonere woulde I tortured bee toe deathe ;
Botte—Birtha ys the pryze; ahe! ytte were ethe[4]
To gayne so gayne[5] a pryze wythe losse of breathe ;
Botte thanne rennome æterne[6]—ytte ys botte ayre ;
Bredde ynne the phantasie, and alleyn lyvynge there.

Albeytte everyche thynge yn lyfe conspyre
To telle me of the faulte I now schulde doe,
Yette woulde I battentlie[7] assuage mie fyre,
And the same menes, as I scall nowe, pursue.
The qualytyes I fro mie parentes drewe,
Were blodde, and morther, masterie, and warre ;
Thie[8] I wylle holde to now, and hede ne moe
A wounde yn rennome, yanne a boddie scarre.
Nowe, Ælla, nowe Ime plantynge of a thorne,
Bie whyche thie peace, thie love, and glorie shalle be
    torne.

---

1 Prepare.   2 Relief, ease.   3 Smoke.   4 Easy.
5 Great, advantageous.   6 Eternal.   7 Boldly, or violently.
8 'Thie' is a mistake, or, at least misprint for ' these.'—DEAN MILLES.

Brystowe.

BIRTHA, EGWINA.

BIRTHA.

Gentle Egwina, do notte preche[1] me joie;
I cannotte joie ynne anie thynge botte weere.[2]
Oh! yatte aughte schulde oure sellynesse[3] destroie,
Floddynge the face wythe woe, and brynie teare!

EGWINA.

You muste, you muste endeavour for to cheere
Youre harte unto somme cherisaunied[4] reste.
Youre loverde[5] from the battelle wylle appere,
Ynne honnoure, and a greater love, be dreste;
Botte I wylle call the mynstrelles roundelaie;
Perchaunce the swotie[6] sounde maie chase your wiere
     awaie.

BIRTHA, EGWINA, MYNSTRELLES.

MYNSTRELLES SONGE.[*]

I.

O! synge untoe mie roundelaie,
O! droppe the brynie teare wythe mee,

---

1 Exhort, recommend.   2 Grief.   3 Happiness.   4 Comfortable.
5 Lord.   6 Sweet.   7 Grief.

* The roundelay, introduced to assuage the grief of Birtha, is most
natural and expressive in its description, and not less harmonious in
its numbers. Several of these ditties, composed before Shakspeare's
time, are preserved in his plays; and such songs as these, which he
observes were *old* and *plain*, and
            " The spinsters and the knitters in the sun
              Did use to chant them."—*Twelfth Night*, Act ii. Sc. 4.
Or, as the Queen in Hamlet calls Ophelia's songs, 'the snatches of old
tunes.' The 'willow,' which is the burden of this roundelai, was an
emblem of grief, either on death or forsaken love. It is the burden of
Desdemona's song in Othello; she says her mother's maid

Daunce ne moe atte hallie daie,
Lycke a reynynge[1] ryver bee;
   Mie love ys dedde,
   Gon to hys death-bedde,
   Al under the wyllowe tree.

II.

Blacke hys cryne as the wyntere nyghte,[2]
Whyte hys rode[3] as the sommer snowe,

———— "had a song of *willow*,
An old song 'twas, but it expressed her fortune,
And she died singing it."

  " The poor soul sat singing by a sycamore-tree,
    Sing all a green willow ;
    Her hand on her bosom, her head on her knee,
    Sing willow, willow, willow," &c.—Act iv.

So the burden of the ballad called *Corydon's Doleful Knell*, (Percy,
vol. ii. p. 265),

    " I'll stick a branch of *willow*,
     Now Phillida is dead."—DEAN MILLES.

As to internal arguments, an unnatural affectation of ancient spelling
and of obsolete words, not belonging to the period assigned to the poems,
strikes us at first sight. Of these old words combinations are not unfre-
quently formed, which never existed in the unpolished state of the
English language : and sometimes the antiquated diction is most in-
artificially misapplied, by an improper contexture with the present
modes of speech. The attentive reader will also discern, that our poet
sometimes forgets his assumed character, and does not always act his
part with consistency : for the chorus, or interlude, of the damsel who
drowns herself (in the tragedy of Ella), is much more intelligible, and
free from uncouth expressions, than the general phraseology of these
compositions.—WARTON.

1 Running.

2 [' Black his hair as the winter night,' &c.
  " His beard was white as snow,
    All flaxen was his poll ;
    He's gone, and he's gone, and we'll cast away moan,
    Gramercy on his soul."—*Hamlet*, Act iv. Sc. 3.

On the expression ' White his neck as the summer snow,' Dean Milles
makes this remark: " As to the whiteness of summer snow, the idea
must be borrowed from those mountainous countries where the snow
lies all the year, and reflects a dazzling whiteness from the sun shining
upon it. The lover's shroud in Hamlet is compared to the whiteness
of mountain snow ; but by Rowley to the whiteness of the moon."
In the romance of *Sir Launfal*, quoted by Warton, we have
    " Har faces was white as snowe on downe,
    Har *rode* was red, har eyne were browne."—ED.]

3 Neck.

Rodde hys face as the mornynge lyghte,
Cale[1] he lyes ynne the grave belowe;
    Mie love ys dedde,
    Gon to hys deathe-bedde,
    Al under the wyllowe tree.

III.

Swote[2] hys tyngue as the throstles note,
Quycke ynn daunce as thoughte canne bee,
Defte[3] hys taboure, codgelle stote,
O! hee lyes bie the wyllowe tree;
    Mie love ys dedde,
    Gonne to hys deathe-bedde,
    Alle underre the wyllowe tree.

IV.

Harke! the ravenne flappes hys wynge,
In the briered delle belowe;
Harke! the dethe-owle loude dothe synge,
To the nyghte-mares[4] as heie goe;
    Mie love ys dedde,
    Gonne to hys deathe-bedde,
    Al under the wyllowe tree.

---

1 Cold.   2 Sweet.   3 Neat.

4 The 'night-mares, portunni, or incubi,' were supposed to oppress persons in their sleep. See Mr. Tyrwhit's note on Fairies in Chaucer, 6441. Lye calls them 'spectres, or night-hags.' They made a part of the fairy system, and as such are mentioned in Edgar's mad speech in King Lear:

    "St. Withold footed thrice the wold;
      He met the *night-mare* and her nine-fold;
   Bid her alight, and her troth plight,
   And aroynt thee, witch, aroynt thee."—Act iii. Sc. 4.

The burden to this roundelay very much resembles that in Hamlet—

    "And will he not come again?
    And will he not come again?
   No, no, he's dead, go to thy death-bed,
   He never will come again."—Act iv. Sc. 3.—DEAN MILLES.

v.

See! the whyte moone sheenes onne hie;
Whyterre ys mie true loves shroude;
Whyterre yanne the mornynge skie,
Whyterre yanne the evenynge cloude;
  Mie love ys dedde,
  Gon to hys deathe-bedde,
  Al under the wyllowe tree.

vi.

Heere, uponne mie true loves grave,
Schalle the baren fleurs be layde,
Nee one hallie[1] Seyncte to save
Al the celness[2] of a mayde.
  Mie love ys dedde,
  Gonne to hys deathe-bedde,
  Alle under the wyllowe tree.

vii.

Wythe mie hondes I'lle dente[3] the brieres
Rounde his hallie corse to gre,[4]
Ouphante[5] fairie, lyghte youre fyres,
Heere mie boddie stylle schalle bee.
  Mie love ys dedde,
  Gon to hys deathe-bedde,
  Al under the wyllowe tree.

viii.

Comme, wythe acorne-coppe and thorne,
Drayne mie hartys blodde awaie;
Lyfe and all yttes goode I scorne,
Daunce bie nete,[6] or feaste by daie.

---

1 Holy.	2 Coldness.	3 Fasten.
4 Grow.	5 Elfin.	6 Night.

Mie love ys dedde,
Gon to hys death-bedde,
Al under the wyllowe tree.

IX.

Waterre wytches, crownede wythe reytes,[1]
Bere mee to yer leathalle[2] tyde.
I die! I comme! mie true love waytes.
Thos the damselle spake and dyed.[*]

BIRTHA.

Thys syngeyng haveth whatte coulde make ytte
    please;
Butte mie uncourtlie[3] shappe[4] benymmes[5] mee of all
    ease.

ÆLLA, *atte* WATCHETTE.

Curse onne mie tardie woundes! brynge mee a stede!
I wylle awaie to Birtha bie thys nyghte;
Albeytte fro mie woundes mie soul doe blede,
I wylle awaie, and die wythynne her syghte.
Brynge mee a stede, wythe eagle-wynges for flyghte;
Swefte as mie wyshe, and, as mie love ys, stronge.
The Danes have wroughte mee myckle woe ynne
    fyghte,
Inne kepeynge mee from Birtha's armes so longe.
O! whatte a dome was myne, sythe masterie
Canne yeve[6] ne pleasaunce, nor mie londes goode leme[7]
    myne eie!

---

1 Water-flags.   2 Deadly.
* [This very beautiful song has been lately set to music by my esteemed
friend, Henry Hugh Pearson, Esq., of Trinity College, Cambridge.—ED.]
3 Unpleasant, cruel.   4 Fate.   5 Bereaves.   6 Give.   7 Enlighten.

Yee goddes, howe ys a loverres temper formed !
Sometymes the samme thynge wylle bothe bane,[1] and
    blesse ;
One tyme encalede,[2] yanne[3] bie the same thynge
    warmd,
Estroughted[4] foorthe, and yanne ybrogten less.
'Tys Birtha's loss whyche doe mie thoughtes possesse ;
I wylle, I muste awaie : whie staies mie stede ?
Mie huscarles,[5] hyther haste ; prepare a dresse,
Whyche couracyers[6] yn hastie journies nede.
O heavens ! I moste awaie to Byrtha eyne,
For yn her lookes I fynde mie beynge doe entwyne.

CELMONDE, *atte* BRYSTOWE.

The worlde ys darke wythe nyghte ; the wyndes are
    stylle ;*
Fayntelie the mone her palyde lyghte makes gleme ;

---

1 Curse.   2 Frozen, cold.   3 Then.   4 Stretched forth.
5 ' Huscarles,' or ' house-carles,' were servants living in the house, in
attendance upon their king or lord.—DEAN MILLES.
6 Horse coursers, couriers.

* To have been dull would not have suited Chatterton's purpose, nor
indeed was it consistent with his genius. His aim was to dazzle and
surprise, by producing such high-wrought pieces of ancient poetry as
never before existed. But to secure our credulity, he should have
pleased us less. He has shewn too much genius, and too little skill.
Overacting his part, and unable or unwilling to repress his abilities, he
awakened our suspicions, and exposed his want of address in attempt-
ing to deceive. He sacrificed his veracity to an imprudent ambition.
Instead of wondering at his contrivance, we find he had none. A medi-
ocrity of poetical talents would have succeeded much better in this
imposture. He was too good a poet to conduct and execute such a
forgery. He conceived that his old poetry would be sufficiently marked
by old words and old spelling. But he took no caution about thoughts

The upryste[1] sprytes the sylente letten[2] fylle,
Wythe ouphant[3] faeryes joynyng ynne the dreme;
The forreste sheenethe wythe the sylver leme;[4]
Nowe maie mie love be sated ynn yttes treate;
Uponne the lynche[5] of somme swefte reynyng[6] streme,
At the swote banquette I wylle swotelie eate.
Thys ys the howse; yee hyndes, swythyn appere.

CELMONDE, SERVYTOURE.

CELMONDE.

Go telle to Birtha strayte, a straungerr waytethe here.

CELMONDE, BIRTHA.

BIRTHA.

Celmonde! yee seynctes! I hope thou haste goode newes.

CELMONDE.

The hope ys loste; for heavie newes prepare.

BIRTHA.

Is Ælla welle?

---

and imagery, the sentiment and the substance. He had forgot, or never knew, or was not inclined to believe, that the garb of antiquity would but ill become the elegance of Pope, or the spirit of Dryden.—WAR-TON.

1 Risen.
2 Church-yard. The term 'litten' is still used in many parts of England.
3 Elfin.   4 Light.   5 Brink, border.   6 Running.

CELMONDE.

Hee lyves; and stylle maie use
The behylte¹ blessynges of a future yeare.

BIRTHA.

Whatte heavie tydynge thenne have I to feare?
Of whatte mischaunce dydste thou so latelie saie?

CELMONDE.

For heavie tydynges swythyn nowe prepare.
Ælla sore wounded ys, yn bykerous² fraie;
In Wedecester's wallid toune he lyes.

BIRTHA.

O mie agroted³ breast!

CELMONDE.

Wythoute your syghte, he dyes.

BIRTHA.

Wylle Birtha's presence ethe⁴ her Ælla's payne?
I flie; newe wynges doe from mie schoulderrs sprynge.

CELMONDE.

Mie stede wydhoute wylle deftelie⁵ beere us twayne.

---

1 [Chaucer uses this word in the sense of 'promised;' but Dean Milles, deriving it from the Saxon, prefers the signification 'hidden,' which certainly suits better with the meaning of the passage. In line 1101, however, it will not bear this interpretation.—ED.]

2 Warlike.   3 Swelling, or bursting.

4 Relieve, ease.   5 Easily, commodiously.

BIRTHA.

Oh! I wyll flie as wynde, and no waie lynge;[1]
Sweftlie caparisons for rydynge brynge;
I have a mynde wynged wythe the levyn ploome.[2]
O Ælla, Ælla! dydste thou kenne the stynge,
The whyche doeth canker ynne mie hartys roome,
Thou wouldste see playne thieselfe the gare[3] to bee;
Aryse, uponne thie love, and flie to meeten me.

CELMONDE.

The stede, on whyche I came, ys swefte as ayre;
Mie servytoures doe wayte mee nere the wode;
Swythynne wythe mee unto the place repayre;
To Ælla I wylle gev you conducte goode.
Youre eyne, alyche a baulme, wylle staunche hys
    bloode,
Holpe oppe hys woundes, and yev[4] hys harte alle
    cheere;
Uponne your eyne he holdes hys lyvelyhode;[5]
You doe hys spryte, and alle hys pleasaunce bere.
Comme, lette's awaie, albeytte ytte ys moke,[6]
Yette love wille be a tore[7] to tourne to feere[8] nyghtes
    smoke.

BIRTHA.

Albeytte unwears[9] dyd the welkynn[10] rende,
Reyne[11] alyche fallynge ryvers, dyd ferse[12] bee,

---

1 Linger.   2 Feathered l'ghtning.   3 Cause.   4 Give.
5 Life.   6 Dark.   7 Torch.   8 Fire.
9 Tempests. The interpretation of this word rests solely on the tes-
timony of Chatterton. It is used again in the third Eclogue.
10 Sky, or heaven.   11 Rain.   12 Fierce.

Erthe wythe the ayre enchafed[1] dyd contende,
Everychone breathe of wynde wythe plagues dyd slee,
Yette I to Ælla's eyne eftsoones woulde flee;
Albeytte hawethornes dyd mie fleshe enseme,[2]
Owlettes, wythe scrychynge, shakeynge everyche tree,
And water-neders[3] wrygglynge yn eche streme,
Yette woulde I flie, ne under coverte staie,
Botte seke mie Ælla owte; brave Celmonde, leade the
    waie.

A Wode.

HURRA, DANES.

HURRA.

Heere ynn yis forreste lette us watche for pree.
Bewreckeynge[4] on oure foemenne oure ylle warre;
Whatteverre schalle be Englysch wee wylle slea,
Spreddynge our ugsomme[5] rennome[6] to afarre.
Ye Dacyanne menne, gyff Dacyanne menne yee are,
Lette nete[7] botte blodde suffycyle[8] for yee bee;
On everich breaste yn gorie letteres scarre,[9]
Whatt sprytes you have, and howe those sprytes
    maie dree.[10]
And gyf yee gette awaie to Denmarkes shore,
Eftesoones[11] we will retourne, and wanquished bee
    ne moere.

---

1 Heated.	2 Furrow, or make seams in.	3 Water serpents.
4 Revenging.	5 Terrible.	6 Renown.
7 Nought.	8 Sufficient.	9 Mark.
10 Drive.	11 Quickly.	

The battelle loste, a battelle was yndede;
Note queedes[1] hemselfes culde stonde so harde a fraie;
Oure verie armoure, and oure heaulmes[2] dyd blede,
The Dacyannes sprytes, lyche dewe drops, fledde
    awaie,
Ytte was an Ælla dyd commaunde the daie;
Ynn spyte of foemanne, I moste saie hys myghte;
Botte wee ynn hynd-lettes[3] blodde the loss wylle paie,
Brynnynge,[4] thatte we knowe howe to wynne yn
    fyghte;
Wee wylle, lyke wylfes[5] enloosed from chaynes,
    destroie ;—
Oure armoures—wynter nyghte shotte[6] oute the daie
    of joie.*

Whene swefte-fote tyme doe rolle the daie alonge,
Somme hamlette scalle onto oure fhuyrie[7] brende ;[8]
Brastynge[9] alyche a rocke, or mountayne stronge,
The talle chyrche-spyre upon the grene shalle bende;
Wee wylle the walles, and auntyante[10] tourrettes
    rende,
Pete[11] everych tree whych goldyn fruyte doe beere,
Downe to the goddes the ownerrs dhereof sende,
Besprengynge[12] alle abrode sadde warre and bloddie
    weere.[13]

---

1 Devils.   2 Helmets.   3 Peasants.
4 Shewing.   5 Wolves.   6 Shut.
* The meaning may probably be, that their arms shall exclude every gleam of joy, just as a winter night excludes every gleam of day.—DEAN MILLES.
7 Fury.   8 Burn.   9 Bursting.
10 Ancient.   11 Pluck up.   12 Scattering.
13 Tempest.

Botte fyrste to yynder oke-tree wee wylle flie ;
And thence wylle yssue o wte onne all yatte commeth
   bie.

Anodher parte of the Woode.

CELMONDE, BIRTHA.

BIRTHA.

Thys merkness[1] doe affraie mie wommanns breaste.
Howe sable ys the spreddynge skie arrayde !
Hallie[2] the bordeleire,[3] who lyves to reste,
Ne ys att nyghtys flemynge[4] hue dysmayde ;
The starres doe scantillie[5] the sable brayde ;[6]
Wyde ys the sylver lemes[7] of comforte wove ;
Speke, Celmonde, does ytte make thee notte afrayde?

CELMONDE.

Merker[8] the nyghte, the fitter tyde[9] for love.

BIRTHA.

Saiest thou for love? ah ! love is far awaie.
Faygne would I see once moe the roddie lemes[10] of daie.

CELMONDE.

Love maie bee nie, woulde Birtha calle ytte here.

BIRTHA.

How, Celmonde, dothe thou mene ?

---

1 Darkness.	2 Happy.	3 Cottager.
4 Terrifying.	5 Scarcely, sparingly.	6 Embroider.
7 Rays, beams.	8 Darker.	9 Time.
10 Beams.		

CELMONDE.

Thys Celmonde menes,
No leme, no eyne, ne mortalle manne appere,
Ne lyghte, an acte of love for to bewreene;[1]
Nete in thys forreste, botte thys tore,[2] dothe sheene,
The whych, potte oute, do leave the whole yn nyghte;
See! howe the brauncynge[4] trees doe here entwyne,
Makeynge thys bower so pleasynge to the syghte
Thys was for love fyrste made, and heere ytt stondes,
Thatte hereynne lovers maie enlyncke yn true loves
    bondes.

BIRTHA.

Celmonde, speake whatte thou menest, or alse mie
    thoughtes
Perchaunce maie robbe thie honestie so fayre.

CELMONDE.

Then here, and knowe, hereto I have you broughte,
Mie longe hydde love unto you to make clere.

BIRTHA.

Oh heaven and earthe! whatte ys ytt I doe heare?
Am I betraste?[5] where ys my Ælla, saie!

CELMONDE.

O! do nete[6] nowe to Ælla syke love bere,
Botte geven some onne Celmondes hedde.

---

1 Discover.   2 Nought.   3 Torch.
4 Branching.   5 Betrayed.   6 Not.

BIRTHA.

Awaie!

I wylle be gone, and groape mie passage oute,
Albeytte neders[1] stynges mie legs do twyne aboute.

CELMONDE.

Nowe bie the seynctes I wylle notte lette thee goe,
Ontylle thou doeste mie brendynge[2] love amate.[3]
Those eyne have caused Celmonde myckle woe,
Yenne lette yer smyle fyrst take hymm yn regrate.[4]
O! didst thou see mie breastis troblous state,
Theere love doth harrie[5] up mie joie, and ethe![6]
I wretched bee, beyonde the hele[7] of fate,
Gyff Birtha stylle wylle make mie harte-veynes blethe.[8]
Softe as the sommer flowreets, Birtha, looke,
Fulle ylle I canne thie frownes and harde dyspleasaunce
    brooke.

BIRTHA.

Thie love ys foule; I woulde bee deafe for aie,
Radher thanne heere syche deslavatie[9] sedde.
Swythynne flie from mee, and ne further saie;
Radher thanne heare thie love, I woulde bee dead.
Yee seynctes! and shal I wronge mie Ælla's bedde,
And wouldst thou, Celmonde, tempte me to the
    thynge?
Lett mee be gone—alle curses onne thie hedde!
Was ytte for thys thou dydste a message brynge?

---

1 Adders.	2 Burning.	3 Quench.
4 Favor.	5 Tear up.	6 Ease.
7 Help.	8 Bleed.	9 Lust.

Lette mee be gone, thou manne of sable harte!
Or welkyn[1] and her starres wyll take a maydens parte.

CELMONDE.

Sythence you wylle notte lette mie suyte avele,[2]
Mie love wylle have yttes joie, altho wythe guylte;
Youre lymbes shall bende, albeytte strynge as stele;
The merkye[3] seesonne wylle your bloshes hylte.[4]

BIRTHA.

Holpe, holpe, yee seynctes! oh thatte mie blodde
    was spylte!

CELMONDE.

The seynctes att distaunce stonde ynn tyme of nede.
Strev[5] notte to goe; thou canste notte, gyff thou
    wylte.
Unto mie wysche[6] bee kinde, and nete alse hede.

BIRTHA.

No, foule bestoykerre,[7] I wylle rende the ayre,
Tylle dethe do staie mie dynne, or some kynde roder[8]
    heare.
Holpe! holpe! oh godde!

CELMONDE, BIRTHA, HURRA, DANES.
HURRA.

        Ah! thatts a wommanne cries.
I kenn hem; saie who are you, yatte be theere?

---

1 Heaven.   2 Prevail.   3 Dark.   4 Hide.
5 Strive.   6 Wish.   7 Deceiver.   8 Traveller.

CELMONDE.

Yee hyndes, awaie! orre bie thys swerde yee dies.

HURRA.

Thie wordes wylle ne mie hartis sete¹ affere.²

BIRTHA.

Save mee, oh! save me from thys royner³ heere!

HURRA.

Stonde thou bie mee; nowe saie thie name and londe;
Or swythyne schall mie swerde thie boddie tare.

CELMONDE.

Bothe I wylle shewe thee bie mie brondeous⁴ honde.

HURRA.

Besette hym rounde, yee Danes.

CELMONDE.

Comme onne, and see
Gyff mie strynge anlace⁵ maie bewryen⁶ whatte I bee.
[*Fyghte al anenste Celmonde, meynte Danes he sleath,
and faleth to Hurra.*]

CELMONDE.

Oh! I forslagen⁷ be! ye Danes, now kenne,
I amme yatte Celmonde, seconde yn the fyghte,
Who dydd, atte Watchette, so forslege⁸ youre menne;

---

1 Stability.	2 Affright.	3 Ruiner.	4 Furious.
5 Sword.	6 Discover.	7 Slain.	8 Slew.

I fele myne eyne to swymme yn æterne[1] nyghte;—
To her be kynde.   [*Dieth.*

HURRA.

          Thenne felle a wordhie knyghte.
Saie, who bee you?

BIRTHA.

                    I am greate Ælla's wyfe.

HURRA.

Ah!

BIRTHA.

Gyff anenste[2] hym you harboure foule despyte,
Nowe wythe the lethal[3] anlace[4] take mie lyfe,
Bie thankes* I ever onne you wylle bestowe,
From ewbryce[5] you mee pyghte,[6] the worste of mortal
     woe.

HURRA.

I wylle; ytte scalle bee soe: yee Dacyans, heere.
Thys Ælla havethe been oure foe for aie.
Thorrowe the battelle he dyd brondeous[7] teare,
Beyng the lyfe and head of everych fraie;
From everych Dacyanne power he won the daie,
Forslagen[8] Magnus, all our schippes ybrente;[9]

---

1 Eternal.   2 Against.   3 Deadly.   4 Sword.
5 Adultery.
* [It should be 'my thanks.' Mr. Bryant snatches greedily at this
error; but it has been justly observed that it is 'such a mistake as
every man in the hurry of writing is subject to.'—ED.]
6 Plucked.   7 Furious.   8 Slew.   9 Burnt.

Bie hys felle arme wee now are made to straie ;
The speere of Dacya he ynne pieces shente ;[1]
Whanne hantoned[2] barckes unto oure londe dyd comme,
Ælla the gare[3] dheie sed, and wysched[4] hym bytter dome.[5]

BIRTHA.

Mercie !

HURRA.

    Bee stylle.
Botte yette he ys a foemanne goode and fayre ;
Whanne wee are spente, he soundethe the forloyne ;[6]
The captyves chayne he tosseth ynne the ayre,
Cheered* the wounded bothe wythe bredde and wyne;
Has hee notte untoe somme of you bynn dygne ?[7]
You woulde have smethd[8] onne Wedecestrian fielde,
Botte hee behylte[9] the slughorne[10] for to cleyne,[11]
Throwynge onne hys wyde backe, hys wyder spred-
    dynge shielde.
Whanne you, as caytysned,[12] yn fielde dyd bee,
He oathed[13] you to be stylle, and strayte didd sette you
    free.

Scalle wee forslege[14] hys wyfe, because he's brave ?
Bicaus hee fyghteth for hys countryes gare?[15]
Wylle hee, who havith bynne yis Ælla's slave,
Robbe hym of whatte percase[16] he holdith deere ?

---

1 Broke.   2 Accustomed.   3 Cause.   4 Wished.   5 Fate.
6 Retreat.   7 Noble, worthy of praise.   8 Smoked.
* [So in all the copies. It should however be ' cheereth.'—Ed.]
9 Forbid.   10 Warlike instrument of music.   11 Sound.
12 Captives.   13 Swore.   14 Slay.   15 Cause.   16 Perhaps.

Or scalle we menne of mennys ¹ sprytes appere,
Doeynge hym favoure for hys favoure donne,
Swefte to hys pallace thys damoiselle² bere,
Bewrynne³ oure case, and to oure waie be gonne?
The last you do approve; so lette ytte bee;
Damoyselle, comme awaie; you safe scalle bee wythe
mee.

BIRTHA.

Al blessynges maie the seynctes unto yee gyve!
Alpleasauncemaie youre longe-straughte⁴lyvyngesbee!
Ælla, whanne knowynge thatte bie you I lyve,
Wylle thyncke too smalle a guyfte⁵ the londe and sea.
O Celmonde! I maie deftlie⁶ rede by thee,
Whatte ille betydethe⁷ the enfouled⁸ kynde;
Maie ne thie cross-stone⁹ of thie cryme bewree!¹⁰
Maie alle menne ken thie valoure, fewe thie mynde!
Soldyer! for syke thou arte ynn noble fraie,
I wylle thie goinges 'tende, and doe thou lede the waie.

HURRA.

The mornynge' gyns alonge the easte to sheene;
Darklinge the lyghte doe onne the waters plaie;
Thefeynte rodde leme¹¹slowe creepeth oerethegreene,
Toe chase the merkyness¹² of nyghte awaie;
Swiftefliethehowersthatte wyllebrynge outethe daie;
The softe dewe falleth onne the greeynge¹³ grasse;

1 Mens. 2 Damsel. 3 Declare. 4 Lengthened.
5 Gift. 6 Properly. 7 Awaiteth. 8 Vicious.
9Monument. 10 Declare. 11 Ray. 12 Darkness.
13 Growing.

The shepster mayden,[1] dyghtynge[2] her arraie,
Scante[3] sees her vysage yn the wavie glasse ;
Bie the fulle daylieghte wee scalle Ælla see,
Or Brystowes wallyd towne ; damoyselle, followe mee.

At Brystowe.

ÆLLA AND SERVITOURES.

ÆLLA.

Tys nowe fulle morne ; I thoughten, bie laste nyghte
To have been heere ; mie stede han notte mie love ;
Thys ys mie pallace ; lette mie hyndes[4] alyghte,
Whylste I goe oppe, and wake mie slepeynge dove.
Staie here, mie hyndlettes ; I shal goe above.
Nowe, Birtha, wyll thie loke enhele[5] mie spryte,
Thie smyles unto mie woundes a baulme wylle proove ;
Mie ledanne[6] boddie wylle bee sette aryghte.
Egwina, haste, and ope the portalle doore,
Yatte I on Birtha's breste maie thynke of warre ne more.

ÆLLA, EGWINA.

EGWINA.

Oh Ælla ! *

---

1 Shepherdess.   2 Preparing.   3 Scarce.   4 Servants.
5 Heal, cure.   6 Heavy.

* Nothing can be more in the manner of modern tragedy than the
following dialogue, to mention no other, consisting of exclamations,
short and hasty sentences, sudden transitions, and frequent interrup-
tion. A better scene for shewing the shrug and start to the greatest
advantage, never appeared at Drury-lane theatre.—WARTON.

ÆLLA.

Ah! that semmlykeene[1] to mee
Speeketh a legendary tale of woe.

EGWINA.

Birtha is —

ÆLLA.

Whatt? where? how? saie, whatte of shee?

EGWINA.

Gone—

ÆLLA.

Gone! ye goddes!

EGWINA.

Alas! ytte ys toe true.
Yee seynctes, hee dies awaie wythe myckle woe!
Ælla! what? Ælla! oh! hee lyves agen!

ÆLLA.

Cal mee notte Ælla; I am hymme ne moe.
Where ys shee gon awaie? ah! speake! how? when?

EGWINA.

I will.

ÆLLA.

Caparyson a score of stedes; flie, flie!
Where ys shee? swythynne speeke, or instante thou
shalte die.

---

1 Appearance. In other places it is written 'semlykeed.' It seems
plain to me, that both these words owe their original to the following
article in Kersey, 'Semelſhecd, (O.) seemliness, comeliness.'—TYR-
WHITT.

EGWINA.

Stylle thie loud rage, and here thou whatte I knowe.

ÆLLA.

Oh! speek.

EGWINA.

Lycbe prymrose, droopynge wythe the heavie rayne,
Laste nyghte I lefte her, droopynge with her wiere,[1]
Her love the gare,[2] thatte gave her harte syke peyne—

ÆLLA.

Her love! to whomme?

EGWINA.

       To thee, her spouse, alleyne.[3]
As ys mie hentylle[4] everyche morne to goe,
I wente, and oped her chamber doore ynn twayne,
Botte found her notte, as I was wont to doe;
Thanne alle arounde the pallace I dyd seere,[5]
Botte culde (to mie hartes woe) ne fynde her anie
    wheere.

ÆLLA.

Thou lyest, foul hagge! thou lyest; thou art her ayde
To chere her louste;—botte noe; ytte cannotte bee.

EGWINA.

Gyff trouthe appear notte inne whatte I have sayde,
Drawe forthe thie anlace swythyn, thanne mee slea.

ÆLLA.

Botte yette ytte muste, ytte must bee soe; I see,
Shee wythe somme loustie[6] paramoure ys gone;

---

1 Grief.	2 Cause.	3 Only, alone.
4 Custom.	5 Search.	6 Lustful.

Itte moste bee soe—oh! howe ytte wracketh mee!
Mie race of love, mie race of lyfe ys ronne;
Nowe rage, and brondeous¹ storm, and tempeste
    comme;
Nete lyvynge upon erthe can now enswote² mie domme.

ÆLLA, EGWINA, SERVYTOURE.

SERVYTOURE,

Loverde!³ I am aboute the trouthe to saie.
Laste nyghte, fulle late I dydde retourne to reste.
As to mie chamber I dydde bende mie waie,
To Birtha one hys name and place addreste;
Downe to hym camme shee; butte thereof the reste
I ken ne matter; so, mie hommage made—

ÆLLA.

O! speake ne moe; mie harte flames yn yttes heste;⁴
I once was Ælla: nowe bee notte yttes shade.
Hanne alle the fuirie of mysfortunes wylle
Fallen onne mie benned⁵ headde I hanne been Ælla stylle.

Thys alleyn was unburied⁶ of alle mie spryte:
Mie honnoure, honnoure, frownd on the dolce⁷ wynde,
Thatte steeked⁸ on ytte: nowe wyth rage Im pyghte;⁹
A brondeous¹⁰ unweere¹¹ ys mie engyned¹² mynde.

---

1 Furious.   2 Sweeten.   3 Lord.
4 Command.   5 Cursed, tormented.   6 Unarmed.
7 Soft, gentle. [If Chatterton did not glean this word from some
music-book that fell in his way, it would be a satisfactory proof that he
used Bailey's Dictionary in constructing his forgery, as 'dolce' is not
to be found in Kersey or Speght. From his father's musical turn, how-
ever, the former is most likely.—ED.]
8. Stealed.   9 Tortured.   10 Furious.   11 Tempest.
12 Racked.

Mie hommeur[1] yette somme drybblet[2] joie maie fynde,
To the Danes woundes I wylle another yeve ;[3]
Whanne thos mie rennome[4] and mie peace ys rynde,[5]
Itte were a recrandize[6] to thyncke toe lyve ;
Mie huscarles,[7] untoe everie asker telle,
Gyffe noblie Ælla lyved, as noble Ælla felle.

                        [*Stabbeth hys breste.*

SERVITOURE.

Ælla ys sleene ; the flower of Englonde's marrde !

ÆLLA.

Be stylle : stythe lette the chyrches rynge mie knelle.
Call hyther brave Coernyke ; he, as warde
Of thys mie Brystowe castle, wylle doe welle.

                        [*Knelle ryngeth.*

ÆLLA, EGWINA, SERVYTOURE, COERNYKE.

ÆLLA.

Thee I ordeyne the warde ; so alle maie telle.
I have botte lyttel tym to dragge thys lyfe ;
Mie lethal[8] tale, alyche a lethalle belle,
Dynne[9] yn the eares of her I wyschd[10] mie wyfe !
Botte, ah ! shee maie bee fayre.

EGWINA.

        Yatte shee moste bee,

---

1 Honour.   2 Inconsiderable.   3 Give.   4 Renown.
5 Ruined.   6 Cowardice.   7 Servants.   8 Deadly.
9 Sound.   10 Wished.

ÆLLA.

Ah! saie notte soe; yatte worde woulde Ælla dobblie slee.

ÆLLA, EGWINA, SERVYTOURE, COERNYKE, BIRTHA, HURRA.

ÆLLA.

Ah! Birtha here!

BIRTHA.

Whatte dynne[1] ys thys? whatte menes yis leathalle
knelle?
Where ys mie Ælla? speeke; where? howe ys hee?
Oh Ælla! art thou yanne alyve and welle!

ÆLLA.

I lyve yndeed; botte doe notte lyve for thee.

BIRTHA.

Whatte menes mie Ælla?

ÆLLA.

              Here mie meneynge see.
Thie foulness urged mie honde to gyve thys wounde,
Ytte mee unsprytes.[2]

BIRTHA.

              Ytte hathe unspryted mee.

ÆLLA.

Ah heavens! mie Birtha fallethe to the grounde!
Botte yette I am a manne, and so wylle bee.

---

1 Sound.   2 Unsouls, 'deprives of life.'

HURRA.

Ælla! I amme a Dane; botte yette a friende to thee.
Thys damoyselle I founde wythynne a woode,
Strevynge fulle harde anenste[1] a burled[2] swayne ;
I sente hym myrynge[3] ynne mie compheeres[4] blodde,
Celmonde hys name, chief of thie warrynge trayne.
Yis damoiselle soughte to be here agayne ;
The whyche, albeytte foemen, wee dydd wylle ;
So here wee broughte her wythe you to remayne.

COERNIKE.

Yee nobylle Danes! wythe goulde I wyll you fylle.

ÆLLA.

Birtha, mie lyfe! mie love! oh! she ys fayre.
Whatte faultes coulde Birtha have; whatte faultes could
        Ælla feare?

BIRTHA.

Amm I yenne thyne? I cannotte blame thie feere.
Botte doe reste mee uponne mie Ælla's breaste ;
I wylle to thee bewryen[5] the woefulle gare.[6]
Celmonde dyd comme to mee at tyme of reste.
Wordeynge[7] for mee to flie, att your requeste,
To Watchette towne, where you deceasynge laie ;
I wyth hym fledde; thro' a murke[8] wode we preste,
Where hee foule love unto mie eares dyd saie:
The Danes —

---

1 Against.   2 Armed.   3 Wallowing.   4 Companions.
5 Declare.   6 Cause.   7 Bringing me word. 8 Dark.

ÆLLA.

Oh! I die contente.—   [*Dieth.*

BIRTHA.

Oh! ys mie Ælla dedde?
Oh! I wyll make hys grave mie vyrgyn spousal bedde.
[*Birtha feyncteth.*

COERNYKE.

Whatte? Ælla deadde! and Birtha dyynge toe!
Soe falles the fayrest flourettes of the playne.
Who canne unplyte[1] the wurchys[2] heaven can doe,
Or who untweste the role of shappe[3] yn twayne?
Ælla, thie rennome[4] was thie onlie gayne;
For yette, thie pleasaunce, and thie joie was loste,
Thie countrymen shall rere thee on the playne,
A pyle of carnes,[5] as anie grave can boaste:
Further, a just amede[6] to thee to bee,
Inne heaven thou synge of Godde, on erthe we'lle
    synge of thee.[*]

---

1 Unfold.   2 Works.   3 Fate.   4 Renown.
5 Stones. Thus the Scotch 'cairn.'
            "I will add a stone to thy cairn."
6 Reward.
  * The Tragedy of Ælla, with the Epistle, Letter, and Entroductionne,
was originally printed from a folio M.S. in Chatterton's hand-writing,
furnished by Mr. Catcott, in the beginning of which he has written
"Chatterton's transcript. 1769."

ADDITIONAL NOTES TO ÆLLA.

I. *" Ælla wythe thys I sende, and hope that you*
Wylle from ylle caste awaie, whatte lynes maie be untrue."
EPISTLE TO CANYNGE, page 25.

It must be observed, for the honour of our poet, that although Ella is composed in stanzas, which continue with great exactness and regularity through the whole play, and are no inconsiderable check to the genius of a dramatic poet; yet the dialogue is carried on with the same ease and freedom, as if it was entirely unencumbered with measure and rhyme. In the Ludus Coventriæ, or play of Corpus Christi, which is the only performance of the kind extant of equal antiquity with Rowley's age, the Dramatis Personæ begin and terminate their speeches with the stanzas. In that of Ælla, the poet, without sacrificing a strict conformity to the metre, has improved the spirit of the dialogue. For the stanza in Ælla is not the measure of every speech, or of the passion which the poet wishes to raise and represent. The effect of surprise—the violence of resentment—the irritable senses of pride and jealousy are finely and strongly marked by sudden changes of the dialogue in the different parts of the stanza, and by making the finest-modelled poetry speak the feelings and actings of the human heart.

Dramatical pieces of this kind usually close with a moral reflection: our poet is peculiarly happy in the application of this talent. He admires the unsearchable ways of Providence; observes both on the merit and misfortunes of Ælla, and assigns him his posthumous reward, marking out the place of his interment with peculiar tokens of distinction, and eternising his name in song; honours adapted to the custom of the age in which he is supposed to have lived. But with the piety of a christian, and the judgment of a critic, he has properly distinguished the God from the hero, by giving to each his respective homage.

"Inne heaven thou synge of Godde, on erthe we'lle synge of thee."—
DEAN MILLES.

II. *" Playes made from hallie tales I holde unmeete,"* &c.
EPISTLE TO CANYNGE, page 26.

It is well known to every searcher into our ancient stage, that the miserable interludes, even of the decline of the sixteenth century, are infinitely subordinate to every other species of poetry then subsisting: that they are utterly destitute of contrivance, character, sentiment, and even of common decorum. The truth is, the tragedy of Ælla, to which I will add the imperfect tragedy of Godwyn, in which is the fine Ode on Freedom, is indebted to the Grecian school, revived in the eighteenth century. Both are the effusions of a young mind, warm from studying Mason's *Elfrida* and *Caractacus.*

It is another unsurmountable objection to the antiquity and authenticity of Ælla, that the subject is historical or civil. Representations of religious subjects, were only fashionable in the reign of Edward the Fourth. And these, exclusive of the subject, by no means resembled what we call a play. They made a part of the great drama of superstition. Rowley, as a priest, was very unlikely to have begun this heterodox innovation, and to have been the first to compose a play not religious. The pious mayor of Bristol never would have patronised so profane a confessor. Churches were our chief theatres before the Reformation: and the *dygne maistre* Canynge, the builder of a church, would have more naturally employed the dramatic talents of Rowley, to decorate his new edifice with the exhibition of a splendid Mystery. If Rowley had penetration and taste, yet he had caution, he had prudence, and a reverence for his establishment. But Rowley proceeds still farther. He openly defends his new attempt, not in a palliative apology, but in a peremptory declaration of his opinion of the absurdity of scriptural plays.

" Playes made from hallie tales I holde unmeete,
Lette somme greate storie of a manne be songe."

This was too bold and too refined a philosophy for a priest of the fifteenth century. The first line is absolute heresy, and would have exposed the writer to the censure of the church. But this passage is perfectly consistent with the general spirit and turn of the epistle in which it appears: and which, according to the Dean of Exeter, contains "specimens of the author's abilities in judicious criticism, and pleasant raillery, in neither of which does he appear at all inferior to Pope." This is an unlucky concession.—WARTON.

III. " *Arounde the alestake, mynstrelles synge the songe.*"
Page 42.

Warton supposes the word 'alestake' to mean a sign-post before an alehouse.

In Chaucer the hoste says—

—— " Here at this alehouse stake,
I wol both drinke, and etin of a cake."

And in 'The Ship of Fools.'

" By the alestake knowe we the alehouse,
And everie inne is known by the signe."

IV.   "*Angelles bee wrogte to bee of neidher kynde.*"—Page 44.

A higher authority has pronounced the sex of angels to be masculine.

——— "Oh! why did God,
Creator wise, that peopled highest heaven,
With spirits masculine, create at last
This novelty on earth, this fair defect
Of nature, and not fill the world at once
With men, as angels, without feminine!"
                           Paradise Lost, book x.

V. "*I speke, mie loverde, alleyne to upryse
Youre wytte from marveile, and the warriour to alyse.*"—Page 49.

In this passage the word 'alyse' is rightly interpreted 'to set free.' In other places it has received the various and erroneous meanings of 'to allow,' 'to desert,' &c. [Chatterton probably took it from Kersey, "Ⅎⅼⅈ𝔰𝔢𝔡 (o.) allowed." From whence Kersey took it is less material; but I am inclined to believe that it was formed originally from a mistaken reading of the article Ⅎⅼⅈ𝔣𝔢𝔡 in Skinner. The very distinct signification of the two words are thus stated by Verstegan, p. 227. 'Ⅎⅼⅈ𝔣𝔢𝔡, allowed, licensed.—Ⅎⅼⅈ𝔰𝔢. release.—Ⅎⅼⅈ𝔰𝔢𝔡, released.— TYRWHITT.

VI.   "*Depycte wythe skylledd honde uponne thie wyde aumere.*"
                                               Page 57.

The word 'aumere' does not occur in any of our ancient poets, except in Chaucer's *Romaunt of the Rose*, v. 2271—

"Weare streighte gloves with *aumere*
Of silk."

The French original stands thus:

"De gans et de bourse de soye,
Et de saincture te cointoye."

Skinner, who probably did not think of consulting the original, supposes 'aumere' to be something belonging to gloves, and so at a venture expounded it *fimbria, institia*; a fringe or border. It seemed, and still seems most probable to me, that 'aumere of silk' is Chaucer's translation of *bourse de soye*; and consequently that 'aumere' was sometimes equivalent to a purse. In short, 'aumere' upon the face of this passage, must probably signify, either 'something belonging to gloves,' or 'a purse,' or 'a girdle;' and I think I might safely trust the intelligent reader with the determination, in which of these three senses it is here used by Chaucer. But I have also referred to another passage of the same poem (ver. 2087), in which he uses 'aumener' in this same sense of a purse.

"Then from his aumener he drough
A little key fetise enough."

The original is

"Adonc de sa *bourse* il traict
Un petit clef bien fait."

Where 'aumener' is undoubtedly the translation of *bourse*. I must observe farther, that in what I take to be the most accurate and authentic edition of the French *Roman de la Rose* (Paris 1727), these two lines are thus written, v. 2028—

> " Lors a de l' *aumoniere* traicte
> Une petite clef bien faicte."

Which, I apprehend, adds no small strength to my conjecture, that both 'aumener' and 'aumere,' are derivatives from the French *aumoniere*. If so, it becomes still clearer, that the proper signification of 'aumere' is, a purse; a signification which will not suit any one of the passages, in which the word occurs in these poems.—Tyrwhitt.

[Chatterton's interpretation was derived from Kersey or Bailey—for one has literally copied the other,—where we have 'aumere, O. welt, skirt or border.—Ed.]

VII. " *As Severn's hyger lyghethe banckes of sonde,*" &c.—Page 69.

The following is Drayton's 'picturesque description' of the 'hygra' to which Dean Milles alludes in the note to this passage.

> " Shut up in narrower bounds the Higre wildly raves,
> And frights the straggling flocks, the neighboring shores to fly,
> Afar as from the main it comes with hideous cry,
> And on the angry front the curled foam doth bring:
> The billows 'gainst the banks when fiercely it doth fling,
> Hurls up the slimy ooze, and makes the scaly brood
> Leap madding to the land affrighted from the flood;
> O'erturns the toiling barge, whose steersman doth not launch,
> And thrusts the furrowing beak into her ireful paunch."
>
> *Poly-olbion.* Bk. VII. l. 10—18.

VIII. " *Sheenynge upon the borne whych stondeth bie,*" &c.—Page 76.

The author of the 'Tragycal Enterlude' is describing the morning of that day, when Ælla obtained the signal victory over the Dacians or Danes. Among other things he mentions the rays of light shining upon the 'borne,' which by Chatterton is interpreted—'burnish.' As the description is remarkably fine, I will present the reader with the whole; as he will from the context more readily perceive the true meaning of this term.

> " Bryghte sonne han ynne hys roddie robes byn dyghte,
> From the rodde easte he flyited wythe hys trayne;
> The Howers drewe awaie the geete of nyghte,
> Her sable tapistrie was rent yn twayne.
> The dauncynge streakes bedecked heavennes playne,
> And on the dewe dyd smyle wythe shemrynge eie,
> Lyche gottes of blodde, whyche doe blacke armoure steyne,
> Sheenynge upon the *borne*, whych stondeth bie;
> The souldyers stoode uponne the hillis syde,
> Lyche yonge enlefed trees, whyche yn a forreste byde."
>
> *Ælla,* line 734.

Chatterton not knowing the meaning of the term 'borne' looked into Skinner, and found 'Borne pro burnish;' and accordingly interpreted 'the borne, whych stondeth bie,' by the 'burnish, whiche stondeth bie.' He was probably still further led to this notion by the word 'armour' being mentioned in the preceding line. That 'borne' may signify burnish, we grant, but not here; for how can it be with the least propriety said that the 'burnish' of armour 'stands by?' The purport of the term is totally mistaken. There are two words in our language, which I believe are sometimes spelt alike. These are 'bourne' and 'borne.' The first signifies a small stream or rivulet:

> "I was weary of wandering, and went me to rest,
> Under a brode bank by a *bourne* side."
> *Pierce Plowman*, p. 1.

The other is from the French word *borne* and *borné*; and denotes any extremity, limit, or boundary. It is used in this sense by Shakspeare; and we find Hamlet speaking of

> "That undiscovered country from whose bourne
> No traveller returns." ——

By this is meant, 'from whose *limit* and *boundary*, no traveller comes back.' It is also used for the extreme part or ridge of a hill; and for a hill itself.

> "From the dire summit of this chalky bourne,
> Look up a height."—*King Lear*.

Hence a person in the Comus of Milton, says—

> "I know each lane, and every alley green,
> Dingle, or bushy dell of this wild wood;
> And every bosky *bourn* from side to side."

Every 'bosky bourn' signifies *every woody hill* or *ridge* of a hill. 'Bosky bourn' is here opposed by the poet to 'bushy dell,' in the foregoing line. This is the true meaning of the passage in Rowley. He mentions the rising sun shining upon the 'bourne,' that is, upon the upper and *extreme part* or *ridge* of that hill, which was near the army. The soldiers were lower down.

> "The souldyers stoode uponne the hillis syde."

It is used in the same sense in the second battle of Hastings; where there is a noble description of a mountain convulsed by an earthquake,

> "Now here, now there, majestic nods the bourne."—Line 198.

The word 'bourne' is here introduced in its true sense; and perfectly analogous in application to the same word mentioned before. This is what in the notes is interpreted 'burnish,' though it in reality signifies, 'the highest range and extremity of an hill.'—BRYANT.

[Bailey has copied from Kersey, (*To* BORN, to burnish, O), and BOURN, a town hard by, a **Bourn**, *i.e.* a river.—ED.] .

GODDWYN,

a

Tragedie,

Bie THOMAS ROWLEIE.

This fragment (the manuscript in Chatterton's hand-writing, mentioned in page 107), purports likewise to be the composition of Thomas Rowley. The very existence of any such person as Rowley is questioned, and on good ground. He is not so much as noticed by William of Worcestre, who lived nearly about the supposed time of Rowley, was himself of Bristol, and makes frequent mention of Canynge. Bale, who lived two hundred years nearer to Rowley than we, and who by unwearied industry dug a thousand bad authors out of obscurity, has never taken the least notice of such a person; nor yet Leland, Pitts, or Tanner, nor indeed any other literary biographer. That no copies of any of his works should exist, but those deposited in Redcliff church, is also an unaccountable circumstance not easy to be surmounted.—DR. GREGORY.

PROLOGUE.

MADE BIE MAISTRE WILLIAM CANYNGE.

———

WHYLOMME[1] bie pensmenne[2] moke[3] ungentle[4] name
Have upon Goddwynne Erle of Kente bin layde,
Dherebie benymmynge[5] hymme of faie[6] and fame;
Unliart[7] divinistres[8] haveth saide,
Thatte he was knowen toe noe hallie[9] wurche;[10]
Botte thys was all hys faulte, he gyfted ne[11] the churche.

The aucthoure[12] of the piece whiche we enacte,
Albeytte[13] a clergyon,[14] trouthe wyll wrytte.
Inne drawynge of hys menne no wytte ys lackte;
Entyn[15] a kynge mote[16] bee full pleased to nyghte.
Attende, and marcke the partes nowe to be done;
Wee better for toe doe do champyon[17] anie onne.

---

1 Of old, formerly. 2 Writers, historians. 3 Much.
4 Inglorious. 5 Bereaving. 6 Faith.
7 Unforgiving. 8 Divines, clergymen, monks. 9 Holy.
10 Work. 11 Not. 12 Author.
13 Though, notwithstanding. 14 Clerk, or clergyman.
15 Even. 16 Might.
17 Challenge. The word 'champyon' is not used as a verb by any writer
before Shakspeare.—TYRWHITT.

GODDWYN.

PERSONS REPRESENTED.

HAROLDE,   bie T. ROWLEIE, the Aucthoure.
GODDWYN,   JOHAN DE ISCAMME.
ELWARDE,   SYRR THYBBOT GORGES.
ALSTAN,   SYRR ALAN DE VERE.
KYNGE EDWARDE, MASTRE WILLYAM CANYNGE.

Odhers bie KNYGHTES MYNSTRELLES.

GODDWYN AND HAROLDE.

GODDWYN.

HAROLDE!

HAROLDE.

Mie loverde !¹

GODDWYN.

O ! I weepe to thyncke,
What foemen ² riseth to ifrete ³ the londe.

1 Lord.   2 Foes, enemies.
3 Devour, destroy. To 'ifrete' the land is not as Chatterton has ex-
plained the word, to *devour* or *destroy*, but to *fret* or *consume* the land,
just as rust consumes iron.— DEAN MILLES.
[The worthy Dean might have spared this observation. In reading

Theie batten[1] onne her flesh, her hartes bloude dryncke,
And all ys graunted from the roieal honde.

HAROLDE.

Lette notte thie agreme[2] blyn,[3] ne aledge[4] stonde ;
Bee I toe wepe? I wepe in teres of gore :
Am I betrassed?[5] syke[6] shulde mie burlie[7] bronde
Depeyncte[8] the wronges on hym from whom I bore.

GODDWYN.

I ken thie spryte[9] ful welle ; gentle thou art,
Stringe,[10] ugsomme,[11] rou,[12] as smethynge[13] armyes
    seeme ;
Yett efte,[14] I feare, thie chefes[15] toe grete a parte,
And that thie rede[16] bee efte borne downe bie breme.[17]
What tydynges from the kynge !

HAROLDE.

His Normans knowe.
I make noe compheere[18] of the shemrynge[19] trayne.

Chaucer, Chatterton could not be so dull as to mistake the meaning of
the word in the following instance out of many others :

> " And forth is ladde this woful yongè knight,
> Unto the countre' of minds full of might ;
> And in a prison fettrid fast is he,
> Tyl that ilke time he shulde YFRETIN be."

And if he had recourse to his favourite Bailey, he would have found the
word in question thus resolved—'IFRETEN,' devoured, O. (meaning
the word was obsolete.) ED.]

1 Fatten.	2 Grievance ; a sense of it.	3 Cease, desist.
4 Allege. idly.	5 Deceived, betrayed.	6 So.
7 Fury, anger, rage.	8 Paint, display.	9 Soul.
10 Strong.	11 Terrible.	12 Ugly, froward.
13 Smoking, bleeding.		14 Oft.
15 Heat, rashness.	16 Advise, counsel, help.	
17 Strength, also strong.		18 Companions.
19 Taudry, glimmering.		

GODDWYN.

Ah Harolde! tis a syghte of myckle woe,
To kenne these Normannes everich rennome gayne.
What tydynge withe the foulke?[1]

HAROLDE.

Stylle mormorynge atte yer shap,[2] stylle toe the kynge
Theie rolle theire trobbles, lyche a sorgie sea.
Hane Englonde thenne a tongue, butte notte a stynge?
Dothe alle compleyne, yette none wylle ryghted bee?

GODDWYN.

Awayte the tyme, whanne Godde wylle sende us ayde.

HAROLDE.

No, we muste streve to ayde oureselves wyth powre.
Whan Godde wylle sende us ayde! tis fetelie[3] prayde.
Moste we thos calke[4] awaie the lyve-longe howre?
Thos croche[5] oure armes, and ne toe lyve dareygne,[6]
Unburled,[7] undelievre,[8] unespryte![9] *
Far fro mie harte be fled thyk[10] thoughte of peyne,
Ile free mie countrie, or Ille die yn fyghte.

GODDWYN.

Botte lette us wayte untylle somme season fytte
Mie Kentyshmen, thie Summertons shall ryse;

---

1 People.   2 Fate, destiny.   3 Nobly, dexterously.
4 Cast.   5 Cross, from 'crouche,' a cross.
6 Attempt, or endeavour.   7 Unarmed.
8 Unactive.   9 Unspirited.   10 Such.
        * ' Unhousell'd, unanointed, unaneal'd!'—*Hamlet.*

Adented[1] prowess[2] to the gite[3] of witte,
Agayne the argent[4] horse shall daunce yn skies.
Oh Harolde, heere forstraughteynge[5] wanhope[6] lies.
Englonde, oh Englonde, tis for thee I blethe.[7]
Whylste Edwarde to thie sonnes wylle nete alyse,[8]
Shulde anie of thie sonnes fele aughte of ethe?[9]
Upponne the trone[10] I sette thee, helde thie crowne;
Botte oh! twere hommage nowe to pyghte[11] thee downe.
Thou arte all preeste, and notheynge of the kynge.
Thou arte all Norman, nothynge of mie blodde.
Know, ytte beseies[12] thee notte a masse to synge;
Servynge thie leegefolcke · thou arte servynge Godde.

HAROLDE.

Then Ille doe heaven a servyce.   To the skyes
The dailie contekes[14] of the londe ascende.
The wyddowe, fahdrelesse, and bondemennes cries
Acheke[15] the mokie[16] aire and heaven astende.[17]
On us the rulers doe the folcke depende;
Hancelled[18] from erthe these Normanne hyndes[19] shalle
     bee;
Lyche a battently[20] low,[21] mie swerde shalle brende;[22]
Lyche fallynge softe rayne droppes, I wyll hem[23] slea;[24]

1 Fastened, annexed.   2 Might, power.   3 Mantle, or robe.
4 White, alluding to the arms of Kent, a horse saliant, argent.
5 Distracting.   6 Despair.   7 Bleed.
8 Allow.   9 Ease.   10 Throne.
11 Pluck.   12 Becomes.   13 Subjects.
14 Contentions, complaints.   This word is used more frequently by
Spenser, than by any other writer.
15 Choke. The participle 'acheked' is in Kersey.
16 Dark, cloudy.   17 Astonish.   18 Cut off, destroyed.
19 Slaves.   20 Loud roaring.   21 Flame of fire.
22 Burn, consume.   23 Them.   24 Slay.

Wee wayte too longe; oure purpose wylle defayte;[1]
Abounne[2] the hyghe empryze,[3] and rouze the champyones
    strayte.

GODDWYN.

Thie suster—

HAROLDE.

       Aye, I knowe, she is his queene.
Albeytte,[4] dyd shee speeke her foemen[5] fayre,
I wulde dequace[6] her comlie semlykeene,[7]
And foulde mie bloddie anlace[8] yn her hayre.

GODDWYN.

Thye fhuir[9] blyn,[10]

HAROLDE.

      No, bydde the leathal[11] mere,[12]
Upriste[13] withe hiltrene[14] wyndes and cause unkend,[15]
Beheste[16] it to be lete;[17] so twylle appeare,
Eere Harolde hyde hys name, his countries friende.
The gule-steynct[18] brygandyne,[19] the adventayle,[20]
The feerie anlace brede[21] shal make mie gare[22] prevayle.

---

1 Decay, fail.   2 Make ready.   3 Enterprise.
4 Notwithstanding.   5 Foes.
6 Mangle, destroy. In KERSEY, whom BAILEY has copied, its mean-
ing is simply, 'To dash.
7 Beauty, countenance.   8 An ancient sword.   9 Fury.
10 Cease.   11 Deadly.   12 Lake.
13 Swollen.   14 Hidden.   15 Unknown.
16 Command.   17 To be still, to cease.   18 Red-stained.
19 Coat of armour.
20 Falchion or sword, shaped like a sword. [BAILEY; and in SPEGHT,
with an explanatory note attached.—ED.]
21 Broad.   22 Cause.

GODDWYN.

Harolde, what wuldest doe?

HAROLDE.

Bethyncke thee whatt.
Here liethe Englonde, all her drites[1] unfree,
Here liethe Normans coupynge[2] her bie lotte,
Caltysnyng[3] everich native plante to gre,[4] —
Whatte woulde I doe? I brondeous[5] wulde hem slee ;[6]
Tare owte theyre sable harte ble ryghtefulle breme ;[7]
Theyre deathe a meanes untoe mie lyfe shulde bee,
Mie spryte shulde revelle yn theyr harte-blodde
streme.
Eftsoones I wylle bewryne[8] mie ragefulle ire,
And Goddis anlace[9] wielde yn furie dyre.

GODDWYN.

Whatte wouldest thou wythe the kynge?

HAROLDE.

Take offe hys crowne ;
The ruler of somme mynster[10] hym ordeyne ;
Sette uppe som dygner[11] than I han pyghte[12] downe ;
And peace in Englonde shulde be brayd[13] agayne.

---

1 Rights, liberties. 2 Cutting, mangling. 3 Forbidding, restraining.
4 Grow. 5 Furious. 6 Slay.
7 Strength. 8 Declare, betray. 9 Sword.
10 Monastery. 11 More worthy. 12 Pulled, plucked.
13 Displayed. [The word is in KERSEY, BAILEY, and SPEGHT, but with
meanings somewhat different to Chatterton's interpretation ('to break
out.'—BAILEY and KERSEY.) ('Arose, awaked, took, brake out.'—
SPEGHT).—ED.]

GODDWYN.

No, lette the super-hallie[1] seyncte kynge reygne,
Ande somme moe reded[2] rule the untentyff[3] reaulme;
Kynge Edwarde, yn hys cortesie, wylle deygne
To yielde the spoiles, and alleyne[4] were[5] the heaulme:
Botte from mee harte bee everych thoughte of gayne,
Not anie of mie kin I wysche him to ordeyne.

HAROLDE.

Tell me the meenes, and I wylle boute ytte strayte;
Bete[6] mee to slea[7] mieselfe, ytte shalle be done.

GODDWYN.

To thee I wylle swythynne[8] the menes unplayte,[9]
Bie whyche thou, Harolde, shalte be proved mie sonne.
I have longe seen whatte peynes were undergon,
Whatte agrames[10] braunce[11] out from the general tree;
The tyme ys commynge, whan the mollock[12] gron[13]
Drented[14] of alle yts swolynge[15] owndes[16] shalle bee;
Mie remedie is goode; our menne shall ryse:
Eftsoons the Normans and owre agrame[17] flies.

---

1 Over-righteous.   2 Counselled, more wise.   3 Uncareful, neglected.
4 Alone.   5 Wear.   6 Bid, command.
7 Slay.   8 Presently.
9 Explain. [To 'unplite.'—KERSEY and BAILEY. 'Unpliten,' make
plain.—SPEGHT.—ED.]
10 Grievances.   11 Branch.
12 Wet, moist. ['Mollock' is properly a substantive, and is used as
such by old writers. So, in Chatterton's usual authorities, KERSEY
and SPEGHT.—ED.]
13 Fen, moor.   14 Drained.   15 Swelling.
16 Waves.   17 Grievance.

HAROLDE.

I will to the West, and gemote[1] alle mie knyghtes,
Wythe bylles that pancte for blodde, and sheeldes as
brede[2]
As the ybroched[3] moon,[4] when blaunch[5] she dyghtes[6]
The wodeland grounde or water-mantled mede ;
Wythe hondes whose myghte canne make the dough-
tiest[7] blede,
Who efte have knelte upon forslagen[8] foes,
Whoe wythe yer fote orrests[9] a castle-stede,[10]
Who dare on kynges for to bewrecke[11] yiere woes ;

---

1 Assemble.   2 Broad.   3 Horned.
4 See the description of Satan's shield.—*Paradise Lost*, bk. 1.
5 White.   6 Decks.   7 Mightiest, most valiant.
8 Slain. BAILEY. [It is observable, as in the present instance,
that Chatterton frequently had recourse to alterations in the orthogra-
phy of the obsolete words which he assiduously gleaned from old
Glossaries, Dictionaries, &c. And, as Tyrwhitt has justly remarked,
the mere proof that particular words were obtained from particular
sources, is no argument whatever in favour of their authenticity or
genuineness. Bailey, to whom we have seen Chatterton to have been
more indebted than to any other lexicographer, compiled his Dictionary
from authorities which had preceded him, and especially from Speght
and Kersey. In fact, he has very often done nothing more than copy
their meanings, and even their misprints, without any examination as
to their correctness. Now Kersey has often mistaken the sense of *his*
authority—Skinner ; and it is notorious, that, in almost every instance,
where he has published a false interpretation, Bailey has committed
the same error ;—the reason is evident. Bailey servilely, and at the
same time ignorantly, transcribed the inaccuracies of his predecessor.
And, as Speght was not always fully possessed of the meaning of his
author, and has, therefore, given currency to gross and palpable blun-
ders, there can be little wonder that the explanations afforded by Chat-
terton, would be sometimes at variance with the real interpretation of
the word in question.—ED.] After this note was written, the Editor
discovered the word ' forslagen ' in Kersey, spelt as in the text.
9 Oversets.   10 A castle.   11 Revenge.

Nowe wylle the menne of Englonde haile the daie,
Whan Goddwyn leades them to the ryghtfulle fraie.

GODDWYN.

Botte firste we'll calle the loverdes[1] of the West,
The erles of Mercia, Conventrie and all;
The moe wee gayne, the gare[2] wylle prosper beste,
Wythe syke a nomber wee can never fall.

HAROLDE.

True, so wee sal doe best to lyncke the chayne,
And alle attenes[3] the spreddynge kyngedomme bynde.
No crouched champyone[4] wythe an harte moe feygne[5]
Dyd yssue owte the hallie[6] swerde to fynde,
Than I nowe strev to ryd mie londe of peyne.
Goddwyn, what thanckes owre laboures wylle enhepe![7]
I'lle ryse mie friendes unto the bloddie pleyne;
I'lle wake the honnoure thatte ys now aslepe.
When wylle the chiefes mete atte thie feastive halle,
That I wythe voice alowde maie there upon 'em calle?

GODDWYN.

Next eve, mie sonne.

HAROLDE.

              Nowe, Englonde, ys the tyme,
Whan thee or thie felle foemens cause moste die.
Thie geason[8] wronges bee reyne[9] ynto theyre pryme;
Now wylle thie sonnes unto thie succoure flie.

---

1 Lords.   2 Cause.   3 At once.
4 One who takes up the cross in order to fight against the Saracens.
5 Willing.   6 Holy.   7 Heap upon us.
8 Rare, extraordinary, strange.   9 Run, shot up.

Alyche a storm egederinge[1] yn the skie,
Tys fulle ande brasteth[2] on the chaper[3] grounde ;
Sycke shalle mie fhuirye on the Normans flie,
And alle theyre mittee[4] menne be sleene[5] arounde.
Nowe, nowe, wylle Harolde or oppressionne falle,
Ne moe the Englyshmenne yn vayne for hele[6] shal calle.

KYNGE EDWARDE AND HYS QUEENE.

QUEENE.

Botte, loverde,[7] whie so manie Normannes here?
Mee thynckethe wee bee notte yn Englyshe londe.
These browded[8] straungers alwaie do appere,
Theie parte yor trone,[9] and sete at your ryghte honde.

KYNGE.

Go to, goe to, you doe ne understonde :
Theie yeave[10] mee lyffe, and dyd mie bowkie[11] kepe ;
Theie dyd mee feeste, and did embowre[12] me gronde;
To trete hem yll wulde lette mie kyndnesse slepe.

QUEENE.

Mancas,[13] you have yn store, and to them parte ;
Youre leege-folcke[14] make moke,[15] dole,[16] you have theyr
worthe asterte.[17]

---

1 Assembling, gathering. 2 Bursteth. 3 Dry, barren.
4 Mighty. 5 Slain. 6 Help.
7 Lord. 8 Embroidered. 9 Throne.
10 Give. 11 Person, body. 12 Lodge.
13 Marks, rather 'mancuses.' 14 Subjects. 15 Much.
16 Lamentation. 17 Neglected, or passed by.

KYNGE.

I heste[1] no rede of you. I ken mie friendes.
Hallie[2] dheie are, fulle ready mee to hele.[3]
Theyre volundes[4] are ystorven[5] to self endes ;
No denwere[6] yn mie breste I of them fele :
I muste to prayers ; goe yn, and you do wele ;
I muste ne lose the dutie of the daie ;
Go inne, go ynne, ande viewe the azure rele,[7]
Fulle welle I wote you have noe mynde toe praie.

QUEENE.

I leeve youe to doe hommage heaven-were ;[8]
To serve yor leege-folcke toe is doeynge hommage there.

KYNGE AND SYR HUGHE.

KYNGE.

Mie friende, Syr Hughe, whatte tydynges brynges
    thee here?

HUGHE.

There is no mancas yn mie loverdes ente ;[9]
The hus[10] dyspense[11] unpaied doe appere ;
The laste receivure[12] ys eftsoones[13] dispente.[14]

---

1 Require, ask.   2 Holy.   3 Help.
4 Will.   5 Dead.   6 Doubt.
7 Waves.   8 Heaven-ward, or God-ward.
9 Purse, used here probably as a treasury.   10 House.
11 Expence.   12 Receipt.   13 Soon.
14 Expended.

KYNGE.

Thenne guylde the Weste.

HUGHE.

Mie loverde, I dyd speke
Untoe the mitte[1] Erle Harolde of the thynge;
He raysed hys honde, and smoke me onne the cheke,
Saieynge, go beare thatte message to the kynge.

KYNGE.

Arace[2] hym of hys powere; bie Goddis worde,
Ne moe thatte Harolde shall ywield the erlies swerde.

HUGHE.

Atte seeson fytte, mie loverde, lette itt bee;
Botte nowe the folcke doe soe enalse[3] hys name,
Inne strevvynge to slea hymme, ourselves we slea;
Syke ys the doughtyness[4] of hys grete fame.

KYNGE.

Hughe, I bethyncke, thie rede[5] ys notte to blame.
Botte thou maiest fynde fulle store of marckes yn Kente.

HUGHE.

Mie noble loverde, Godwynn ys the same;
He sweeres he wylle notte swelle the Normans ent.[6]

---

1 A contraction of ' mighty.'   2 Divest.   3 Embrace.
4 Mightiness.   5 Counsel.   6 Purse.

KYNGE.

Ah traytoure ! botte mie rage I wylle commaunde.
Thou arte a Normanne, Hughe, a straunger to the launde.

Thou kenneste howe these Englysche erle doe bere
Such stedness [1] in the yll and evylle thynge,
Botte atte the goode theie hover yn denwere, [2]
Onknowlachynge [3] gif thereunto to clynge.

HUGHE.

Onwordie [4] syke a marvelle [5] of a kynge!
O Edwarde, thou deservest purer leege; [6]
To thee heie [7] shulden al theire mancas brynge;
Thie nodde should save menne, and thie glomb [8] for-
slege. [9]
I amme no curriedowe, [10] I lacke no wite, [11]
I speke whatte bee the trouthe, and whatte all see is ryghte.

KYNGE.

Thou arte a hallie [12] manne, I doe thee pryze.
Comme, comme, and here and hele [13] mee ynn mie
praires.
Fulle twentie mancas I wylle thee alise, [14]
And twayne of hamlettes [15] to thee and thie heyres.
Soe shalle all Normannes from mie londe be fed,
Theie alleyn [16] have syke love as to acquyre yer bredde.

---

1 Firmness, stedfastness.	2 Doubt, suspense.	3 Not knowing.
4 Unworthy.	5 Wonder.	6 Homage, obeysance.
7 They.	8 Frown.	9 Kill.
10 Flatterer.	11 Reward.	12 Holy.
13 Help.	14 Allow.	15 Manors.
16 Alone.		

CHORUS.

Whan Freedom, dreste yn blodde-steyned veste,
  To everie knyghte her warre-songe sunge,
Uponne her hedde wylde wedes were spredde;
  A gorie anlace bye her honge.
    She daunced onne the heathe;
    She hearde the voice of deathe;
Pale-eyned affryghte, hys harte of sylver hue,
In vayne assayled[1] her bosomme to acale;[2]
She hearde onflemed[3] the shriekynge voice of woe,
And sadnesse ynne the owlette shake the dale.
    She shooke the burled[4] speere,
    On hie she jeste[5] her sheelde,
    Her foemen[6] all appere,
    And flizze[7] alonge the feelde.
Power, wythe his heafod[8] straught[9] ynto the skyes,
Hys speere a sonne-beame, and hys sheelde a starre,
Alyche[10] twaie[11] brendeynge[12] gronfyres[13] rolls hys eyes,
Chaftes[14] with hys yronne feete and soundes to war.
    She syttes upon a rocke,
    She bendes before hys speere,
    She ryses from the shocke,
    Wieldynge her owne yn ayre.
Harde as the thonder dothe she drive ytte on,
Wytte scillye[15] wympled[16] gies[17] ytte to hys crowne,
Hys longe sharpe speere, hys spreddynge sheelde ys
  gon,

1 Endeavoured.   2 Freeze.   3 Undismayed.
4 Armed, pointed.   5 Hoisted on high, raised.
6 Foes, enemies.   7 Fly.   8 Head.
9 Stretched.   10 Like.   11 Two.
12 Flaming.   13 Meteors.   14 Beats, stamps.
15 Closely.   16 Mantled, covered.   17 Guides.

He falles, and fallynge rolleth thousandes down.
   War, goare-faced war, bie envie burld,[1] arist,[2]
Hys feerie heaulme[3] noddynge to the ayre,
Tenne bloddie arrowes ynne hys streynynge fyste—[*]
      *   *   *   *   *   *

---

1 Armed.   2 Arose.   3 Helmet.

[*] This Ode, or Chorus, is undoubtedly one of the most sublime compositions of Rowley's pen; a rival even in its present imperfect state to the song on Ælla, and, if complete, would probably gain an indisputable preference. It scarcely contains a redundant word, or fails in a deficient expression, nor can its powerful imagery be conveyed in more concise and emphatical language. Freedom never appeared in a more original dress, than in her summons to war—in her wild attire—her undaunted spirit—her enduring fortitude; and, the effectual manner in which she avenges herself of her enemy.—DEAN MILLES.

As a complete specimen of his abilities in Lyric composition, it is only necessary to cite the incomparable Ode or Chorus in Goddwyn, a tragedy which he has left imperfect.—DR. GREGORY.

We find, among these Poems, Odes in irregular metres, Eclogues of the Pastoral kind, and Discoursing Tragedies; compositions, for not one of which any example could be found in England in the XVth century. Even in those compositions, of which the species was not entirely unknown, it is impossible not to observe a striking difference from the other compositions of that age, with respect to the *manner* in which they are constructed, and the *subjects* to which they are applied. Instead of tedious chronicles we have here interesting portions of history, selected and embellished with all the graces of epic poetry; instead of devotional hymns, legendary tales, and moralizations of scripture, we have elegant little poems upon *charitie* and *happinesse*, a *new church*, a *living worthy*, and other occurrences of the moment: no translations from the French, no allusions to the popular authors of the middle ages; nothing, in short, of what we see in so many other writers about that time. If Rowley really lived and wrote these poems in the XVth century, he must have stalked about, like Tiresias among the *Homeric ghosts*—

    " He only wise, the rest mere fleeting shades."—
                            TYRWHITT.

𝔈𝔫𝔤𝔩𝔶𝔰𝔥 𝔐𝔢𝔱𝔞𝔪𝔬𝔯𝔭𝔥𝔬𝔰𝔦𝔰:*

𝔅𝔦𝔢 𝔗. 𝔯𝔬𝔴𝔩𝔢𝔦𝔢.

BOOKE 1ST.[1]

I.

Whanne Scythyannes, salvage as the wolves theie
    chacde,
Peyncted in horrowe[2] formes bie nature dyghte,[3]
Heckled[4] yn beastskyns, slepte uponne the waste,
And wyth the morneynge rouzed the wolfe to fyghte,
Swefte as descendeynge lemes[5] of roddie lyghte
Plonged to the hulstred[6] bedde of laveynge[7] seas,
Gerd[8] the blacke mountayn okes yn drybblets[9] twighte,[10]
And ranne yn thoughte alonge the azure mees,[11]
Whose eyne dyd feerie sheene, like blue-hayred defs[12],
That dreerie hange upon Dover's emblaunched[13] clefs.

---

* This poem was originally printed from a single sheet in Chatterton's
hand-writing, communicated by Mr. Barrett, who received it from
Chatterton.
  1 [" I will endeavour to get the remainder of these poems."—CHAT-
TERTON.]

2 Unseemly, disagreeable.	3 Dressed.	4 Wrapped.
5 Rays.	6 Hidden, secret.	7 Washing.
8 Broke, rent.	9 Small pieces.	10 Pulled, rent.
11 Meadows.	12 Vapours, meteors.	
13 Whitened.		

II.

Soft boundeynge ov·'r swelleynge azure reles 1
The salvage natyves sawe a shyppe appere ;
An uncouthe² denwere ³ to theire bosomme steles ;
Theyre myghte ys knopped ⁴ ynne the frost of fere.
The headed javlyn lisseth ⁵ here and there ;
Theie stonde, theie ronne, theie loke wythe ger eyne ;
The shyppes sayle, boleynge⁶ wythe the kyndelie ayre,
Ronneth to harbour from the beateynge bryne ;
Theie dryve awaie aghaste, whanne to the stronde
A burled⁷ Trojan lepes, wythe Morglaien sweerde yn
    honde.

III.

Hymme followede eftsoones hys compheeres,⁸ whose
    swerdes
Glestred lyke gledeynge ⁹ starres ynne frostie nete,
Hayleynge theyre capytayne in chirckynge¹⁰ wordes
Kynge of the lande, whereon theie set theyre fete.
The greete kynge Brutus thanne theie dyd hym greete,
Prepared for battle, mareschalled the fyghte ;
Theie urged the warre, the natyves fledde, as flete
As fleaynge cloudes that swymme before the syghte ;
Tyll tyred wythe battles, for to ceese the fraie,
Theie uncted¹¹ Brutus kynge, and gave the Trojanns
    swaie.

---

1 Ridges, rising waves.   2, 3 Unknown tremor.
4 Fastened, chained, congealed, rather, nipped.
5 Boundeth.   6 Swelling.   7 Armed.
8 Companions.   9 Lived.   10 A confused noise.
11 Anointed.

IV.

Twayne of twelve years han lemed[1] up the myndes,
Leggende[2] the salvage unthewes[3] of theire breste,
Improved in mysterk[4] warre, and lymmed[5] theyre
    kyndes,
Whenne Brute from Brutons sonke to æterne reste.
Eftsoons the gentle Locryne was possest
Of swaie, and vested yn the paramente ;[6]
Halceld[7] the bykrous[8] Huns, who dyd infeste
Hys wakeynge kyngdom wyth a foule intente ;
As hys broade swerde oer Homberres heade was honge,
He tourned toe ryver wyde, and roarynge rolled alonge.

V.

He wedded Gendolyne of roieal sede,
Upon whose countenance rodde healthe was spreade ;
Bloushing, alyche[9] the scarlette of herr wede,[10]
She sonke to pleasaunce on the marryage bedde.
Eftsoons her peacefull joie of mynde was fledde ;
Elstrid ametten[11] with the kynge Locryne ;
Unnombered beauties were upon her shedde,
Moche fyne, moche fayrer thanne was Gendolyne ;
The mornynge tynge, the rose, the lillie floure,
In ever ronneynge race on her dyd peyncte theyre
    powere.

---

1 Enlightened.   2 Alloyed.   3 Savage barbarity.
4 Mystic.   5 Polished.   6 A princely robe.
7 Defeated.   8 Warring.   9 Like.
10 Garment.   11 Met with.

VI.

The gentle suyte of Locryne gayned her love ;*
Theie lyved soft momentes to a swotie[1] age ;
Eft[2] wandringe yn the coppyce, delle, and grove,
Where ne one eyne mote theyre disporte engage ;
There dydde theie tell the merrie lovynge fage,[3]
Croppe the prymrosen floure to decke theyre headde ;
The feerie Gendolyne yn woman rage
Gemoted[4] warriours to bewreck[5] her bedde ;

* Above all, the internal evidence arising from the poems themselves, has always appeared to us to convey decisive marks of modern origin. The smoothness of the verse, which, in most cases, resembles the most correct modern poetry, as well as the complicated nature of the stanza, are highly suspicious. It is no doubt true, that, in some compositions of a lyrical nature, the old English poets attained a considerable degree of ease and fluency, chiefly such as were adapted to the music of the minstrels, when the necessity of following the tune compelled the poet to observe a regularity of rhythm. Such, for example, are the poems of Lawrence Minot. But these poems are flimsy songs, in which the same idea, and often the same words, are repeated and chimed upon, in order to attain the necessary smoothness. Take, for example, a verse of Minot, which for the sake of the uninitiated we have stripped of the antique spelling :

‘ Sir David the Bruce
    Was at distance,
When Edward the Baliolfe
    Rode with his lance :
The north end of England
    Teached him to dance.
When he was met on the moor
    With mickell mischaunce,
Sir Philip the valayse
    Might not him advance ;
The flowers that fair were
    Ar fallen in France :
The flowers are now fallen,
    That fair were and fell :
A boar with his battaille
    Has don them to dwell.'

The ease of these lines is the smoothness of mere ballad, attained by the tenuity of idea, and the tautology of expression.—SIR WALTER SCOTT.

1 Sweet.   2 Oft.   3 A tale.   4 Assembled.   5 Revenge.

Theie rose ; ynne battle was greete Locryne sleene ;
The faire Elstrida fledde from the enchafed[1] queene.

VII.

A tye of love, a dawter fayre she hanne,
Whose boddeynge[2] morneyng shewed a fayre daie,
Her fadre Locrynne, once an hailie manne.
Wyth the fayre dawterre dydde she haste awaie,
To where the western mittee[3] pyles of claie
Arise ynto the cloudes, and doe them beere ;
There dyd Elstrida and Sabryna staie ;
The fyrste tryckde out a whyle yn warryours gratch[4]
    and gear,
Vyncente was she ycleped, butte fulle soone fate
Sente deathe to telle the dame she was notte yn regrate[5].

VIII.

The queene Gendolyne sente a gyaunte knyghte,
Whose doughtie heade swepte the emmertleynge[6] skies,
To slea her wheresoever she shulde be pyghte,[7]
Eke everychone who shulde her ele[5] emprize.[9]
Swefte as the roareynge wyndes the gyaunte flies,
Stayde the loude wyndes, and shaded reaulmes yn
    nyghte,
Stepte over cytties, on meint[10] acres lies,
Meeteynge the herehaughtes of morneynge lighte ;
Tyll mooveynge to the weste, myschaunce hys gye,[11]
He thorowe warriours gratch fayre Elstrid did espie.

---

1 Heated, enraged.   2 Budding.   3 Mighty.   4 Apparel.
5 Esteem, favour.   6 Glittering.   7 Settled.   8 Help.
9 Adventure.   10 Many.   11 Guide.

IX.

He tore a ragged mountayne from the grounde,
Harried[1] uppe noddynge forrests to the skie,
Thanne wythe a fuirie, mote the erthe astounde,[2]
To meddle ayre he lette the mountayne flie.
The flying wolfynnes sente a yelleynge crie;
Onne Vyncente and Sabryna felle the mount;
To lyve æternalle dyd theie eftsoones die;
Thorowe the sandie grave boiled up the pourple founte,
On a broade grassie playne was layde the hylle,
Staieynge the rounynge course of meint a limmed[3] rylle.

X.

The goddes, who kenned the actyons of the wyghte,
To leggen[4] the sadde happe of twayne so fayre,
Houton[5] dyd make the mountaine bie theire mighte.
Forth from Sabryna ran a ryverre cleere,[6]
Roarynge and rolleynge on yn course bysmare;[7]
From female Vyncente shotte a ridge of stones,
Eche syde the ryver rysynge heavenwere;[8]
Sabrynas floode was helde ynne Elstryds bones.
So are theie cleped; gentle and the hynde
Can telle, that Severnes streeme bie Vyncentes rocke's
    ywrynde.[9]

XI.

The bawsyn[10] gyaunt, hee who dyd them slee,
To telle Gendolyne quycklie was ysped;[11]
Whanne, as he strod alonge the shakeynge lee,

---

1 Tost.   2 Astonish.   3 Glassy, reflecting.
4 Lessen, allay.   5 Hollow.   6 Famous.
7 Bewildered, curious.   8 Towards heaven.
9 Hid, covered.   10 Huge, bulky.   11 Dispatched.

The roddie levynne[1] glesterrd on hys headde:
Into hys hearte the azure vapoures spreade;
He wrythde arounde yn drearie dernie[2] payne;
Whanne from his lyfe-bloode the rodde lemes[3] were fed,
He felle an hepe of ashes on the playne :
Stylle does hys ashes shoote ynto the lyghte,
A wondrous mountayne hie, and Snowdon ys ytte
hyghte.[*]

---

1 Red lightning.   2 Cruel.   3 Flames, rays.

[*] When I read the researches of those learned antiquaries who have endeavoured to prove, that the poems attributed to Rowley were really written by him, I observe many ingenious remarks in confirmation of their opinion, which it would be tedious if not difficult to controvert; but I no sooner turn to the poems, than the labours of the antiquaries appear only a waste of time and ingenuity, and I am involuntarily forced to join in placing that laurel, which he seems so well to have deserved, on the brow of Chatterton.

The poems bear so many marks of superior genius, that they have deservedly excited the general attention of polite scholars, and are considered as the most remarkable productions in modern poetry. We have many instances of poetical eminence at an early age; but neither Cowley, Milton, nor Pope, ever produced anything, while they were boys, which can justly be compared to the poems of Chatterton. The learned antiquaries do not indeed dispute their excellence. They extol it in the highest terms of applause. They raise their favourite Rowley to a rivalry with Homer; but they make the very merit of the works an argument against the real author. Is it possible, say they, that a boy could produce compositions so beautifully and so masterly? That a common boy should produce them is not possible; but that they should be produced by a boy of an extraordinary genius, such a genius as is that of Homer and Shakspeare, such a genius as appears not above once in many centuries, though a prodigy, is such an one as by no means exceeds the bounds of rational credibility.

That Chatterton was such a genius, his manners and his life in some degree evince. He had all the tremulous sensibility of genius, all its eccentricities, all its pride, and all its spirit. Even his death, unfortunate and wicked as it was, displayed a magnitude of soul, which urged him to spurn a world where even his exalted genius could not vindicate him from contempt, indigence, and contumely.—VICESIMUS KNOX.

An Excelente Balade of Charitie:*

As wroten bie the gode prieste Thomas Rowleie,[1] 1464.

I.

In Virgyne[2] the sweltrie sun gan sheene,
And hotte upon the mees[3] did caste his raie:
The apple rodded[4] from its palie greene,
And the mole[5] peare did bende the leafy spraie ;
The peede chelandri[6] sunge the livelong daie;
'Twas nowe the pride, the manhode of the yeare,
And eke the grounde was dighte[7] in its mose defte[8]
    aumere.[9]

---

* The "Ballad of Charity" is an imitation of the most beautiful and affecting of our Saviour's parables, "The good Samaritan." The poetical descriptions are truly picturesque. We feel the horror of the dark cold night; we see "the big drops fall," and the "full flocks driving o'er the plain." "The welkin opens, and the yellow lightning flies," &c.—DR. GREGORY.

1 Thomas Rowley, the author, was born at Norton Mal-reward, in Somersetshire, educated at the Convent of St. Kenna, at Keynesham, and died at Westbury, in Gloucestershire.—CHATTERTON.

2 The sign of Virgo.   3 Meads.   4 Reddened, ripened.
5 Soft.   6 Pied goldfinch.   7 Drest, arrayed.
8 Neat, ornamented.   9 A loose robe or mantle.

II.

The sun was glemeing in the midde of daie,
Deadde still the aire, and eke the welken[1] blue,
When from the sea arist[2] in drear arraie
A hepe of cloudes of sable sullen hue,
The which full fast unto the woodlande drewe,
Hiltring[3] attenes[4] the sunnis fetyve[5] face,
And the blacke tempeste swolne and gatherd up apace.*

III.

Beneathe an holme, faste by a pathwaie side,
Which dyde unto Seyncte Godwine's covent† lede,

---

1 The sky, the atmosphere.   2 Arose.   3 Hiding, shrouding.
4 At once.   5 Beauteous, festive.

* The smoothness of Rowley is combined with all the graces and re-
finement of modern poetry. Take two stanzas at hazard, divested of
the artificial *patina*, or rust of antique orthography :

"The sun was gleaming in the midst of day,
    Dead-still the air, and eke the welkin blue,
When from the sea arose in drear array,
A heap of clouds, of sable sullen hue,
The which full fast unto the woodland drew,
    Hiding at once the sunnes festive face ;
And the black tempest swell'd, and gathered up apace.

*   *   *   *

The gather'd storm is ripe; the big drops fall;
    The sun-burnt meadows smoke, and drink the rain ;
The coming *ghastness* doth the cattle 'pal ;
    And the full flocks are driving o'er the plain.
Dash'd from the clouds the waters fly again,
    The welkin opes, the yellow levin flies,
And the hot fiery steam in the wide flashing dies.

Can any one read this beautiful description of a landscape overshaded
by a thunder-storm, and doubt for a moment that it is by a modern
hand? Yet we have only discarded 'heltring,' 'fetive,' 'forswat,' and
'smothe;' all other differences betwixt our copy and the text being
merely in spelling.—Sir Walter Scott.

† 'Seyncte Godwine's Covent.' It would have been *charitable* if the
author had not pointed at personal characters in this "Ballad of
Charity." The Abbott of St. Godwin's at the time of the writing of this
was Ralph de Bellomont, a great stickler for the Lancastrian family.
Rowley was a Yorkist.—Chatterton.

A hapless pilgrim moneynge dyd abide,
Pore in his viewe, ungentle[1] in his weede,[2]
Longe bretful[3] of the miseries of neede,
Where from the hail-stone coulde the almer[4] flie?
He had no housen theere, ne anie covent nie.

IV.

Look in his glommed[5] face, his sprighte there scanne;
Howe woe-be-gone, how withered, forwynd,[6] deade!
Haste to thie church-glebe-house,[7] asshrewed[8] manne!
Haste to thie kiste,[9] thie onlie dortoure[10] bedde.
Cale,[11] as the claie whiche will gre on thie hedde,
Is Charitie and Love aminge[12] highe elves;
Knightis and Barons live for pleasure and themselves.[*]

---

1 Beggarly.   2 Dress.
3 Filled with.   4 Beggar.
5 'Glommed,' clouded, dejected. A person of some note in the lite-
rary world is of opinion, that 'glum' and 'glom' are modern cant
words; and from this circumstance doubts the authenticity of Rowley's
manuscripts. 'Glummong' in the Saxon, signifies twilight, a dark or
dubious light; and the modern word 'gloomy' is derived from the
Saxon 'glum.'—CHATTERTON.

6 Dry, sapless.   7 The grave.   8 Accursed, unfortunate.
9 Coffin.   10 A sleeping room.   11 Cold.   12 Among.
[*] Chatterton probably alluded to his own deserted situation, since, it
is said, he gave this ballad to the publisher of the 'Town and Country
Magazine,' only a month before his death.—DR. GREGORY.

The poet in the truly excellent "Balade of Charitie," describes a
person overtaken by a sudden storm, whom he styles an 'almer.' It is
not impossible, but that there might have been such a word to denote
'an asker of alms;' but it is contrary to analogy: and I think, impro-
bable.—BRYANT.

v.

The gatherd storme is rype; the bigge drops falle;
The forswat[1] meadowes smethe,[2] and drenche[3] the
   raine;
The comyng ghastness[4] do the cattle pall,[5]
And the full flockes are drivynge ore the plaine;
Dashde from the cloudes the waters flott[6] againe;
The welkin opes; the yellow levynne[7] flies;
And the hot fierie smothe[8] in the wide lowings[9] dies.

vi.

Liste! now the thunder's rattling clymmynge[10] sound
Cheves[11] slowlie on, and then embollen[12] clangs,
Shakes the hie spyre, and losst, dispended, drown'd,
Still on the gallard[13] eare of terroure hanges;
The windes are up; the lofty elmen swanges;
Again the levynne and the thunder poures,
And the full cloudes are braste[14]attenes in stonen showers.

vii.

Spurreynge his palfrie oere the watrie plaine,
The Abbote of Seyncte Godwynes convente came;
His chapournette[15] was drented with the reine,
And his pencte[16] gyrdle met with mickle shame;

---

1 Sun-burnt.   2 Smoke.   3 Drink.   4 Ghastliness.
5 Pall, a contraction from ' appal', to fright.
6 Fly.   7 Lightning.   8 Steam, or vapours.
9 Flames.   10 Noisy.   11 Moves.
12 Swelled, strengthened.   13 Frighted.   14 Burst.
15 A small round hat, not unlike the shapournette in heraldry, formerly
worn by ecclesiastics and lawyers.—CHATTERTON.
16 Painted.

He aynewarde tolde his bederoll [1] at the same ;
The storme encreasen, and he drew aside,
With the mist [2] almes-craver neere to the holme to bide.

VIII.

His cope [3] was all of Lyncolne clothe so fyne,
With a gold button fasten'd neere his chynne ;
His autremete [4] was edged with golden twynne,
And his shoone pyke [5] a loverds [6] mighte have binne ;
Full well it shewn he thoughten coste no sinne :
The trammels of the palfrye pleasde his sighte,
For the horse-millanare [7] his head with roses dighte.

---

1 He told his beads backwards ; a figurative expression to signify
cursing.—CHATTERTON.

2 Poor, needy.   3 A cloke.

4 [According to Chatterton's interpretation, the meaning of this word
is 'a loose white robe worn by priests.' Skinner, as quoted by Dean
Milles, calls it *vestimentum*, but adds *forsan quasi altera nitra*. And
in the picture which Chaucer has drawn of the fearful reverse of Zeno-
bia's fortunes, he says—

> " And she that helmid was in starke stouris,
> And won by force tounis strong, and touris
> Shall on her hedde now werin *autremite*."

And the signification which Speght gives to it in that sense, is 'another
attire.' Kersey calls it 'a kind of vestment,' one of the rare instances
in which he differs from Speght. Bailey has copied the latter. It
seems probable, however, that it was more properly a 'coif' or 'head-
dress.'—ED.]

5 Picked shoe.   6 A lord.

7 One morning while Mr. Tyrwhitt and I were at Bristol, in 1776, we
had not proceeded far from our lodging before he found he had left on
his table a memorandum-book, which it was necessary he should have
about him. He therefore returned to fetch it while I stood still in the
very place we parted at, looking on the objects about me. By this spot,
as I was subsequently assured, the young Chatterton would naturally
pass to the charity school, on St. Augustine's back, where he was edu-
cated. But whether this circumstance be correctly stated or not, is
immaterial to the general tendency of the following remark. On the

IX.

An almes, sir prieste ! the droppynge pilgrim saide,
O! let me waite within your covente dore,
Till the sunne sheneth hie above our heade,
And the loude tempeste of the aire is oer ;
Helpless and ould am I alas ! and poor :
No house, ne friend, ne moneie in my pouche ;
All yatte 1 calle my owne is this my silver crouche.[1]

X.

Varlet, replyd the Abbatte, cease your dinne ;
This is no season almes and prayers to give ;
Mie porter never lets a faitour[2] in ;
None touch mie rynge who not in honour live.
And now the sonne with the blacke cloudes did stryve,
And shettynge[3] on the grounde his glairie[4] raie,
The Abbatte spurrde his steede, and eftsoones roadde
awaie.

---

spot, however, where I was standing, our retentive observer had picked
up an idea which afterwards found its way into his " Excelente Balade
of Charitie, as wroten by the gode prieste Thomas Rowleie, 1464."

"For the 'horse-millanare' his head with roses dighte."

The considerate reader must obviously have stared on being informed
that such a term and such a trade had been extant in 1464; but his
wonder would have ceased, had he been convinced, as I am, that in a
public part of Bristol, full in sight of every passer by, was a sadler's
shop, over which was inscribed ' A' or ' B,' no matter which, 'horse-
milliner.' On the outside of one of the windows of the same operator
stood (and I suppose yet stands) a wooden horse dressed out with rib-
bons, to explain the nature of horse-millinery. We have here perhaps
the history of this modern image, which was impressed by Chatterton
into his description of an " Abbote of Seyncte Godwynes Convente."—
STEEVENS.

1 Crucifix.   2 A beggar, or vagabond.
3 Shooting.   4 Glaring.

XI.

Once moe the skie was blacke, the thounder rolde;
Faste reyneynge[1] oer the plaine a prieste was seen;
Ne dighte full proude, ne buttoned up in golde;
His cope and jape[2] were graie, and eke were clene;
A Limitoure[3] he was of order seene;
And from the pathwaie side then turned hee,
Where the pore almer laie binethe the holmen tree.

XII.

An almes, sir priest! the droppynge pilgrim sayde,
For sweete Seyncte Marie and your order sake.
The Limitoure then loosen'd his pouche threade,
And did thereoute a groate of silver take;
The mister[4] pilgrim dyd for halline[5] shake.
Here take this silver, it maie eathe[6] thie care;
We are Goddes stewards all, nete[7] of oure owne we bare.

XIII.

But ah! unhailie[8] pilgrim, lerne of me,
Scathe[9] anie give a rentrolle to their Lorde.
Here take my semecope,[10] thou arte bare I see;
Tis thyne; the Seynctes will give me mie rewarde.
He left the pilgrim, and his waie aborde.[11]
Virgynne and hallie Seyncte, who sitte yn gloure,[12]
Or give the mittee[13] will, or give the gode man power!

---

1 ;Running.
2 A short surplice, worn by friars of an inferior class, and secular priests.
3 A licensed begging friar.

4 Needy, hapless.	5 Joy.	6 Ease.
7 Nought.	8 Unhappy.	9 Scarce.
10 A short under-cloke.	11 Went on.	12 Glory.
13 Mighty, rich.		

To Johne Ladgate.

[Sent with the following Songe to Ella.]

Well thanne, goode Johne, sythe[1] ytt must needes be
  soe,
Thatt thou and I a bowtynge matche[2] must have,
Lette ytt ne breakynge of oulde friendshyppe bee,
Thys ys the onelie all-a-boone[3] I crave.

Rememberr Stowe,[4] the Bryghtstowe Carmalyte,
Who whanne Johne Clarkynge, one of myckle lore,[5]
Dydd throwe hys gauntlette-penne, wyth hym to fyghte,
Hee showd smalle wytte, and showd hys weaknesse
  more.

Thys ys mie formance, whyche I nowe have wrytte,
The best performance of mie lyttel wytte.

---

1 Since.   2 Contest.

3 Favour. [Speght, Kersey, and Bailey interpret it 'a made request.'
The orthography in the former is the same as in the text. In Bailey
and Kersey it is spelt 'All-a-Bone.' See note to the same word in the
third Eclogue.—Ed.]

4 'Stowe' should be 'Stone,' a Carmelite friar of Bristol, educated at
Cambridge, and a famous preacher.—Warton.

5 Learning.

SONGE TO ÆLLA,

LORDE OF THE CASTEL OF BRYSTOWE YNNE DAIES OF YORE.

Oh thou, orr what remaynes of thee,
  Ælla, the darlynge of futurity,
Lett thys mie songe bolde as thie courage be,
  As everlastynge to posteritye.
Whanne Dacya's sonnes, whose hayres of bloude redde
      hue
Lyche kynge-cuppes brastynge wythe the morning due,
  Arraung'd ynne dreare arraie,
  Upponne the lethale daie,
Spredde farre and wyde onne Watchets shore;
  Than dyddst thou furiouse stande,
  And bie thie valyante hande
Beesprengedd¹ all the mees² wythe gore.

  Drawne bie thyne anlace³ felle,
  Downe to the depthe of helle
  Thousandes of Dacyanns went;
  Brystowannes, menne of myghte,
  Ydar'd the bloudie fyghte,
  And actedd deeds full quent.⁴

  Oh thou, whereer (thie bones att reste)
  Thye Spryte to haunte delyghteth beste,
Whetherr upponne the bloude-embrewedd pleyne,
  Orr whare thou kennst fromm farre
  The dysmall crye of warre,
Orr seest somme mountayne made of corse of sleyne;

---

1 Sprinkled   2 Meadows.   3 Sword.   4 Strange.

Orr seest the hatchedd [1] stede,
Ypraunceynge o'er the mede,
And neighe to be amenged [2] the poynctedd speeres ;
Orr ynne blacke armoure staulke arounde
Embattel'd Brystowe, once thie grounde,
And glowe ardurous [3] onn the Castle steeres ;

Orr fierye round the mynsterr glare ;
Lette Brystowe stylle be made thie care ;
Guarde ytt fromme foemenne and consumynge fyre;
Lyche Avones streme ensyrke [4] ytte rounde,
Ne lette a flame enharme the grounde,
Tylle ynne one flame all the whole worlde expyre. [*]

---

1 Covered with achievements.   2 Among.
3 Burning.   4 Encircle.

[*] The stanza of old English poetry is most commonly formed of lines
of equal feet, and constantly preserves an uniform recurrence of the
same systematic alternation of rhyme. The 'Songe to Ælla' is com-
posed in that devious and irregular measure, which has been called the
'Pindaric.' What shall we think of a Pindaric ode in the reign of
Edward the Fourth? It is well known, that this novelty was reserved
for the capricious ambition of Cowley's muse. The writers of the fif-
teenth century were not so fond of soaring. They had neither skill
nor strength for such towering flights.—WARTON.

Chatterton's verses have been shown to be too smooth and harmo-
nious to be genuine compositions of antiquity: they are liable at the
same time to the very opposite objection; they are too old for the era
to which they are ascribed. This sounds like a paradox; yet it will be
found to be true. The versification is too modern; the language often
too ancient. It is not the language of any particular period of an-
tiquity, but of *two entire centuries!* This is easily accounted for.
Chatterton had no other means of writing old language, but by applying
to glossaries and dictionaries, and these comprise all the antiquated
words of preceding times; many provincial words used perhaps by
a northern poet, and entirely unknown to a southern inhabitant;
many words also, used in a singular sense by our ancient bards, and
perhaps by them only once. — MALONE.

The underwritten Lines were
Composed by John Ladgate, a Priest in London,
And sent to Rowlie, as an Answer to the preceding
Songe of Ella.[1]

Havynge wythe mouche attentyon redde
    Whatt you dydd to mee sende,
Admyre the varses mouche I dyd,
    And thus an answer lende.

Amongs the Greeces Homer was
    A Poett mouche renownde,
Amongs the Latyns Vyrgilius
    Was beste of Poets founde.

The Brytish Merlyn oftenne hanne
    The gyfte of inspyration,
And Afled[1] to the Sexonne menne
    Dydd synge wythe elocation.[2]

Ynne Norman tymes, Turgotus and
    Goode Chaucer dydd excelle,
Thenn Stowe, the Bryghtstowe Carmelyte,
    Dydd bare awaie the belle.

---

1 Alfred.   2 Elocution.

Nowe Rowlie ynne these mokie [1] dayes
Lendes owte hys sheenynge lyghtes,
And Turgotus and Chaucer lyves
Ynne ev'ry lyne he wrytes.*

---

1 Dark, gloomy.

* All the poets who thus owe their existence to Chatterton, write in the same harmonous style, and display the same tact and superiority of genius. Other poets living in the same or different ages, exhibit a wide diversity in judgment, fancy, and the higher creative faculty of imagination, so that a discriminating mind can distinguish an individual character in almost every separate writer, but here are persons living in different ages; moving in different stations; exposed to different circumstances; and expressing different sentiments; yet all of whom betraying the same peculiar habits, with the same talents and facilities of composition. This is evidenced, whether it be

The Abbatte, John, (living in the year 1186).	Maystre John à Iscam.
Carpenter, Bishoppe of Worcester	Seyncte Baldwynne, 1247.
Ecca, Bishoppe of Hereforde.	Seyncte Warburghe, 1247.
Elmar, Bishoppe of Selseie.	John de Bergham, 1320.
The Rawfe Chedder Chappmanne, 1356.	John Ladgate.
Syr William Canynge, 1469.	Syr Thybbot Gorges, 1440.
	Thomas Rowley, 1469.

And the whole of these poets, with the exception of Ladgate, completely unknown to the world, till called from their dormitory by Chatterton! Such a fact would be a phenomenon unspeakably more inexplicable than that of ascribing Rowley to a youth of less than sixteen, who had made 'Antique Lore' his peculiar study, and who was endowed with precocious, and almost unlimited genius. — COTTLE's *Early Recollections of Coleridge.*

Mr. Tyrwhitt compared the copy of the 'Songe to Ælla' and 'Ladgate's Answer,' supplied by Mr. Catcott, with one made by Mr. Barrett, from the piece of vellum which Chatterton gave to him as the original MS. These are the variations of importance, exclusive of many in the spelling.

VERSES TO LADGATE.

In the title, for 'Ladgate,' r. 'Lydgate.' ver. 3. for "bee,' r. ' goe.'
ver. 2. r. ' Thatt I and thee.'   7. for ' fyghte,' r. ' wryte.'

SONGE to ÆLLA.

The title in the vellum MS. was simply ' Songe toe Ælla,' with a small mark of reference to a note below, containing the following wordes— ' Lord of the Castelle of Brystowe ynne daies of yore.' It may be proper also to take notice, that the whole song was there written like prose, without any breaks, or divisions into verses.

ver. 6. for ' brastynge,' *r.* ' burstynge.' ver. 23. for ' dysmall,' *r.* honore.'
11. for ' valyante,' *r.* ' burlie.'

LADGATE'S ANSWER.

No title in the Vellum MS.

ver 3. for ' varses' *r.* ' peue.'   ult. for lyne,' *r.* ' thynge.'
antep. for 'Lendes,' *r.* ' Sendes.

Mr. Barrett had also a copy of these Poems by Chatterton, which differed from that which Chatterton afterwards produced as the original, in the following particulars, among others:

IN THE TITLE OF THE VERSES TO LADGATE.

	Orig. ' Lydgate.'	— Chat. ' Ladgate.'
ver. 3.	Orig. ' goe.'	— Chat. ' doe.'
7.	Orig. ' wryte.'	— Chat. ' fyghte.'

SONGE TO ÆLLA.

ver. 5.	Orig. ' Dacyane.'	— Chat. ' Dacya's.
	Orig. ' whose lockes.'	— Chat. ' whose hayres.'
11.	Orig. ' burlie.'	— Chat. ' bronded.'
22.	Orig. ' kennest.'	— Chat. ' hearst.'
23.	Orig. ' honore.'	— Chat. ' dysmall.'
26.	Orig. ' Yprauncynge.'	— Chat. ' Ifrayning.'
30.	Orig. ' gloue.'	— Chat. ' glare.'

TYRWHITT's *Edition of Rowley.*

Upon these variations we have these remarks: " In one copy of the ' Songe to Ælla,' which Chatterton gave to Mr. Barrett, these lines were found :

" Or seest the hatched steed,
Ifrayning o'er the meed."

Being called upon for the original, he the next day produced a parchment, containing the same poem, in which he had written ' yprauncing,' instead of ' ifrayning;' but by some artifice he had obscured the MS. so much to give it an ancient appearance, that Mr. Barrett could not make out the word without the use of galls. What follows from all this, but that Chatterton found on examination that there was no such word as ' ifrayning,' and that he substituted another in its place ? In the same poem he at one time wrote 'locks,'—' burlie'—' brasting,' and ' kennest;' at another, ' hairs'—' valiant'—' bursting,' and ' hearest.' Variations of this kind he could have produced without end. What he called originals indeed, were probably in general more perfect than what he called copies; because the former were always produced after the other, and were, in truth, nothing more than second editions of the same pieces."—MALONE.

The Tournament.

An Interlude.

.

This Poem was originally printed from a copy made by Mr. Catcott, from one in Chatterton's hand-writing.

Sir Simon de Bourton, the hero of this poem, is supposed to have been the first founder of a church dedicated to "oure Ladie," in the place where the church of St. Mary Redcliffe now stands.

The following account is transcribed from one of the parchment manuscripts produced by Chatterton:—

"Symonne de Byrtonne eldest sonne of Syrre Baldwynus de Byrtonne, was born on the eve of the annunciation, M.C.C.XXXXXXV. hee was desyrabelle of aspect, and in hys yowthe much yeven to Tourneyeynge, and M.C.C.XXXXXXXX at Wynchestre yule games won myckle honnoure, he abstaynyd from marryage, he was myckle learned and ybuylded a house in the Yle of Wyghte after fashyon of a pallayse royaul,goodlye to beholude, wyth carveily'd pyllars on whych was thys ryme wroten :

<blockquote>
Fulle nobille is thys Kyngelie howse
And eke fulle nobille thee,
Echone is for the other fytte
As sayncies for heaven bee.
</blockquote>

Hee ever was fullen of almesdeeds, and was of the poore beloved: in M.C.C.LXXXV Kynge Edwarde* kepte hys Chrystmasse at Bryghtstowe and proceeded agaynste the Welchmenne ebroughtenne manye stronge and dowghtee knyghts, amongst whom were Syrre Ferrars Nevylle, Geoffroie Freeman, Clymar Percie, Heldebrand Gournie, Ralph Mohun, Syr Lyster Percie, and Edgare Knyvet, knyghtes of renowne, who established a three days' jouste on Sayncts Maryes Hylle: Syrre Ferrars Nevylle appeared dyghte in ruddy armoure bearyng a rampaunte lyon Gutte de Sangue, agaynste hym came Syr Gervayse Teysdylle, who bearyd a launce issuynge proper but was quycklie overthrowen : then appeared Leonarde Ramsay, who had a honde issuante holdeynge a bloudie swerde peercynge a couroune wyth a sheelde peasenue with sylver; he ranne twayne tyltes, but Neville thrown hym on the thyrde rencountre : then dyd the aforesayd Syrre Symonne de Byrtonne avow that if he overthrowen Syrre Ferrars Neville, he woulde there erecte and buylde a chyrche to owre Ladye: allgate there stoode anigh Lamyngtonnes Ladies chamber: hee then encountred vygorously and bore Syrre Ferrars horse and man to the grounde, remaynynge konynge, victore knyght of the Jouste, ande settynge atte the ryghte honde of K. Edwarde. Inne M.CCLXXXXI hee performed hys vowen ybuylden a godelye chyrche from a pattern of St. Oswaldes Abbyes Chyrche and the day of our Lordes natyvyty M.C.CCI. Gylbert de Sante Leonfardoe Byshope of Chychestre dyd dedicate it to the Holie Vyrgynne Marye moder of Godde."

This MS., one of the pretended originals, entitled "Vita Burtoni," is 6½ inches square, partly written with *brown* ink, and partly with perfectly *black*. It is smeared in the centre with glue or brown varnish, but for the most part is in an attorney's regular engrossing hand. The parchment, where it has not been disfigured, appears new and of its natural colour. Some drops of red ink appear in different parts of the parchment.—SOUTHEY's *Edition of Chatterton.*

---

* This circumstance is proved by our old chronicles under the year 1285, "Rex Edw. 1. per Walliam progrediens occidentalem intravit Glamorganciam, quæ ad Comitem Gloveruiæ noscitur pertinere: Rex dein Bristolliam veniens festum Dominicæ nativitatis eo Anno ibi tenuit."—BARRETT.

THE TOURNAMENT.

ENTER AN HERAWDE.

THE Tournament begynnes; the hammerrs sounde ;
The courserrs lysse [1] about the mensuredd [2] fielde ;
The shemrynge [3] armoure throws the sheene [4] arounde ;
Quayntyssed [5] fons [6] depicted [7] onn eche sheelde.
The feerie [8] heaulmets, wythe the wreathes amielde, [9]
Supportes the rampynge lyoncell [10] orr beare,
Wythe straunge depyctures, [11] nature maie nott
    yeelde,
Unseemelie to all orderr doe appere,
Yett yatte [12] to menne, who thyncke and have a spryte, [13]
Makes knowen thatt the phantasies unryghte.

I, sonne of honnoure, spencer [14] of her joies,

---

1 Sport, or play.	2 Bounded, or measured.	3 Shining.
4 Lustre.	5 Curiously devised.	
6 Fancies or devices.	7 Painted, or displayed.	
8 Fiery.	9 Ornamented, enamelled.	
10 A young lion.	11 Drawings, paintings.	12 That.
13 Soul.		

14   " I, sonne of honour, spencer of her joyes
         Must swythen goe to yeve the speeres arounde,
         Wyth advantayle and borne. I meynte emploie,
         Who withoute me woulde fall untoe the grounde."
So it should be stopt. After the herald had mentioned that he was to
present to the knights what belonged to them, he magnifies his own

Muste swythen ¹ goe to yeve ² the speeres arounde;
Wythe advantayle ³ and borne ⁴ I meynte ⁵ emploie,
Who withoute mee woulde fall untoe the grounde.
Soe the tall oake the ivie twysteth rounde;
Soe the neshe⁶flowerr grees⁷ynne the woodeland shade.
The worlde bie diffraunce ⁸ ys ynne orderr founde;
Wydhoute unlikenesse nothynge could bee made.
As ynn the bowke ⁹ nete ¹⁰ alleyn ¹¹ cann bee donne,
Syke ¹² ynn the weal ¹³ of kynde all thynges are partes of
    onne.

ENTERR SYRR SYMONNE DE BOURTONNE.

Herawde,¹⁴ bie heavenne these tylterrs staie too longe,
Mie phantasie ys dyinge forr the fyghte.
The mynstrelles have begonne the thyrde warr songe,
Yett notte a speere of hemm ¹⁵ hath grete mie syghte.
I feere there be ne manne wordhie mie myghte.
I lacke a Guid,¹⁶ a Wyllyamm ¹⁷ to entylte.

office, and speaks of himself as the dispencer of all honour. "I," says
he, "employ many, who without me would sink to nothing." In short,
he intimates, that all honours and badges of honour, come through the
hands of the herald; which seems to have been not at all understood
by Chatterton.

Such, I imagine, is the purport of the two words in question, 'adven-
tayle' and 'borne'. By the former of these is meant, ' an helmet with
a sliding beaver;' by the other, a kind of 'cuirass' or 'gorget;' which
two, by Chatterton, have been interpreted 'armour' and 'burnish.'—
BRYANT.

1 Quickly.	2 Give.	3 Armour.	4 Burnish.
5 Many.	6 Young, weak, tender.	7 Grows.	
8 Variety.	9 Body.	10 Nothing.	11 Alone.
12 So.	13 Government.	14 Herald.	
15 A contraction of 'them.'			

16 Guie de Sancta Egidio, the most famous tiltor of his age.—CHAT-
TERTON. Rather Guy of Warwick.—DEAN MILLES.

17 William Rufus.—CHATTERTON. Rather William the Conqueror.
—DEAN MILLES.

To reine[1] anente[2] a fele[3] embodiedd knyghte,
Ytt gettes ne rennome[4] gyff hys blodde bee spylte.
Bie heavenne and Marie ytt ys tyme they're here ;
I lyche nott unthylle[5] thus to wielde the speare.

HERAWDE.

Methynckes I heare yer slugghornes[6] dynn[7] fromm
farre.

BOURTONNE.

Ah ! swythenn[8] mie shielde and tyltynge launce bee
bounde.[9]
Eftsoones[10] beheste[11] mie Squyerr to the warre.
I flie before to clayme a challenge grownde.

[*Goeth oute.*

HERAWDE.

Thie valourous actes woulde meinte[12] of menne as-
tounde ;
Harde bee yer shappe[13] encontrynge thee ynn fyghte ;
Anenst[14] alle menne thou berest to the grounde,
Lyche the hard hayle dothe the tall roshes pyghte.[15]
As whanne the mornynge sonne ydronks[16] the dew,
Syche dothe thie valourous actes drocke[17] eche
knyghte's hue.

---

1 Run.　　2 Against.　　3 Feeble.　　4 Honour, glory.
5 Useless.　　6 A kind of clarion, or war trumpet.
7 Sound.　　8 Quickly.　　9 Ready.　　10 Soon.
11 Command.　12 Most.　　13 Fate, or doom.
14 Against.　　15 Pitched, or bent down.　　16 Drinks.
17 Drink.

THE LYSTES. THE KYNGE. SYRR SYMONNE DE BOUR-
TONNE, SYRR HUGO FERRARIS, SYRR RANULPH NE-
VILLE, SYRR LODOVICK DE CLYNTON, SYRR JOHAN DE
BERGHAMME, AND ODHERR KNYGHTES, HERAWDE,
MYNSTRELLES, AND SERVYTOURS.[1]

KYNGE.

The barganette;[2] yee mynstrelles tune the strynge,
Somme actyonn dyre of auntyante kynges now synge.

MYNSTRELLES.

I.

Wyllyamm, the Normannes floure botte Englondes
       thorne,
The manne whose myghte delievretie[3] hadd knite,[4]
Snett[5] oppe hys long strunge bowe and sheelde
       aborne,[6]
Behesteynge[7] all hys hommageres[8] to fyghte.
Goe, rouze the lyonn fromm hys hylted[9] denne,
Lett thie floes[10] drenche the blodde of anie thynge bott
       menne.

II.

Ynn the treed forreste doe the knyghtes appere;
Wyllyamm wythe myghte hys bowe enyronn'd[11] plies;[12]
Loude dynns[13] the arrowe ynn the wolfynn's eare;
Hee ryseth battent,[14] roares, he panctes, hee dyes.

---

1 Servants, attendants.   2 Song, or ballad.   3 Activity.
4 Joined.   5 Bent.
6 Burnished. See note to page 112.   7 Commanding.
8 Servants.   9 Hidden.   10 Arrows.
11 Worked with iron.   12 Bends.   13 Sounds.
14 Loudly.

Forslagenn[1] att thie feete lett wolvynns bee,
Lett thie floes drenche theyre blodde, bott do ne
bredrenn slea.

III.

Throwe the merke[2] shade of twistynde trees hee rydes;
The flemed[3] owlett[4] flapps herr eve-speckte[5] wynge;
The lordynge[6] toade ynn all hys passes bides;
The berten[7] neders[8] att hymm darte the stynge;
Stylle, stylle, hee passes onn, hys stede astrodde,
Nee hedes the daungerous waie gyff leadynge untoe
bloodde.

IV.

The lyoncel, fromme sweltrie[9] countries braughte,
Coucheynge binethe the sheltre of the brierr,
Att commyng dynn[10] doth rayse hymselfe distraughte,[11]
Hee loketh wythe an eie of flames of fyre.
Goe, stycke the lyonn to hys hyltren[12] denne,
Lette thie floes[13] drenche the blood of anie thynge botte
menn.

V.

Wythe passent[14] steppe the lyonn mov'th alonge;
Wyllyamm hys ironne-woven bowe hee bendes,
Wythe myghte alych the roghlynge[15] thonderr stronge;
The lyonn ynn a roare hys spryte foorthe sendes.
Goe, slea the lion ynn hys blodde-steyn'd denne,
Botte bee thie takelle[16] drie fromm blodde of odherr
menne.

---

1 Slain.	2 Dark, or gloom.	3, 4 Frighted owl.
5 Marked with evening dew.		6 Heavy, sluggish.
7 Venemous, rather brown.		8 Adders.
9 Hot, sultry.	10 Sound, noise.	11 Distracted.
12 Hidden.	13 Arrows.	14 Walking leisurely.
15 Rolling.	16 Arrow.	

VI.

Swefte fromm the thyckett starks the stagge awaie ;
The couraciers' as swefte doe afterr flie.
Hee lepethe hie, hee stondes, hee kepes at baie,
Botte metes the arrowe, and eftsoones² dothe die.
Forslagenn³ atte thie fote lette wylde beastes bee,
Lette thie floes drenche yer blodde, yett do ne bredrenn
          slee.

VII.

Wythe murtherr tyredd, hee sleynges hys bowe alyne.⁴
The stagge ys ouch'd⁵ wythe crownes of lillie flowerrs.
Arounde theire heaulmes theie greene verte⁶ doe
          entwyne ;
Joying and rev'lous ynn the grene wode bowerrs.
Forslagenn wyth thie sloe lette wylde beastes bee,
Feeste thee upponne theire fleshe, doe ne thie bredrenn
          slee.

KYNGE.

Nowe to the Tourneie ;⁷ who wylle fyrste affraie ?⁸

HERAULDE.

Nevylle, a baronne, bee yatte⁹ honnoure thyne.

BOURTONNE.

I clayme the passage.

---

1 Horse coursers.   2 Full soon.   3 Slain.
4 Across his shoulders, rather unstrung.
5 Garlands of flowers being put round the neck of the game, it was
said to be 'ouch'd,' from 'ouch,' a chain worn by earls round their
necks.—CHATTERTON.
6 Leaves and branches.   7 Tournament.
8 Fight, or encounter.   9 That.

NEVYLLE.

I contake[1] thie waie,

BOURTONNE.

Thenn there's mie gauntlette[2] on mie gaberdyne.[3]

HEREHAULDE.

A leegefull[4] challenge, knyghtes and champyonns
    dygne,
A leegefull challenge, lette the slugghorne sounde.
        [*Syrr Symonne and Nevylle tylte.*
Nevylle ys goeynge, manne and horse, toe grounde.
              [*Nevylle falls.*
Loverdes,[6] how doughtilie[7] the tylterrs joyne!
Yee champyonnes, heere Symonne de Bourtonne
    fyghtes,
Onne hee hathe quacedd,[8] assayle[9] hymm, yee knyghtes.

FERRARIS.

I wylle anente[10] hymm goe; mie squierr, mie shielde;
Orr onne orr odherr wyll doe myckle[11] scethe[12]
Before I doe departe the lissedd fielde,
Mieselfe orr Bourtonne hereupponn wyll blethe.[41]
Mie shielde!

---

1 Dispute.	2 Glove.	3 A piece of armour.
4 Lawful.	5 Worthy.	6 Lords.
7 Furiously.	8 Vanquished.	9 Oppose.
10 Against.	11 Much.	12 Damage, mischief.
13 Bounded.	14 Bleed.	

BOURTONNE,

Comme onne, and fitte thie tylte-launce ethe.[1]
Whanne Bourtonn fyghtes, hee metes a doughtie[2] foe.

[*Theie tylte.   Ferraris falleth.*

Hee falleth ; nowe bie heavenne thie woundes doe
    smethe ;[3]
I feere mee, I have wroughte thee myckle woe.[4]

HERAWDE.

Bourtonne hys seconde beereth to the feelde.
Comme onn, yee knyghtes, and wynn the honnour'd
    sheeld.

BERGHAMME.

I take the challenge ; squyre, mie launce and stede.
I, Bourtonne, take the gauntlette; forr mee staie.
Botte, gyff thou fyghteste mee, thou shalt have mede ;[5]
Somme odherr I wylle champyonn toe affraie ;[6]
Perchaunce fromme hemm I maie possess the daie,
Thenn I schalle be a foemanne forr the spere.
Herehawde, toe the bankes of Knyghtys faie,
De Berghamme wayteth forr a foemann heere.

CLINTON.

Botte longe thou schalte ne tende ;[7] I doe thee fie.[8]
Lyche forreying[9] levyn,[10] schalle mie tylte-launce flie.
    [*Berghamme and Clinton tylte.   Clinton fallethe.*

---

1 Easy.   2 Valiant.   3 Smoke.   4 Hurt, or damage.
5 Reward.   6 Fight, or engage.   7 Attend, or wait.
8 Defy.   9, 10 Destroying lightning.

BERGHAMME.

Nowe, nowe, Syrr Knyghte, attoure[1] thie beeveredd[2]
    eyne.
I have borne downe, and efte[3] doe gauntlette thee.
Swythenne[4] begynne, and wrynn[5] thie shappe[6] orr
    myne ;
Gyff thou dyscomfytte, ytt wylle dobblie bee.
[*Bourtonne and Burghamm tylteth. Berghamme falls.*

HERAWDE.

Symonne de Bourtonne haveth borne downe three,
And bie the thyrd hathe honnoure of a fourthe.
Lett hymm bee sett asyde, tylle hee doth see
A tyltynge forr a knyghte of gentle wourthe.
Heere commethe straunge knyghtes ; gyff corteous[7]
    heie,[8]
Ytt welle beseies[9] to yeve[10] hemm ryghte of fraie.[11]

FIRST KNYGHTE.

Straungerrs wee bee, and homblie doe wee clayme
The rennome[12] ynn thys Tourneie[13] forr to tylte;
Dherbie to proove fromm cravents[14] owre goode name,
Bewrynnynge[15] thatt wee gentile blodde have spylte.

HEREHAWDE.

Yee knyghtes of cortesie, these straungerrs, saie,
Bee you fulle wyllynge forr to yeve[16] hemm fraie?
    [*Fyve Knyghtes tylteth wythe the straunge Knyghte,
    and bee everichone[17] overthrowne.*

1 Turn.	2 Beavered.	3 Again.	4 Quickly.
5 Declare.	6 Fate.	7 Worthy.	8 They.
9 Becomes.	10 Give.	11 Fight.	12 Honour.
13 Tournament.	14 Cowards.	15 Declaring.	16 Give.
17 Every one.			

BOURTONNE.

Nowe bie Seyncte Marie, gyff onn all the fielde
Ycrasedd[1] speres and helmetts bee besprente,[2]
Gyff everyche knyghte dydd houlde a piercedd[3] sheeld,
Gyff all the feelde wythe champyonne blodde be stente,[4]
Yett toe encounterr hymm I bee contente.
Annodherr launce, Marshalle, anodherr launce.
Albeytte hee wythe lowes[5] of fyre ybrente,[6]
Yett Bourtonne woulde agenste hys val[7] advance.
Fyve haveth fallenn downe anethe[8] hys speere,
Botte hee schalle bee the next thatt falleth heere.

Bie thee, Seyncte Marie, and thy Sonne I sweare,
Thatt ynn whatte place yonn doughtie knyghte shall fall
Anethe[9] the stronge push of mie straught out[10] speere,
There schalle aryse a hallie[11] chyrches walle,
The whyche, ynn honnoure, I wylle Marye calle,
Wythe pillars large, and spyre full hyghe and rounde.
And thys I faifullie[12] wylle stonde to all,
Gyff yonderr straungerr falleth to the grounde.
Straungerr, bee boune;[13] I champyonn[14] you to warre.
Sounde, sounde the slughornes,[15] to be hearde fromm
　　farre.
[*Bourtonne and the Straungerr tylt.　Straunger falleth.*

---

1 Broken.　Thus in Chaucer's *Dreme*—
　　　　　　——— " My chambre was
　　　　　Ful wel depainted, and with glas
　　　　　Were al the windowes wel yglased,
　　　　　Ful clere, and nat an hole *ycrased.*
2 Scattered.　3 Broken, or pierced through with darts.　4 Stained.
5 Flames.　6 Burnt.　　7 Healm.　　8 Beneath.
9 Against.　10 Stretched out.　11 Holy.　　12 Faithfully.
13 Ready.　14 Challenge.　15 War trumpets.

KYNGE.

The Mornynge Tyltes now cease.

HERAWDE.

Bourtonne ys kynge.

Dysplaie the Englyshe bannorre onn the tente ;*
Rounde hymm, yee mynstrelles, songs of achments[1]
synge ;
Yee Herawdes, getherr upp the speeres besprente ;[2]
To Kynge of Tourney-tylte bee all knees bente.
Dames faire and gentle, forr youre loves hee foughte ;
Forr you the longe tylte-launce, the swerde hee
shente ;[3]
Hee joustedd,[4] alleine[5] havynge you ynn thoughte.
Comme, mynstrells, sound the strynge, goe onn eche
syde,
Whylest hee untoe the Kynge ynn state doe ryde.

MYNSTRELLES.

I.

Whann Battayle, smethynge[6] wythe new quickenn'd
gore,
Bendynge wythe spoiles, and bloddie droppynge hedde,
Dydd the merke'[7] wood of ethe[8] and rest explore,
Seekeynge to lie onn Pleasures downie bedde,

---

* " Advance our waving colours on the walls !"
    SHAKSPEARE, *Henry VI.* Part I.

1 Achievements, glorious actions.   2 Broken spears.
3 Broke, destroyed.   4 Tilted.   5 Only, alone.
6 Smoking, steaming.   7 Dark. gloomy.   8 Ease.

Pleasure, dauncyng fromm her wode,
Wreathedd wythe floures of aiglintine,[1]
From hys vysage washedd the bloude,
Hylte[2] hys swerde and gaberdyne.

II.

Wythe syke an eyne shee swotelie[3] hymm dydd view,
Dydd soe ycorvenn[4] everrie shape to joie,
Hys spryte dydd chaunge untoe anodherr hue,
Hys armes, ne spoyles, mote anie thoughts emploie.
  All delyghtsomme and contente,
  Fyre enshotynge[5] fromm hys eyne,
  Ynn hys armes hee dydd herr hente,[6]
  Lyche the merk-plante[7] doe entwyne.
Soe, gyff thou lovest Pleasure and herr trayne,
Onknowlachynge[8] ynn whatt place herr to fynde,
Thys rule yspende,[9] and ynn thie mynde retayne;
Seeke Honnoure fyrste, and Pleasaunce lies behynde.[*]

---

1 Sweetbrier.   2 Hid, scattered.   3 Sweetly.   4 Moulded.
5 Shooting, darting.   6 Grasp, hold.   7 Night-shade.
8 Ignorant, unknowing.   9 Consider.

[*] In identifying the priest of the 15th century with the bard of the 18th, as far as intellect extends, Chatterton must ever be considered as an almost miraculous being, on whom was showered "the pomp and prodigality of heaven." Independently of his creative faculty, he is to be recognized as one who seemed intuitively to possess what others imperfectly acquire by labour. All difficulties vanished before him, and every branch of knowledge became familiar to which he momentarily directed his luminous attention.

When we consider the wonderful acquirements of Chatterton, in his short life, the maturity of his understanding, the brilliancy of his fancy, and the accuracy of his taste, the mind indulges in a melancholy but luxurious anticipation of what *another* seventeen years might have produced! But, as it is, he has reared to himself an immortal cenotaph; and it is high time for the public, with a decisive hand, to pluck the borrowed plumes from a fictitious Rowley, and to place them on the brow of a real Chatterton. His fame should no longer be divided, but the present generation should boast the honorable distinction of having produced, perhaps, the greatest genius that ever appeared in the "tide of times."—COTTLE.

Battle of Hastings.

In printing the first of these poems two copies have been made use of, both taken from copies of Chatterton's hand-writing—the one by Mr. Catcott, and the other by Mr. Barrett. The principal difference between them is at the end, where the latter has fourteen lines from stanza 55, which are wanting in the former The second poem is printed from a single copy, made by Mr. Barrett, from one in Chatterton's hand-writing.

It should be observed, that the Poem marked No. 1, was given to Mr. Barrett by Chatterton, with the following title: " Battle of Hastings, wrote by Turgot the Monk, a Saxon, in the tenth century, and translated by Thomas Rowlie, parish preeste of St. Johns, in the city of Bristol, in the year 1465.—The remainder of the poem I have not been happy enough to meet with." Being afterwards pressed by Mr. Barrett to produce any part of this poem in the original hand-writing, he at last said that he wrote this poem himself for a friend ; but that he had another, the copy of an original by Rowley : and being then desired to produce that other poem, he, after a considerable interval of time, brought to Mr. Barrett the poem marked No. 2, as far as stanza 52 inclusive, with the following title: "Battle of Hastyngs by Turgotus, translated by Roulie for W. Canynge, Esq." The lines from stanza 52 inclusive, were brought some time after, in consequence of Mr. Barrett's repeated solicitations for the conclusion of the poem.—*Note to Tyrwhitt's Edition.*

BATTLE OF HASTINGS.*

(NO. 1.)

I.

O CHRYSTE, it is a grief for me to telle,
How manie a nobil erle and valrous knyghte

---

* I cannot but observe, that Chatterton could not have chosen from our history, a more commodious subject for a poem than the ' Battle of Hastings,' exclusive of its susceptibility of poetical ornament, and of its coincidence with his predominant predilection for antiquarian imagery.—WARTON.

There are extant two parts, or rather two different parts, of the ' Battle of Hastings.' These appear to have been higher in the estimation of Chatterton, as well as of Dr. Milles, than most of the other productions of Rowley. When Chatterton brought the first part to Mr. Barrett, being greatly pressed to produce the poem in the original hand-writing, he at last said that he had written this poem himself for a friend; but that he had another, the copy of an original by Rowley: and being then desired to produce that poem, he brought, after some time, to Mr. Barrett, the poem which is marked in Mr. Tyrwhitt's and Dr. Milles's editions, as "No. 2." The first of these poems I cannot help classing among the most inferior of Rowley's. The mere detail of violence and carnage, with nothing to interest curiosity, or engage the more tender passions can be pleasing to few readers. There is not a single episode to enliven the tedious narrative, and but few of the beauties of poetry to relieve the mind from the disgusting subject. The second part is far superior. There is more of poetical description in it, more of nature, more of character. The imagery is more ani-

In fyghtynge for Kynge Harrold noblie fell,
Al sleyne in Hastyngs feeld in bloudie fyghte.
O sea, our teeming[1] donore! han thy floude,
Han anie fructuous[2] entendement,[3]
Thou wouldst have rose and sank wyth tydes of bloude,
Before Duke Wyllyam's knyghts han hither went;
    Whose cowart arrowes manie erles sleyne,
    And brued[4] the feeld wyth bloude as season rayne.

II.

And of his knyghtes did eke full manie die,
All passyng hie, of mickle myghte echone,
Whose poygnant arrowes, typp'd with destynie,
Caus'd manie wydowes to make myckle mone.
Lordynges, avaunt, that chycken-harted are,
From out of hearynge quicklie now departe;
Full well I wote,[5] to synge of bloudie warre
Will greeve your tenderlie and mayden harte.
    Go, do the weaklie womman inn mann's geare,[6]
    And scond[7] your mansion if grymm war come there.

---

mated, the incidents more varied. The character of Tancarville is
well drawn, and the spirit of candour and humanity which pervades it,
is perhaps unparalleled in any writer before the age of Shakspeare.
The whole episode of Gyrtha is well conducted, and the altercation
between him and his brother Harold, is interesting. But the descrip-
tion of 'Morning,' and that of 'Salisbury plain,' would be alone suffi-
cient to rescue the whole poem from oblivion, and to entitle it to a place
upon a classic shelf. The utmost efforts of the author however cannot
always impart interest or variety to the dull catalogue of names, which
have ceased to be remembered, and the unvaried recital of wounds and
deaths. But Homer himself nods when engaged upon a topic so un-
favourable to genius.—DR. GREGORY.

1 Prolific.   2 Useful.   3 Meaning.   4 Embrued.
5 Know.   6 Apparel.   7 Abscond from.

III.

Soone as the erlie maten[1] belle was tolde,
And sonne was come to byd us all good daie,
Bothe armies on the feeld, both brave and bolde,
Prepar'd for fyghte in champyon arraie.
As when two bulles, destynde for Hocktide fyghte,
Are yoked bie the necke within a sparre,[2]
Theie rend the erthe, and travellyrs affryghte,
Lackynge to gage[3] the sportive bloudie warre;
 Soe lacked Harroldes menne to come to blowes,
 The Normans lacked for to wielde their bowes.

IV.

Kynge Harrolde turnynge to hys leegemen[4] spake:
My merrie men, be not cast downe in mynde;
Your onlie lode[5] for aye to mar or make,
Before yon sunne has donde his welke[6] you'll fynde.
Your lovyng wife, who erst dyd rid the londe
Of Lurdanes,[7] and the treasure that you han,[8]
Wyll falle into the Normanne robber's honde,[9]

---

1 Morning. 2 Enclosure. 3 Engage in. 4 Subjects.
5 Praise. 6 Finished his course. 7 Lord Danes.
8 The capital blunder which runs through all these poems, and would
alone be sufficient to destroy their credit, is the termination of verbs of
the singular number in *n*; 'han' is in twenty-six instances used in
these poems, for the present or past time singular of the verb 'have.'
But 'han,' being an abbreviation of 'haven,' is never used by any
ancient writer, except in the present time plural, and the infinitive
mood.—TYRWHITT.

9 There is a transposition of the words in this speech of Harold,
which renders it obscure; the meaning may be thus expressed:
  ———— You, who erst
  Did rid the land of the Lord Danes, will find
  Your loving wife and treasure which you had
  Will fall into the Norman robber's hand.
        DEAN MILLES.

Unlesse with honde and harte you plaie the manne.
   Cheer up youre hartes, chase sorrowe farre awaie,
   Godde and Seyncte Cuthbert be the worde to daie.

V.

And thenne Duke Wyllyam to his knyghtes did saie :
My merrie menne, be bravelie everiche ;[1]
Gif I do gayn the honore of the daie,
Ech one of you I wyll make myckle riche.
Beer you in mynde, we for a kyngdomm fyghte ;
Lordshippes and honores echone shall possesse ;
Be this the worde to daie, God and my Ryghte ;
Ne doubte but God will oure true cause blesse.
   The clarions then sounded sharpe and shrille ;
   Deathdoeynge blades were out intent to kille.

VI.

And brave Kyng Harrolde had nowe donde[2] hys saie ;[3]
He threwe wythe myghte amayne[4] hys shorte horse-
   spear,
The noise it made the duke to turn awaie,
And hytt his knyghte, de Beque, upon the ear.
His cristede[5] beaver dyd him smalle abounde ;[6]
The cruel spear went thorough all his hede ;
The purpel bloude came goushynge[7] to the grounde,
And at Duke Wyllyam's feet he tumbled deade :
   So fell the myghtie tower of Standrip, whenne
   It felte the furie of the Danish menne.

---

1 Every one.   2 Put on.   3 Military cloak.   4 Main force.
5 Crested.   6 Benefit.   7 Gushing.

VII.

O Afflem, son of Cuthbert, holie Sayncte,
Come ayde thy freend, and shewe Duke Wyllyams
    payne;
Take up thy pencyl, all hys features paincte;
Thy coloryng excells a synger strayne.
Duke Wyllyam sawe hys freende sleyne piteouslie,
His lovynge freende whome he muche honored,
For he han lovd hym from puerilitie,
And theie together bothe han bin ybred:
    O! in Duke Wyllyam's harte it raysde a flame,
    To whiche the rage of emptie wolves is tame.

VIII.

He tooke a brasen crosse-bowe in his honde,
And drewe it harde with all hys myghte amein,
Ne doubtyng but the bravest in the londe
Han by his soundynge arrowe-lede[1] bene sleyne.
Alured's stede, the fynest stede alive,
Bye comelie forme knowlached[2] from the rest;
But nowe his destind howre dyd aryve,
The arrowe hyt upon his milkwhite breste:
    So have I seen a ladie-smock soe white,
    Blown in the mornynge, and mowd downe at night.

IX.

With thilk[3] a force it dyd his bodie gore,
That in his tender guttes it entered,
In veritee[4] a fulle clothe yarde or more,[5]

---

1 Arrow-head.   2 Known.   3 Such.   4 Truth.
5   " With such a force and vehement might,
        He did his body gore;
      The spear went thro' the other side,
        A large cloth yard and more."—*Chevy Chace.*

And downe with flaiten[1] noyse he sunken dede.
Brave Alured, benethe his faithfull horse,
Was smeerd all over withe the gorie duste,
And on hym laie the recer's lukewarme corse,
That Alured coulde not hymself aluste.[2]
   The standyng Normans drew theyr bowe echone,
   And broght full manie Englysh champyons downe.

x.

The Normans kept aloofe, at distaunce stylle,
The Englysh nete but short horse-spears could welde;
The Englysh manie dethe-sure dartes did kille,
And manie arrowes twang'd upon the sheelde.
Kynge Haroldes knyghts desir'de for hendie[3] stroke,
And marched furious o'er the bloudie pleyne,
In bodie close, and made the pleyne to smoke;
Theire sheelds rebounded arrowes back agayne.
   The Normans stode aloofe, nor hede[4] the same,
   Their arrowes woulde do dethe, tho' from far off
   they came.

xi.

Duke Wyllyam drewe agen hys arrowe strynge,
An arrowe withe a sylver-hede drewe he;
The arrowe dauncynge in the ayre dyd synge,
And hytt the horse Tosselyn on the knee.
At this brave Tosslyn threwe his short horse-speare;
Duke Wyllyam stooped to avoyde the blowe;
The yrone weapon hummed in his eare,
And hitte Sir Doullie Naibor on the prowe;[5]

---

1 Terrific.   2 Disengage.   3 Hand to hand.
4 Regarded.   5 Forehead.

Upon his helme soe furious was the stroke,
It splete[1] his bever, and the ryvets broke.

XII.

Downe fell the beaver by Tosslyn splete in tweine,
And onn his hede expos'd a punie wounde,
But on Destoutvilles sholder came ameine,
And fell'd the champyon to the bloudie grounde.
Then Doullie myghte his bowestrynge drewe,
Enthoughte to gyve brave Tosslyn bloudie wounde,
But Harolde's asenglave[2] stopp'd it as it flewe,
And it fell bootless on the bloudie grounde.
　　Siere Doullie, when he sawe hys venge[3] thus broke,
　　Death-doynge blade from out the scabard toke.

XIII.

And nowe the battail closde on everych syde,
And face to face appeard the knyghts full brave;
They lifted up theire bylles with myckle pryde,
And manie woundes unto the Normans gave.
So have I sene two weirs[4] at once give grounde,
White fomyng hygh to rorynge combat runne;
In roaryng dyn and heaven-breaking sounde,
Burste waves on waves, and spangle in the sunne;
　　And when their myghte in burstynge waves is fled,
　　Like cowards, stele alonge their ozy bede.

XIV.

Yonge Egelrede, a knyghte of comelie mien,
Affynd[5] unto the kynge of Dynefarre,

---

1 Split.　　2 Lance.　　3 Revenge.　　4 Torrents.　　5 Related.

At echone tylte and tourney he was seene,
And lov'd to be amonge the bloudie warre;
He couch'd hys launce, and ran wyth mickle myghte
Ageinste the brest of Sieur de Bonoboe;
He grond and sunken on the place of fyghte,
O Chryste! to fele his wounde, his harte was woe,
   Ten thousand thoughtes push'd in upon his mynde,
   Not for hymselfe, but those he left behynde.

xv.

He dy'd and leffed[1] wyfe and chyldren tweine,
Whom he wyth cheryshment did dearlie love;
In England's court, in goode Kynge Edwarde's regne,
He wonne the tylte, and ware her crymson glove;
And thence unto the place where he was borne,
Together with hys welthe and better wyfe,
To Normandie he dyd perdie[2] returne,
In peace and quietnesse to lead his lyfe;
   And now with sovrayn Wyllyam he came,
   To die in battel, or get welthe and fame.

xvi.

Then, swefte as lyghtnynge, Egelredus set
Agaynst du Barlie of the mounten head;
In his dere hartes bloude his longe launce was wett,
And from his courser down he tumbled dede.
So have I sene a mountayne oak, that longe
Has caste his shadowe to the mountayne syde,
Brave all the wyndes, tho' ever they so stronge,
And view the briers belowe with self-taught pride;

---

1 Left.   2 Certainly.

But, whan throwne downe by mightie thunderstroke,
He'de rather bee a bryer than an oke.

XVII.

Then Egelred dyd in a declynie[1]
Hys launce uprere wyth all hys myghte ameine,
And strok Fitzport upon the dexter eye,
And at his pole [2] the spear came out agayne.
Butt as he drewe it forthe, an arrowe fledde
Wyth mickle myght sent from de Tracy's bowe,
And at hys syde the arrowe entered,
And oute the crymson streme of bloude gan flowe;
In purple strekes it dyd his armer staine,
And smok'd in puddles on the dustie plaine.

XVIII.

But Egelred, before he sunken downe,
With all his myghte amein his spear besped,[3]
It hytte Bertrammil Manne upon the crowne,
And bothe together quicklie sunken dede.
So have I seen a rocke o'er others hange,
Who stronglie plac'd laughde at his slippry state,
But when he falls with heaven-peercynge bange
That he the sleeve[4] unravels all theire fate,
And broken onn the beech thys lesson speak,
The stronge and firme should not defame the weake.

XIX.

Howel ap Jevah came from Matraval,
Where he by chaunce han slayne a noble's son,

---

1 Stooping, declination.   2 Crown of his head.
3 Dispatched.   4 Clue.

And now was come to fyghte at Harold's call,
And in the battel he much goode han done;
Unto Kyng Harold he foughte mickle near,
For he was yeoman of the bodie guard;
And with a targyt and a fyghtyng spear,
He of his boddie han kepte watch and ward:
   True as a shadow to a substant[1] thynge,
   So true he guarded Harold hys good kynge.

xx.

But when Egelred tumbled to the grounde,
He from Kynge Harolde quicklie dyd advaunce,
And strooke de Tracie thilk[2] a crewel wounde,
Hys harte and lever came out on the launce.
And then retreted for to guarde his kynge,
On dented[3] launce he bore the harte awaie;
An arrowe came from Auffroie Griel's strynge,
Into hys heele betwyxt hys yron staie;
   The grey-goose pynion, that thereon was sett,
   Eftsoons[4] wyth smokyng crymson bloud was wett.[5]

xxi.

His bloude at this was waxen flaminge hotte,
Without adoe[6] he turned once agayne,
And hytt de Griel thilk a blowe, God wote,
Maugre[7] hys helme, he splete his hede in twayne.
This Auffroie was a manne of mickle pryde,
Whose featliest bewty ladden[8] in his face;

---

1 Substantial.   2 Such.   3 Bruised.   4 Quickly.
5   "The grey-goose wing that was thereon,
        In his heart's blood was wet."—*Chevy Chace.*
6 Delay.   7 Notwithstanding.   8 Lay.

His chaunce in warr he ne before han tryde,
But lyv'd in love and Rosaline's embrace ;
   And like a useless weede amonge the haie
   Amonge the sleine warriours Griel laie.

XXII.

Kynge Harolde then he putt his yeomen bie,
And ferslie[1] ryd into the bloudie fyghte;
Erle Ethelwolf, and Goodrick, and Alfie,
Cuthbert, and Goddard, mical menne of myghte,
Ethelwin, Ethelbert, and Edwin too,
Effred the famous, and Erle Ethelwarde,
Kynge Harolde's leegemenn,[2] erlies[3] hie and true,
Rode after hym, his bodie for to guarde ;
   The reste of erlies, fyghtynge other wheres,
   Stained with Norman bloude theire fyghtynge speres.

XXIII.

As when some ryver with the season-raynes
White fomynge hie doth breke the bridges oft,
O'erturns the hamelet and all conteins,
And layeth o'er the hylls a muddie soft ;
So Harold ranne upon his Normanne foes,
And layde the greate and small upon the grounde,
And delte among them thilke a store of blowes,
Full manie a Normanne fell by him dede wounde ;
   So who he be that ouphant[4] faieries strike,
   Their soules will wander to Kynge Offa's dyke.

---

1 Furiously.   2 Subjects.   3 Earls.   4 Elfin.

XXIV.

Fitz Salnarville, Duke William's favourite knyghte,
To noble Edelwarde his life dyd yielde;
Withe hys tylte launce hee stroke with thilk a myghte,
The Norman's bowels steemde upon the feeld.
Old Salnarville beheld hys son lie ded,
Against Erle Edelwarde his bowe-strynge drewe;
But Harold at one blowe made tweine his head;
He dy'd before the poignant arrowe flew.
   So was the hope of all the issue gone,
   And in one battle fell the sire and son.

XXV.

De Aubignee rod fercely thro' the fyghte,
To where the boddie of Salnarville laie;
Quod he; And art thou ded, thou manne of myghte?
I'll be reveng'd, or die for thee this daie.
Die then thou shalt, Erle Ethelwarde he said;
I am a cunnynge erle, and that can tell;
Then drew hys swerde, and ghastlie cut hys hede,
And on his freend eftsoons he lifeless fell,
   Stretch'd on the bloudie pleyne; great God forefend,[1]
   It be the fate of no such trustie freende!

XXVI.

Then Egwin Sieur Pikeny did attaque;
He turned aboute and vilely souten[2] flie;
But Egwyn cutt so deepe into his backe,
He rolled on the grounde and soon dyd die.

---

1 Forbid.   2 Sought.

His distant sonne, Sire Romara de Biere,
Soughte to revenge his fallen kynsman's lote,
But soone Erle Cuthbert's dented fyghtyng spear
Stucke in his harte, and stayd his speed, God wote.
   He tumbled downe close by hys kynsman's syde,
   Myngled their stremes of pourple bloude, and dy'd.

XXVII.

And now an arrowe from a bowe unwote[1]
Into Erle Cuthbert's harte eftsoons dyd flee;
Who dying sayd; Ah me! how hard my lote!
Now slayne, mayhap, of one of lowe degree.
So have I seen a leafie elm of yore
Have been the pride and glorie of the pleine;
But, when the spendyng landlord is growne poore,
It falls benethe the axe of some rude sweine;
   And like the oke, the sovran of the woode,
   It's fallen boddie tells you how it stoode.

XXVIII.

When Edelward perceevd Erle Cuthbert die,
On Hubert strongest of the Normanne crewe,
As wolfs when hungred on the cattel flie,
So Edelward amaine upon him flewe.
With thilk a force he hyt hym to the grounde;
And was demasing[2] howe to take his life,
When he behynde received a ghastlie wounde
Gyven by De Torcie, with a stabbyng knyfe;
   Base trecherous Normannes, if such actes you doe,
   The conquer'd maie clame victorie of you.

---

1 Unknown.   2 Considering.

XXIX.

The erlie felt de Torcie's treacherous knyfe
Han made his crymson bloude and spirits floe;
And knowlachyng[1] he soon must quyt this lyfe,
Resolved Hubert should too with hym goe.
He held hys trustie swerd against his breste,
And down he fell, and peerc'd him to the harte;
And both together then did take their reste,
Their soules from corpses unaknell'd[2] depart;
    And both together soughte the unknown shore,
    Where we shall goe, where manie's gon before.

XXX.

Kynge Harolde Torcie's trechery dyd spie,
And hie alofe[3] his temper'd swerde dyd welde,
Cut offe his arme, and made the bloude to flie,
His proofe steel armoure did him littel sheelde;
And not contente, he splete his hede in twaine,
And down he tumbled on the bloudie grounde;
Meanwhile the other erlies on the playne
Gave and received manie a bloudie wounde,
    Such as the arts in warre han learnt with care,
    But manie knyghtes were women in men's geer.

XXXI.

Herrewald, borne on Sarim's[4] spreddyng plaine,
Where Thor's fam'd temple manie ages stoode;
Where Druids, auncient preests dyd ryghtes ordaine,
And in the middle shed the victyms bloude;

---

1 Knowing.   2 Without the funeral knell being rung.
         " Unhousell'd, unanointed, *unaknell'd*."
                   HAMLET *in Pope's Edition.*
3 Aloft.   4 Salisbury's.

Where auncient Bardi dyd their verses synge,
Of Cæsar conquer'd, and his mighty hoste,
And how old Tynyan, necromancing kynge,
Wreck'd all hys shyppyng on the Brittish coaste,
  And made hym in his tatter'd barks to flie,
  'Till Tynyan's dethe and opportunity.

XXXII.

To make it more renomed[1] than before,
(I, tho' a Saxon, yet the truthe will telle)
The Saxonnes steynd the place wyth Brittish gore,
Where nete but bloud of sacrifices felle.
Tho' Chrystians, stylle they thoghte mouche of the pile,
And here theie mette when causes dyd it neede;
'Twas here the auncient Elders of the Isle
Dyd by the trecherie of Hengist bleede;
  O Hengist! han thy cause bin good and true,
  Thou wouldst such murdrous acts as these eschew.

XXXIII.

The erlie was a manne of hie degree,
And han that daie full manie Normannes sleine;
Three Norman Champyons of hie degree
He lefte to smoke upon the bloudie pleine:
The Sier Fitzbotevilleine did then advaunce,
And with his bowe he smote the erlies hede;
Who eftsoons gored hym with his tylting launce,
And at his horses feet he tumbled dede:
  His partyng spirit hovered o'er the floude
  Of soddayne roushynge mouche lov'd purple blonde.

1 Renowned.

XXXIV.

De Viponte then, a squier of low degree,
An arrowe drewe with all his myghte ameine;
The arrowe graz'd upon the erlies knee,
A punie wounde, that caus'd but littel peine.
So have I seene a Dolthead place a stone,
Enthoghte[1] to staie a driving rivers course;
But better han it bin to lett alone,
It onlie drives it on with mickle force;
    The erlie, wounded by so base a hynde,
    Rays'd furyous doyngs in his noble mynde.

XXXV.

The Siere Chatillion, yonger of that name,
Advaunced next before the erlie's syghte;
His fader was a manne of mickle fame,
And he renomde and valorous in fyghte.
Chatillion his trustie swerd forth drewe,
The erle drawes his, menne both of mickle myghte;
And at eche other vengouslie[2] they flewe,
As mastie[3] dogs at Hocktide set to fyghte;
    Bothe scorn'd to yeelde, and bothe abhor'de to flie,
    Resolv'd to vanquishe, or resolv'd to die.

XXXVI.

Chatillion hyt the erlie on the hede,
Thatt splytte eftsoons his cristed helm in twayne;
Whiche he perforce withe target covered,
And to the battel went with myghte ameine.
The erlie hytte Chatillion thilke a blowe
Upon his breste, his harte was plein to see;

---

1 Thinking.   2 Revengefully.   3 Mastiff.

He tumbled at the horses feet alsoe,
And in dethe-panges he seez'd the recer's knee:
    Faste as the ivy rounde the oke doth clymbe,
    So faste he dying gryp'd[1] the racer's lymbe.

XXXVII.

The recer then beganne to flynge and kicke,
And toste the erlie farr off to the grounde;
The erlie's squier then a swerde did sticke
Into his harte, a dedlie ghastlie wounde;
And downe he felle upon the crymson pleine,
Upon Chatillion's soulless corse of claie;
A puddlie streme of bloude flow'd oute ameine;
Stretch'd out at length besmer'd with gore he laie;
    As some tall oke fell'd from the greenie plaine,
    To live a second time upon the main.

XXXVIII.

The erlie nowe an horse and beaver han,
And nowe agayne appered on the feeld;
And manie a mickle knyghte and mightie manne
To his dethe-doyng swerd his life did yeeld;
When Siere de Broque an arrowe longe lett flie,
Intending Herewaldus to have sleyne;
It miss'd; butt hytte Edardus on the eye,
And at his pole came out with horrid payne.
    Edardus felle upon the bloudie grounde,
    His noble soule came roushyng from the wounde.[2]

---

1 Grasped.
2   " And the disdainful soul came rushing through the wound."
                              DAYDEN's *Virgil.*
[This is the last line in the translation, and as such, is very likely to
have attracted the attention of Chatterton.—ED.]

XXXIX.

Thys Herewald perceev'd, and full of ire
He on the Siere de Broque with furie came;
Quod he; thou'st slaughtred my beloved squier,
But I will be revenged for the same.
Into his bowels then his launce he thruste,
And drew thereout a steemie[1] drerie[2] lode;
Quod he; these offals are for ever curst,
Shall serve the coughs,[3] and rooks, and dawes for
        foode.
    Then on the pleine the steemie lode hee throwde,
    Smokynge wyth lyfe, and dy'd with crymson bloude.

XL.

Fitz Broque, who saw his father killen lie,
Ah me! sayde he; what woeful syghte I see!
But now I must do somethynge more than sighe;
And then an arrowe from the bowe drewe he.
Beneth the erlie's navil came the darte;
Fitz Broque on foote han drawne it from the bowe;
And upwards went into the erlie's harte,
And out the crymson streme of bloude 'gan flowe.
    As fromm a hatch,[4] drawne with a vehement geir,[5]
    White rushe the burstynge waves, and roar along the
        weir.

XLI.

The erle with one honde grasp'd the recer's mayne,
And with the other he his launce besped;[6]

---

1 Steeming.   2 Dreadful.   3 Choughs, or ravens.
4 Pen, or lock.   5 Turn, or twist. 6 Dispatched.

And then felle bleedyng on the bloudie plaine,
His launce it hytte Fitz Broque upon the hede;
Upon his hede it made a wounde full slyghte,
But peerc'd his shoulder, ghastlie wounde inferne,
Before his optics[1] daunced a shade of nyghte,
Whyche soone were closed ynn a sleepe eterne.
   The noble erlie than, withote a grone,
    Took flyghte, to fynde the regyons unknowne.

XLII.

Brave Alured from binethe his noble horse
Was gotten on his leggs, with bloude all smore;[2]
And now eletten[2] on another horse,
Eftsoons he withe his launce did manie gore.
The cowart Norman knyghtes before hym fledde,
And from a distaunce sent their arrowes keene;
But noe such destinie awaits his hedde,
As to be sleyen[4] by a wighte[5] so meene.
   Tho' oft the oke falls by the villen's[6] shock,
    'Tys moe than hyndes can do, to move the rock.

XLIII.

Upon Du Chatelet he ferselie sett,
And peerc'd his bodie with a force full grete;
The asenglave[7] of his tylt-launce was wett,
The rollynge bloude alonge the launce did fleet.
Advauncynge, as a mastie at a bull,
He rann his launce into Fitz Warren's harte;

---

1 Eyes.   2 Besmeared.   3 Alighted.
4 Slain.   5 Person.   6 Vassal, peasant.
7 The neck or steel part of the lance.

From Partaies bowe, a wight unmercifull,
Within his owne he felt a cruel darte;
 Close by the Norman champyons he han sleine,
 He fell; and mixd his bloude with theirs upon the
  pleine.

XLIV.

Erle Ethelbert then hove,[1] with clinie[2] just,
A launce, that stroke Partaie upon the thighe,
And pinn'd him downe unto the gorie duste;
Cruel, quod he, thou cruellie shalt die.
With that his launce he enterd at his throte;
He scritch'd[3] and screem'd in melancholie mood;
And at his backe eftsoons came out, God wote,
And after it a crymson streme of bloude:
 In agonie and peine he there dyd lie,
 While life and dethe strove for the masterrie.

XLV.

He gryped hard the bloudie murd'ring launce,
And in a grone he left this mortel lyfe.
Behynde the erlie Fiscampe did advaunce,
Bethoghte[4] to kill him with a stabbynge knife;
But Egward, who perceev'd his fowle intent,
Eftsoons his trustie swerde he forthwyth drewe,
And thilke a cruel blowe to Fiscampe sent,
That soule and bodie's bloude at one gate flewe.
 Thilk deeds do all deserve, whose deeds so fowle
 Will black theire earthlie name, if not their soule.

---

1 Heaved. 2 Inclination. 3 Shrieked. 4 Thinking.

XLVI.

When lo! an arrowe from Walleris honde,
Winged with fate and dethe daunced alonge;
And slewe the noble flower of Powyslonde,
Howel ap Jevah, who yclepd[1] the stronge.
Whan he the first mischaunce received han,
With horsemans haste he from the armie rodde;
And did repaire unto the cunnynge manne,
Who sange a charme, that dyd it mickle goode;
    Then praid Seyncte Cuthbert, and our holie Dame,
    To blesse his labour, and to heal the same.

XLVII.

Then drewe the arrowe, and the wounde did seck,[2]
And putt the teint of holie herbies[3] on;
And putt a rowe of bloude-stones round his neck;
And then did say; 'go, champyon, get agone.'
And now was comynge Harrolde to defend,
And metten with Walleris cruel darte;
His sheelde of wolf-skinn did him not attend,[4]
The arrow peerced into his noble harte;
    As some tall oke, hewn from the mountayne hed,
    Falls to the pleine; so fell the warriour dede.

XLVIII.

His countryman, brave Mervyn ap Teudor,
Who love of hym han from his country gone,
When he perceev'd his friend lie in his gore,
As furious as a mountayn wolf he ranne.

1 Called.   2 Suck.   3 Herbs.   4 Protect.

As ouphant faieries, whan the moone sheenes bryghte,
In littel circles daunce upon the greene,
All living creatures flie far from their syghte,
Ne by the race of destinie be seen ;
 For what he be that ouphant faieries stryke,
 Their soules will wander to Kyng Offa's dyke.

XLIX.

So from the face of Mervyn Tewdor brave
The Normans eftsoons fled awaie aghaste ;[1]
And lefte behynde their bowe and asenglave,
For fear of hym, in thilk a cowart haste.
His garb sufficient were to meve affryghte ;
A wolf skin girded round his myddle was ;
A bear skyn, from Norwegians wan in fyghte,
Was tytend[2] round his shoulders by the claws :
 So Hercules, 'tis sunge, much like to him,
 Upon his shoulder wore a lyon's skin.[3]

L.

Upon his thyghes and harte-swefte[4] legges he wore
A hugie[5] goat skyn, all of one grete peice ;
A boar-skyn sheelde on his bare armes he bore ;
His gauntletts were the skynn of harte of greece.

---

1 Terrified.   2 Tightened.

3   " And then about his shoulders broad he threw
   A hoary hide of some wild beast, whom he
   In salvage forest by adventure slew,
   And reft the spoil his ornament to be ;
   Which spreading all his back with dreadful view,
   Made all that him so horrible did see,
  Think him Alcides in a lion's skin,
  When the Nemean conquest he did win."
        SPENSER's *Muiopotmos*, Stanza IX.

4 Swift as deer.   5 Huge.

They fledde; he followed close upon their heels,
Vowynge vengeance for his deare countrymanne;
And Siere de Sancelotte his vengeance feels;
He peerc'd hys backe, and out the bloude ytt ranne.
  His bloude went downe the swerde unto his arme,
  In springing rivulet, alive and warme.

LI.

His swerde was shorte, and broade, and myckle keene,
And no mann's bone could stonde to stoppe itts wale;
The Normann's harte in partes two cutt cleane,
He clos'd his eyne, and clos'd hys eyne for aie.
Then with his swerde he sett on Fitz du Valle,
A knyghte mouch famous for to runne at tylte;
With thilk a furie on hym he dyd falle,
Into his neck he ranne the swerde and hylte;
    As myghtie lyghtenynge often has been founde,
    To drive an oke into unfallow'd grounde.

LII.

And with the swerde, that in his neck yet stoke,
The Norman fell unto the bloudie grounde;
And with the fall ap Tewdore's swerde he broke,
And bloude afreshe came trickling from the wounde.
As whan the hyndes, before a mountayne wolfe,
Flie from his paws, and angrie vysage grym;
But when he falls into the pittie golphe,[1]
They dare hym to his bearde, and battone[2] hym;
    And cause he fryghted them so muche before,
    Lyke cowart hyndes, they battone hym the more.

1 Pit.   2 Beat him.

LIII.

So, whan they sawe ap Tewdore was bereft
Of his keen swerde, thatt wroghte thilke great dismaie:
They turned about, eftsoons upon hym lept,
And full a score engaged in the fraie.
Mervyn ap Tewdore, ragyng as a bear,
Seiz'd on the beaver of the Sier de Laque;
And wring'd his hedde with such a vehement gier,[1]
His visage was turned round unto his backe.
   Backe to his harte retyr'd the useless gore,
   And felle upon the pleine to rise no more.

LIV.

Then on the mightie Siere Fitz Pierce he flew,
And broke his helm and seiz'd hym bie the throte:
Then manie Normann knyghtes their arrowes drew,
That enter'd into Mervyn's harte, God wote.
In dying panges he gryp'd his throte more stronge,
And from their sockets started out his eyes;
And from his mouthe came out his blameless tonge;
And bothe in peyne and anguishe eftsoon dies.
   As some rude rocke torne from his bed of claie,
   Stretch'd onn the pleine the brave ap Tewdore
   laie.

LV.

And now Erle Ethelbert and Egward came
Brave Mervyn from the Normannes to assist;
A myghtie siere, Fitz Chatulet bie name,
An arrowe drew that dyd them littel list.[2]

---

1 Twist.   2 Concern.

Erle Egward points his launce at Chatulet,
And Ethelbert at Walleris set his:
And Egward dyd the siere a hard blowe hytt,
But Ethelbert by a myschaunce dyd miss:
    Fear laide Walleris flat upon the strande,
    He ne deserved a death from erlies hande.

LVI.

Betwyxt the ribbes of Sire Fitz Chatelet
The poynted launce of Egward did ypass;
The distaunt syde thereof was ruddie wet,
And he fell breathless on the bloudie grass.
As cowart Walleris laie on the grounde,
The dreaded weapon hummed o'er his heade,
And hytt the squier thylke a lethal[1] wounde,
Upon his fallen lorde he tumbled dead:
    Oh shame to Norman armes! a lord a slave,
    A captyve villeyn than a lorde more brave!

LVII.

From Chatelet hys launce Erle Egward drew,
And hit Wallerie on the dexter cheek;
Peerc'd to his braine, and cut his tongue in two:
There, knyght, quod he, let that thy actions speak[2]—

    *   *   *   *

---

1 Deadly.

2 Chatterton owned that he was the author of the first "Battle of Hastings." The very same day that he acknowledged this forgery, he informed Mr. Barrett that he had another poem, the copy of an original by Rowley; and at a *considerable interval of time* (which indeed was requisite for writing his new piece); he produced *another* "Battle of Hastings," much longer than the former;—a fair copy from an undoubted original!—MALONE.

BATTLE OF HASTINGS.*

(NO. 2.)

I.

On Truth! immortal daughter of the skies,
Too lyttle known to wryters of these daies,
Teach me, fayre Saincte! thy passynge worthe to pryze,
To blame a friend and give a foeman prayse.
The fickle moone, bedeckt wythe sylver rays,
Leadynge a traine of starres of feeble lyghte,
With look adigne[1] the worlde belowe surveles,
The world, that wotted[2] not it coud be nyghte;
Wyth armour dyd, with human gore ydeyd,[3]
She sees Kynge Harolde stande, fayre Englands curse
          and pryde.

---

* We may consider this poem, not as a continuation of the former,
but as an improved work of the same author, on the same subject; in
which he has diversified many of the historical events, and introduced
new personages, but preserved the same style and metre, and used the
same kind of allusion and similes with those in the former poem, be-
ginning with the "History of the Battle," and leaving the conclusion
imperfect.—DEAN MILLES.

1 Noble.   2 Knew.   3 Dyed.

II.

With ale and vernage¹ drunk his souldiers lay;
Here was an hynde,² anie an erlie spredde;
Sad keepynge of their leaders natal daie!
This even in drinke, too-morrow with the dead!
Thro' everie troope disorder reer'd her hedde;
Dancynge and heideignes³ was the onlie theme;
Sad dome was theires, who lefte this easie bedde,
And wak'd in torments from so sweet a dream.
Duke Williams menne, of comeing dethe afraide,
All nyghte to the great Godde for succour ask'd and praied.

III.

Thus Harolde to his wites⁴ that stoode arounde;
Goe, Gyrthe and Eilward, take bills halfe a score.
And search how farre our foeman's campe doth bound;
Yourself have rede;⁵ I nede to saie ne more.
My brother best belov'd of anie ore,⁶
My Leofwinus, goe to everich wite,
Tell them to raunge the battel to the grore,
And waiten tyll I sende the hest⁷ for fyghte.
He saide; the loieaul broders lefte the place,
Success and cheerfulness depicted on ech face.

---

1 A sort of wine.   2 Peasant.
3 'Heydegnes' signified a rustic dance, and is called by Drayton
'Heydegies.'
     "The Nereids on Trent's brim danced wanton *heydegies.*"
Hence the word 'hoyden' is given to a romping female, and dancing
the 'heys' seems to be a contraction of the same word.—DEAN
MILLES.
4 People.   5 Wisdom.   6 Other.   7 Command.

IV.

Slowelie brave Gyrthe and Eilwarde dyd advaunce,
And markd wyth care the armies dystant syde,
When the dyre clatteryuge of the shielde and launce
Made them to be by Hugh Fitzhugh espy'd.
He lyfted up his voice, and lowdlie cry'd;
Like wolfs in wintere did the Normanne yell;
Girthe drew hys swerde, and cutte hys buried hyde;
The proto-slene[1] manne of the fielde he felle;
Out streemd the bloude, and ran in smokynge curles,
Reflected bie the moone seemd rubies mixt wyth pearles.

V.

A troope of Normannes from the mass-songe came,
Rousd from their praiers by the flotting[2] crie;
Thoughe Girthe and Ailwardus perceev'd the same,
Not once theie stoode abash'd, or thoghte to flie.
He seizd a bill, to conquer or to die;
Fierce as a clevis[3] from a rocke ytorne,
That makes a vallie wheresoe're it lie;
Fierce as a ryver burstynge from the borne;[4]
So fiercelie Gyrthe hitte Fitz du Gore a blowe,
And on the verdaunt playne he layde the champyone
        lowe.

VI.

Tancarville thus; alle peace in Williams name;
Let none edraw his arcublaster[5] bowe.
Girthe cas'd[6] his weppone, as he hearde the same,
And vengynge[7] Normannes staid the flyinge floe.

---

1 First-slain.   2 Undulating.   3 Cleft.   4 Brook.
5 Cross-bow.   6 Sheathed.   7 Revenging.

The sire wente onne; ye menne, what mean ye so
Thus unprovok'd to courte a bloudie fyghte?
Quod Gyrthe; oure meanynge we ne care to showe,
Nor dread thy duke wyth all his men of myghte;
Here single onlie these to all thie crewe
Shall shewe what Englysh handes and heartes can doe.

VII.

Seek not for bloude, Tancarville calme reply'd,
Nor joie in dethe, lyke madmen most distraught;[1]
In peace and mercy is a Chrystian's pryde;
He that dothe contestes pryze is in a faulte.
And now the news was to Duke William brought,
That men of Haroldes armie taken were;
For they're good cheere all caties[2] were enthoughte,[3]
And Gyrthe and Eilwardus enjoi'd goode cheere.
Quod Willyam; thus shall Willyam be founde
A friend to everie manne that treads on English ground.

VIII.

Erle Leofwinus throwghe the campe ypass'd,
And sawe bothe men and erlies on the grounde;
They slepte, as thoughe they woulde have slepte
    theyr last,
And hadd alreadie felte theyr fatale wounde.
He started backe, and was wyth shame astownd;[4]
Loked wanne[5] wythanger, and he shooke wyth rage;
When throughe the hollow tentes these wordes dyd
    sound,

---

1 Distracted.   2 Delicacies.   3 Thought of.
4 Astonished.   5 Pale.

Rowse from your sleepe, detratours[1] of the age !
Was it for thys the stoute Norwegian bledde?
Awake, ye huscarles,[2] now, or waken wyth the dead.

IX.

As when the shepster[3] in the shadie bowre
In jintle[4] slumbers chase[5] the heat of daie,
Hears doublyng echoe wind[6] the wolfins rore,
That neare hys flocke is watchynge for a praie,
He tremblynge for his sheep drives dreeme awaie,
Gripes faste hys burled[7] croke, and sore adradde[8]
Wyth fleeting[9] strides he hastens to the fraie,
And rage and prowess fyres the coistrell[10] lad ;
With trustie talbots[11] to the battel flies,
And yell of men and dogs and wolfins[12] tear the skies.

X.

Such was the dire confusion of eche wite,
That rose from sleep n walsome[13] power of wine ;
Theie thoughte the foe by trechit[14] yn the nyghte
Had broke theyr camp and gotten paste the line ;
Now here, now there, the burnysht sheeldes and byll-
    spear shine ;
Throwote the campe a wild confusionne spredde ;
Eche bracd hys armlace[15] siker[16] ne desygne,[17]
The crested helmet nodded on the he de ;

---

1 Traitors.   2 Servants.   3 Shepherd.   4 Gentle.
5 Drives away.   6 Sound.   7 Armed.   8 Frighted.
9 Flying.   10 Servant.   11 Dogs.   12 Wolves.
13 Loathsome.   14 Treachery.   15 Accoutrements for the arms.
16 Sure.   17 It means, each put on his neighbour's armour.

Some caught a slughorne,[1] and an onsett[2] wounde;
Kynge Harolde hearde the charge, and wondred at the
   sounde.

XI.

Thus Leofwine; O women cas'd in stele!
Was itte for thys Norwegia's stubborn sede
Throughe the black armoure dyd the anlace fele,
And rybbes of solid brasse were made to bleede?
Whylst yet the worlde was wondrynge at the deede.
You souldiers, that shoulde stand with byll in hand,
Get full of wine, devoid of any rede.[3]
O shame! oh dyre dishonoure to the lande!
He sayde; and shame on everie visage spredde,
Ne sawe the erlies face, but addawd[4] hung their head.

XII.

Thus he; rowze yee, and forme the boddie tyghte.
The Kentysh menne in fronte, for strenght renown'd,
Next the Brystowans dare the bloudie fyghte,
And last the numerous crewe shall presse the grounde.
I and my king be wyth the Kenters founde;
Bythric and Alfwold hedde the Brystowe bande;
And Bertrams sonne, the man of glorious wounde,
Lead in the rear the menged[5] of the lande;
And let the Londoners and Sussers plie
Bie Herewardes memuine[6] and the lighte skyrts anie.[7]

XIII.

He saide; and as a packe of hounds belent,[8]
When that the trackyng of the hare is gone,

If one perchaunce shall hit upon the scent,
With twa[1] redubbled fhuir[2] the alans[3] run;
So styrrd the valiante Saxons everych one;
Soone linked man to man the champyones stoode;
To 'tone for their bewrate[4] so soone 'twas done,
And lyfted bylls enseem'd an yron woode;
Here glorious Alfwold towr'd above the wites,[5]
And seem'd to brave the fuir of twa ten thousand fights.

XIV.

Thus Leofwine; to-day will Englandes dome
Be fyxt for aie, for gode or evill state;
This sunnes aunture[6] be felt for years to come;
Then bravelie fyghte, and live till deathe of date.
Thinke of brave Ælfridus, yclept[7] the grete,
From porte to porte the red-hair'd Dane he chas'd,,
The Danes, with whomme not lyoncels[8] cou'd mate,
Who made of peopled reaulms a barren waste;
Thinke how at once by you Norwegia bled
Whilste dethe and victorie for magystrie[9] bested.[10]

XV.

Meanwhile did Gyrthe unto Kynge Harolde ride,
And tolde howe he dyd with Duke Willyam fare.
Brave Harolde look'd askaunte,[11] and thus reply'd;
And can thie fay[12] be bowght wyth drunken cheer?
Gyrthe waxen hotte; fhuir in his eyne did glare;
And thus he saide; oh brother, friend, and kynge,

---

1 Twice.	2 Fury.	3 Hounds.	4 Treachery.
5 Men, people.	6 Adventure.	7 Called.	8 Young lions.
9 Mastery.	10 Contended.	11 Obliquely.	12 Faith.

Have I deserved this fremed[1] speche to heare?
Bie Goddes hie hallidome[2] ne thoughte the thynge.
When Tostus sent me golde and sylver store,
I scorn'd hys present vile, and scorn'd hys treason more.

XVI.

Forgive me, Gyrthe, the brave Kynge Harolde cry'd;
Who can I trust, if brothers are not true?
I think of Tostus, once my joie and pryde.
Girthe saide, with looke adigne;[3] my lord, I doe.
But what oure foemen are, quod Girthe, I'll shewe;
By Gods hie hallidome they preestes are.
Do not, quod Harolde, Girthe, mystell[4] them so,
For theie are everich one brave men at warre.
Quod Girthe; why will ye then provoke theyr hate?
Quod Harolde; great the foe, so is the glorie grete.

XVII.

And now Duke Willyam mareschalled his band,
And stretch'd his armie owte a goodlie rowe.
First did a ranke of arcublastries[5] stande,
Next those on horsebacke drew the ascendyng flo,[6]
Brave champyones, eche well lerned in the bowe,
Theyr asenglave[7] acrosse theyr horses ty'd,
Or with the loverds[8] squier behinde dyd goe,
Or waited squier lyke at the horses syde.
When thus Duke Willyam to a Monke dyd saie,
Prepare thyselfe wyth spede, to Harolde haste awaie.

---

1 Strange.   2 Holy church.   3 Noble.   4 Miscall.
5 Cross-bowmen.   6 An arrow.   7 Lances.   8 Lords.

XVIII.

Telle hym from me one of these three to take;
That hee to mee do homage for thys lande,
Or mee hys heyre, when he deceasyth, make,
Or to the judgment of Chrysts vicar stande.
He saide; the Monke departyd out of hande,
And to Kyng Harolde dyd this message bear;
Who said; tell thou the Duke, at his likand[1]
If he can gette the crown hee may itte wear.
He said, and drove the Monke out of his syghte,
And with his brothers rouz'd each manne to bloudie
    fyghte.

XIX.

A standarde made of sylke and jewells rare,
Wherein alle coloures wroughte aboute in bighes,[2]
An armyd knyghte was seen deth-doynge there,
Under this motte,[3] ' He conquers or he dies.'
This standard rych, endazzlyng mortal eyes,
Was borne neare Harolde at the Kenters heade,
Who charg'd hys broders for the grete empryze[4]
That straite the hest[5] for battle should be spredde.
To evry erle and knyghte the worde is gyven,
And cries *a guerre* and slughornes shake the vaulted
    heaven.

XX.

As when the erthe, torne by convulsyons dyre,
In reaulmes of darkness hid from human syghte,

---

1 Choice.   2 Jewels.   3 Motto.   4 Undertaking.   5 Command.

The warring force of water, air, and fyre,
Brast[1] from the regions of eternal nyghte,
Thro the darke caverns seeke the reaulmes of lyght;
Some loftie mountaine, by its fury torne,
Dreadfully moves, and causes grete affryght;
Nowe here, now there, majestic nods the bourne,[2]
And awfulle shakes, mov'd by the almighty force,
Whole woods and forests nod, and ryvers change theyr
    course.

XXI.

So did the men of war at once advaunce,
Link'd man to man, enseemed one boddie light;
Above a wood, yform'd of bill and launce,
That noddyd in the ayre most straunge to syght.
Harde as the iron were the menne of mighte,
Ne neede of slughornes[3] to enrowse theyr minde;
Eche shootynge spere yreaden[4] for the fyghte,
More feerce than fallynge rocks, more swefte than
    wynd;
With solemne step, by ecchoe made more dyre,
One single boddie all theie march'd, theyr eyen on fyre.

XXII.

And now the greie-ey'd morne with vi'lets drest,
Shakyng the dewdrops on the flourie meedes,
Fled with her rosie radiance to the west:
Forth from the easterne gatte the fyerie steedes
Of the bright sunne awaytynge spirits leedes:
The sunne, in fierie pompe enthron'd on hie,

---

1 Burst.   2 Hill, or rock.   3 War trumpets.   4 Made ready.

Swyfter than thoughte alonge hys jernie[1] gledes,[2]
And scatters nyghtes remaynes from oute the skie :
He sawe the armies make for bloudie fraie,
And stopt his driving steedes, and hid his lyghtsome
    raye.

XXIII.

Kynge Harolde hie in ayre majestic rays'd
His mightie arme, deckt with a manchyn[3] rare,
With even hande a mighty javlyn paizde,[4]
Then furyouse sent it whystlynge thro' the ayre.
It struck the helmet of the Sieur de Beer;
In vayne did brasse or yron stop its waie;
Above his eyne it came, the bones dyd tare,
Peercynge quite thro', before it dyd allaie;[5]
He tumbled, scritchyng[6] wyth hys horrid payne;
His hollow cuishes[7] rang upon the bloudie pleyne.

XXIV.

This Willyam saw, and soundynge Rowlaudes songe
He bent his yron interwoven bowe,
Makynge bothe endes to meet with myg.ite full stronge,
From out of mortals syght shot up the floe;[8]
Then swyfte as fallynge starres to earthe belowe
It slaunted down on Alfwoldes payncted sheelde;
Quite thro' the silver-bordur'd crosse did goe,
Nor loste its force, but stuck into the feelde;
The Normannes, like theyr sovrin, dyd prepare,
And shotte ten thousande floes uprysynge in the aire.

---

1 Journey.   2 Glides.   3 Sleeve.   4 Poised.   5 Stop.
6 Shrieking.   7 Armour for the thighs.   8 Arrow.

XXV.

As when a flyghte of cranes, that takes their waie
In householde armies thro' the flanched[1] skie,
Alike the cause, or companie or prey,
If that perchaunce some boggie fenne is nie,
Soon as the muddie natyon theie espie,
Inne one blacke cloude theie to the erth descende ;
Feirce as the fallynge thunderbolte they flie ;
In vayne do reedes the speckled folk defend :
So prone to heavie blowe the arrowes felle,
And peercd thro' brasse, and sente manie to heaven or
    helle.

XXVI.

Ælan Adelfred, of the stowe[2] of Leigh,
Felte a dire arrowe burnynge in his breste ;
Before he dyd, he sente hys spear awaie,
Thenne sunke to glorie and eternal reste.
Nevylle, a Normanne of alle Normannes beste,
Throw the joint cuishe dyd the javlyn feel,
As hee on horsebacke for the fyghte address'd,
And sawe hys bloude come smokynge o'er the steele ;
He sente the avengynge floe into the ayre,
And turn'd hys horses hedde, and did to leeche[3] repayre.

XXVII.

And now the javelyns, barb'd with death his wynges,
Hurl'd from the Englysh handes by force aderne,[4]
Whyzz dreare[5] alonge, and songes of terror synges,
Such songes as alwaies clos'd in lyfe eterne.

---

1 Arched.   2 Place, or city.   3 Physician.   4 Dire.   5 Terrible.

Hurl'd by such strength along the ayre theie burne,
Not to be quenched butte ynn Normannes bloude;
Wherere theie came they were of lyfe forlorn,
And alwaies followed by a purple floude;
Like cloudes the Normanne arrowes did descend,
Like cloudes of carnage full in purple drops dyd end.

XXVIII.

Nor, Leofwynus, dydst thou still estande;
Full soon thie pheon[1] glytted[2] in the aire;
The force of none but thyne and Harold's hande
Could hurle a javlyn with such lethal[3] geer;[4]
Itte whyzz'd a ghastlie dynne in Normannes ear,
Then thund'ryng dyd upon hys greave[5] alyghte,
Peirce to his hearte, and dyd hys bowels tear,
He clos'd hys eyne in everlastynge nyghte;[6]
Ah! what avayld the lyons on his creste!
His hatchments rare with him upon the grounde was prest.

XXIX.

Willyam agayne ymade his bowe-ends meet,
And hie in ayre the arrowe wynged his waie,
Descendyng like a shafte of thunder fleete,
Lyke thunder rattling at the noon of daie,
Onne Algars sheelde the arrowe dyd assaie,[7]
There throghe dyd peerse, and stycke into his groine;
In grypynge torments on the feelde he laie,
Tille welcome dethe came in and clos'd his eyne;

---

1 Spear.   2 Gilded.   3 Deadly.   4 Turn.
5 A part of armour.
6   " Clos'd his eyes in endless night."—GRAY's *Bard*.
7 Make an attempt.

Distort[1] with peyne he laie upon the borne,[2]
Lyke sturdie elms by stormes in uncothe[3] wrythynges
    torne.

XXX.

Alrick his brother, when hee this perceev'd,
He drewe his swerde, his lefte hande helde a speere,
Towards the duke he turn'd his prauncyng steede,
And to the Godde of heaven he sent a prayre ;
Then sent his lethale javlyn in the ayre,
On Hue de Beaumontes backe the javelyn came,
Thro his redde armour to hys harte it tare,
He felle and thondred on the place of fame ;
Next with his swerde he 'sayl'd the Seiur de Roe,
And braste[4] his sylver helme, so furyous was the blowe.

XXXI.

But Willyam, who had seen hys prowesse great,
And feered muche how farre his bronde[5] might goe,
Tooke a stronge arblaster,[6] and bigge with fate
From twangynge iron sente the fleetynge floe.[7]
As Alric hoistes hys arme for dedlie blowe,
Which, han it came, had been Du Roees laste,
The swyfte-wyng'd messenger from Willyams bowe
Quite throwe his arme into his syde ypaste ;
His eyne shotte fyra, lyke blazyng starre at nyghte,
He gryp'd his swerde, and felle upon the place of fyghte.

XXXII.

O Alfwolde, saie, how shalle I synge of thee
Or telle how manie dyd benethe thee falle ;

---

1 Distorted, writhing.   2 Burnished armour.   3 Strange.
4 Broke, burst.   5 Fury.   6 Cross-bow.   7 Arrow.

Not Haroldes self more Normanne knyghtes did slee,
Not Haroldes self did for more praises call;
How shall a penne like myne then shew it all?
Lyke thee, their leader, eche Bristowyanne foughte;
Lyke thee, their blaze must be canonical,
Fore theie, like thee, that daie bewrecke¹ yroughte:
Did thirtie Normannes fall upon the grounde,
Full half a score from thee and theie receive their fatale
    wounde.

XXXIII.

First Fytz Chivelloys felt thie direful force;
Nete² did hys helde out brazen sheelde availe;
Eftsoones throwe that thie drivynge speare did peerce,
Nor was ytte stopped by his coate of mayle;
Into his breaste it quicklie did assayle;³
Out ran the bloude, like hygra⁴ of the tyde;
With purple stayned all hys adventayle;⁵
In scarlet was his cuishe⁶ of sylver dyde:
Upon the bloudie carnage house he laie,
Whylst hys longe sheelde dyd gleem⁷ with the sun's
    rysing ray.

XXXIV.

Next Fescampe felle; O Chrieste, howe harde his fate
To die the leckedst⁸ knyghte of all the thronge;
His sprite was made of malice deslavate,⁹
Ne shoulden find a place in anie songe.
The broch'd¹⁰ keene javlyn hurld from honde so stronge

---

1 Revenge.   2 Nought.   3 Attempt.   4 Bore of the Severn.
5 Armour.   6 Armour for the thigh.   7 Pointed.
8 Cowardliest.   9 Disloyal.   10 Pointed.

As thine came thundrynge on his crysted[1] beave;[2]
Ah! neete avayld the brass or iron thonge,
With mightie force his skulle in twoe dyd cleave;
Fallyng he shooken out his smokyng braine,
As wither'd oakes or elmes are hewne from off the playne.

xxxv.

Nor, Norcie, could thie myghte and skilfulle lore[3]
Preserve thee from the doom of Alfwold's speere;
Couldste thou not kenne,[4] most skyll'd After la goure,[5]
How in the battle it would wythe thee fare?
When Alfwold's javelyn, rattlynge in the ayre,
From hande dyvine on thie habergeon[6] came,
Oute at thy backe it dyd thie hartes bloude bear,
It gave thee death and everlastynge fame;
Thy deathe could onlie come from Alfwolde arme,
As diamondes onlie can its fellow diamonds harme.

xxxvi.

Next Sire du Mouline fell upon the grounde,
Quite throughe his throte the lethal javlyn preste,
His soule and bloude came roushynge from the wounde;
He clos'd his eyen, and op'd them with the blest.
It can ne be I should behight[7] the rest,
That by the myghtie arme of Alfwolde felle,
Paste bie a penne to be counte or expreste,
How manie Alfwolde sent to heaven or helle;

---

1 Crested.   2 Beaver.   3 Learning.   4 Know.
5 There can be no doubt that this singular word is used by some in-
advertency for 'asterlagour,' or 'astrologer.'—ED.]
6 Coat of mail.   7 Name.

As leaves from trees shook by derne[1] Autumns hand,
So laie the Normannes slain by Alfwold on the strand.[*]

XXXVII.

As when a drove of wolves withe dreary yelles
Assayle some flocke, ne care if shepster ken't,[2]
Besprenge[3] destructione oer the woodes and delles;
The shepster swaynes in vayne theyr lees[4] lement;
So foughte the Brystowe menne; ne one crevent,[5]
Ne onne abashed enthoughten for to flee;
With fallen Normans all the playne besprent,
And like theyr leaders every man did slee;
In vayne on every syde the arrowes fled;
The Brystowe menne styll rag'd, for Alfwold was not
　　dead.

XXXVIII.

Manie meanwhile by Haroldes arm did falle,
And Leofwyne and Gyrthe encreas'd the slayne;
'Twould take a Nestor's age to synge them all,
Or telle how manie Normannes preste the playne;
But of the erles, whom record nete hath slayne,
O Truthe! for good of after-tymes relate
That, thowe they're deade, theyr names may lyve
　　agayne,
And be in deathe, as they in life were, greate;

---

1 Dreary.
　* The minute enumeration of the Norman names in the "Battle of
Hastings," may be explained by supposing Chatterton to have copied
them from "Fuller's Church History," while the Saxon names not
being so easily attainable, are but sparingly interspersed.—TYRWHITT.
2 Know it.　　3 Spread.　　4 Sheep-pastures.　　5 Coward.

So after-ages maie theyr actions see,
And like to them æternal alwaie stryve to be. ·

XXXIX.

Adhelm, a knyghte, whose holie deathless sire*
For ever bended to St. Cuthbert's shryne,
Whose breast for ever burn'd with sacred fyre,
And ee'n on erthe he myghte be call'd dyvine;
To Cuthbert's church he dyd his goodes resygne,
And lefte hys son his God's and fortunes knyghte;
His son the Saincte behelde with looke adigne,[1]
Made him in gemot[2] wyse, and greate in fyghte;
Saincte Cuthberte dyd him ayde in all hys deedes,
His friends he lets to live, and all his foemen bleedes.

XL.

He married was to Kenewalchae faire,
The fynest dame the sun or moone adave;[3]
She was the myghtie Aderedus' heyre,
Who was alreadie hastynge to the grave;
As the blue Bruton, rysinge from the wave,
Like sea-gods seeme in most majestic guise,
And rounde aboute the risynge waters lave,[4]
And their longe hayre arounde their bodie flies,
Such majestie was in her porte displaid,
To be excell'd bie none but Homer's martial maid.

XLI.

White as the chaulkie clyffes of Brittaines isle,
Red as the highest colour'd Gallic wine,

---

* [The next seven stanzas may compete with almost anything in
English poetry.—Ed.]

1 Worthy.   2 Counsel.   3 Arose upon.   4 Wash.

Gaie as all nature at the mornynge smile,
Those hues with pleasaunce on her lippes combine—
Her lippes more redde than summer evenynge skyne,[1]
Or Phœbus rysinge in a frostie morne,
Her breste more white than snow in feeldes that
    lyene,[2]
Or lillie lambes that never have been shorne,
Swellynge like bubbles in a boillynge welle,
Or new-braste[3] brooklettes gently whyspringe in the
    delle.

XLII.

Browne as the fylberte droppyng from the shelle,
Browne as the nappy ale at Hocktyde game,
So browne the erokyde[4] rynges, that featlie[5] fell
Over the neck of the all-beauteous dame.
Greie as the morne before the ruddie flame
Of Phœbus' charyotte rollynge thro the skie;
Greie as the steel-horn'd goats Conyan made tame,
So greie appear'd her featly sparklyng eye:
Those eyne, that dyd oft mickle pleased look
On Adhelm valyaunt man, the virtues doomsday book.

XLIII.

Majestic as the grove of okes that stoode
Before the abbie buylt by Oswald kynge;
Majestic as Hybernics holie woode,
Where sainctes and soules departed masses synge;*
Such awe from her sweete looke forth issuynge

---

1 Sky.   2 Lies.   3 Newly burst.
4 Curling, crooked.   5 Genteely.
* [This appears to be a mistake. It should be—
    " Where saints *for* souls departed masses sing."—Ed.]

At once for reveraunce and love did calle;
Sweet as the voice of thraslarks[1] in the Spring,
So sweet the wordes that from her lippes did falle;
None fell in vayne; all shewed some entent;
Her wordies did displaie her great entendement.[2]

XLIV.

Tapre as candles layde at Cuthberts shryne,
Tapre as elmes that Goodrickes abbie shrove,[3]
Tapre as silver chalices for wine,
So tapre was her armes and shape ygrove.[4]
As skyllful mynemenne[5] by the stones above
Can ken what metalle is ylach'd[6] belowe,
So Kennewalcha's face, ymade for love,
The lovelie ymage of her soule did shewe;
Thus was she outward form'd; the sun her mind
Did guilde her mortal shape and all her charms refin'd.

XLV.

What blazours[7] then, what glorie shall he clayme,
What doughtie[8] Homere shall hys praises synge,
That lefte the bosome of so fayre a dame
Uncall'd, unaskt, to serve his lorde the kynge?
To his fayre shrine goode subjects oughte to bringe
The armes, the helmets, all the spoyles of warre,
Throwe everie reaulm the poets blaze the thynge,
And travelling merchants spredde hys name to farre;
The stoute Norwegians had his anlace[9] felte,
And nowe amonge his foes dethe-doynge blowes he delte.

---

1 Thrushes.	2 Understanding.	3 Shrouded.	4 Formed.
5 Miners.	6 Confined.	7 Praisers.	8 Powerful.
9 Sword.			

XLVI.

As when a wolfyn gettynge in the meedes
He rageth sore, and doth about hym slee,
Nowe here a talbot,[1] there a lambkin bleeds,
And alle the grasse with clotted gore doth stree;[2]
As when a rivlette rolles impetuouslie,
And breaks the bankes that would its force restrayne,
Alonge the playne in fomynge rynges doth flee,
Gaynste walles and hedges doth its course maintayne;
As when a manne doth in a corn-fielde mowe,
With ease at one felle stroke full manie is laide lowe.

XLVII.

So manie, with such force, and with such ease,
Did Adhelm slaughtre on the bloudie playne;
Before hym manie dyd theyr hearts bloude lease,[3]
Ofttymes he foughte on towres of smokynge slayne.
Angillian felte his force, nor felte in vayne;
He cutte hym with his swerde athur[4] the breaste;
Out ran the bloude, and did hys armoure stayne,
He clos'd his eyen in æternal reste;
Lyke a tall oke by tempeste borne awaie,
Stretch'd in the armes of dethe upon the plaine he laie.

XLVIII.

Next thro' the ayre he sent his javlyn feerce,
That on De Clearmoundes buckler did alyghte,
Throwe the vaste orbe the sharpe pheone[5] did peerce,
Rang on his coate of mayle and spente its mighte.

---

1 Species of dog.   2 Strew, or scatter.   3 Lose.
4 Across.   5 Spear.

But soon another wing'd its aiery flyghte,
The keen broad pheon to his lungs did goe;
He felle, and groan'd upon the place of fighte,
Whilst lyfe and bloude came issuynge from the blowe.
Like a tall pyne upon his native playne,
So fell the mightie sire and mingled with the slaine.

XLIX.

Hue de Longeville, a force doughtre mere,[1]
Advauncyd forwarde to provoke the darte,
When soone he founde that Adhelmes poynted speere
Had founde an easie passage to his hearte.
He drewe his bowe, nor was of dethe astarte,[2]
Then fell down brethlesse to encrease the corse;
But as he drewe hys bowe devoid of arte,
So it came down upon Troyvillain's horse;
Deep thro' hys hatchments[3] wente the pointed floe;
Now here, now there, with rage bleedyng he rounde
     doth goe.

L.

Nor does he hede his mastres known commands,
Tyll, growen furiouse by his bloudie wounde,
Erect upon his hynder feete he staundes,
And throwes hys mastre far off to the grounde.
Near Adhelms feete the Normanne laie astounde,[4]
Besprengd[5] his arrowes, loosend was his sheelde,
Thro' his redde armoure, as he laie ensoond,[6]
He peerc'd his swerde, and out upon the feelde

---

1 Exile.   2 Afraid.   3 Comparisons.   4 Stunned.
5 Scattered.   6 In a swoon.

The Normannes bowels steem'd,[1] a deadlie syghte!
He op'd and clos'd hys eyen in everlastynge nyghte.

LI.

Caverd, a Scot, who for the Normannes foughte,
A man well skill'd in swerde and soundynge strynge,
Who fled his country for a crime enstrote,[2]
For darynge with bolde worde hys loiaule kynge,
He at Erle Aldhelme with grete force did flynge
An heavie javlyn, made for bloudie wounde,
Alonge his sheelde askaunte[3] the same did ringe,
Peerc'd thro' the corner, then stuck in the grounde;
So when the thonder rauttles in the skie,
Thro' some tall spyre the shaftes in a torn clevis[4] flie.

LII.

Then Addhelm hurl'd a croched javlyn stronge,
With mighte that none but such grete championes know;
Swifter than thoughte the javlyn past alonge,
Ande hytte the Scot most feirclie on the prowe;[5]
His helmet brasted[6] at the thondring blowe,
Into his brain the tremblyn javlyn steck;[7]
From eyther syde the bloude began to flow,
And run in circling ringlets rounde his neck;
Down fell the warriour on the lethal strande,
Lyke some tall vessel wreckt upon the tragick sande.

---

1 Reeked.   2 To be punished.   3 Slanting.   4 Cleft.
5 Forehead.   6 Burst.   7 Stuck.

(*Continued.*)*

LIII.

Where fruytless heathes and meadowes cladde in greie,
Save where derne¹ hawthornes reare theyr humble
    heade,
The hungrie traveller upon his waie
Sees a huge desarte alle arounde hym spredde,
The distaunte citie scantlie² to be spedde,
The curlynge force of smoke he sees in vayne,
'Tis too far distaunte, and his onlie bedde
Iwimpled³ in hys cloke ys on the playne,
  Whylste rattlynge thonder forrey⁴ oer his hedde,
And raines come down to wette hys harde uncouthlie
    bedde.

LIV.

A wondrous pyle of rugged mountaynes standes,
Plac'd on eche other in a dreare arraie,
It ne could be the worke of human handes,
It ne was reared up bie menne of claie.
Here did the Brutons adoration paye
To the false god whom they did Tauran name,
Dightynge⁵ hys altarre with greete fyres in Maie,
Roastynge theyr vyctualle⁶ round aboute the flame,
  Twas here that Hengyst did the Brytons slee,
As they were mette in council for to bee.

---

* [See note at page 166 respecting this continuation. The description
of Stonehenge which follows is unrivalled.—ED.]
  1 Dreary, melancholy.   2 Scarcely.   3 Muffled.—BAILEY.
  4 Destroy.   5 Dressing.
  6 [Mr. Bryant is of opinion that this word should be "victims."—ED.

LV.

Neere on a loftie hylle a citie standes,
That lyftes yts scheafted[1] heade ynto the skies,
And kynglie lookes arounde on lower landes,
And the longe browne playne that before itte lies.
Herewarde, borne of parentes brave and wyse,
Within thys vylle[2] fyrste adrewe the ayre,
A blessynge to the erthe sente from the skies,
In anie kyngdom nee coulde fynde his pheer;[3]
Now rybbd in steele he rages yn the fyghte,
And sweeps whole armies to the reaulmes of nyghte.

LVI.

So when derne Autumne wyth hys sallowe hande
Tares the green mantle from the lymed[4] trees,
The leaves besprenged[5] on the yellow strande
Flie in whole armies from the blataunte[6] breeze;
Alle the whole fielde a carnage-howse he sees,
And sowles unknelled hover'd o'er the bloude;
From place to place on either hand he slees,
And sweepes alle neere hym lyke a bronded[7] floude;
Dethe honge upon his arme; he sleed so maynt,[8]
'Tis paste the pointel[9] of a man to paynte.

LVII.

Bryghte sonne in haste han drove hys fierie wayne
A three howres course alonge the whited skyen,[10]
Vewynge the swarthless[11] bodies on the playne,
And longed greetlie to plonce[12] in the bryne.

---

1 Adorned with turrets.	2 Parish.	3 Equal.	4 Smooth.
5 Scattered.	6 Noisy.	7 Furious.	8 Many.
9 Pen. 10 Sky.	11 Without souls, lifeless.		12 Plunge.

For as hys beemes and far-stretchynge eyne
Did view the pooles of gore yn purple sheene,
The wolsomme¹ vapours rounde hys lockes dyd twyne,
And dyd disfygure all hys semmlikeen ;²
Then to harde actyon he hys wayne dyd rowse,
In hyssynge ocean to make glair³ hys browes.

LVIII.

Duke Wyllyam gave commaunde, eche Norman
    knyghte,
That beer war-token in a shielde so fyne,
Shoulde onward goe, and dare to closer fyghte
The Saxonne warryor, that dyd so entwine,
Lyke the neshe⁴ bryon⁵ and the eglantine,⁶
Orre Cornysh wrastlers at a Hocktyde game.
The Normannes, all emarchialld in a lyne,
To the ourt⁷ arraie of the thight⁸ Saxonnes came ;
There 'twas the whaped⁹ Normannes on a parre
Dyd know that Saxonnes were the sonnes of warre.

LIX.

Oh Turgotte, wheresoeer thie spryte dothe haunte,
Whither wyth thie lovd Adhelme by thie syde,
Where thou mayste heare the swotie¹⁰ nyghte larke
    chaunte,
Orre wyth some mokynge¹¹ brooklette swetelie glide,
Or rowle in ferselie¹² wythe ferse Severnes tyde,

---

1 Loathsome.   2 Countenance.   3 Clear.   4 Tender.
5 Wild-vine.   6 Sweetbrier.   7 Open.
8 Closed, consolidated.   9 Astonished.
10 Sweet.   11 Mocking, bubbling.
12 Tumult.

Whereer thou art, come and my mynde enleme[1]
Wyth such greete thoughtes as dyd with thee abyde,
Thou sonne, of whom I ofte have caught a beeme,
Send mee agayne a drybblette, of thie lyghte,
That I the deeds of Englyshmenne maie wryte.

LX.

Harolde, who saw the Normannes to advaunce,
Seiz'd a huge byll, and layd hym down hys spere;
Soe dyd ech wite laie downe the broched[3] launce,
And groves of bylles did glitter in the ayre.
Wyth showtes the Normannes did to battel steere;
Campynon famous for his stature highe,
Fyrey wythe brasse, benethe a shyrte of lere,[4]
In cloudie daie he reech'd into the skie;
Neere to Kyng Harolde dyd he come alonge,
And drewe hys steele Morglaien sworde so stronge.

LXI.

Thryce rounde hys heade hee swung hys anlace[5] wyde,
On whyche the sunne his visage did agleeme,[6]
Then straynynge, as hys membres would dyvyde,
Hee stroke on Haroldes sheelde yn manner breme;[7]
Alonge the fielde it made an horrid cleembe,[8]
Coupeynge[9] Kyng Harolds payncted sheeld in twayne,
Then yn the bloude the fierie swerde dyd steeme,
And then dyd drive ynto the bloudie playne;
So when in ayre the vapours do abounde,
Some thunderbolte tares trees and dryves ynto the
　　　grounde.

---

1 Enlighten.　2 Small portion.　3 Pointed.　4 Leather.　5 Sword.
6 Shine.　　　7 Furious.　　　8 Sound.　　9 Cutting.

LXII.

Harolde upreer'd hys bylle, and furious sente
A stroke, lyke thondre, at the Normannes syde;
Upon the playne the broken brasse besprente[1]
Dyd ne hys bodie from dethe-doeynge hyde;
He tournyd backe, and dyd not there abyde;
With straught oute sheelde hee ayenwarde[2] did goe,
Threwe downe the Normannes, did their rankes divide,
To save himselfe lefte them unto the foe;
So olyphauntes,[3] in kingdomme of the sunne,
When once provok'd doth throwe theyr owne troopes
    runne.

LXIII.

Harolde, who ken'd hee was his armies staie,
Nedeynge the rede[4] of generaul so wyse,
Byd Alfwoulde to Campynon haste awaie,
As thro the armie ayenwarde he 'hies,
Swyfte as a feether'd takel[5] Alfwoulde flies,
The steele bylle blushynge oer wyth lukewarm bloude;
Ten Kenters, ten Bristowans for th' emprize[6]
Hasted wyth Alfwoulde where Campynon stood,
Who aynewarde went, whylste everie Normanne
    knyghte
Dyd blush to see their champyon put to flyghte.

LXIV.

As painctyd Bruton, when a wolfyn wylde,
When yt is cale[7] and blustrynge wyndes do blowe,
Enters hys bordelle,[8] taketh hys yonge chylde,
And wyth his bloude bestreynts[9] the lillie snowe,

---

1 Scattered.   2 Backward.   3 Elephants.   4 Advice.   5 Arrow.
6 Enterprise. 7 Cold.   8 Cottage.   9 Sprinkles.

He thoroughe mountayne hie and dale doth goe,
Throwe the quyck torrent of the bollen¹ ave,²
Throwe Severne rollynge oer the sandes belowe
He skyms alofe,³ and blents⁴ the beatynge wave,
Ne stynts,⁵ ne lagges the chace, tylle for hys eyne
In peecies hee the morthering theef doth chyne.⁶

LXV.

So Alfwoulde he dyd to Campynon haste ;
Hys bloudie bylle awhap'd⁷ the Normannes eyne ;
Hee fled, as wolfes when bie the talbots chac'd,
To bloudie byker⁸ he dyd ne enclyne.
Duke Wyllyam stroke hym on hys brigandyne,
And sayd ; Campynon, is it thee I see ?
Thee ? who dydst actes of glorie so bewryen,⁹
Now poorlie come to hyde thieselfe bie mee ?
Awaie ! thou dogge, and acte a warrior's parte,
Or with mie swerde I'll perce thee to the harte.

LXVI.

Betweene Erle Alfwoulde and Duke Wyllyam's bronde¹⁰
Campynon thoughte that nete but deathe coulde bee,
Seezed a huge swerde Morglaien yn his honde,
Mottrynge¹¹ a praier to the Vyrgyne:
So hunted deere the dryvynge houndes will slee,
When theie dyscover they cannot escape ;
And feerful lambkyns, when theie hunted bee,
Theyre ynfante hunters doe theie ofte awhape ;
Thus stoode Campynon, greete but hertlesse knyghte,
When feere of dethe made hym for deathe to fyghte.

---

1 Swelling.   2 Wave.   3 Aloft.   4 Mixes with.
5 Stops.   6 Divide.   7 Astonished.   8 Contest.
9 Shew.   10 Sword.   11 Muttering.

LXVII.

Alfwoulde began to dyghte[1] hymselfe for fyghte,
Meanewhyle hys menne on everie syde dyd slee,
Whan on hys lyfted sheelde withe alle hys myghte
Campynon's swerde in burlie-brande[2] dyd dree;[3]
Bewopen[4] Alfwoulde fellen on his knee;
Hys Brystowe menne came in hym for to save;
Eftsoons upgotten from the grounde was hee,
And dyd agayne the touring Norman brave;
Hee grasp'd hys bylle in syke a drear arraie,
Hee seem'd a lyon catchynge at hys preie.

LXVIII.

Upon the Normannes brazen adventayle[5]
The thondrynge bill of myghtie Alfwould came;
It made a dentful[6] bruse, and then dyd fayle;
Fromme rattlynge weepons shotte a sparklynge flame;
Eftsoons agayne the thondrynge bill ycame,
Peers'd thro hys adventayle and skyrts of lare;[7]
A tyde of purple gore came wyth the same,
As out hys bowells on the feelde it tare;
Campynon felle, as when some cittie-walle
Inne dolefulle terrours on its myuours falle.

LXIX.

He felle, and dyd the Norman rankes dyvide;
So when an oke, that shotte ynto the skie,*

---

1 Prepare.　　2 Armed fury.　　3 Drive.　　4 Stupefied.
5 Armour.　　6 Indented.　　7 Leather.
* 　　"As when the mountain oak, or poplar tall,
　　　Or pine, fit mast for some great admiral,
　　　Groans to the oft-heaved axe with many a wound,
　　　Then spreads a length of ruin on the ground."—POPE's HOMER.

Feeles the broad axes peersynge his broade syde,
Slowlie hee falls and on the grounde doth lie.
Pressynge all downe that is wyth hym anighe,
And stoppynge wearie travellers on the waie;
So straught[1] upon the playne the Norman hie
*   *   *   *
Bled, gron'd, and dyed: the Normanne knyghtes
    astound
To see the bawsin[2] champyon preste upon the grounde.

LXX.

As when the hygra[3] of the Severne roars,
And thunders ugsom[4] on the sandes below,
The cleembe[5] reboundes to Wedecester's shore,
And sweeps the black sande rounde its horie prowe;[6]
So bremie[7] Alfwoulde thro' the warre dyd goe;
Hys Kenters and Brystowans slew ech syde,
Betreinted[8] all alonge with bloudless foe,
And seem'd to swymm alonge with bloudie tyde;
Fromme place to place besmear'd with bloud they went,
And rounde aboute them swarthless[9] corse besprente.[10]

LXXI.

A famous Normanne who yclepd[11] Aubene,
Of skyll in bow, in tylte, and handesworde fyghte,
That daie yn feelde han manie Saxons sleene,
Forre hee in sothen[12] was a manne of myghte;
Fyrste dyd his swerde on Adelgar alyghte,

<hr>

1 Stretched out.	2 Huge.	3 Bore. See note to page 69.
4 Turrible. 5 Noise.	6 Brow.	7 Furious. 8 Sprinkled.
9 Lifeless.	10 Scattered.	11 Called. 12 Truth.

As hee on horseback was, and peers'd hys gryne,[1]
Then upwarde wente: in everlastynge nyghte
Hee closd hys rollyng and dymsyghted eyne.
Next Eadlyn, Tatwyn, and fam'd Adelred,
Bie various causes sunken to the dead.

LXXII.

But now to Alfwoulde he opposynge went,
To whom compar'd hee was a man of stre,[2]
And wyth bothe hondes a myghtie blowe he sente
At Alfwoulde's head, as hard as hee could dree;[3]
But on hys payncted sheelde so bismarlie[4]
Aslaunte[5] his swerde did go ynto the grounde;
Then Alfwould him attack'd most furyouslie,
Athrowe hys gaberdyne[6] hee dyd him wounde,
Then soone agayne hys swerde hee dyd upryne,[7]
And clove his creste and split hym to the eyne.[*]

*   *   *   *

---

1 Groin.	2 Straw.	3 Drive.	4 Curiously.
5 Slanting.	6 Cloak.	7 Lift up.	

[*] This is the last event recorded in the poem which does not appear to be drawing to a conclusion. The death of Harold, that great prelude to the event of this decisive battle, remains unsung. How much cause then have we to lament, that the same pen which has so classically adorned the recital of this engagement, should not have completed the poem, by describing the more important and interesting conclusion of that remarkable event!—DEAN MILLES.

Of the merit of the " Rowley Poems " in a critical point of view, it is not here the place, or now the time to speak. They have been long subjected to the public; and in spite of their being written in a dialect which resembles the ancient or modern language of England, hardly more nearly than the vocabulary of George Psalmanazar did that of Formosa; they have been ever esteemed compositions of the highest merit. The drama called "Ælla," many parts of the " Battle of Hastings," the " Ballad of Charity," that of Sir Charles Bawdin (which somewhat resembles the antique style of minstrel poetry), the " Dirge," and several of the " Eclogues," may rank with the labours of our most distinguished poets. Pity it is, that the circumstances and temper of the author combined to shorten a life distinguished by such works of excellence during its limited career.—SIR WALTER SCOTT.

Mr. Bryant is of opinion, that the "Battle of Hastings" contains a *mass of occult intelligence*, in many *obscure references*, and *dark hints*. This is a mass which I cannot penetrate. The poem, as we have seen, is supposed to have been originally written by Turgott, a coeval ecclesiastic. But a writer so connected with the times, a professed historian, and who was here the author of a separate and distinct narrative of this single event, must have treated the subject with minuteness and particularity. He was drawing from the life, and recording recent facts. This newly discovered manuscript of Turgott must have mentioned anecdotes not now to be found in our histories, or have related those already recorded, with additional circumstances, with a less degree of generality, and a variety of new particulars. But, unluckily, we see little more than the well-known, established, leading incidents. Some few poetical or imaginary insertions excepted, this memorable Battle is much the same in Hollinshed as in Turgott. I am speaking of real facts, such as properly belong to this event as a piece of history, and such as Turgott would have naturally told. As to those *occult intelligences*, instanced by Mr. Bryant, *Tynyan's necromancy*, the *goats of Conyan made tame*, and the souls of the *fairy-stricken* people that wander to *Offa's dyke*, they are extraneous, and the sport of the poet. Tynyan is an old British king in Geoffrey of Monmouth. So little is known of this monarch, that he was safely and easily converted into a necromancer. The *goats of Conyan* might be an allusion, to amuse and deceive, without any meaning at the bottom. We must not always treat fancies as mysteries. There are now remembered many romantic traditions, such as that of the souls of the *fairy-stricken people*. But this might have sprung from Chatterton's imagination, for it is by no means out of the style and cast of modern fiction. All these may be said to have been added to Turgott by Rowley. It is at least as probable that they came from Chatterton. They certainly did not fall from the pen of an archdeacon, a prior of an episcopal church, and a conscientious annalist. At least they would not have been introduced by Turgott into the grave dignity of an historic detail.— WARTON.

𝕿𝖍𝖊 𝕽𝖔𝖒𝖆𝖚𝖓𝖙𝖊¹ 𝖔𝖋 𝖙𝖍𝖊 𝕮𝖓𝖞𝖌𝖍𝖙𝖊.²*

BY JOHN DE BERGHAM.

———

THE Sunne ento Vyrgyne was gotten,
The floureys al arounde onspryngede,ᵃ
The woddie⁴ Grasse blaunched⁵ the Fenne,
The Quenis Ermyne arised fro Bedde;
Syr Knyghte dyd ymounte oponn a Stede
Ne Rouncie⁶ ne Drybblette⁷ of make,
Thanne asterte⁸ for dur'sie⁹ dede

---

1 Romance.   2 Knight.
* Mr. Burgum (the Bristol pewterer) is one of the first persons who
expresses an opinion of the authenticity and excellence of Rowley's
poems. Chatterton, pleased with this first blossom of credulity, and
from which he presaged an abundant harvest, with an elated and a grate-
ful heart, presents him with the 'Romaunte of the Cnyghte,' a poem
written by 'JOHN DE BERGHAM,' one of *his own* ancestors, about four
hundred and fifty years before; and, the more effectually to exclude
suspicion, he accompanies it with the same poem modernized by him-
self.—COTTLE. See the 'Romance of the Knight' in Chatterton's ac-
knowledged Poems.
3 Faded, fallen.   4 Woody.
5 Whitened.   6 A cart horse, or one put to menial services.
7 Small, little.   8 Passed, or went forth.
9 From 'duress,' hardship, signifying hardy.

Wythe Morglaie! hys Fooemenne[1] to make blede
Eke[3]swythyn[4]as wynde. Trees, theyre Hartys to shake,[*]
Al doune in a Delle, a merke[5] dernie[6] Delle,
Wheere Coppys eke Thighe Trees there bee,
There dyd hee perchaunce Isee
A Damoselle askedde for ayde on her kne,
An Cnyghte uncourteous dydde bie her stonde
Hee hollyd herr faeste bie her honde,
Discorteous Cnyghte, I doe praie nowe thou telle
Whirst doeste thou bee so to thee Damselle?
The Knyghte hym assoled[7] eftsoones,[8]
Itte beethe ne mattere of thyne.
Begon for I wayte notte thye boones.

The Knyghte sed I proove on thie Gaberdyne,[9]
Alyche[10] Boars enchafed[11] to fyghte heie flies.
The Discoorteous Knyghte bee strynge[12] botte stryn-
    ger the righte,
The dynne[13] bee herde a'myle for fuire[14] in the fyghte,
Tyl thee false Knyghte yfallethe and dyes.

Damoysel, quod the Knyghte, now comme thou wi me,
Y wotte[15] welle quod shee I nede thee ne fere.
The Knyghte yfallen badd wolde Ischulde bee,
Butte loe he ys dedde maie itte spede Heavenwere.[16]

---

1 A fatal sword.   2 Foes.   3 Also.   4 Quickly.
* [The sense is,—to make the blood of his enemies flow as swift as *the wind*; and their hearts shake like the branches of trees.—Ed.]
5 Dark.   6 Gloomy, solitary.
7 Answered. Used by Rowley in the same sense.—Chatterton.
8 Quickly, presently.
9 A manner of challenging. So in Rowley's Tournament,
"Thanne theeres my Gauntelette on thie Gaberdyne"—Chatterton.
10 Like.   11 Heated, furious, vexed.   12 Strong.
13 Sound, noise.   14 Fury.   15 Know.   16 To God.

𝔈𝔠𝔩𝔬𝔤𝔲𝔢𝔰.

———

ECLOGUE THE FIRST.*

Whanne Englonde, smeethynge[1] from her lethal[2]
   wounde,
From her galled necke dyd twytte[3] the chayne awaie,
Kennynge her legeful sonnes falle all arounde,
(Myghtie theie fell, 'twas Honoure ledde the fraie,)
Thanne inne a dale, bie eve's dark surcote[4] graie,
Twayne lonelie shepsterres[5] dyd abrodden[6] flie,
(The rostlyng[7] liff doth theyr whytte hartes affraie,[8])
And wythe the owlette trembled and dyd crie;
Firste Roberte Neatherde hys sore boesom struke,
Then fellen on the grounde and thus yspoke.

---

* The "Eclogues" are to be accounted some of the most perfect
specimens among the poems of Rowley. Indeed I am not acquainted
with any pastorals superior to them, either ancient or modern. The
first of them bears a remote resemblance to the first Eclogue of
Virgil, and contains a beautiful andpathetic picture of the state of
England during the civil wars between the houses of York and Lan-
caster. The thoughts and images are all truly pastoral, and it is im-
possible to read it without experiencing those lively yet melancholy
feelings, which a true delineation of nature alone can inspire.—DR.
GREGORY.
1 Smoking.   2 Deadly.   3 Pluck or pull.
4 'Surcote,' a cloak or mantle, which hid all the other dress.
5 Shepherds.
6 Abruptly. So Chaucer—
     "Syke he abredden dyde attourne."—CHATTERTON.
7 Rustling.   8 Affright.

ROBERTE.

Ah, Raufe! gif thos the howres do comme alonge,
Gif thos wee flie in chase of farther woe,
Oure fote wylle fayle, albeytte wee bee stronge,
Ne wylle oure pace swefte as oure danger goe.
To oure grete wronges we have enheped[1] moe,
The Baronnes warre! oh! woe and well-a-daie!
I haveth lyff, bott have escaped soe
That lyff ytsel mie senses doe affraie.
Oh Raufe, comme lyste, and hear mie dernie[2] tale,
Comme heare the balefull[3] dome[4] of Robynne of the
     dale.

RAUFE.

Saie to mee nete;[5] I kenne thie woe in myne;
O! I've a tale that Sabalus[6] mote[7] telle.
Swote[8] flouretts, mantled meedows, forestes dygne;[9]
Gravots[10] far-kend[11] arounde the Errmiets.[12] cell;
The swote[13] ribible[14] dynning[15] yn the dell;
The joyous daunceynge ynn the hoastrie[16] courte;
Eke[17] the highe songe and everych joie farewell,
Farewell the verie shade of fayre dysporte:[18]
Impestering[19] trobble onn mie heade doe comme,
Ne one kynde Seyncte to warde[20] the aye[21] encreasynge
     dome.

---

1 Added.   2 Sad.   3 Woeful, lamentable.   4 Lot.
5 Nought.   6 The devil.   7 Might.   8 Sweet.
9 Good, neat, genteel.   10 Groves, sometimes used for a coppice.
11 Far-seen.   12 Hermit.   13 Sweet.   14 Violin.
15 Sounding.   16 Inn, or public house.   17 Also.
18 Pleasure.   19 Annoying.   20 To keep off.   21 Ever, always.

ROBERTE.

Oh! I coulde waile mie kynge-coppe-decked mees,[1]
Mie spreedynge flockes of shepe of lillie white,
Mie tendre applynges ;[2] and embodyde[3] trees,[*]
Mie Parker's Grange,[4] far spreedynge to the syghte,
Mie cuyen[5] kyne,[6] mie bullockes stringe[7] yn fyghte,
Mie gorne[8] emblaunched[9] with the comfreie[10] plante,
Mie floure[11] Seyncte Marie shotteyng[12] wythe the
    lyghte,
Mie store of all the blessynges Heaven can grant.
I amm duressed[13] unto sorrowes blowe,
I hantend[14] to the peyne, will lette ne salte teare flowe.

1 Meadows.   2 Grafted trees.   3 Thick, stout.
[*] In the notes it is explained *grafted trees*, but very untruly. 'Ap-
plynge' is a diminutive of apple. It is to be observed that the fruit is
often put for the tree which bears it. Nothing is more common than
to say, "we plant a codling or a fig; and cut down a crab or a sloe."
Moreover, all words terminating like the word in question, betoken
something diminutive and tender, and which has not arrived at matu-
rity. This may be seen in the word 'codling' before mentioned : also
in 'yearling, firstling, bantling, nursling, fondling, sapling, foundling.'
These are all diminutives, and relate to the most early part of life, and
to that imbecility with which it is attended. An 'appling' is a young
apple-tree, and *tendre* is for *tender:* when therefore the poet men-
tions—
        "Mie tendre applynges and embodyde trees,"
he opposes his young and weak plants of late growth, to the trees
which are strong and full bodied.—BRYANT.
[Mr. Tyrwhitt, however, asserts that the word 'applynge' is not to
be found elsewhere.—ED.]
4 Liberty of pasture given to the Parker.   5 Tender.
6 Cows.   7 Strong.   8 Garden.   9 Whitened.
10 'Cumfrey,' a favourite dish at that time.   11 Marygold.
12 Shutting.   13 Hardened.   14 Accustomed.

BAUFE.

Here I wille obaie [1] untylle Dethe doe 'pere,
Here lyche a foule empoysoned leathel [2] tree,
Whyche sleaeth [3] everichone that commeth nere,
Soe wille I, fyxed unto thys place, gre. [4]
I to bement [5] haveth moe cause than thee;
Sleene in the warre mie boolie [6] fadre lies;
Oh! joieous I hys mortherer would slea,
And bie hys syde for aie enclose myne eies.
Calked [7] from everych joie, heere wylle I blede;
Fell ys the Cullys-yatte [8] of mie hartes castle stede.

ROBERTE.

Oure woes alyche, alyche our dome [9] shal bee.
Mie sonne, mie sonne alleyn, [10] ystorven [11] ys; •
Here wylle I staie, and end mie lyff with thee;
A lyff lyche myne a borden ys ywis. [12]

---

1 Abide. This line is also wrote—
    " Here wyll I obaie untill dethe appere,"
but this is modernized.—CHATTERTON.
2 Deadly.   3 Destroyeth, killeth.   4 Grow.   5 Lament.
6 Much-loved, beloved.   7 Cast out, ejected.
8 Alluding to the portcullis, which guarded the gate, on which often
depended the castle.
9 Fate.   10 My only son.   11 Dead.
• ' Alone' is never used for ' only;' *solus* for *unicus; seul* for *unique.*
The distinction, I believe, exists in most languages. If the learned
persons do not yet apprehend it, I would advise them, in the following
passage of Shakspeare—
        " Ah! no—it is my only son,"
to substitute *my son alone,* and to judge for themselves whether the
difference in the idea suggested arises merely from the different posi-
tion of the words.—TYRWHITT
    12 I think.

Now from e'en logges¹ fledden is selyness,²
Mynsterres³ alleyn⁴ can boaste the hallie⁵ Seyncte,
Now doeth Englonde weare a bloudie dresse
And wyth her champyonnes gore her face depeyncte;⁶*
Peace fledde, disorder sheweth her dark rode,⁷
And thorow ayre doth flie, yn garments steyned with
  bloude.

ECLOGUE THE SECOND.†

NYGELLE.

SPRYTES⁸ of the bleste, the pious Nygelle sed,
Poure owte yer pleasaunce⁹ onn mie fadres hedde.

I.

Rycharde of Lyons harte to fyghte is gon,
Uponne the brede¹⁰ sea doe the banners gleme,¹¹
The amenused¹² nationnes be aston,¹³
To ken¹⁴ syke¹⁵ large a flete, syke fyne, syke breme,¹⁶

---

1 Cottages.   2 Happiness.   3 Monasteries.   4 Only.
5 Holy.   6 Paint.

  *   " When I will wear a garment all of blood,
            And stain my favours in a bloody mask."
                                    Henry IV. Part 1.

7 Complexion.

† The second Eclogue is an eulogium on the actions of Richard the
First in the Holy Land. The poem is supposed to be sung by a young
shepherd, whose father is absent in the Holy War; and the Epode, or
burthen, is happily imagined. Before he has concluded his song, he is
cheered by the sight of the vessel in which his father returns victorious.—
DR. GREGORY.

8 Spirits, souls.   9 Pleasure.   10 Broad.   11 Shine, glimmer.
12 Diminished, lessened.   13 Astonished, confounded.
14 See, discover, know.   15 Such, so.   16 Strong.

The barkis heafods' coupe[2] the lymed[3] streme;
Oundes[4] synkeynge oundes upon the hard ake[5] riese;
The water slughornes[6] wythe a swotye[7] cleme[8]
Conteke[9] the dynnynge[10] ayre, and reche the skies.
Sprytes of the bleste, on gouldyu trones[11] astedde,[12]
Poure owte yer pleasaunce onn mie fadres hedde.

II.

The gule[13] depeyncted[14] oares[15] from the black tyde,
Decorn[16] wyth fonnes[17] rare, doe shemrynge[18] ryse;
Upswalynge[19] doe heie[20] shewe ynne drierie[21] prydé,
Lyche gore-red estells[22] in the eve[23]-merk[24] skyes;
The nome-depeyncted[25] shields, the speres aryse,
Alyche,[26] talle roshes on the water syde;
Alenge[27] from bark to bark the bryghte sheene[28] flyes;
Sweft-kerv'd[29] delyghtes doe on the water glyde.
Sprytes of the bleste, and everich Seyncte ydedde,
Poure owte youre pleasaunce on mie fadres hedde.

III.

The Sarasen lokes owte: he doethe feere,
That Englondes brondeous[30] sonnes do cotte the waie.

---

1 Heads. 2 Cut. 3 Glassy, reflecting.
4 Waves, billows. 5 Oak.
6 A musical instrument, not unlike a hautboy, ' rather a war trumpet.'
7 Sweet. 8 Sound. 9 Confuse, contend with.
10 Sounding. 11 Thrones. 12 Seated.
13 Red. 14 Painted. 15 Wherries.
16 Carved. 17 Devices. 18 Glimmering.
19 Rising high, swelling up. 20 They.
21 Terrible. 22 A corruption of *estoile*, a star.
23 Evening. 24 Dark.
25 Rebused shields; a herald term, when the charge of the shield implies the name of the bearer.—CHATTERTON.
26 Like. 27 Along. 28 Shine.
29 Short-lived. 30 Furious.

Lyke honted bockes,* theye reineth[1] here and there,
Onknowlachynge[2] inne whatte place to obaie.[3]
The banner glesters on the beme of daie;
The mitte[4] crosse Jerusalim ys seene;
Dhereof the syghte yer corragedoe affraie,[5]
In balefull[6] dole their faces be ywreene.[7]
Sprytes of the bleste, and everich Seyncte ydedde,
Poure owte your pleasaunce on mie fadres hedde.

IV.

The bollengers[8] and cottes,[8] so swyfte yn fyghte,
Upon the sydes of everich bark appere;
Foorthe to his office lepethe everych knyghte,
Eftsoones[9] hys squyer, with hys shielde and spere.
The jynynge[10] shieldes doe shemre and moke glare;[11]
The dosheynge[12] oare doe make gemoted[13] dynne;
The reynyng[14] foemen,[15] thynckeynge gif[16] to dare,
Boun[17] the merk[18] swerde, theie seche to fraie,[19] theie
blyn.[20]
Sprytes of the bleste, and everyche Seyncte ydedde,
Poure owte yer pleasaunce onne mie fadres hedde.

V.

Now comm the warrynge Sarasyns to fyghte;
Kynge Rycharde, lyche a lyoncel[21] of warre,

---

* ['Bockes' in this line should undoubtedly be 'brockes.' The word
has been passed over without a meaning in previous editions. 'Brock'
is a badger; or, as Kersey has it, a hart of the third year.—Ed.]

1 Runneth.	2 Not knowing.	3 Abide.	4 Mighty.
5 Affright.	6 Woeful.	7 Covered.	
8 Different kinds of boats.		9 Full soon, presently.	
10 Joining.	11 Glitter.	12 Dashing.	
13 United, assembled.		14 Running.	15 Foes.
16 If.	17 Make ready.	18 Dark.	19 Engage.
20 Cease, stand still.		21 A young lion.	

Inne sheenynge goulde, lyke feerie[1] gronfers,[2] dyghte,[3]
Shaketh alofe hys honde, and seene afarre.
Syke haveth I espyde a greter starre
Amenge[4] the drybblett[5] ons to sheene fulle bryghte;
Syke sunnys wayne[6] wyth amayl'd[7] beames doe barr
The blaunchie[8] mone or estells[9] to gev lyghte.
Sprytes of the bleste, and everich Seyncte ydedde,
Poure owte your pleasaunce on mie fadres hedde.

VI.

Distraughte[10] affraie,[11] wythe lockes of blodde-red die.
Terroure, emburled[12] yn the thonders rage,
Deathe, lynked to dismaie, dothe ugsomme[13] flie,
Enchafynge[14] echone champyonne war to wage.
Speeres bevyle[15] speres; swerdes upon swerdes
    engage;
Armoure on armoure dynn,[16] shielde upon shielde;
Ne dethe of thosandes can the warre assuage,
Botte falleynge nombers sable[17] all the feelde.
Sprytes of the bleste, and everych Seyncte ydedde,
Poure owte youre pleasaunce on mie fadres hedde.

VII.

The foemen fal arounde; the cross reles[18] hye;
Steyned ynne goere,[19] the harte of warre ys seen;

---

1 Flaming.
2 A meteor, from 'gron' a fen, and 'fer' a corruption of fire; that is,
a fire exhaled from a fen.—CHATTERTON.   3 Decked.
4 Among.   5 Small, insignificant.   6 Car.   7 Enamelled.
8 White, silver. 9 Stars.   10 Distracting.
11 Affright.   12 Armed.   13 Terribly.
14 Encouraging, heating.
15 The idea of *breaking*, which is quite foreign from *beryle*, might
perhaps have been suggested by the following passage in Kersey:
" 𝕭𝖊𝖇𝖎𝖑𝖊 (in heraldry) broken or open, like a bevel or carpenter's rule."
—TYRWHITT.
16 Sounds   17 Blacken.   18 Waves.   19 Blood, gore.

Kyng Rycharde, thorough everyche trope dothe flie,
And beereth meynte[1] of Turkes onto the greene;
Bie hymm the floure of Asies menn ys sleene;[2]
The waylynge[3] mone doth fade before hys sonne;
Bie hym hys knyghtes bee formed to actions deene,[4]
Doeynge syke marvels,[5] strongers be aston.[6]
Sprytes of the bleste, and everych Seyncte ydedde,
Poure owte your pleasaunce onn mie fadres hedde.

VIII.

The fyghte ys wonne; Kynge Rycharde master is;
The Englonde bannerr kisseth the hie ayre;
Full of pure joie the armie is iwys,[7]
And everych one haveth it onne his bayre;[8]
Agayne to Englonde comme, and worschepped there,
Twyghte[9] into lovynge armes, and feasted eft;[10]
In everych eyne aredynge nete of wyere,[11]
Of all remembrance of past peyne berefte.
Sprytes of the bleste, and everich Seyncte ydedde,
Syke pleasures powre upon mie fadres hedde.

Syke Nigel sed, whan from the bluie sea
The upswol[12] sayle dyd daunce before hys eyne;
Swefte as the wishe, hee toe the beeche dyd flee,
And founde his fadre steppeynge from the bryne.
Lette thyssen menne, who haveth sprite of loove,
Bethyncke untoe hemselves how mote the meetynge
proove.

---

1 Many.   2 Slain.
3 Decreasing.   4 Glorious, worthy.   5 Wonders.
6 Astonished.   7 Certainly.   8 Brow.
9 Plucked, pulled.   10 Often.
11 Grief, trouble.   12 Swollen.

ECLOGUE THE THIRD.*

MANNE, WOMANNE, SIR ROGERRE.

WOULDST thou kenn nature in her better parte?
Goe, serche the logges¹ and bordels² of the hynde;³
Gyff⁴ theie have anie, itte ys roughe-made arte,
Inne hem⁵ you see the blakied⁶ forme of kynde.⁷
Haveth your mynde a lycheynge⁸ of a mynde?
Woulde it kenne everich thynge, as it mote⁹ bee?
Woulde ytte here phrase of vulgar from the hynde,
Withoute wiseegger¹⁰ wordes and knowlache¹¹ free?
Gyfsoe, rede thys, whyche Iche dysportynge¹² pende;
Gif nete besyde, yttes rhyme maie ytte commende.

MANNE.

Botte whether, fayre mayde, do ye goe?
    O where do ye bende yer waie?
I wille knowe whether you goe,
    I wylle not bee asseled¹³ naie.

WOMANNE.

To Robin and Nell, all downe in the delle,
    To hele¹⁴ hem at makeynge of haie.

---

* The third pastoral is chiefly to be admired for its excellent morality;
it is, however, enlivened by a variety of appropriate images, and many
of the ornaments of true poetry.—DR. GREGORY.

1 Lodges, huts.   2 Cottages.   3 Servant, slave, peasant.
4 If.   5 A contraction of *them.*
6 Naked, original.   7 Nature.   8 Liking.
9 Might. The sense of this line is, Would you see every thing in its
primæval state?—CHATTERTON.
10 Wise-egger, a philosopher.   11 Knowledge.
12 Sporting.   13 Answered.   14 Aid, or help.

MANNE.

Syr Roggerre, the parsone, hav hyred mee there,
Comme, comme, lett us tryppe ytte awaie,
We'lle wurke¹ and we'lle synge, and weylle drenche²
    of stronge beer
As longe as the merrie sommers daie.

WOMANNE.

How harde ys mie dome to wurch!
        Moke is mie woe.
Dame Agnes, whoe lies ynne the Chyrche
        With birlette ³ golde,
Wythe gelten⁴ aumeres⁵ stronge ontolde,
What was shee moe than me, to be soe?

MANNE.

    I kenne Syr Roger from afar
        Tryppynge over the lea;
    Ich ask whie the loverds⁶ son
        Is moe than mee.

SYR ROGERRE.

The sweltrie⁷ sonne dothe hie apace hys wayne,⁸
From everich beme a seme⁹ of lyfe doe falle;
Swythyn ¹⁰ scille ¹¹ oppe the haie uponne the playne;
Methynckes the cockes begynneth to gre¹² talle.

---

1 Work.   2 Drink.
3 A hood, or covering for the back part of the head.   4 Gilded.
5 Borders of gold and silver, on which was laid thin plates of either
metal counterchanged, not unlike the present spangled laces.—CHAT-
TERTON.
6 Lord.   7 Sultry.   8 Car.   9 Seed.
10 Quickly, presently.   11 Gather.   12 Grow.

Thys ys alyche oure doome ;[1] the great, the smalle,
Moste withe[2] and bee forwyned[3] by deathis darte.
See ! the swote[4] flourette[5] hathe noe swote at alle ;
Itte wythe the ranke wede bereth evalle[6] parte.
The cravent,[7] warrioure, and the wyse be blente,[8]
Alyche to drie awaie wythe those theie dyd bemente.[9]

MANNE.

All-a-boon,[10] Syr Priest, all-a-boon.
　Bye yer preestschype[11] nowe saye unto mee ;
Syr Gaufryd the knyghte, who lyvethe harde bie,
　Whie shoulde hee than mee
　　　　　Bee more greate,
Inne honnoure, knyghtehoode and estate ?

SYR ROGERRE.

Attourne[12] thy eyne arounde thys haied mee,[13]
Tentyflie, loke arounde the chaper[15] delle ;[16]
An answere to thie barganette[17] here see,
Thys welked[18] flourette wylle a leson telle :
Arist[19] it blew,[20] itte florished, and dyd well,
Lokeynge ascaunce[21] upon the naighboure greene ;
Yet with the deigned[22] greene yttes rennome[23] felle,

---

1 Fate.　　　2 A contraction of wither.　　3 Dried.
4 Sweet.　　　5 Flower.　　6 Equal.　　　7 Coward.
8 Ceased, dead, no more.　　　　　　　　9 Lament.
10 The only passage, I believe, in which these eight letters are to be
found together in the same order is in Chaucer, *Canterbury Tales*, v.
9492.
　　　" And alderfirst he bade hem all a bone."—TYRWHITT.
11 Priesthood.　　12 Turn.　　13 Hay-field.
14 Carefully, with circumspection.
15 Dry, sun-burnt. 16 Valley.　17 A song or ballad.
18 Withered.　　19 Arisen, or arose.　　　20 Blossomed.
21 Disdainfully.　22 Disdained.　　　　　23 Glory.

Eftsoones¹ ytte shronke upon the daie-brente² playne,
Didde not yttes loke, whilest ytte there dyd stonde,
To croppe ytte in the bodde move somme dred³ honde.

Syke⁴ ys the waie of lyffe; the loverds⁵ ente⁶
Mooveth the robber hym therfor to slea;⁷
Gyf thou has ethe,⁸ the shadowe of contente,
Beleive the trothe,⁹ theres none moe haile¹⁰ yan thee.
Thou wurchest;¹¹ welle, canne thatte a trobble bee?
Slothe moe wulde jade thee than the roughest daie.
Couldest thou the kivercled¹² of soughlys¹³ see,
Thou wouldst eftsoones¹⁴ see trothe ynne whatte I saie;
Botte lette me heere thie waie of lyffe, and thenne
Heare thou from me the lyffes of odher menne.

MANNE.

I ryse wythe the sonne,
Lyche hym to dryve the wayne,¹⁵
And eere mie wurche is don
I synge a songe or twayne.¹⁶
I followe the plough-tayle,
Wythe a longe jubb¹⁷ of ale.
   Botte of the maydens, oh!
Itte lacketh notte to telle;
Syre Preeste mote notte crie woe,
Culde hys bull do as welle.

---

1 Quickly.	2 Sun-burnt.	3 Bold.	4 Such.
5 Lord's.	6 A purse or bag.	7 Slay.	8 Ease.
9 Truth.	10 Happy.	11 Workest.	
12 The hidden or secret part of.		13 Souls.	
14 Full soon, or presently.		15 Car.	
16 Two.		17 A bottle.	

I daunce the beste heiedeygnes,[1]
And foile[2] the wysest feygnes.[3]
　　On everych Seynctes hie daie
Wythe the mynstrelle[4] am I seene,
All a footeynge it awaie,
Wythe maydens on the greene.
But oh! I wyshe to be moe greate,
In rennome, tenure, and estate.

SYR ROGERRE.

Has thou ne seene a tree uponne a hylle,
Whose unliste[5] braunces[6] rechen far toe syghte;
Whan fuired[7] unwers[8] doe the heaven fylle,
Itte shaketh deere[9] yu dole[10] and moke[11] affryghte.
Whylest the congeon[12] flowrette abessie[13] dyghte,[14]
Stondethe unhurte, unquaced[15] bie the storme:
Syke is a picte[16] of lyffe: the manne of myghte
Is tempest-chaft,[17] hys woe greate as hys forme;
Thieselfe a flowrette of a small accounte,
Wouldst harder felle[18] the wynde, as hygher thee dydste
　　mounte.

---

1 A country dance, still practised in the North. See note to page 193.
2 Baffle.   3 A corruption of *feints*.   4 A minstrel is a musician.
5 Unbounded.   6 Branches.   7 Furious.
8 Tempests, storms.
9 Dire.   10 Dismay.   11 Much.   12 Dwarf.
13 Humbly.   14 Decked.   15 Unhurt.   16 Picture.
17 Tempest-beaten.   18 Feel.

Elinoure and Juga.*

Onne Ruddeborne¹ bank twa pynynge Maydens sate,
Theire teares faste dryppeynge to the waterre cleere;
Echone bementynge² for her absente mate,
Who atte Seyncte Albonns shouke the morthynge³
　　speare.
The nottebrowne Elinoure to Juga fayre
Dydde speke acroole,⁴ wythe languishment of eyne,
Lyche droppes of pearlie dew, lemed⁵ the quyvryng
　　brine.

---

* The last of these pastorals, called "Elinoure and Juga," is one of
the finest pathetic tales I have ever read. The complaint of two young
females lamenting their lovers slain in the wars of York and Lancaster,
was one of the happiest subjects that could be chosen for a tragic pas-
toral.—Dr. Gregory.

1 'Rudborne' (in Saxon, red-water) a river near Saint Albans,
famous for the battles there fought between the Houses of Lancaster
and York.—Chatterton.

2 Lamenting.　　　　　　　3 Murdering.

4 [' Acroole.' This word has no authority whatever. 'To crool,'
however, is in Bailey, with the interpretation, *to growl, to mutter, to
mumble.* A similar word is said likewise to have denoted the sound
made by the dove.—Ed]

5 Glistened.

ELINOURE.

O gentle Juga! heare mie dernie' plainte,
To fyghte for Yorke mie love ys dyghte² in stele;
O maie ne sanguen steine the whyte rose peyncte,
Maie good Seyncte Cuthberte watche Syrre Roberte
    wele.
  Moke³ moe thanne deathe in phantasie I feele;
See! see! upon the grounde he bleedynge lies;
Inhild⁴ some joice⁵ of lyfe, or else mie deare love dies.

JUGA.

Systers in sorrowe on thys daise-ey'd banke,
Where melancholych broods, we wyll lamente;
Be wette wythe mornynge dewe and evene danke;⁶
Lyche levynde⁷ okes in eche the odher bente,
Or lyche forlettenn⁸ halles of merriemente,
  Whose gastlie mitches⁹ holde the traine of fryghte,¹⁰
Where lethale¹¹ ravens bark, and owlets wake the
    nyghte.

ELINOURE.

No moe the miskynette¹² shall wake the morne,✦
The minstrelle daunce, good cheere, and morryce plaie;

---

1 Sad complaint.   2 Arrayed, or cased.   3 Much.   4 Infuse.
5 Juice.   6 Damp.   7 Blasted.
8 Abandoned, forsaken—
      "Whilst hush'd, and by the mace of ruin rent,
        Sinks the forsaken hall of merriment."—BOWLES.
9 Ruins.   10 Fear.   11 Deadly, or death boding.
12 A small bagpipe.
✦ In the spirit of Gray's Elegy—
      "The breezy call of incense breathing morn,
        The swallow twittering from her straw-built shed;
      The cock's shrill clarion, or the echoing horn,
        No more shall rouse them from their lowly bed.

No moe the amblynge palfrie and the horne
Shall from the lessel [1] rouze the foxe awaie ;
I'll seke the foreste alle the lyve-longe daie ;
Alle nete [2] amenge [3] the gravde chyrche-glebe [4] wyll goe,
And to the passante Spryghtes lecture [5] mie tale of woe.

JUGA.

Whan mokie [6] cloudes do hange upon the leme
Of leden [7] Moon, ynn sylver mantels dyghte ;
The tryppeynge Faeries weve the golden dreme
Of Selyness, [8] whyche flyethe wythe the nyghte ;
Thenne (botte the Seynctes forbydde !) gif to a spryte
Syrr Rychardes forme ye lyped [9] I'll holde dystraughte
Hys bledeynge claie-colde corse, and die eche daie ynn
          thoughte.

ELINOURE.

Ah woe bementynge [10] wordes ; what wordes can shewe !
Thou limed [11] ryver, on thie linche [12] maie bleede
Champyons, whose bloude wylle wythe thie waterres
          flowe,
And Rudborne streeme be Rudborne streeme indeede !
Haste, gentle Juga, tryppe ytte oere the meade,
To knowe, or wheder we muste waile agayne,
Or wythe oure fallen knyghtes be menged [13] onne the plain.

---

1 In a confined sense, a bush or hedge, though sometimes used as a
forest.

2 Night.	3 Among.	4 Church-yard.	5 Relate.
6 Black.	7 Decreasing.	8 Happiness.	9 Linked.
10 Lamented.	11 Glassy.	13 Bank.	14 Mingled.

Soe sayinge, lyke twa levyn-blasted trees,
Or twayne of cloudes that holdeth stormie rayne;
Theie moved gentle oere the dewie mees,[1]
To where Seyncte Albons holie shrynes remayne.
There dyd theye fynde that bothe their knyghtes
    were slayne,
Distraughte[2] theie wandered to swoll'n Rudbornes syde,
Yelled theyre leathalle knelle, sonke ynn the waves, and
    dyde.*

---

   1 Meads.   2 Distracted.

  * In return for the pleasure I have received from thy poems, I pay
thee, poor boy, the trifling tribute of my praise. Thyself thou hast em-
blazoned; thine own monument thou hast erected. But they whom
thou hast delighted feel a pleasure in vindicating thine honour from
the rude attacks of detraction. Thy sentiments, thy verse, thy rhythm,
all are modern, all are thine. By the help of glossaries and dictio-
naries, and the perusal of many old English writers, thou hast been able
to translate the language of the present time into that of former centu-
ries. Thou hast built an artificial ruin. The stones are mossy and
old, the whole fabric appears really antique to the distant and careless
spectator; even the connoisseur, who pores with spectacles on the
single stones, and inspects the mossy concretions with an antiquarian
eye, boldly authenticates its antiquity; but they who examine without
prejudice, and by the criterion of common sense, clearly discover the
cement and the workmanship of a modern mason.—VICESIMUS KNOX.

  To speak of Chatterton is to touch upon a name from which time
neither has taken nor will take any of its interest. Boyse, in his
blanket, Savage in a prison, and Smart scrawling his most impassioned
verses with charcoal upon the walls of a madhouse, are not the most
mournful examples which might be held up as a warning to kindred
spirits. There are even more pitiable objects in the world than Chat-
terton himself with the poison at his lips. His mighty mind brought
with it into the world a taint of hereditary insanity, which explains the
act of suicide, and divests it of its fearful guilt.—SOUTHEY.

The Storie of William Canynge.*

I.

Anent[1] a brooklette as I laie reclynd,
Listeynge to heare the water glyde alonge,
Myndeynge how thorowe the grene mees'[2] yt twynd,
Awhilst the cavys respons'd[3] yts mottring[4] songe,
At dystaunt rysyng Avonne to be sped,
Amenged[5] wyth rysyng hylles dyd shewe yts head;

---

* The first thirty-four lines of this poem are extant upon another of
the vellum fragments, given by Chatterton to Mr. Barrett.† The re-
mainder is printed from a copy furnished by Mr. Catcott, with some
corrections from another copy, made by Mr. Barrett from one in Chat-
terton's hand-writing. This poem makes part of a prose work, attri-
buted to Rowley, giving an account of painters, carvellers, poets, and
other eminent natives of Bristol, from the earliest times to his own.
The transaction alluded to in the last stanza is related at large in
some prose memoirs of Rowley. It is there said that Mr. Canynge
went into orders, to avoid a marriage, proposed by King Edward,
between him and a lady of the Widdevile family. It is certain, from
the register of the Bishop of Worcester, that Mr. Canynge was ordained
Acolythe by Bishop Carpenter, on 19th September, 1467, and received
the higher orders of subdeacon, deacon, and priest, on the 12th of
March, 1467, O.S., the 2d and 16th of April, 1468, respectively.—TYR-
WHITT's *Edition.*

† These thirty-four lines and one more short poem are the only
scraps of poetry which Chatterton ever produced as the originals of
Rowley.—*Cottle's Account of Rowley's MSS.*

1 Opposite. 2 Meadows. 3 Answered. 5 Murmuring. 5 Mingled.

II.

Engarlanded wyth crownes of osyer weedes
And wraytes[1] of alders of a bercie scent,
And stickeynge out wyth clowde-agested[2] reedes,
The hoarie Avonne show'd dyre semblamente,[3]
Whylest blataunt[4] Severne, from Sabryna clepde,
Rores flemie[6] o'er the sandes that she hepde.

III.

These eynegears[7] swythyn[8] bringethe to mie thowghte
Of hardie champyons knowen to the floude,
How onne the bankes thereof brave Ælle foughte,
Ælle descended from Merce kynglie bloude,
Warden of Brystowe towne and castel stede,
Who ever and anon made Danes to blede.

IV.

Methoughte such doughtie[9] menn must have a sprighte
Dote[10] yn the armour brace[11] that Mychael bore,
Whan he wyth Satan, kynge of helle, dyd fyghte,
And earthe was drented[12] yn a mere[13] of gore;
Orr, soone as theie dyd see the worldis lyghte,
Fate had wrott downe, thys mann ys borne to fyghte.

---

1 Wreaths. 2 Heaped up. 3 Appearance. 4 Noisy.
5 Named—
    "Sabrine, Locrine's child, who of her life bereft,
    Her ever-living name to thee, fair river, left."
                    DRAYTON's *Poly-olbion*, bk. 6.
6 Frighted. 7 Objects. 8 Quickly. 9 Valiant.
10 Dressed. 11 Suit of armour. 12 Drenched. 13 Lake.

v.

Ælle, I sayd, or els my mynde dyd saie,
Whie ys thy actyons left so spare yn storie?
Were I toe dispone,[1] there should lyvven aie
In erthe and hevenis rolles thie tale of glorie;
Thie actes soe doughtie should for aie abyde,
And bie theyre teste all after actes be tryde.

vi.

Next holie Wareburghus fylld mie mynde,
As fayre a sayncte as anie towne can boaste,
Or bee the erthe wyth lyghte or merke[8] ywrynde,[2]
I see hys ymage waulkeyng throwe the coaste:
Fitz Hardynge, Bithrickus, and twentie moe
Ynn visyonn 'fore mie phantasie dyd goe.

vii.

Thus all mie wandrynge faytour[4] thynkeynge strayde,
And eche dygne buylder dequac'd[5] onn mie mynde,
Whan from the distaunt streeme arose a mayde,
Whose gentle tresses mov'd not to the wynde;
Lyche to the sylver moone yn frostie neete,
The damoiselle dyd come soe blythe and sweete.

viii.

Ne browded[6] mantell of a scarlette hue,
Ne shoone pykes[7] plaited o'er wyth ribbande geere,
Ne costlie paraments[8] of woden[9] blue,

---

1 Dispose.	2 Darkness.	3 Covered.
4 Deceiving.	5 Dashed.	6 Embroidered.
7 Picked shoes.	8 Robes of state.	9 Dyed with woad.

Noughte of a dresse, but bewtie[1] dyd shee weere;
Naked shee was, and loked swete of youthe,
All dyd bewryen, that her name was Trouthe.

IX.

The ethie[2] ringletts of her notte-browne hayre
What ne a manne should see dyd swotelie[4] byde,
Whych on her milk-white bodykin[3] so fayre
Dyd showe lyke browne streemes fowlyng[6] the white
     tyde.
Or veynes of brown hue yn a marble cuarr,[7]
Whyche by the traveller ys kenn'd from farr.

X.

Astounded mickle there I sylente laie,
Still scauncing[8] wondrous at the walkynge syghte;
Mie senses forgarde[9] ne coulde reyn[10] awaie;
But was ne forstraughte[11] whan shee dyd alyghte
Anie to mee, dreste up yn naked viewe,
Whych mote yn some ewbrycious[12] thoughtes abrewe.[13]

XI.

But I ne dyd once thynke of wanton thoughte;
For well I mynded what bie vowe I hete,[14]
And yn mie pockate han a crouchee[15] broughte,

Whych yn the blosom woulde such sins anete;[1]
I lok'd wyth eyne as pure as angelles doe,
And dyd the everie thoughte of foule eschewe.

XII.

Wyth sweet semblate[2] and an angel's grace
Shee 'gan to lecture from her gentle breste;
For Trouthis wordes ys her myndes face,
False oratoryes she dyd aie deteste;
Sweetnesse was yn eche worde she dyd ywreene,[3]
Tho' shee strove not to make that sweetnesse sheene.

XIII.

Shee sayd; mie manner of appereynge here
Mie name and sleyghted myndbruch[4] maie thee telle;
I'm Trouthe, that dyd descende fromm heavenwere,[5]
Goulers[6] and courtiers doe not kenne mee welle;
Thie inmoste thoughtes, thie labrynge brayne I sawe,
And from thie gentle dreeme will thee adawe.[7]

---

1 'Anete,' annihilated, unauthorised. Dean Milles says it is the
old English word 'nete' or 'nought,' with the prefix; to which cor-
responds the old French verb 'aneantiaed' (annihilated), used by
Chaucer. But there is no proof that the word 'nete' has ever been
used as a verb, even if it exists.—SOUTHEY.

Waving the discussion, whether there exists such an old English
word as 'nete,' I will be satisfied if the Dean will produce a single in-
stance in which 'nete' or 'anete,' or 'nought' or 'anought,' is used as
a verb. Till that is done, he should not require us to believe that any
one of those words corresponds to a French verb, or can signify 'anni-
hilate.'—TYRWHITT.

2 Appearance.   3 Display.
4 Firmness. [In Kersey the interpretation is, 'a hurting of honour
and worship.'—ED.]
5 Towards heaven.   6 Usurers.   7 Awaken.

XIV.

Full manie champyons and menne of lore,[1]
Payncters and carvellers[2] have gain'd good name,
But there's a Canynge, to encrease the store,
A Canynge, who shall buie uppe alle theyre fame.
Take thou mie power, and see yn chylde and manne
What troulie[3] noblenesse yn Canynge ranne.

XV.

As when a bordelier[4] onn ethie[5] bedde,
Tyr'd wyth the laboures maynt[6] of sweltrie daie,
Yn slepeis bosom laieth hys deft[7] headde,
So, senses sonke to reste, mie boddie laie;
Eftsoons[8] mie sprighte, from erthlie bandes untyde,
Immengde[9] yn flanched[10] ayre wyth Trouthe asyde.

XVI.

Strayte was I carry'd back to tymes of yore,
Whylst Canynge swathed yet yn fleshlie bedde,
And saw all actyons whych han been before,
And all the scroll of Fate unravelled;
And when the fate-mark'd babe acome to syghte,
I saw hym eager gaspynge after lyghte.

XVII.

In all hys shepen[11] gambols and chyldes plaie,
In everie merriemakeyng, fayre or wake,

---

1 Learning.   2 Carvers, sculptors.   3 True, truly.   4 Cottager.
5 Easy.   6 Many.   7 Neat, cleanly.
8 Quickly, immediately.   9 Mingled.   10 Arched.
11 Innocent, simple.

I kenn'd a perpled[1] lyghte of Wysdom's raie;
He eate downe learnynge wyth the wastle cake.[*]
As wise as anie of the eldermenne,
He'd wytte enowe toe make a mayre at tenne.[*]

XVIII.

As the dulce[2] downie barbe beganne to gre,[4]
So was the well thyghte[3] texture of hys lore ;
Eche daie enhedeynge[6] mockler[7] for to bee,
Greete yn hys councel for the daies he bore.
All tongues, all carrols dyd unto hym synge,
Wondryng at one soe wyse, and yet soe yinge.[8]

XIX.

Encreaseynge yn the yeares of mortal lyfe,
And hasteynge to hys journie ynto heaven,
Hee thoughte ytt proper for to cheese[9] a wyfe,
And use the sexes for the purpose gevene.[10]
Hee then was yothe of comelie semelikeede,[11]
And hee had made a mayden's herte to blede.

---

1 Scattered.   2 Cake of the whitest bread.
[*] Of his native city he was mayor five times; and beside several
other charities, founded an alms-house or hospital (which is yet in
being) at Redcliffe-hill; and built a chapel, and that noble church of
St. Mary Redcliffe, the finest parish church in England—
     " The maystrie of a human hande,
     The pryde of Bristowe and the Westerne land."
Full of good works, he died in the year 1474, and was buried in Red-
cliff church, where two monuments were erected to his memory; one
with his effigies in the robes of a magistrate, the other in those of
a priest cut in white marble.—*Memoirs of Sir William Canynge.*
3 Soft. See note to page 103.   4 Grow.   5 Connected.
6 Being careful.   7 Stronger, greater.
8 Young.   9 Choose.   10 Given.   11 Countenance.

XX.

He had a fader, (Jesus rest hys soule!)
Who loved money, as hys charie ¹ joie;
Hee had a broder (happie manne be's dole!)
Yn mynde and boddie, hys owne fadre's boie;
What then could Canynge wissen ² as a parte
To gyve to her whoe had made chop ³ of hearte?

XXI.

But landes and castle tenures, golde and bighes,⁴
And hoardes of sylver rousted yn the ent,⁵
Canynge and hys fayre sweete dyd that despyse,
To change of troulie love was theyr content;
Theie lyv'd togeder yn a house adygne,⁶
Of goode sendaument ⁷ commilie ⁸ and fyne.

XXII.

Butte soone hys broder and hys syre dyd die,
And lefte to Willyam states and renteynge rolles,
And at hys wyll hys broder Johne* supplie.
Hee gave a chauntrie to redeeme theyre soules;
And put hys broder ynto syke a trade,
That he lorde mayor of Londonne towne was made.†

XXIII.

Eftsoones hys mornynge tourn'd to gloomie nyghte;
Hys dame, hys seconde selfe, gave upp her brethe,

---

1 Dear.   2 Wish.   3 Exchange.   4 Jewels.
5 Purse.   6 Creditable.   7 Appearance.
8 Decent, comely.
* Called 'Thomas,' by Stow, in his list of mayors.
† This is true; Canning was Lord Mayor of London in 1456.

Seekeynge for eterne lyfe and endless lyghte,
And fleed good Canynge; sad mystake of dethe !
Soe have I seen a flower ynn Sommer tyme
Trodde downe and broke and widder[1] ynn ytts pryme.

xxiv.

Next Radcleeve chyrche (oh worke of hande of heav'n,
Whare Canynge sheweth as an instrumente,)
Was to my bismarde[2] eyne-syghte newlie giv'n ;
'Tis past to blazonne ytt to good contente.
You that woulde faygn the fetyve[3] buyldynge see
Repayre to Radcleve, and contented bee.

xxv.

I sawe the myndbruch[4] of hys nobille soule
Whan Edwarde meniced[5] a seconde wyfe;
I saw what Pheryons yn hys mynde dyd rolle ;
Nowe fyx'd fromm seconde dames a preeste for lyfe.
Thys ys the manne of menne, the vision spoke ;
Then belle for even-songe mie senses woke.

---

1 Wither.   2 Astonished, deluded.   3 Elegant.
4 Firmness, *rather* wounded honour.   5 Menaced.

To this poem we may add the following *prose* "account of this ex-
traordinary person, written by Rowley the priest;" printed in the
"Town and Country Magazine for Nov. 1775," and republished with
several corrections in Southey's edition.

It forms one of the MSS. communicated by Chatterton as original,
and is preserved with the others in the British Museum.

" It is written with red ink, the letters are perfectly distinct, and the
first line is written in the common attorney's text-hand. The parch-
ment appears brown from some liquid that has been applied to it, but
for which it is difficult to assign any reason, except to give the parch-
ment a *mistaken* appearance of age. The letters are remarkably

legible, and being *red ink*, they could not require oak bark, or any similar composition to render them more so. We must conclude that this brown tint was communicated by Chatterton, but it is singular that he should not have discoloured the *whole* of the surface, as one corner of the parchment discovers its natural colour."—*Cottle's Account of Rowley's MSS.*

Some further Account of this extraordinary person, written by Rowley the Priest.

"I was fadre confessor to masteres Roberte and Mastre William Cannings. Mastre Robert was a man after his fadre's own harte, greedie of gaynes and sparynge of alms deedes; but master William was mickle courteous, and gave me many marks in my needs. At the age of 22 years deaces'd master Roberte, and by master William's desyre bequeathd me one hundred marks; I went to thank master William for his mickle courtesie, and to make tender of myselfe to him.—Fadre, quod he, I have a crotchett in my brayne, that will need your aide. Master William, said I, if you command me I will go to Roome for you; not so farr distant, said he: I ken you for a mickle learned priest; if you will leave the parysh of our ladie, and travel for for mee, it shall be mickle to your profits.

" I gave my hands, and he told mee I must goe to all the abbies and pryorys, and gather together auncient drawyings, if of anie account, at anyprice. Consented I to the same, and pursuant sett out the Mundaie following for the minster of our Ladie and Saint Goodwyne, where a drawing of a steeple, contryvd for the belles when runge to swaie out of the syde into the ayre, had I thence; it was done by Syr Symon de Mambrie, who, in the troublesomme rayne of kyng Stephen, devoted himselfe, and was shorne.

" Hawkes showd me a manuscript in Saxonne, but I was onley to bargayne for drawyings.—The next drawyngs I metten with was a church to be reard, so as in form of a cross, the end standing in the ground; a long nanuscript was annexed. Master Canning thought no workman culd be found handie enough to do it.—The tale of the drawers deserveth relation. — Thomas de Blunderville, a preeste, although the preeste had no allows, lovd a fair mayden, and on her begatt a sonn. Thomas educated his sonn; at sixteen years he went into the warrs, and neer did return for five years.—His mother was married to a knight, and bare a daughter, then sixteen, who was seen

and lovd by Thomas, sonn of Thomas, and married to him, unknown
to her mother, by Ralph de Mesching, of the minster, who invited, as
custom was, two of his brothers, Thomas de Blunderville and John
Heschamme.   Thomas nevertheless had not seen his sonn for five
years, yet kennd him instantly; and learning the name of the bryde,
took him asydde and disclosed to him that he was his sonn, and was
weded to his own sistre. Yoynge Thomas toke on so that he was
shorne.

" He drew manie fine drawyinges on glass.

" The abott of the minster of Peterburrow sold it me; he might
have bargayned 20 marks better, but master William would not part
with it.   The prior of Coventree did sell me a picture of great account,
made by Badilian Y'allyanne, who did live in the reign of Kynge
Henrie the First, a mann of fickle temper, havyng been tendred syx
pounds of silver for it, to which he said naie, and afterwards did give
it to the then abott of Coventriee.   In brief, I gathered together manie
marks value of fine drawyings, all the works of mickle cunning.—Mas-
ter William culld the most choise parts, but hearing of a drawying in
Durham church hee did send me.

" Fadree, you have done mickle well, all the chatils are more worth
than you gave; take this for your paynes: so saying, he did put into
my hands a purse of two hundreds good pounds, and did say that
I should note be in need; I did thank him most heartily.—The choise
drawyng, when his fadre did dye, was begunn to be put up, and somme
houses near the old church erased; it was drawn by Afiema, preeste of
St. Cutchberts, and offered as a drawyng for Westminster, but cast
asyde, being the tender did not speak French.—I had now mickle of
ryches, and lyvd in a house on the hill, often repayrings to mastere
William, who was now lord of the house.   I sent him my verses touch-
ing his church, for which he did send me mickle good things.—In the
year kyng Edward came to Bristow, master Cannings send for me to
avoid a marrige which the kyng was bent upon between him and
a ladie he ne'er had seen, of the familee of the Winddevilles; the
danger were nigh, unless avoided by one remidee, an holie one, which
was, to be ordained a sonn of holy church, beyng franke from the
power of kynges in that cause, and cannot be wedded.—Mr. Cannings
instauntly sent me to Carpenter, his good friend, bishop of Worcester,
and the Fryday following was prepaird and ordaynd the next day, the
daie of St. Mathew, and on Sunday sung his first mass in the church of
our ladie, to the astonishing of kyng Edward, who was so furiously
madd and ravyngs withall, that master Cannings was wyling to give
him 3000 marks, which gave him peace again, and he was admyted to

the presence of the kyng, staid in Bristow, partook of all his pleasures and pastimes till he departed the next year.

"I gave master Cannings my Bristow tragedy, for which he gave me in hands twentie pounds, and did praise it more than I did think myself did deserve, for I can say in troth I was never proud of my verses since I did read master Chaucer; and now haveing nought to do, and not wyling to be ydle, I went to the minster of our Ladie and Saint Goodwin, and then did purchase the Saxon manuscripts, and sett my selfe diligentley to translate and worde it in English metre, which in one year I performed and styled it the Battle of Hastyngs; master William did bargyin for one manuscript, and John Pelham, an esquire of Ashley, for another.—Master William did praise it muckle greatly, but advised me to tender it to no man, beying the menn whose name were therein mentioned would be offended. He gave me 20 markes, and I did goe to Ashley, to master Pelham, to be payd of him for the other one I left with him.

"But his ladie being of the family of the Fiscamps, of whom some things are said, he told me he had burnt it, and would have me burnt if I did not avaunt. Dureing this dinn his wife did come out, and made a dinn to speake by a figure, would have over sounded the bells of our Ladie of the Cliffe; I was fain content to get away in a safe skin.

"I wrote my Justice of Peace, which master Cannings adviad me secrett to keep, which I did; and now being grown auncient I was seizd with great pains, which did cost me mickle of marks to be cured off.—Master William offered me a cannon's place in Westbury College, which gladly had I accepted but my pains made me to stay at home. After this mischance I livd in a house by the Tower, which has not been repaird since Robert Consull of Gloucester repayrd the castle and wall; here I livd warm, but in my house on the hyll the ayer was mickle keen: some marks it cost me to put in repair my new house; and brynging my chattels from the ould; it was a fine house, and I much marville it was untenanted. A person greedy of gains was the then possessour, and of him I did buy it at a very small rate, having lookd on the ground works and mayne supports, and fynding them staunch, and repayrs no need wanting, I did buy of the owner, Geoffry Coombe, on a repayring lease for 99 years, he thinkying it would fall down everie day; but with a few marks expence did put it up in a manner neat, and therein I lyvd."

Onn oure Ladies Chyrche.*

As onn a hylle one eve sittynge,
At oure Ladie's Chyrche mouche wonderynge,
The counynge handieworke so fyne,
Han well nighe dazeled mine eyne;
Quod I; some counynge fairie hande
Yreer'd this chapelle in this lande;
Fulle well I wote¹ so fine a syghte
Was ne yreer'd of mortall wighte.
Quod Trouthe; thou lackest knowlachynge;²
Thou forsoth ne wotteth of the thynge.
A Rev'rend Fadre, William Canynge hight,
Yreered uppe this chapelle brighte;
And eke another in the Towne,
Where glassie bubblynge Trymme doth roun.³
Quod I; ne doubte for all he's given
His sowle will certes goe to heaven.
Yea, quod Trouthe; than goe thou home,
And see thou doe as hee hath donne.
Quod I; I doubte, that can ne bee;
I have ne gotten markes three.
Quod Trouthe; as thou hast got, give almes-dedes soe;
Canynges and Gaunts culde doe ne moe.

* From a copy made by Mr. Catcott, from one in Chatterton's hand-writing.—TYRWHITT's *Edition.*
1 Know.   2 Knowledge.   3 Run.

ON THE SAME.*

STAY, curyous traveller, and pass not bye,
Until this fetive¹ pile astounde² thine eye.
Whole rocks on rocks with yron joynd surveie,
And okes with okes entremed³ disponed⁴ lie.
This mightie pile, that keeps the wyndes at baie,
Fyre-levyn⁵ and the mokie⁶ storme defie,
That shootes aloofe into the reaulmes of daie,
Shall be the record of the Buylders fame for aie.

Thou seest this maystrie of a human hand,
The pride of Brystowe and the Westerne lande,
Yet is the Buylders vertues much moe greete,
Greeter than can bie Rowlies pen be scande.
Thou seest the saynctes and kynges in stonen state,
That seem'd with breath and human soule dispande,⁷
As payrde⁸ to us enseem these men of slate,
Such is greete Canynge's mynde when payrd⁹ to God
        elate.

---

* From a MS. in Chatterton's hand-writing, furnished by Mr. Cat-
cott, entitled, " A Discorse on Bristowe, by Thomas Rowlie."—TYR-
WHITT's *Edition.*

1 Elegant.	2 Astonish.	3 Intermixed.	4 Disposed.
5 Lightning.	6 Gloomy.	7 Expanded.	8 & 9 Compared.

Well maiest thou be astounde, but view it well;
Go not from hence before thou see thy fill;
And learn the Builder's vertues and his name;
Of this tall spyre in every countye tell,
And with thy tale the lazing[1] rych men shame ;
Showe howe the glorious Canynge did excelle ;
How hee, good man, a friend for kynges became,
And gloryous paved at once the way to heaven and fame.[*]

---

1 Inactive.

[*] It is asked with some degree of plausibility, how could Chatterton, who was educated in a charity school, where only writing and arithmetic were taught, produce such fine pieces of poetry, which shew marks of more liberal pursuits, and studies of another nature? In the same general way of putting a question, it may be asked, how could that idle and illiterate fellow Shakspeare, who was driven out of Warwickshire for deer-stealing, write the tragedy of Othello? I give as general an answer, that the powers of unconquerable mind outgo plans of education and conditions of life. The enthusiasm of intellectual energy surmounts every impediment to a career that is pressing forward to futurity.

> " Ergo vivida vis animi pervicit, et extra
> Processit longe flammantia mœnia mundi."[†]—WARTON.

[†] Lucretius, I. 73.

𝔒n the 𝔇edication of our 𝔏adie's 𝔆hurch.*

Soone as bryght sonne alonge the skyne,
   Han sente hys ruddie lyghte;
And fayryes hyd ynne 'slyppe cuppes,
   Tylle wysh'd approche of nyghte,
The mattyn belle wyth shryllie sounde,
   Reeckode throwe the ayre;
A troop of holie freeres dyd,
   For Jesus masse prepare.
Arounde the highe unsaynted chyrche,
   Wythe holie relyques wente;
And every door and poste aboute
   Wythe godlie thynges besprent.
Then Carpenter yn scarlette dreste,
   And mytred holylie:
From Mastre Canynge hys greate howse,
   Wyth rosarie dyd hie.
Before hym wente a throng of freeres
   Who dyd the masse songe synge,
Behynde hym Mastre Canynge came,
   Tryck'd lyke a barbed kynge,

---

* This poem was given by Chatterton in a note to the Parlyamente
of Sprytes. The lines are here divided into the ballad length.—
Southey's *Edition.*

And then a rowe of holie freeres
  Who dyd the mass songe sound ;
The procurators and chyrche reeves
  Next prest upon the ground,
And when unto the chyrche theye came
  A holie masse was sange,
So lowdlie was theyr swotie voyce,
  The heven so hie it range.
Then Carpenter dyd puryfie
  The chyrche to Godde for aie,
Wythe holie masses and good psalmes
  Whyche hee dyd thereyn saie.
Then was a sermon preeched soon
  Bie Carpynterre holie,
And after that another one
  Ypreechen was bie mee :
Thenn alle dyd goe to Canynges house
  An Enterlude to playe,
And drynk hys wyne and ale so goode
  And praie for him for aie.*

---

* The whole of Chatterton's life presents a fund of useful instruction
to young persons of brilliant and lively talents, and affords a strong
dissuasive against that impetuosity of expectation, and those delusive
hopes of success, founded upon the consciousness of genius and merit,
which lead them to neglect the ordinary means of acquiring competence
and independence. The early disgust which Chatterton conceived for
his profession, may be accounted one of the prime sources of his mis-
fortunes.—DR. GREGORY.

𝔉ragment,

by

John, second Abbatte of Seynete Austyns Mynsterre.*

————

Harte of lyone! shake thie sworde,
Bare thie mortheynge[1] steinede honde :
Quace[2] whole armies to the queede,[3]
Worke thie wylle yn burlie bronde.[4]
Barons here on bankers-browded,[5]
Fyghte yn furres gaynste the cale ;[6]
Whilest thou ynne thonderynge armes
Warriketh[7] whole cyttyes bale.[8]
Harte of lyon ! Sound the beme![9]
Sounde ytte ynto inner londes,
Feare flies sportine ynne the cleeme,[10]
Inne thie banner terror stondes.†

———

* From Barrett's History of Bristol. It was sent by Chatterton to
Horace Walpole, as a note to Rowleie's Historie of Peyncters. 'This
John," he says, "was inducted abbot in the year 1186, and sat in the
dies 29 years. He was the greatest poet of the age in which he lived ;
he understood the learned languages. Take a specimen of his poetry
on King Richard Ist."—Southey's *Edition.*

 1 Murdering. 2 Vanquish, 3 Devil. 4 Fury, anger.
 5 Embroidered couches. 6 Cold. 7 Worketh, dealeth.
 8 Destruction.   9 Trumpet. 10 Sound.

 † If any one can perceive any difference of hand between this poem,
attributed to Abbot *John,* and those which pass under the name of the
supposed Rowley, he must possess much greater powers of discrimina-
tion, than fall to the share of common critics.—Tyrwhitt.

The

Parlyamente

of

Sprytes.

A most merrie Enterlude.

The lively and vigorous imagination of Chatterton contributed, doubtless, to animate him with that spirit of enterprise, which led him to form so many impracticable and visionary schemes for the acquisition of fame and fortune. His ambition was evident from his earliest youth; and perhaps the inequality of his spirits might, in a great measure, depend upon the fairness of his views, or the dissipation of his projects. His melancholy was extreme on some occasions, and at those times he constantly argued in favour of suicide. Mr. Catcott left him one evening totally depressed; but he returned the next morning with unusual spirits. He said, "he had sprung a mine," and produced a parchment, containing the *Parliament of Sprytes*, a poem *

His natural melancholy was not corrected by the irreligious principles, which he had so unfortunately imbibed. To these we are certainly to attribute his premature death; and, if he can be proved guilty of the licentiousness which is by some laid to his charge, it is reasonable to believe that a system, which exonerates the mind from the apprehension of future punishment, would not contribute much to restrain the criminal excesses of the passions. Had Chatterton lived, and been fortunate enough to fall into settled and sober habits of life, his excellent understanding would, in all probability, have led him to see the fallacy of those principles which he had hastily embraced; as it was, the only preservatives of which he was possessed against the contagion of vice, were the enthusiasm of literature, and that delicacy of sentiment which taste and reading inspire. But though these auxiliaries are not wholly to be despised, we have too many instances of their inefficacy in supporting the cause of virtue, to place any confident reliance on them.—Dr. GREGORY.

Chatterton's answer to the strong objection arising from the smoothness of Rowley's poetry, when stated to him by Horace Walpole, is very remarkable—' The harmony is not so extraordinary, as Joseph Iscam is altogether as harmonious.' Now, as Joseph Iscam is equally a person of dubious existence, this is a curious instance of *placing the elephant upon the tortoise*. His ruling passion was not the vanity of a poet, who depends upon the opinion of others for its gratification, but the stoical pride of talent, which felt nourishment in the solitary contemplation of superiority over the dupes who fell into his toils.—SIR WALTER SCOTT.

* Now preserved in the British Museum. It was first printed in Barrett's History of Bristol.

A MOST MERRIE ENTYRLUDE,

Plaied bie the Carmelyte Freeres at Mastre Canynges hys greete howse, before Mastre Canynges and Byshoppe Carpenterre,* on dedicatynge the chyrche of *Oure Ladie of Redclefte*, hight

THE PARLIAMENTE OF SPRYTES.

WROTEN BIE T. ROWLEIE AND J. ISCAMME.†

Entroductyon bie Queene Mabbe.
(Bie Iscamme.)

Whan from the erthe the sonnes hulstred,[1]
Than from the flouretts straughte[2] with dewe ;

---

* John Carpenter, bishop of Worcester, who, in conjunction with Mr. Canynge, founded the Abbey at Westbury.

† John Iscam, according to Rowley, was a canon of the monastery of Saint Augustine in Bristol. He wrote a dramatic piece called "The Pleasaunt Dyscorses of Lamyngeton:" also, at the desire of Mr. Canynge (Rowley being then collecting of Drawings for Mr. Canynge) he translated a Latin piece called "Miles Brystolli," into English metre. The place of his birth is not known.—CHATTERTON.

1 Hidden.

2 Stretched. I think this line is borrowed from a much better one of Rowley's, viz. "Like kynge cuppes brasteynge wyth the mornynge dew." The reason why I think Iscam guilty of the plagiary is, that the 'Songe to Ella', from whence the above line is taken, was wrote when Rowley was in London collecting of drawings for Mr. Canynge to build the church, and Iscam wrote the above little before the finishing of the church.—CHATTERTON.

Mie leege menne makes yee awhaped,[1]
And wytches theyre wytchencref[2] doe.
Then ryse the sprytes ugsome[3] and rou,[4]
And take theyre walke the letten[5] throwe.
Than do the sprytes of valourous menne,
Agleeme along the barbed[6] halle;
Pleasaunte the moultrynge[7] banners kenne,
Or sytte arounde yn honourde stalle.
Oure sprytes atourne[8] theyr eyne[9] to nyghte,
And looke on Canynge his chyrche bryghte.
In sothe yn alle mie bismarde[10] rounde,
Troolie the thynge muste be bewryen:[11]
Inne stone or woden worke ne founde,
Nete so bielecoyle[12] to myne eyne
As ys goode Canynge hys chyrche of stone,
Whych blatauntlie[13] wylle shewe his prayse alone.

To Johannes Carpenterre Byshoppe of Worcesterre.
(Bie Rowleie.)

To you goode Byshoppe, I address mie saie,
To you who honoureth the clothe you weare;
Lyke pretious bighes[14] ynne golde of beste allaie
Echone dothe make the other seeme more fayre:
Other than you* where coulde a manne be founde
So fytte to make a place bee holie grounde.

---

1 Astonished.   2 Witchcraft.   3 Terrible.   4 Ugly.
5 This is a word peculiar to the West, and signifies a 'churchyard.'
6 Hung with banners or trophies.   7 Mouldering.   8 Turn.
9 Eyes.   10 Curious.   11 Declared or made known.
12 Well-pleasing or welcome.   13 Loudly.   14 Jewels.
* 'Other than you,' &c. Carpenter dedicated the church, as appears
by a poem written by Rowley.—CHATTERTON.

The sainctes ynne stones so netelie carvelled,[1]
Theie scantlie[2] are whatte theie enseeme to be;
Bie fervente praier of yours myghte rear theyre heade
And chaunte owte masses to oure Vyrgyne.
Was everie prelate lyke a Carpenterre,
The chyrche would ne blushe at a Wynchesterre.

Learned as Beauclerke, as the confessour
Holie ynne lyfe, lyke Canynge charitable,
Busie in holie chyrche as Vavasour,
Slacke yn thynges evylle, yn alle goode thynges stable,
Honest as Saxonnes was, from whence thou'rt sprunge,
Tho' boddie weak thie soule for ever younge.

Thou knowest welle thie conscience free from steyne,
Thie soule her rode[3] no sable batements have;
Yclenchde[4] oer wythe vyrtues beste adaygne,
A daie æterne[5] thie mynde does aie adave.[6]
Ne spoyled widdowes, orphyans dystreste,
Ne starvvynge preestes ycrase[7] thie nyghtlie reste.

Here then to thee let me for one and alle
Give lawde to Carpenterre and commendatyon,
For hys grete vyrtues but alas! too smalle
Is mie poore skylle to shewe you hys juste blatyon,[8]
Or to blaze forthe hys publicke goode alone,
And alle hys pryvate goode to Godde and hym ys
knowne.

---

1 Carved.   2 Scarcely.   3 Complexion.   4 Covered.
5 Eternal.   6 Enjoy.   7 To break.
8 Renown, praise.

Spryte of Nymrodde speaketh.
(Bie Iscamme.)

Soon as the morne but newlie wake,
Spyed Nyghte ystorven lye;
On herre corse dyd dew droppes shake,
Then fore the sonne upgotten was I.
The rampynge lyon, felle tygere,
The bocke that skyppes from place to place,
The olyphaunte[1] and rhynocere,[2]
Before mee throughe the greene wood I dyd chace.
Nymrodde as scryptures hyght mie name,
Baalle as jetted[3] stories saie;
For rearynge Babelle of greete fame,
Mie name and renome[4] shalle lyven for aie:
But here I spie a fyner rearynge,
Genst whych the clowdes dothe not fyghte,
Onne whych the starres doe sytte to appearynge:
Weeke menne thynke ytte reache the kyngdom of
    lyghte.
O where ys the manne that buylded the same,
Dyspendynge[5] worldlie store so welle;
Fayn woulde I chaunge wyth hym mie name,
And stande ynne hys chaunce ne to goe to helle.

---

1 Elephant. So an ancient anonymous author:
      " The olyphaunt of beastes is
        The wisest I wis,
      For hee alwaie dothe eat
      Lyttle store of meat."—*Note by* CHATTERTON.
2 Rhinoceros.
3 Devised or faigned.   4 Renown.   5 Expending.

Spryte of Assyrians syngeth.

Whan toe theyre caves æterne abeste,[1]
The waters ne moe han' dystreste
    The worlde so large;
    Butte dyde dyscharge
Themselves ynto theyre bedde of reste.

Then menne besprenged[3] alle abroade,
Ne moe dyde worshyppe the true Godde;
    Butte dyd create
    Hie temples greate
Unto the ymage of Nymrodde.

But nowe the Worde of Godde is come,
Borne of Maide Marie toe brynge home
    Mankynde hys shepe,
    Them for to keepe
In the folde of hys heavenlie kyngdome.

Thys chyrche whych·Canynge he dyd reer,
To bee dispente[4] in prayse and prayer,
    Mennes soules to save,
    From vowrynge[5] grave,
And puryfye them heaven-were.[6]

---

1 According to Rowley, ' Humbled or brought down.' And Rowleie saies " thie pryde wylle be abeste." Entroductyon to the Entyrlude of the Apostate.—CHATTERTON.

2 Preterite of 'have.'   3 Scattered.   4 Used.

5 Devouring.

6 Heavenward.

    " Not goulde or bighes will bring thee heaven-were,
    Ne kyne or mylkie flockes upon the playne,
    Ne mannours rych nor banners brave and fayre,
    Ne wife the sweetest of the erthlie trayne.
      " Entroductyon to the Enterlude of the Apostate."
          Note by CHATTERTON.

Sprytes of Elle,[1] *Bythryeke,*[2] *Fytz-hardynge, Frampton,*
   Gauntes, Segowen, Lanyngeton, Knyghtes, Templars,
   and Byrtonne.

(Bie Rowleie.)

Spryte of Bythrycke speeketh.

Elle, thie Brystowe is thie onlie care,
Thou arte lyke dragonne vyllant[3] of yts gode :
Ne lovynge dames toe kynde moe love can bear,
Ne Lombardes over golde moe vyllaunt[4] broode.

Spryte of Elle speeketh.

Swythyn,[5] yee sprytes forsake the bollen[6] floude,
And browke[7] a sygthe wyth mee, a syghte enfyne ;
Welle have I vended myne for Danyshe bloude,
Syth thys greete structure greete mie whaped[8] eyne.
Yee that have buylden on the Radclefte syde,
Tourne there your eyne and see your workes outvyde.

Spryte of Bythrycke speeketh.

What wondrous monumente ! what pyle ys thys !
That byndes in wonders chayne entendemente ![9]
That dothe aloof the ayrie skyen kyss,
And seemeth mountaynes joyned bie cemente.
From Godde hys greete and wondrous storehouse sente.

---

1 Keeper of Bristol Castle in the time of the Saxons.
2 An Anglo-Saxon, who in William the Conqueror's time had Bristol.
—Chatterton.
3 & 4 Vigilant.   5 Quickly.   6 Swelled.   7 Enjoy.
8 Amazed.   9 Understanding.

Fulle welle myne eyne arede[1] ytte canne ne bee,
That manne coulde reare of thylke agreete extente,
A chyrche so bausyn fetyve[2] as wee see:
The flemed[3] cloudes disparted from it flie,
Twylle bee, I wis, to alle eternytye.

Elle's spryte speeketh.

Were I once moe caste yn a mortalle frame,
To heare the chauntrie songe sounde ynne myne eare,
To heare the masses to owre holie dame,
To viewe the cross yles and the arches fayre!
Throughe the halfe hulstred sylver twynklynge glare
Of yon bryghte moone in foggie mantles dreste,
I must contente the buyldynge to aspere,[4]
Whylste ishad[5] cloudes the hallie[6] syghte arreste.
Tyll as the nyghtes growe wayle[7] I flie the lyghte,
O were I manne agen to see the syghte!
There sytte the canons; clothe of sable hue
Adorne the boddies of them everie one;
The chaunters whyte with scarfes of woden blewe,
And crymson chappeaus[8] for them toe put onne,
Wythe golden tassyls glyttrynge ynne the sunne;
The dames ynne kyrtles alle of Lyncolne greene,
And knotted shoone pykes[9] of brave coloures done:
A fyner syghte yn sothe was never seen.

Byrtonnes spryte speeketh.

Inne tyltes and turnies was mie dear delyghte,
For manne and Godde hys warfare han renome;

---

1 Conceive.   2 Elegantly large.   3 Frighted.   4 To view.
5 Broken.   6 Well pleasing, also holy.   7 Old.
8 Hats or caps of estates.   9 Shoe-strings.

At everyche tyltynge yarde mie name was byghte,
I beare the belle awaie whereer I come.
Of Redclefte chyrche the buyldynge newe I done,
And dyd fulle manie holie place endowe,
Of Maries house made the foundacyon,
And gave threescore markes to Johnes hys toe.
Then clos'd myne eyne on erthe to ope no moe,
Whylst syx moneths mynde upon mie grave was doe.
Full gladde am I mie chyrche was pyghten[1] down,
Syth thys brave structure doth agreete myne eye.
Thys geason[2] buyldynge, limedst[3] of the towne,
Like to the donours soule, shalle never die;
But if, percase, Tyme, of hys dyre envie,
Shalle beate ytte to rude walles and throckes[4] of stone;
The faytour[5] traveller that passes bie
Wyllesee yttes royend[6] auntyaunte splendoure shewne
Inne the crasd[7] arches and the carvellynge,
And pyllars theyre greene heades to heaven rearynge.

Spryte of Segowen[8] speeketh.

Bestoykynge[8] golde was once myne onlie toie,
Wyth ytte mie soule wythynne the coffer laie:
Itte dyd the mastrie of mie lyfe emploie,
Bie nyghte mie leman[10] and mie jubbe[11] bie daye.
Once as I dosynge yn the wytch howre laie,
Thynkynge howe to benym[12] the orphyans breadde,
And from the redeless[13] take theyre goodes awaie,

---

1 Pulled down.	2 Rare.	3 Most noble.	4 Heaps.
5 Wandering.	6 Ruined.	7 Broken, old.	
8 A usurer, a native of Lombardy.	9 Deceiving.		10 Mistress.
11 Bottle.	12 To take away.		13 Helpless.

I from the skien hear'd a voyce, which said,
Thou sleepest, but loe Sathan is awake;
Some deede that's holie doe, or hee thie soule wylle take.

I swythyn was upryst[1] wyth feere astounde;[2]
Methoughte yn merke[3] was plaien devylles felle:
Strayte dyd I nomber twentie aves rounde,
Thoughten full soone for to go to helle.
In the morne mie case to a goode preeste dyd telle,
Who dyd areede[4] mee to ybuild that daie
The chyrche of Thomas, thenne to pieces felle.
Mie heart dispanded[5] into heaven laie:
Soon was the sylver to the workmenne given,—
'Twas beste astowde,[6] a karynte[7] gave to heaven.

But welle, I wote, thie causalies were not soe,
'Twas love of Godde that set thee on the rearynge
Of this fayre chyrch, O Canynge, for to doe
Thys lymed[8] buyldynge of so fyne appearynge:
Thys chyrch owre lesser buyldyngs all owt-darynge,
Lyke to the moone wythe starres of lyttle lyghte;
And after tymes the feetyve[9] pyle reverynge,
The prynce of chyrches buylders thee shall hyghte;
Greete was the cause, but greeter was the effecte,
So alle wyll saie who doe thys place prospect.

Spryte of Fytz Hardynge speeketh.

From royal parentes dyd I have retaynynge,
The redde-hayrde Dane confeste to be mie syre;

---

1 Risen up.　　2 Astonished.　　3 Darkness.　　4 Counsel.
5 Expanded.　　6 Bestowed.　　7 A loan.　　8 Noble.
9 Handsome or elegant.

The Dane who often throwe thys kyngdom draynynge,
Would mark theyre waie athrowgh wythe bloude and
　　fyre.
As stopped ryvers alwaies ryse moe hygher,
And rammed stones bie opposures stronger bee;
So thie[1] whan vanquyshed dyd prove moe dyre,
And for one peysan[2] theie dyd threescore slee.
From them of Denmarques royalle bloude came I,
Welle myghte I boaste of mie gentylytie.
The pypes maie sounde and bubble forth mie name,
And tellen what on Radclefte syde I dyd:
Trinytie Colledge ne agrutche mie fame,
The fayrest place in Brystowe ybuylded.
The royalle bloude that thorow mie vaynes slydde
Dyd tyncte mie harte wythe manie a noble thoughte;
Lyke to mie mynde the mynster[3] yreared,
Wythe noble carvel workmanshyppe was wroughte.
Hie at the deys,[4] lyke to a kynge on's throne,
Dyd I take place and was myself alone.

But thou, the buylder of this swotie[5] place,
Where alle the saynctes in sweete ajunctyon stande,
A verie heaven for yttes fetyve grace,
The glorie and the wonder of the lande,
That shewes the buylders mynde and fourmers hande,
To bee the beste that on the erthe remaynes;
At once for wonder and delyghte commaunde,
Shewynge howe muche hee of the godde reteynes.
Canynge the great, the charytable, and good,
Noble as kynges if not of kyngelie bloude.

---

1 'Thie,' for these.　　2 Countryman, foot soldier.　　3 Monastery.
4 First table in a monastery, where the superior sat.
5 Sweet or delighting.

Spryte of Framptone speeketh.

Brystowe shall speeke mie name, and Radclefte toe,
For here mie deedes were goddelye everychone;
As Owdens mynster bie the gate wylle shewe,
And Johnes at Brystowe what mie workes han done.
Besydes anere[1] howse that I han begunne;
Butte myne comparde to thyssen ys a groffe;[2]
Nete to bee mencioned or looked upon,
A verie punelstre[3] or verie scoffe;
Canynge, thie name shall lyven be for aie,
Thie name ne wyth the chyrche shall waste awaie.

Spryte of Gaunts speeketh.

I dyd fulle manie reparatyons give,
And the bonne Hommes dyd fulle ryche endowe;
As tourynge to mie Godde on erthe dyd lyve,
So alle the Brystowe chronycles wylle shewe.
Butte alle mie deedes wylle bee as nothynge nowe,
Syth Canynge have thys buyldynge fynyshed,
Whych seemeth to be the pryde of Brystowe,
And bie ne buyldeyng to bee overmatched:
Whyche aie shalle laste and bee the prayse of alle,
And onlie in the wrecke of nature falle.

A Knyghte Templars spryte speeketh.

In hallie land where Sarasins defyle
The grounde whereon oure Savyour dyd goe,
And Chryste hys temple make to moschyes[4] vyle,
Wordies of despyte genst oure Savyour throwe.
There 'twas that we dyd owre warfarage doe,

---

1 Another.   2 A laughing-stock.
3 An empty boat.   4 Mosques.

Guardynge the pylgryms of the Chrystyan faie;[1]
And dyd owre holie armes in bloude embrue,
Movynge lyke thonder-boultes yn drear arraie.
Owre strokes lyke levyn[2] tareynge the tall tree
Owre Godde owre arme wyth lethalle force dyd dree.[3]
Maint[4] tenures fayre, ande mannoures of greete welthe,
Greene woodes, and brooklettes runnynge throughe
    the lee,
Dyd menne us gyve for theyre deare soule her helthe,
Gave erthlie ryches for goodes heavenlie.
Nee dyd we lette oure ryches untyle[5] bee,
But dyd ybuylde the Temple chyrche so fyne,
The whyche ya wroughte abowte so bismarelie;[6]
Itte seemeth camoys[7] to the wondrynge eyne;
And ever and anon when belles rynged,
From place to place ytte moveth yttes hie heade:
Butte Canynge from the sweate of hys owne browes,
Dyd gette hys golde and rayse thys fetyve howse.

Lamyngetonnes spryte speeketh.

Lette alle mie faultes bee buried ynne the grave:
Alle obloquyes be rotted wythe mie duste;
Lette him fyrst carpen that no wemmes[8] have:
'Tys paste mannes nature for to bee aie juste.
But yette in sothen to rejoyce I muste,
That I dyd not immeddle for to buylde;
Sythe thys quaintissed[9] place so gloryous,
Seemeynge alle chyrches joyned yn one guylde,[10]
Has nowe supplied for what I had done,
Whych toe mie clerge[11] is a gloryous sonne.

1 Faith.	2 Lightning.	3 Drive.	4 Many.
5 Useless.	6 Curiously.	7 Crooked upwards.—KEARSLEY.
8 Faults.	9 Curiously devised.	10 Company.	11 Candle.

Elle's spryte speeketh.

Then lette us alle do jyntelie reveraunce here,
The beste of menne and Byshoppes here doe stande :
Who are Goddes shepsterres¹ and do take good care,
Of the goode shepe hee putteth yn theyre hand ;
Ne one is loste butte alle in well likande²
Awayte to heare the Generalle Byshoppes calle,
When Mychaels trompe shall sound to ynmoste lande,
Affryghte the wycked and awaken alle:
Then Canynge ryses to eternal reste,
And fyndes hee chose on erthe a lyfe the beste. *

---

1 Shepherds. 2 Liking.

* I cannot dismiss Mr. Bryant without taking notice of a position
which he has laid down, and is indeed the basis of almost all the argu-
ments that he has urged to prove the authenticity of the Bristol MSS.
It is this; that as every author must know his own meaning, and as
Chatterton has sometimes given wrong interpretations of words that
are found in the poems attributed to Rowley, he could not be the
author of those poems.

If Chatterton had originally written these poems, in the form in
which they now appear, this argument might in a doubtful question
have some weight. But although I have as high an opinion of his
abilities as perhaps any person whatsoever, and do indeed believe him
to have been the greatest genius that England has produced since the
days of Shakspeare, I am not ready to acknowledge that he was endued
with any miraculous powers. Devoted as he was from his infancy to
the study of antiquities, he could not have been so conversant with
ancient language, or have had all the words necessary to be used so
present to his mind, as to write antiquated poetry of any considerable
length, off hand. He, without doubt, wrote his verses in plain English,
and afterwards embroidered them with such old words as would suit
the sense and metre. With these he furnished himself, sometimes
probably from memory, and sometimes from glossaries; and annexed
such interpretations as he found or made. When he could not readily
find a word that would suit his metre, he invented one. If then his old
words afford some sense, and yet are sometimes interpreted wrong,

nothing more follows than that his glossaries were imperfect, or his knowledge inaccurate; (still however he might have had a confused, though not complete, idea of their import:) if, as the commentator asserts, the words that he has explained not only suit the places in which they stand, but are often more apposite than he imagined, and have a latent and significant meaning, that never occurred to him, this will only show, that a man's book is sometimes wiser than himself; a truth of which we have every day so many striking instances, that it was scarcely necessary for this learned antiquarian to have exhibited a new proof of it.

Let it be considered too, that the glossary and the text were not always written at the same time; that Chatterton might not always remember the precise sense in which he had used antiquated words; and from a confused recollection, or from the want of the very same books that he had consulted while he was writing his poems, might add sometimes a false, and sometimes an imperfect interpretation. This is not a mere hypothesis; for in one instance we know that the comment was written at some interval of time after the text. "The glossary of the poem entitled, 'The English Metamorphosis' (Mr. Tyrwhitt informs us) was written down by Chatterton extemporally, without the assistance of any book, at the desire and in the presence of Mr. Barrett." —MALONE.

On the Mynster.*

Wythe daityve¹ steppe relygyon dyghte yn greie,
　　Her face of doleful hue,
Swyfte as a takel² thro'we bryghte heav'n tooke her
　　waie,
　　　And ofte and ere anon dyd saie
　　　"Aie! mee! what shall I doe;
"See Brystoe citie, whyche I nowe doe kenne,
　　"Arysynge to mie view,
"Thycke throng'd wythe soldyers and wythe traffyck-
　　menne;
　　　"Butte saynctes I seen few."

---

* This poem is reprinted from Barrett's History of Bristol. It is said
by Chatterton to be translated by Rowley, "as nie as Englyshe wyll
serve, from the original, written by Abbot John, who was ynductyd
20 yeares, and dyd act as abbatt 9 yeares before hys inductyon for
Phillip then abbatt: he dyed yn M.CC.XV. beynge buryed in his albe in
the mynster."—SOUTHEY's *Edition of Chatterton.*

John, seconde abbotte of Seyncte Augustynns, was a manne well
skyllde ynn the languages of yore; hee wrote ynn the Greke tonge a
poem onne Roberte Fitz Hardynge, whyche as nie as Englyshe wylle
serve I have thus transplacedd:
　　　" Wythe daityve steppe relygyon dyghte yn greie,
　　　　Her face of doleful hue," &c.
As above.—ROWLEY's *History of Painters and Carvellers.*

1 Perhaps 'haltive,' or 'haiftiff' hasty, from the French 'haity'
hasty.

2 Arrow.

Fytz-Hardynge rose!—he rose lyke bryghte sonne in
   the morne,
            "Faire dame adryne thein eyne,
            " Let alle thie greefe bee myne,
  " For I wylle rere thee uppe a Mynster hie ;
 " The toppe whereof shall reach ynto the skie ;
            " And wylle a monke be shorne ;"
            Thenne dyd the dame replie,
            " I shall ne be forelourne ;
 " Here wyll I take a cherysaunied reste,
 " And spend mie daies upon Fytz-Hardynges breste."*

---

* Setting aside the opinion of those uncharitable biographers whose
imaginations have conducted Chatterton to the gibbet, it may be owned,
that his unformed character exhibited strong and conflicting elements
of good and evil. Even the momentary project of the infidel boy to be-
come a methodist preacher, betrays an obliquity of design, and a con-
tempt of human credulity, that is not very amiable. But had he been
spared, his pride and ambition would have come to flow in proper
channels ; his understanding would have taught him the practical value
of truth, and the dignity of virtue, and he would have despised artifice
when he had felt the strength and security of wisdom.—CAMPBELL.

   Chatterton was a prodigy of genius, and would have proved the first
of English poets, had he reached a maturer age.—WARTON.

   To speak of Chatterton, is to touch upon a name from which time
neither has taken nor will take any of its interest.—SOUTHEY.

𝔗𝔥𝔢 𝔚𝔬𝔯𝔩𝔡𝔢.*

Fadre, Sonne, and Mynstrelles.

FADRE.

To the worlde newe and ytts bestoykenynge[1] waie
Thys coistrelle[2] sonne of myne ys all mie care,
Yee mynstrelles warne hymme how wyth rede[3] he straie
Where guylded vyce dothe spredde hys mascill'd[4] snare,
To gettyng wealth I woulde hee shoulde bee bredde,
And couronnes of rudde goulde ne glorie rounde hys
hedde.

FIRST MYNSTREL.

Mie name is Intereste, tis I
Dothe yntoe alle bosoms flie,
Eche one hylten[5] secret's myne,
None so wordie, goode, and dygne,

---

* From Barrett's History of Bristol. A glossary to this poem is now
added for the first time. The interpretations are given from Kersey.
1 Deceiving.   2 A young lad.   3 Advice, counsel, help.
4 Evidently formed from '𝕸𝖆𝖘𝖈𝖑𝖊 (F. in Heraldry) a kind of
short lozenge, that is voided, or has a hole in the middle representing
the mesh of a net."
5 Hidden.

Butte wyll fynde ytte to theyr cost,
Intereste wyll rule the roaste.
I to everichone gyve lawes,
Selfe ys fyrst yn everich cause.

SECOND MYNSTREL.

I amme a faytour[1] flame
Of lemmies[2] melancholi,
Love somme behyghte[3] mie name,
Some doe anemp[4] me follie;
Inne sprytes of meltynge molde
I sette mie burneynge sele;
To mee a goulers[5] goulde
Doeth nete a pyne[6] avele;
I pre upon the helthe,
And from gode redeynge[7] flee,
The manne who woulde gette wealthe
Muste never thynke of mee.

THIRD MYNSTREL.

I bee the Queede[8] of Pryde, mie spyrynge heade
Mote reche the cloudes and stylle be rysynge hie,
Too lyttle is the earthe to bee mie bedde,
Too hannow[9] for mie breetheynge place the skie;

---

1 Wretch, vagabond.
2 This word is uncertain. Kersey has '𝔏𝔢𝔪𝔢𝔰' lights or
flames.
3 Call.   4 Name.   5 Usurer's.   6 Pin.
7 Counsel.   8 Devil, or evil spirit.
9 Narrow. The word is neither in Speght, Kersey, or Bailey.

Daynous[1] I see the worlde bineth me lie
Botte to mie betterres, I soe lyttle gree,
Annenthe[2] a shadow of a shade I bee,
Tys to the smalle alleyn that I canne multyplie.

FOURTH MYNSTREL.

I am the Queed of goulers; look arounde
The ayrs aboute mee thieves doe represente,
Bloudsteyned robbers spryng from oute the grounde,
And airie vysyons swarme around mie ente;[3]
O save mie monies, ytte ys theyre entente
To nymme[4] the redde Godde of mie fremded[5] sprighte,
Whatte joie canne goulers have or daie or nyghte!

FIFTH MYNSTREL.

Vice bee I hyghte, onne golde fulle ofte I ryde,
Fulle fayre unto the syghte for aie I seeme;
Mie ugsomness wythe goldenne veyles I hyde,
Laieynge mie lovers ynne a sylkenne dreme;
Botte whan mie untrue pleasaunce have byn tryde,
Thanne doe I showe alle horrownesse and rou.[6]
And those I have ynne nette woulde feyne mie grype
    eschew.

SIXTH MYNSTREL.

I bee greete Dethe, alle ken mee bie the name,
Botte none can saie howe I doe loose the spryghte,
Goode menne mie tardyinge delaie doethe blame,
Botte moste ryche goulerres from mee take a flyghte;

---

1 Disdainful.   2 Less than.   3 Purse.
4 To take by stealth, to filch.   5 Frighted.   6 Ugliness.

Myckle of wealthe I see whereere I came,
Doethe mie ghastness mockle multyplye
And maketh hem afrayde to lyve or die.

FADRE.

Howe villeyn Mynstrelles, and is this your rede.
Awaie: Awaie: I wyll ne geve a curse,
Mie sonne, mie sonne, of mie speeche take hede,
Nothynge ys goode thatte bryngeth not to purse. *

---

1 Advice.

* Unfortunate boy! poorly wast thou accommodated during thy
short sojourning among us ;—rudely wast thou treated,—sorely did thy
feeling soul suffer from the scorn of the unworthy; and there are, at
last, those who wish to rob thee of thy only meed, thy posthumous glory.
Severe, too, are the censurers of thy morals. In the gloomy moments
of despondency, I fear thou hast uttered impious and blasphemous
thoughts, which none can defend, and which neither thy youth, nor thy
fiery spirit, nor thy situation, can excuse. But let thy more rigid cen-
sors reflect, that thou wast literally and strictly but a boy. Let many
of thy bitterest enemies reflect what were their own religious principles,
and whether they had any, at the age of fourteen, fifteen, and sixteen.
Surely it is a severe and an unjust surmise, that thou wouldest pro-
bably have ended thy life as a victim of the laws, if thou hadst not fin-
ished it as thou didst; since the very act by which thou durst put an
end to thy painful existence, proves that thou thoughtest it better to die,
than to support life by theft or violence.

Malice, if there was any, may surely now be at rest; for "cold he lies
in the grave below." But where were ye, O ye friends to genius, when,
stung with disappointment, distressed for food and raiment, with every
frightful form of human misery painted on his fine imagination, poor
Chatterton sunk in despair? Alas! ye knew him not then, and now it
is too late,—

" For now he is dead;
Gone to his death bed,
All under the willow tree."

So sang the sweet youth, in as tender an elegy as ever flowed from a
feeling heart.

In return for the pleasure I have received from thy poems, I pay
thee, poor boy, the trifling tribute of my praise. Thyself thou hast
emblazoned; thine own monument thou hast erected. But they whom
thou hast delighted, feel a pleasure in vindicating thine honours from
the rude attacks of detraction.—VICESIMUS KNOX.

One Canto of an Ancient Poem,

called

The Unknown Knight or the Tournament.*

I.

The Matten belle han sounded long,
The Cocks han sang their morning songe,
When lo! the tuneful Clarions sound,
(Wherein all other noise was drown'd)
Did echo to the rooms around,
And greet the ears of Champyons stronge;
Arise, arise from downie bedde
For Sunne doth gin to shew his hedde!

II.

Then each did don in seemlie gear,
What armour eche beseem'd to wear,
And on each sheelde devices shone,
Of wounded hearts and battles won,
All curious and nice echon;
With manie a tassild spear;

---

* From the Supplement to Chatterton's Miscellanies. "I offered this as a sample, having two more Cantos. The Author unknown." 1769. —SOUTHEY'S EDITION.

And mounted echeone on a steed
Unwote made Ladies hearts to blede.

III.

Heraulds eche side the Clarions wound,
The Horses started at the sound;
The Knyghtes echeone dyd poynt the launce,
And to the combattes did advaunce;
From Hyberne, Scotland, eke from Fraunce;
Theyre prancyng horses tare the ground;
All strove to reche the place of fyghte,
The first to exercise their myghte—

IV.

O'Rocke upon his courser fleet,
Swift as lightning were his feet,
First gain'd the lists and gatte him fame;
From West Hybernee Isle he came,
His myghte depictur'd in his name.*
All dreded such an one to meet;
Bold as a mountain wolf he stood,
Upon his swerde sat grim dethe and bloude.

V.

But when he threwe downe his Asenglave,
Next came in Syr Botelier bold and brave,
The dethe of manie a Saraceen;
Theie thought him a Devil from Hells black den,
Ne thinking that anie of mortalle menne
Could send so manie to the grave.

---

* Probably alluding to the word 'rock.'

For his life to John Rumsee he render'd his thanks
Descended from Godred the King of the Manks.

VI.

Within his sure rest he settled his speare,
And ran at O'Rocke in full career ;
Their launces with the furious stroke
Into a thousand shivers broke,
Even as the thunder tears the oak,
And scatters splinters here and there :
So great the shock, their senses did depart,
The bloude all ran to strengthen up the harte.

VII.

Syr Botelier Rumsie first came from his traunce,
And from the Marshall toke the launce ;
O'Rocke eke chose another speere,
And ran at Syr Botelier [in] full career ;
His prancynge stede the ground did tare ;
In haste he made a false advance ;
Syr Botelier seeing, with myghte amain
Fellde him down upon the playne.

VIII.

Syr Pigotte Novlin at the Clarions sound,
On a milk-white stede with gold trappings around,
He couchde in his rest his silver-poynt speere,
And ferslie ranne up in full career ;
But for his appearance he payed full deare,
In the first course laid on the ground ;
Besmeer'd in the dust with his silver and gold,
No longer a glorious sight to behold.

IX.

Syr Botelier then having conquer'd his twayne,
Rode Conqueror off the tourneying playne;
Receivying a garland from *Alice's* hand,
The fayrest Ladye in the lande.
Syr Pigotte this viewed, and furious did stand,
Tormented in mind and bodily peyne,
Syr Botelier crown'd, most galantlie stode,
As some tall oak within the thick wode.

X.

Awhile the shrill Clarions sounded the word;
Next rode in Syr John, of Adderleigh Lord,
Who over his back his thick shield did bryng,
In checkee of redde and silver sheeninge,
With steede and gold trappings beseeming a King,
A guilded fine Adder twyned round his swerde.
De Bretville advanced, a man of great myghte
And couched his launce in his rest for the fyghte.

XI.

Ferse as the falling waters of the lough,
That tumble headlonge from the mountain's browe,
Ev'n so they met in drierie sound,
De Bretville fell upon the ground,
The bloude from inward bruised wound,
Did out his stained helmet flowe;
As some tall bark upon the foamie main,
So laie De Bretville on the plain.

XII.

Syr John of the Dale or Compton hight,
Advanced next in lists of fyght,
He knew the tricks of tourneyinge full well,
In running race ne manne culd him excell,
Or how to wielde a sworde better tel,
And eke he was a manne of might :
On a black Stede with silver trappynges dyght
He darde the dangers of the tourneyd fighte.

XIII.

Within their rests their speeres they set,
So furiously ech other met,
That Compton's well intended speere
Syr John his shield in pieces tare,
And wound his hand in furious geir ;
Syr Johns stele Assenglave was wette :
Syr John then toe the marshal turn'd,
His breast with meekle furie burn'd.

XIV.

The tenders of the feelde came in,
And bade the Champyons not begyn ;
Eche tourney but one hour should last,
And then one hour was gone and past.

The Freere of Orderys Whyte.*

There was a Broder of Orderys Whyte,
Hee songe hys masses yn the nyghte;
   Ave Maria, Jesu Maria.
The nonnes al slepeynge yn the Dortoure.
Thoughte hym of al syngeynge Freers the Flowre.
   Ave Maria, Jesu Maria.

Suster Agnes looved his syngeynge well,
And songe with hem too the sothen to tell;
   Ave Maria, &c.
But be ytte ne sed bie Elde or yynge
That ever dheye oderwyse dyd synge
   Than Ave Maria, &c.

This Broder was called evrich wheere
To Kenshamm and to Bristol Nonnere;
   Ave Maria, &c.
Botte seyynge of masses dyd wurch hym so lowe,
Above hys Skynne hys Bonys did growe.
   Ave Maria, &c.

He eaten Beefe ande Dyshes of Mows,†
And hontend everych Knyghtys House
   With Ave Maria, &c.
And beynge ance moe in gode lyken,
He songe to the Nones and was poren agen
   With Ave Maria, &c.

* From a MSS. by Chatterton in the British Museum. There is also
the beginning of a poem called "the Freere of Orderys Black," which
is unfit for publication.—SOUTHEY's *Edition.*

† Probably a preparation of boiled corn.—ED.

Dialogue.

Between Maister Philpot and Walworth Cocknies.*

PHILPOT.

God ye God den,† my good naighbour, howe d'ye ayle?
How does your wyfe, man! what never assole?
Cum rectitate vivas, verborum mala ne cures.

---

* From Dean Milles's Edition of Rowley. "It contains," says the
Dean, "a variety of evidence, tending to confirm the authenticity of
these poems. In the first place, this sort of macaronic verse of mixed lan-
guages, is a style used in the fourteenth and fifteenth centuries. Dante
has some of these amongst his Rime, (p. 226. vol. 2d. Venice 1741)
which are composed of French, Italian, and Latin, and conclude thus:
'Namque locutus sum in lingua trina.'
Skelton, who lived not long after Rowley, has also poems in the same
kind of verse. Secondly, the correctness of the Latin, and the propriety
of the answers in English, shew it to have been written at least by a
better scholar than Chatterton. Thirdly, the low humour of the dialogue,
although suited to the taste of that early and illiterate age, could be no
object of imitation to a modern poet. But it is a most remarkable cir-
cumstance, that he has introduced his two Cockneies under the names
of two most respectable aldermen of the city of London, who lived
about the year 1380, Sir William Walworth and Sir John Philpot; men
of such distinguished reputation, not only in their own city, but also in
the whole kingdom, that the first parliament of Richard the Second,
in granting a subsidy to that king, made it subject to the control and
management of these two citizens." (Walsingham, p. 200. Rapin, vol. 1,
p. 454 and 458.)
† This salutation, which should be written "God ye good Den," is
more than once used by Shakespeare:
In Love's Labour Lost, the clown says,
"God dig you den all." Act iv. Sc. 1.
That is to say, "God give you a good evening;" for 'dig' is undoubt-
edly a mistake for 'give.'
So in the Dialogue between the Nurse and Mercutio, in Romeo and
Juliet, Act ii. Sc. 5, the former says,
"God ye good morrow gentlemen:"
to which the latter replies,
"God ye good den, fair gentlewoman."
And in the Exmoor Courtship,
"Good den, good den:"
which the Glossarist on that pamphlet properly explains by the wish
of a good evening; and Mr. Steevens observes on the passage in Love's
Labour Lost, that this contraction is not unusual in our ancient comic
writers, and quotes the play called the Northern Lass, by R. Brome,
1633, for the following phrase:
"God you good even."—SOUTHEY's *Edition.*

WALWORTH.

Ah, Mastre Phyllepot, evil tongues do saie,
That my wyfe will lyen down to daie :
Tis ne twaine moneths syth shee was myne for

PHILPOT.

Animum submittere noli rebus in adversis,
Nolito quædam referenti semper credere.
But I pity you nayghbour, is it so ?

WALWORTH.

Quæ requirit misericordiam mala causa est,
Alack, alack, a sad dome mine in fay,
But oft with cityzens it is the case ;
Honesta turpitudo pro bonâ
Causâ mori, as auntient pensmen sayse. •

• Mr. Bryant's next argument is drawn from "the many
quotations in the story of John Lamington," and he says that "
of these quotations were obvious, and such as a boy could attain
And I can easily believe that they were *not obvious* to Mr. Br
whose studies we know have generally travelled a higher road;
can say with truth, that I found them in the very first book in v
I looked for them. The three former are transposed out of 'C
Distichs, and the two other out of the *Sentences of Publius S*
usually subjoined to the *Distichs* in a little volume, which, in r
small schools, I believe, is still the first that is put into the han
learners of Latin after the Grammar. They stand thus in an editi
Boxhornius, L. Bat. 1635.
   Cato, Lib. III. Dist. 4.
  Quum recte vivas, ne cures verba malorum.
   — Lib. II. Dist. 26.
  Rebus in adversis animum submittere noli.
   — Lib. II. Dist. 21.
  Noli tu quædam referenti credere semper.

PHILPOT.

Home news welle let alone and latyn too,
    For mee a memorie doth 'gin to fayle ;
Saie, Master Walworth, what gode newes have you,
    Praie have you herdeen of the stouns of hayle ?

WALWORTH.

I have, and that ytte with reddour did sayle,
    Some heutstones were lyke cheryes rege and grete,
And to the grownde there did the trees preveyle,
    But goodmanne Philpotte what dye you ahete
Bowte goods of Laymingtone, nowe holde by you
For certaine monies store to you for chattels due ?

SYRUS, *Sentent. Iamb.* p. 119.
Mala causa est quæ requirit misericordiam.
Sentent. Troch v. 3.
Est honesta turpitudo pro bonâ causâ mori.

In Chatterton's transcript of this last line he had originally inserted *est* after *turpitudo;* and he had written *bonay,* (to rhyme, I suppose more exactly to *fay*). The blunders in the first line of *rectate* for *recte,* and of *verborum mala* for *verba malorum,* seem to shew that he wrote from memory. They must have been overlooked, I presume, by the Dean of Exeter, who considers all these passages, not as quotations, but as original compositions, and argues, in part, *"from the correctness of the Latin,* that they must have been written at least by a better Scholar than Chatterton."* It appears, from the testimony of Mr. Smith, that Chatterton had intimated very frequently both a desire to learn and a design to teach himself Latin ; and though I do not suppose that he ever made any great progress in that language, I really think that he might have attained to these quotations. With respect to their *pertinency,* and their not being *idly and ostentatiously introduced,* it is scarce credible, I think, that such a medley of quotations, from such a book, should have been huddled together in such a dialogue by any one but a boy, who was proud of displaying the little Latin which he had just acquired. So much for the words which Chatterton is supposed to have been incapable of understanding.—TYRWHITT.

PHILPOT.

Ah, I have nymd him specyal, for his wine
  Have ta'en attons twelve pounds, for dayntye cheer,
Though the same time mie wyfe with hym dyd dyne,
  Been payd a mark—non-extra of the beer ;
But when hys synkynge purse did 'gin to wear
  I lent hym full syx markes upon hys faie,
And hee poore Custrols, havynge note to spere
  Favor'd a cleere and now doth runne awaie,
Hys goodes I downe at Bristowe towne wyll selle,
For which I will get forty shenynge marks full well.

WALWORTH.

Tyde lyfe, tyde death, I wyll withe thee go downe,
And selle some goods too yn brave Brystowe towne.*

---

* [This poem in Dean Milles's, and in Southey and Cottle's Editions,
is made to end at the words "as auntient penamen sayse." For the
remainder—now for the first time published in a collection of Chat-
terton's works,—the public are indebted to Richard Smith, Esq. of
Bristol (See appendix to the Rowley Poems.) I have elsewhere ac-
knowledged the favour of much valuable assistance rendered me by
that gentleman.—ED.]

𝕿𝖍𝖊 𝕸𝖊𝖗𝖗𝖎𝖊 𝕿𝖗𝖎𝖈𝖐𝖘 𝖔𝖋 𝕷𝖆𝖒𝖞𝖓𝖌𝖊𝖙𝖔𝖜𝖓𝖊.

𝖁𝖞 𝕸𝖆𝖎𝖘𝖙𝖗𝖊 𝕵𝖔𝖍𝖓 𝖆 𝕶𝖘𝖈𝖆𝖒.

A rygourous doome is myne, upon mie faie :
Before the parent starre, the lyghtsome sonne,
Hath three tymes lyghted up the cheerful daie,
To other reaulmes must Laymingtonne be gonne,
Or else my flymsie thredde of lyfe is spunne ;
And shall I hearken to a cowarts reede,
And from so vain a shade, as lyfe is, runne ?
No ! flie all thoughtes of runynge to the Queed ; [1]
No ! here I'll staie, and let the Cockneies see,
That Laymyntone the brave, will Laymyngetowne
    still be.

To fyght, and not to flee, my sabatans [2]
I'll don, and girth my swerde unto my syde ;
I'll go to ship, but not to foreyne landes,
But act the pyrate, rob in every tyde ;
With Cockneies bloude Thamysis shall be dyde.
Theire goodes in Bristowe markette shall be solde,
My bark the laverd [3] of the waters ryde,
Her sayles of scarlette and her stere of golde ;
My men the Saxonnes, I the Hengyst bee,
And in my shyppe combyne the force of all their three.

---

1 Devil.   2 Boots.   3 Lord.

Go to my trustie menne in Selwoods chace,
That through the lessel [1] hunt the burled [2] boare,
Tell them how standes with me the present case,
And bydde them revel down at Watchets shore,
And saunt [3] about in hawlkes and woods no more;
Let every auntrous [4] knyghte his armour brase,
Their meats be mans fleshe, and theyre beverage gore,
Hancele, [5] or Hanceled, from the human race;
Bid them, like mee theyre leeder, shape theyre mynde
To be a bloudie foe in armes, gaynst all mankynde.

RALPH.

I go my boon companions for to fynde.

Ralph goes out.

LAMYNGETOWNE.

Unfaifull Cockneies dogs! your god is gayne.
When in your towne I spent my greete estate,
What crowdes of citts came flockynge to my traine,
What shoals of tradesmenne eaten from my plate,
My name was alwaies Laymyngeton the greate;
But whan my wealth was gone, ye kennd me not,
I stoode in warde, ye laughed at mie fate,
Nor car'd if Laymyngeton the great did rotte;
But know ye, curriedowes, [6] ye shall soon feele,
I've got experience now, altho' I bought it weele.

You let me know that all the worlde are knaves,
That lordes and cits are robbers in disguise;

| 1 Bushes. | 2 Armed. | 3 Saunter. |
| 4 Adventurous. | 5 Cut off. | 6 Flatterers. |

I and my men, the Cockneies of the waves,
Will profitte by youre lessons and bee wise;
Make you give back the harvest of youre lies;
From deep fraught barques l'le take the mysers soul,
Make all the wealthe of every [man] my prize,
And cheating Londons pryde to Dygner Bristowe
    rolle.

  * * * * *

Lamingstone, Philpott, and Robynne.

LAMINGSTONE.

Thou saiest manne that thou wouldst goe with mee,
 And bare a parte in all mie mennes empryze,
Thinke well upon the daungers of the sea
 And ghess if that wyll no thee recradize,
When throwghe the skies the levyn-brondie flies,
 And levyns sparkel in the whited oundes
Seemynge to ryse at lepestones to the skies,
 And no contentéd bee with its sette bounds.
Then rolles the barque and tosses too and fro,
 Sike drearie scenes as thys will caste thie bloude I
  trowe.
Thynke, when wyth bloudie axes in our handes
 We are to fyghte for goulde and sylver to,
On neighbours myndbruch lyfe no one then standes,
 But all his ayme and end is to death's doo.

ROBYNNE.

I've thowghte on alle and am resolved to goe,
 Fortune, no more I'll bee thie taunted slave,
Once I was greete, nowe plans'd in wante and woe,
 I'll goo and bee a pick-hatch of the wave;

Goodes I have none, and lyfe I do disdayne,
   I'll be a victoar, or I'll break mie gallynge chayne,
I'll washe mie handes in bloude and dele in dethe,
Our shippe shall blowe alonge with windes of dyinge
   breth.

LAMINGSTONE.

I like thy courage, and I'll tell thy doome,
   Thou wilt unyere a brave captaine bee,
Goe thou to Brystowe, staie untylle wee come
   For there we shall happlie have neede of thee,
And for a thight and shapelie warehouse see
   Whareen to put the chattels we shall brynge,
And know if there two Cocknie knaves may bee
   Phillpot and Walworth, soe reporte doth synge.
If soe I'll trounce the gouler bie mie faie,
There's monies maun for thee—Ralph! take the
   things awaie
Which we from Watchetts towne have taken nowe,
Yn the barque's bottom see thee same you stowe.

RALPH.

Mastre of myne, I go as you do saie.

ROBYNNE.

And I to Brystowe town will haste awaie.*

---

* [The remainder of this poem, from the line—
   'And cheating London's pryde to Dygner Bristowe rolle,'
is now for the first time included in a collected edition of Chatterton's
Works. It is taken from Mr. Smith's MS., and was never *printed* till
1838. (See appendix to Rowley Poems.)—ED.]

Songe

Of Seyncte Baldywynne.*

Whann Norrurs¹ end hys menne of myghte,
Uponne thys brydge darde all to fyghte,
Forslagenn manie warriours laie,
And Dacyanns well nie wonne the daie.
Whanne doughty Baldwinus arose,
And scatterd deathe amonge hys foes,
Fromme out the brydge the purlinge bloode
Embolled² hie the runnynge floude.

Dethe dydd uponne hys anlace hange,
And all hys arms were *gutte de sangue*.³
His doughtinesse wrought thilk dismaye,
The foreign warriors ranne awaie,
Erle Baldwynus regardedd well,
How manie menn forslaggen fell;
To Heaven lyft oppe hys holie eye,
And thanked Godd for victorye;
Thenne threw hys anlance ynn the tyde,
Lyvdd ynn a cell, and hermytte died.

---

* According to Chatterton, this and the following poem were sung
when the Bridge at Bristol was completed in 1247.
1 King of Norway.   2 Swelled.
3 Drops of blood; an heraldic allusion, suitable to the genius of that
age.—CHATTERTON.

Songe

Of Seyncte Warburghe.

I.

Whanne Kynge Kynghill[1] ynn hys honde
Helde the sceptre of thys londe,
Sheenynge starre of Chrystes lyghte,
The merkie[2] mysts of pagann nyghte
     Gan to scatter farr and wyde :
Thanne Seyncte Warburghe hee arose,
Doffed hys honnores and fyne clothes ;
Preechynge hys Lorde Jesus name,
Toe the lande of West Sexx came,
     Whare blaeke[3] Severn rolls hys tyde.

II.

Stronge ynn faithfullness, he trodde
Overr the waterrs lyke a Godde,
Till he gaynde the distaunt hecke,[4]
Ynn whose bankes hys staffe dydd steck,
     Wytnesse to the myrracle ;
Thenne he preechedd nyghte and daie,
And set manee ynn ryghte waie.
Thys goode staffe great wonders wroughte,
Moe than gueste bie mortalle thoughte,
     Orr thann mortall tonge can tell.

---

1 King Coenwulf.   2 Dark.   3 Yellow.   4 Height.

III.

Thenn the foulke a brydge dydd make
Overr the streme untoe the hecke,
All of wode eke longe and wyde,
Pryde and glorie of the tyde;
    Whych ynn tyme dydd falle awaie:
Then Erle Leof[1] he bespedde[2]
Thys grete ryverr fromme hys bedde,
Round hys castle for to runne,
T'was in trothe ann ancyante onne,
    But warre and tyme wyll all decaie.

IV.

Now agayne, wythe bremie[3] force,
Severn ynn hys aynciant course
Rolls hys rappyd streeme alonge,
With a sable[4] swifte and stronge,
    Moreying[5] manie ann okie wood:
Wee the menne of Brystowe towne
Have yreerd thys brydge of stone,
Wyshynge echone that ytt maie laste
Till the date of daies be past,
    Standynge where the other stoode.

---

1 Earl Leofwin.   2 Dispatched, turned away.
3 Furious, violent.   4 Sand.
5 Rooting up, so explained in the Glossary to Robert Gloucester.—
'Mored', *i.e.* digged, grubbed. The roots of trees are still called 'mores'
in Devonshire.—CHATTERTON.

Sancte Warbur.*

In auntient dayes, when Kenewalchyn King
Of all the borders of the sea did reigne,
Whos cutting celes,† as the Bardyes synge,
Cut strakyng furrowes in the foamie mayne,
Sancte Warbur cast aside his Earles estate,
As great as good, and eke as good as great.
Tho blest with what us men accounts as store,
Saw something further, and saw something more.

Where smokyng Wasker scours the claiey bank,
And gilded fishes wanton in the sunne,
Emyttynge to the feelds a dewie dank,
As in the twyning path-waye he doth runne ;
Here stood a house, that in the ryver smile
Since valorous Ursa first wonne Bryttayn Isle ;
The stones in one as firm as rock unite,
And it defyde the greatest Warriours myghte.

---

* From the Supplement to Chatterton's Miscellanies. It is there
entitled—Imitation of our Old Poets. On oure Ladyes Chirch. 1769.
—Southey's *Edition*.

† Most probably from the ancient word 'ceolis'; which, in the Saxon,
is 'ships'. But whence 'coelæ', we find in Brompton, are used for large
ships.

Around about the lofty elemens[1] hie
Proud as their planter reerde their greenie crest,
Bent out their heads, whene'er the windes came bie.
In amorous dalliaunce the flete cloudes kest.
Attendynge Squires dreste in trickynge brighte,
To each tenth Squier an attendynge Knyghte,
The hallie hung with pendaunts to the flore,
A coat of nobil armes upon the doore ;

Horses and dogges to hunt the fallowe deere,
Of pastures many, wide extent of wode,
Faulkonnes in mewes, and, little birds to teir,
The Sparrow Hawke, and manie Hawkies gode.
Just in the prime of life, whan others court
Some swottie Nymph, to gain their tender hand,
Greet with the Kynge and *trerdie* greet with the
Court
And as aforesed mickle much of land,

* * * * *

---

1 Elms.

𝔚𝔞𝔯𝔯𝔢.*

𝔅𝔶 𝔍𝔬𝔥𝔫, 𝔰𝔢𝔠𝔬𝔫𝔡 𝔄𝔟𝔟𝔬𝔱𝔱𝔢 𝔬𝔣 𝔖𝔢𝔶𝔞𝔠𝔱𝔢 𝔄𝔲𝔰𝔱𝔶𝔫𝔰 𝔐𝔶𝔫𝔰𝔱𝔢𝔯𝔯𝔢.

Of warres glumm[1] pleasaunce doe I chaunte mie laie,
Trouthe tips the poynctelle,[2] wysdomme skemps[3] the
 lyne,
Whylste hoare experiaunce telleth what toe saie,
And forwyned[4] hosbandrie wyth blearie eyne,
Stondeth and woe bements[5]; the trecklynge bryne
Rounnynge adone hys cheekes which doethe shewe,
Lyke hys unfrutefulle fieldes, longe straungers to the
 ploughe.
Saie, Glowster,[6] whanne besprenged[7] on evrich syde,
The gentle hyndlette and the vylleyn felle ;
Whanne smetheynge[8] sange[9] dyd flow lyke to a tyde,
And sprytes were damned for the lacke of knelle,
Diddest thou kenne ne lykeness to an helle,
Where all were misdeedes doeynge lyche unwise,
Where hope unbarred and deathe eftsoones dyd shote
 theyre eies.

Ye shepster[10] swaynes who the ribibble[11] kenne,
Ende the thyghte[12] daunce, ne loke uponne the spere:
In ugsommnesse[13] ware moste bee dyghte toe menne,
Unseliness[14] attendethe honourewere;[15]
Quaffe your swote[16] vernage[17] and atreeted[18] beere.

---

* From Barrett's History of Bristol. Chatterton says, " As you ap-
prove of the small specimen of his poetry, I have sent you a larger,
which, though admirable is still (in my opinion) inferior to Rowley,
whose works, when I have leisure, I will fairly copy and send you."—
SOUTHEY's *Edition.*
1 Gloomy. 2 Pen. 3 Marks. 4 Blasted, burnt.
5 Lament. 6 Earl or Consul of Glocester
7 Scattered. 8 Smoking 9 Blood. 10 Shepherd.
11 A fiddle. 12 Compact, orderly, tight. 13 Terror.
14 Unhappiness. 15 The place or residence of honour.
16 Sweet. 17 Vintage, wine cyder. 18 Extracted from corn.

A Chronycalle of Brystowe.

Wrote bie Raufe Chedder, Chappmanne 1356.*

Ynne whilomme daies as Stowe saies
  Ynne famous Brystowe towne
Dhere lyved Knyghtes doughtie yn fyghtes
  Of marvellous renowne.
A Saxonne boulde renowned of oulde
  For Dethe and dernie dede
Maint Tanmen slone the Brugge uponne
  Icausynge hem to blede.
Baldwynne hys name, Rolles saie the same
  And yev hymme rennome grate,
Hee lyved nere the Ellynteire
  Al bie Seyncte Lenardes yate.
A mansion hie, made bosmorelie
  Was reered bie hys honde,
Whanne he ysterve, hys name unkerve
  Inne Baldwynne streete doe stonde.
On Ellie then of Mercyann menne
  As meynte of Pentells blase,
Inne Castle-stede made dofull dede
  And dydde the Dans arase.
One Leefwyne of Kyngelie Lyne
  Inne Brystowe towne dyd leve,

---

* From a MS. by Chatterton in the British Museum.

And toe the samme for hys gode name
  The Ackmanne Yate dyd gev.
Hammon a Lorde of hie accorde
  Was ynne the strete nempte brede ;
Soe greate hys Myghte soe strynge yn fyghte
  Onne Byker hee dyd fede.
Fitz Lupons digne of gentle Lyne
  Onne Radclyve made hys Baie,
Inn moddie Gronne the whyche uponne
  Botte Reittes and roshes laie.
Than Radclyve Strete of Mansyonnes meete
  In semelie gare doe stonde,
And Canynge grete of fayre estate
  Bryngeth to Tradynge Londe.
Hardynge dydde comme from longe Kyngddomme
  Inne Knyvesmythe strete to lyne,
Roberte hys Sonne, moche gode thynges donne
  As Abblates doe blasynne.
Roberte the Erle, ne conkered curll
  Inne Castle stede dyd fraie
Yynge Henrie to ynn Brystowe true
  As Hydelle dyd obaie.
A Maioure dheene bee ande Jamne hee
  Botte anne ungentle wyghte,
Seyncte Marie tende eche ammie frende
  Bie hallie Taper lyghte.

On Happienesse.*

By William Canynge.

I.

Maie Selynesse¹ on erthes boundes bee hadde?
Maie yt adyghte² yn human shape be found?
Wote yee, yt was wyth Edin's bower bestadde,³
Or quite eraced⁴ from the scaunce-layd⁵ grounde,
Whan from the secret fontes the waterres dyd abounde?
Does yt agrosed⁶ shun the bodyed waulke,
Lyve to ytself and to yttes ecchoe taulke?

II.

All hayle, Contente, thou mayd of turtle-eyne,
As thie behoulders thynke thou arte iwreene, ⁷
To ope the dore to Selynesse ys thyne,
And Chrystis glorie doth upponne thee sheene.
Doer of the foule thynge ne hath thee seene;
In caves, ynn wodes, ynn woe, and dole⁸ distresse,
Whoere hath thee hath gotten Selynesse.

---

* This, and the two following Poems, attributed to Mr. Canynge, are printed from Mr. Catcott's copies.—TYRWHITT's *Edition.*

1 Happiness.	2 Clothed.	3 Fixed.	4 Banished, erased.
5 Uneven.	6 Frighted.	7 Displayed.	8 Grievous.

The Gouler's Requiem,*

By the same.

I.

Mie boolie[1] entes,[2] adieu ! ne moe the syghte
Of guilden merke shall mete mie joieous eyne,

---

* What was supposed to be dulness in Chatterton was genius. The symptoms of talents were misconstrued by his contemporaries. They were disgusted with his pride, which was a consciousness of preeminence of abilities. Before he was five years old, he was the little tyrant of his playfellows, and the leader of the sport. Mr. Capel, a brother apprentice in the same house with Chatterton, relates, that there was "generally dreariness in his look, and a wildness attended with a visible contempt for others." The silence, the solitude, of this visionary boy, his eccentric habits, his singularities of behaviour, were not attributed to the true cause. His fits of melancholy were mistaken for sullenness. His sister says that he was "sometimes so *gloomed*, that for many days together he would say very little, and that by constraint." An old female relation, who undoubtedly thought him mad, has reported that "he talked very little, was very absent in company, and used very often to walk by the river side, talking to himself, and flourishing his arms about." He despised discretion, a virtue allied to many meannesses; and in the place of worldly prudence, attention to proposals of economy, and a regular profession, substituted his anticipation of immortality. He scorned subsistence, but what his own poetry could alone confer. Silent and unsuspected, he was now soliciting the muse in secret. At the hours allotted him to play, we are told that he constantly retired to read. This was the young Edwin, who forged Rowley's poems.

It was owing to his pride which has been construed into veracity that he so inflexibly persisted to the last, that these poems were written by Rowley. To this secret of his bosom he had vowed eternal fidelity, and there is a degree of heroism in his obstinacy. Although in a state of indigence, and a candidate for reputation, no persuasion, no expectation of gain or of praise, no interest could induce him to depart from his original declaration. When he perceived that the poems were treated as forgeries, and that he was traduced as a cheat, the superiority which he had always maintained was affected, and he became still more determined in asserting what he had once asserted His vanity was piqued in an improper way. He thought it would be more to his advantage, to own than to suppress the truth ; he rather wished to escape the character of falsehood than to claim the merit of excellent poetry. He had formed golden dreams of the success of this imposture. But finding that his forgeries were suspected, and that his hopes of profit were at an end, he would not avail himself of that fame which an open confession would here put into his power, and which now only remained to supply the place of solid emolument. Criticism, the companion and the assistant of truth, has endeavoured to replace those laurels, which he tore from his brows with his own hand. — WARTON.

1 Beloved.   2 Purses.

Ne moe the sylver noble sheenynge bryghte
Schall fyll mie honde with weight to speke ytt fyne;
Ne moe, ne moe, alass! I call you myne:
Whydder[1] must you, ah! whydder must I goe?
I kenn not either; oh mie enmers[2] dygne,
To parte wyth you wyll wurcke mee myckle woe;
I muste be gonne, botte whare I dare ne telle;
O storthe[3] unto mie mynde! I goe to helle.

II.

Soone as the morne dyd dyghte[4] the roddie sunne,
A shade of theves eche streake of lyghte dyd seeme;
Whann ynn the heavn full half hys course was runn,
Eche stirryng nayghbour dyd mie harte afleme:[5]
Thye loss, or quyck or slepe, was aie mie dreme;
For thee, O gould, I dyd the lawe ycrase;[6]
For thee, I gotten or bie wiles or breme;[7]
Ynn thee I all mie joie and good dyd place;
Botte nowe to mee thie pleasaunce ys ne moe,
I kenne notte botte for thee I to the quede[8] must goe.

---

1 Whither   2 Coined money.   3 Death.   4 Dress.
5 Affright.   6 Violate.   7 Violence. 8 Devil.

Heraudyn.

A Fragmente.*

Yynge Heraudyn al bie the grene Wode sate,
Hereynge the swote Chelandrie ¹ ande the Oue.²
Seeinge the kenspecked ³ amaylde⁴ flourettes nete,
Envyngynge ⁵ to the Birds hys Love songs true.
Syrre Preeste camme bie ande forthe hys bede-rolle
    drewe,
Fyve Aves and one Pater moste be sedde ;
Twayne songe, the one his songe of Willowe Rue
The odher one——————

*   *   *   *   *

---

* From a MS. by Chatterton in the British Museum.
1 Goldfinch.   2 Ouzel-blackbird.   3 Marked.
4 Enamelled.   5 Sending.

Epitaph on Robert Canynge.*

Thys mornynge starre of Radcleves rysynge raie,
A true manne good of mynde and Canynge hyghte,
Benethe thys stone lies moltrynge ¹ ynto claie,
Untylle the darke tombe sheene an eterne lyghte.
Thyrde from hys loynes the present Canynge came ;
Houton ² are wordes for to telle hys doe ;
For aye shall lyve hys heaven-recorded name,
Ne shall yt dye whanne tyme shalle bee no moe ;
Whanne Mychael's trumpe shall sounde to rise the
    solle, ³
He'll wynge to heaven with kynne, and happie bee hys
    dolle. ⁴

Onn John a Dalbenie.

By William Canynge.

Johne makes a jarre boute Lancaster and Yorke ;
Bee stille, gode manne, and learne to mynde thie worke.

---

* This is one of the fragments of vellum, given by Chatterton to Mr.
Barrett, as part of his original MSS.
1 Mouldering.   2 Hollow.   3 Soul.   4 Portion.

The Accounte of W. Canynges Feast.*
By the same.

Thorowe the halle the belle han sounde;
Byelecoyle¹ doe the Grave beseeme;²
The ealdermenne doe sytte arounde,
Ande snoffelle³ oppe the cheorte⁴ steeme.
Lyche asses wylde ynne desarte waste
Swotelye the morneynge ayre doe taste.

Syke keene thie ate; the minstrels plaie,
The dynne of angelles doe theie keepe;
Heie stylle, the guestes ha ne to saie,
Butte nodde yer thankes ande falle aslape.
Thus echone daie bee I to deene,
Gyf Rowley, Iscamm, or Tyb. Gorges be ne seene.

---

* This poem is taken from a fragment of vellum, which Chatterton
gave to Mr. Barrett as an original. With respect to the three friends of
Mr. Canynge mentioned in the last line, the name of Rowley is suffici-
ently known from the preceding poems. Iscamm appears as an actor
in the tragedy of Ælla, and in that of Goddwyn; and a poem, ascribed
to him, entitled, "The merry Tricks of Laymington," is inserted in
the "Discorse of Bristow." Sir Theobald Gorges was a knight of an
ancient family seated at Wraxhall, within a few miles of Bristol.
(See Rot. Parl. 3 H. VI. n. 28. Leland's Itin. vol. VII. p. 98.) He has
also appeared as an actor in both the tragedies, and as the author of
one of the Mynstrelles songes in Ælla. His connexion with Mr. Canynge
is verified by a deed of the latter, dated 20th October, 1467, in which
he gives to trustees, in part of a benefaction of £500 to the Church of
St. Mary Redcliffe, "certain jewels of Sir Theobald Gorges, Knt."
which had been pawned to him for £160. TYRWHITT's *Edition*.
1 Fair welcome.   2 Becomes.   3 Snuff up.   4 Cheerful.

APPENDIX

TO THE ROWLEY POEMS.

To the Editor of the Bristol Mirror.

Sir,—I send to you a lost portion of a piece written by
Chatterton. It was the gift of my uncle Mr. George Symes
Catcott, in 1782, to the late Mr. Thos. Eagles, who first pub-
lished the Bristow Tragedy, or the Death of Sir Charles
Bawdin (1772) It has lain amongst the papers of the latter
gentleman many years, together with other autographs, of
which you will probably hear more hereafter. His son, the
Reverend and very highly-talented fellow-citizen, John
Eagles, has kindly presented it to me. Independently of
the history of the sheet, the MS. carries in every line in-
dubitable internal evidence of its parent to all who are
acquainted with the hand and the acknowledged productions
of the unhappy boy. The lines are written on both sides of
a school copy-book. I have searched all the editions extant
of Chatterton's works, but I cannot find it; I presume, there-
fore, that it has never been published. The first portion of
the piece, of which this is a part, will be found in " The in-
troduction to the Discoursynge Tragedy of Ælla, as plaied
before Mastre Cannynge, att his howse nempte the Redde
Lodge," in the reign of Edward ye Fourth. I copy this ex-
tract from the edition of " The works of Rowlie," page 181,
as edited by the learned and very Reverend Dean Milles. In
that folio may also be seen a figure " carvelled in stone,"
representing the hero of the piece, one Johannes Lamynton.

It escaped also the researches of the Poet Laureat and Mr. Cottle in 1803, a portion only of the piece (see Chatterton's works, page 145, vol. 2) having fallen into their hands. The late Mr. Thomas Eagles was applied to by the editors, and was a man of too liberal a mind, wittingly to have refused a contribution; it is probable, therefore, that he had mislaid it, or forgotten that he had such a MS. in his possession.

The aforesaid Laymyngstone, for the name is not always spelled the same, was a man of good family, and at one time "a courteous Sir Knight," and fought bravely on several honest occasions; but he took to dissolute courses—in a word he became the leader of a band of pirates, who infested the THAMES, the NARROW SEAS, and the BRISTOL CHANNEL. At length he was captured, and condemned to be hanged; when under sentence of death the poet makes him say—

" A rygourous doome is mynne, upon my fate
  Before the parent starre, the lyghtsomme sunne
  Hath three times lyghtened uppe the cheerful dale,
  To other realms must Lamyngstone be gonne,
  Or else my fleemsie threede of lyffe is spunne,
  And shall I hearken to a cowart's reede?
  No—flie all thoughts of running to the queede
  No, here I'll stay, and let the Cocknies see
  That Lamyngstone the brave will Lamyngstone still bee.

" To fyght and not to flee my sabatans
  I'll don, and girth my sworde unto my syde,
  I'll go to shippe, but not to forayne land,
  But acte the Pyrate, robbing everie tyde.
  With Cocknies' bloude, Thamysis shall be redde
  My Barque the lavard of the waters rydde,
  Her sayles of scarlette, and her stoure of goulde.
  My menne the Saxonnes, I the Hengyst bee,
  And in my shyppe combyne the force of all the three."

This bravery holds him on during forty lines in Mr. Catcott's manuscript, now before me. There is also "a true, whole, and particular account of his birth, parentage, and education," shewing how, in expiation of his malpractices,

he was ordered to build a church, but it is too long for inser-
tion here.   Besides, although I have spoken of our hero as
a reality, yet there is little doubt that the whole is a fiction
by Chatterton ; but as even in an ordinary novel the rea-
der feels an interest in the catastrophe, I add that King
Henry pardoned him, even after hope had left him.

His propensities were, however, " bred in the bone ;" he
again hoisted the bloody flag, and finally perished in a great
battle, fighting under the white rose, against the Lancas-
trians.

It may be well to apprize the reader that Robynne,
being determined to join the band of free-booters, under
Lamyngstone, applies to him to be enrolled, but the latter
tried to dissuade him, by depicting the horrors of a pirate's
life—with what success the lines will shew.

LAMINGSTONE, PHILPOTT, AND ROBYNNE.

Lam.—Thou saiest manne that thou wouldst goe with mee,
 And bare a parte in all mie mennes empryze,
Thinke well upon the daungers of the sea
 And ghess if that wyll no thee recradize,
When throwghe the skies the levyn-brondie flies,
 And levyns sparkel in the whited oundes
Seemynge to ryse at lepestone to the skies,
 And no contented bee with its sette bounds.
Then rolles the barque and tosses too and fro,
 Sike drearie scenes as thys will coole thie bloude I trowe.
Thynk, when wyth bloudie axes in our handes
 We are to fyghte for goulde and sylver to,
On neighbours myndbuch lyfe no one then standes,
 But all his ayme and end is to death's doo.

Rob.—I've thowghte on alle, and am resolved to goe,
 Fortune no moe I'll bee thie taunted slave,
Once I was greete, nowe plans'd in wante and woe,
 I'll goo and bee a pick hatch of the wave ;
Goodes I have none, and lyfe I do disdayne,
 I'll be a victoar, or I'll break mie gallynge chayne,
I'll washe mie handes in bloude and dele in dethe,
 Our shippe shall blowe alonge with windes of dyinge breth.

Thus far is the autograph of Chatterton.   Upon reference to a copy of the whole piece, now before me, in the hand-writing of Mr. Catcott, I find that which is here subjoined, and which in all probability was upon the next leaf of the copy-book which is now lost.

> *Lam.*—I like thy courage, and I'll tell thy doome,
>   Thou wilt unyere a brave captaine bee,
> Goe thou to Brystowe, staie untylle wee come
>   For there we shall happlie have neede of thee,
> And for a thight and shapelie warehouse see
>   Whareen to put the chattels we shall brynge,
> And know if there two Cocknie knaves may bee
>   Phillpot and Walworth, soe reporte doth synge.
> If soe I'll trounce the gouler bie mie faie,
> There's monies maun for thee—Ralph! take the things awaie
> Which we from Watchets towne have taken nowe,
> Yn the barque's bottom see thee same you stowe.
>
> *Ralph.*—Mastre of myne I go as you do saie.
>
> *Rob.*—And I to Brystowe town will haste awaie.

We must now have recourse to Dean Milles's and Cottle's Edition—in the latter, in vol. ii. page 145, will be found a fragment, being a most strange and unaccountable jumble of Latin and English, ending thus :—

> *Walworth*—Quæ requirit misericordiam mala causa est
>   Alack ! alack ! a sad dome mine in fay.
>   But oft with citizens it is the case.
> Honesta turpitudo pro bonâ
>   Causâ mori, as auntiente pensmene saye.

Here it breaks off, being from "The first part of Discourse the Second, between Master Walworth and Philpot Cock-nies."

Chatterton's autograph supplies the remainder of the *hiatus*—whether it was *valde deflendus* the reader shall judge ; howbeit, at all events, it is a lost sheep driven into the Shepherd's flock.   Thus it runs :—

Phill.—Home news welle let alone and latyn too,
    For mee a memorie doth 'gin to fayle;
Saie, Master Walworth, what gode newes have you,
    Praie have you herdeen of the stouns of hayle ?

Walw.—I have, and that ytte with reddour did sayle,
    Some heutstones were lyke cheryes rege and grete,
And to the grownde there did the trees preveyle,
    But goodmanne Philpotte what dye you ahete
Bowte goods of Laymingtone, nowe holde by you
For certaine monies store to you for chattels due ?

Phille.—Ah, I have nymd him specyal, for his wine
    Have ta'en attons twelve pounds, for dayntye cheer,
Though the same time mie wyfe wyth hym dyd dyne,
    Been payd a mark—non-extra of the beer;
But when hys synkynge purse did 'gin to wear
    I lent hym full syx markes upon hys faie,
And hee, poore Custrols, havynge note to spere
    Favor'd a cleere and now doth runne awaie,
Hys goodes I downe at Brystowe towne wyll selle,
For which I will get forty shenynge marks full well.

Wal.—Tyde lyfe, tyde death, I wyll withe thee go downe,
    And selle some goods too yn brave Brystowe towne.

So much for the autograph—now for a word, by way of
tail-piece. All inquiring strangers are surprised to find
that, although Bristol gave birth to the boy whose innate
talent has rendered him, in spite of all obstacles, a star of
the very first magnitude in the galaxy of national bards, yet
that the noble library in his native city contains not a single
line, or even a word, the actual production of his hand and
pen.

This reproach, for so I consider it to be, shall be speedily
done away, by presenting to the library the last letter he
ever wrote, together with the sketch of the intended pamph-
let against Bishop Newton—also the first 560 lines of the
BATTLE OF HASTYNGS—the TOURNAMENT, OR UNKNOWN
KNIGHT, consisting of 110 lines—CRAISH'S HERALDRY,
consisting of six pages of his manuscript, on which are em-
blazoned by him eight shields, never yet published. For

the three latter pieces the public have to thank the Rev. John Eagles, who, most liberally, presented the autographs to me a short time since.

As an *avant courier*, I have already presented to the Committee, to be hung up in the room, the sheet concerning LAMYNGSTONE, which being placed between two panes of glass and framed, may be read both sides without any risque of damage.*

Although this communication is longer than I intended, yet I have to hope that your readers will pardon it, especially the admirers of that friendless and talented boy, whose transcendant genius has cast upon "auntiente Brightstowe" a never dying lustre, and an interest to be extinguished only by "the crack of doom."

I remain, &c., yours,

RICHARD SMITH,
Surgeon.

38, *Park Street,*
April 27, 1838.

---

* The late Mr. George Symes Catcott, who was termed "Rowley's Midwife" (he having first published "The Poems"), was a most laborious collector of all papers, notices, critiques, and paragraphs, from all the publications, newspapers, journals, and magazines, together with a complete list and index; and all these, fifty-seven in number, he has pasted into two large volumes. He has also, with his own hand, copied all the correspondence between himself and the literati of the day. Amongst these are letters from and to Dean Milles, Lord Dacres, Percy of Alnwick, Dr. Glynn, Rev. (afterwards Sir Herbert) Croft, Tyrwhitt, Villey, Lord Camden, Lord Charlemont, and the celebrated Thomas James Matthias. Now this is nowhere else to be found. The books are now in the possession of Mr. Richard Smith, Senior Surgeon of the Infirmary, who is the nephew of Mr. Catcott. We have reason to believe that the whole, together with Chatterton's autograph letter, and many other things, will be at no very distant period presented to the City Library. This is as it should be.—*Extract from the Bristol Mirror.*

The Rowley Poems bear internal evidence of their being the productions of a boy; of a marvellous boy indeed, but still of a boy. There are no traces of experience, of long observation, of a knowledge of human nature, or indeed of acquirement of any sort; while of strong natural powers of talent, of genius, every page furnishes us with abundant instances. Chatterton's forte, I think, was pathos; and had not his mortal career closed so prematurely, he would probably have devoted himself to Lyrical Poetry. What he has left behind him is full of genius, but full of inequalities and faults. We have hardly sufficient data to enable us to judge what Chatterton's real character, moral or literary,—and it is difficult to separate them in our enquiry,—was, or would have been. I, for one, cannot help thinking, that the vices of the former were adventitious, and that the imperfections of the latter would have been obviated or removed. His tale is but half told. Had not the curtain dropt so abruptly on the hero of the Drama, succeeding scenes might have shewn him triumphing over all his follies, and atoning for all his faults. His ruling passion was the love of fame; and the progress of Fame is like the course of the Thames, which in its native fields will scarcely float the toy-ship which an infant's hand has launched, but when it has once visited the metropolis, mighty vessels may ride upon its bosom, and it rolls on irresistibly to the ocean. This Chatterton knew; and, in a blind confidence on his own unaided powers, he rushed to the capital in pursuit of competence and renown. The result we all know was neglect, penury, and self-destruction.—HENRY NEELE.

The following curious parallel to the fictions of Chatterton is extracted from Hallam's *Introduction to the Literature of Europe.*

"In the days of our fathers it would have been necessary to mention as a forgery the celebrated poems attributed to Thomas Rowley. Probably no one person living believes in their authenticity;—nor should I have alluded to so palpable a fabrication at all, but for the curious circumstance that a very similar trial of literary credulity has not long since been essayed in France. A gentleman of the name of Surville published a collection of poems, alleged to have been written by Clotilde de Surville, a poetess of the fifteenth century. The muse of the Ardèche warbled her notes during a longer life than the monk of Bristow ; and having sung the relief of Orleans by the maid of Arc in 1429, lived to pour her swan-like chant on the battle of Fornova in 1495. Love, however, as well as war, is her theme, and it was a remarkable felicity that she rendered an ode of her prototype Sappho into French verse, many years before any one else in France could have seen it. The forgery is by no means so gross as that of Chatterton.".

Printed in the United States
79304LV00003B/39

9 781430 478881